The Natural Stallion

His Behaviour, Management and Training

Lesley Skipper

First published in 2010

by

Black Tent Publications
145 Durham Road
STOCKTON-ON-TEES
TS19 0DS

www.black-tent.co.uk

©Lesley Skipper 2010

ALL RIGHTS RESERVED

No part of this book may be produced in any form, by photocopying or by any electronic or mechanical means, including information storage or retrieval systems, without pemission in writing from both the copyright owner and the publisher of this book.

The right of Lesley Skipper to be identified as the author of this work has been asserted by her in accordance with the Copyright, Designs and Patents Act 1988

Editing and design by Lesley Skipper

Printed and bound in the UK by

Good News Digital Books
Hallsford Bridge
Ongar
Essex
CM5 9RX

ISBN: 978-1-907212-03-1

A catalogue record for this book is available from the British Library

The Natural Stallion

For Nivalis and Rigel

And all the other stallions who have enriched my life

The Natural Stallion

Contents

Acknowledgements	viii
Author's note	ix
Publisher's note	ix
Introduction	11
Chapter 1: Myths, folk beliefs and 'received wisdom'	15
Chapter 2: Why keep a stallion?	20
Chapter 3: What is a stallion? Part I: Stallion physiology	31
Chapter 4: What is a stallion? Part II: The stallion's role in life	40
Chapter 5: Dominance and the stallion	82
Chapter 6: Mating behaviour	102
Chapter 7: Keeping a stallion happy	122
Chapter 8: What kind of relationship do we want with a stallion?	144
Chapter 9: Training principles	160
Chapter 10: Training good behaviours	182
Chapter 11: Dealing with problem behaviours	191
Chapter 12: The stallion's role in the horse world in general	239
Conclusion	262
Appendix I: Safety	267
Appendix II: Seeking professional help	277
Bibliography	283
Index	294

Acknowledgements

I would like to thank the following people who have helped me in the preparation of this book:

Dr Francis Burton, Chairman of the Equine Behaviour Forum, for all his support and encouragement, especially when I have become despondent over the sheer size of the task ahead of me; Gill Cooper for reading the draft of the book and making many valuable suggestions; Joanne Husband, for all her help and support over the years; Andy Beck of the White Horse Ethology Project in New Zealand, for allowing me to use material from his website, ebook and articles; Catherine Bell, founder of the Thinking Horsemanship online forum; Sylvia Loch, who has unfailingly encouraged me in this project; Anne Wilson, for her support and encouragement and also for her contribution re Palomo Linares (see Chapter 12); Ann Hyland, for so much information about her remarkable stallion Nizzolan; Melanie Gaddas-Brown, for allowing us to acquire our senior stallion, Guisburn Nivalis, aged five months, together with his dam Roxzella; Rachael Johnson, for founding the stallion care discussion group mentioned in the Conclusion and for reading the draft of this book and making some very constructive suggestions; Dr Joanna Hockenhull of the Department of Biological Sciences, University of Chester for kindly sending me material related to the incidence of gastric ulcers in horses; Patti Demers Bailey for information about her great stallion Remington Steele; Jean Peck, for information about her great stallion Dervatiw Gwyddion; Telané Greyling, who has spent years studying the feral horses of the Namib Naukluft, and who very kindly sent me her unpublished theses on the horses of the Namib Naukluft, as well as much interesting and useful information via personal correspondence; Dr Sue McDonnell of University of Pennsylvania School of Veterinary Medicine for allowing me to reproduce the procedure cited in Chapter 10; and finally my husband Brian, whose unfailing support enables me to keep on with projects like this even when despair sets in regarding the sheer scale of the task of trying to change entrenched beliefs.

Thanks to Elsevier B.V. for permission to reproduce the extract from Chapter 4 of *Equine Breeding Management and Artificial Insemination* by Juan C. Samper, Jonathan Pycock and Angus O. McKinnon (Saunders, 1999), given on page 000.

Finally, I would like to thank our two stallions Nivalis (Prince Shalamzar x Roxzella) and Rigel (Guisburn Nivalis x Mikenah), just for being themselves and for giving us so much pleasure. Thanks, boys!

Author's note

By their very nature, horses are dangerous: not because they wish to harm us deliberately, for they are mostly peace-loving creatures, but because of their sheer size, power and reactivity.

Stallions are therefore by definition dangerous: not because they are stallions, but because they are horses. Their emotional and reactive nature, and the fact that their true role in life is to guard their equine family from real or perceived danger, makes them vigilant, and more likely to react to threats, real or imagined.

Anyone who deals with stallions is, or should be, sufficiently experienced with horses to be aware of the possible dangers and how to anticipate them. Readers are therefore expected to be able to take responsibility for their own actions when dealing with stallions.

Every care has been taken to alert readers to safety concerns and warnings are given throughout the text regarding possible dangers associated with training and management procedures. Ultimately, however, the responsibility for safety lies with the person handling the horse. The author and publishers cannot accept any responsibility for any injury or damages which may arise from failure to heed these warnings, or as a result of following procedures mentioned in this book.

Publisher's note

Every effort has been made to trace the copyright ownership of quotations and illustrative material used in this book. If anyone has a claim in this respect, they should contact the publisher.

The Natural Stallion

Introduction

*I*N 2000 I wrote an article about stallions for an online magazine, *The Joy of Horses*, in which I set out to dispel some of the myths and misconceptions that have become part of stallion lore. Stallions are perceived by many people, both inside and outside the horse world, as aggressive and difficult to manage, and in some cases downright dangerous. Comparatively few people have the opportunity to observe stallions in anything like natural surroundings; even fewer will have had the opportunity to study how they interact with their family group in the wild, or in free-ranging situations, when left to get on with their lives without human interference. So for the most part people in the horse world will find it difficult to separate the true nature of stallions from the preconceived ideas and expectations of people who have only ever experienced stallion behaviour in very restricted circumstances. I wanted to encourage people to view stallions in a more sympathetic light, and to understand that a stallion is still a horse, and has much the same needs and priorities as any other horse, albeit with a few 'extras' which need to be taken into account in training and management. I also wanted to demonstrate that for the most part it is the prevalent management practices which create problems in managing and handling stallions, rather than the inherent nature of stallions themselves.

The response to the article was astonishing. I started to receive – and continue to receive to this day – e-mails from horse owners asking a variety of questions about stallions. Some of these relate to breeding, but many more relate to training and management, such as

◊ What causes aggression in stallions, and how can I deal with it?

◊ How can I turn a stallion out safely?

◊ How does the social behaviour of stallions relate to keeping them around other horses?

◊ Can a stallion be kept with geldings or other stallions?

◊ Can stallions be safely run out with mares? What kind of problems can arise?

◊ Can stallions run with mares and still be well-mannered at shows?

◊ What do I do if a stallion 'drops' at a show?

◊ Are stallions difficult to train?

◊ Do people manage to ride their stallions in mixed company?

As I attempted to answer these and many other related questions, it became clear to me that more and more people are either keeping colts entire, acquiring mature stallions, or are thinking about doing either or both of these things. There are a number of reasons for this, as Chapter 2 will show, but they seem to go hand-in-hand with an increase in awareness of the kinds of environment, management and training practices necessary to keep horses happy and healthy, together with a genuine desire to give male entires a better life.

With this in mind, I incorporated some of the material from the stallion article, in revised form, into Chapter 10 of my book *Let Horses Be Horses* (J.A. Allen 2005). However, as the e-mails continued to come in, I began to realize that although this chapter could certainly be of use to the kind of people who were sending me the e-mails, it could not answer more than a few of their questions. I started to search the literature and the internet, and found that not only were there virtually no books dealing with stallions other than from the point of view of stud management, there were also many contradictory opinions and conflicting advice being offered on the many equestrian forums to be found on the internet. Much of the advice given, and many of the opinions offered, were clearly based on assumptions and information that may not necessarily be accurate, and which in many cases could add to the distorted views so many people have about stallions.

So I decided that what was needed was a book which would answer as many of the questions as possible, taking into account the latest scientific research on various aspects of stallion behaviour. This book shows how stallions behave when allowed to live as naturally as a domestic situation permits, and to perform as many of their natural behaviours as possible within the constraints of domestication. It will enable anyone wanting to understand more about the true nature of stallions, and how to keep them as naturally as possible, to

◊ Understand exactly what a stallion is, and what his role in natural horse society consists of

◊ Recognize and deal with preconceived ideas, misconceptions and outright myths about stallions

◊ Understand why established stallion management regimes may create behavioural problems

◊ Decide whether they have the necessary qualities to be able to handle a stallion safely without resorting to coercion or harsh treatment

◊ Acquire new skills, or enhance existing skills, that will enable them to train their stallion (s) positively and humanely

◊ Decide whether they can provide the kind of conditions that will allow the stallion to perform as many of his natural behaviours as possible

I hope the book will also inspire those who already keep stallions in accordance with established management practices to change their management regime, to allow their stallion(s) the kind of lifestyle which will enable them to lead happier, more productive lives and allow their true nature to reveal itself.

It is easy to forget that even though certain aspects of stallion behaviour need special consideration, a stallion is still a horse, and in all basic respects he will behave in much the same way as other horses will. Nevertheless, owning a stallion brings with it extra responsibilities over and above those required from everyone who keeps horses, regardless of sex. Some people who are just considering keeping a stallion may, after considering the matter, find these responsibilities simply too burdensome and if they do so that is no reflection on them: it is a sensible recognition of the realities of keeping a stallion. But those who decide that they can live with this burden will, if they approach the training and managing of their stallion in the right frame of mind, end up with an equine companion who is a joy to observe, to work with and simply to have around. Andy Beck, who has spent many years studying the behaviour of horses kept in natural family groups at his White Horse Equine Ethology Project, has this to say (Beck, 2006):

> For those whose luck it is to experience the magic of partnership with a stallion it can be truly life changing so that they never forget the experience. Isn't this a good enough reason to plead for a change of perception and of management practices?

SOME OF THE MORE PERVASIVE MYTHS ABOUT STALLIONS

Some of the myths listed below do – like many myths – contain an element of truth (however small). Next to my brief remarks about each myth I have listed the chapter(s) in which it is discussed.

'A stallion only respects the person who is more dominant than he. That is a law of nature.' (McCall, 2001) *This is a classic example of the 'self-fulfilling prophecy' discussed on page 17, based on a misunderstanding of the nature of 'dominance' and of the stallion's role in equine society.* Chapters 4, 5, 8 and 11

'Every day can be a fight with a stallion to see who rules.' (McCall, 2001) *Another example of the 'self-fulfilling prophecy'.* Chapters 4, 5, 8 and 11

Stallions play mind games with humans in order to gain dominance. *Extremely unlikely: see 1 and 2 above.* Chapters 4, 5, 8 and 11

You cannot ever trust a stallion. *Yet another example of the 'self-fulfilling prophecy'.* Chapters 4, 5, 8 and 11

Never turn your back on a stallion. *This is based on the faulty assumption that stallions are inherently untrustworthy.* Chapters 4, 5, 8 and 11

Stallions may attack without warning, for no reason. *No animal does anything without a reason, even if that reason is not immediately apparent.* Chapter 11

Allowing stallions to nibble will turn into a habit of savage biting. *Only true if the stallion is psychologically disturbed, for whatever reason, or where training has been inadequate.* Chapters 9, 10 and 11

Women are not capable of handling stallions; it's a man's job. *That this is untrue is proved daily, all over the world.* Chapters 2 and 11

Stallions need to know who is boss. *This depends on your definition of 'boss'; as it is generally defined, this is likely to be untrue.* Chapters 4, 5, 8 and 11

Stallions are run by testosterone, and it overrides their brains. *Only true where the stallion has not been correctly trained and managed.* Chapters 7, 9, 10 and 11

Stallions think and react differently from other horses. *Only partially true: for the most part stallions are just like other horses, apart from a few 'extras'.* Chapters 2, 4, 5, 6, 7, 8, 10 and 11

Stallions will kill foals that are not theirs. *Infanticide in stallions has been observed, but it is very rare.* Chapters 4 and 7

You cannot ever pasture stallions with mares and foals. *That this is untrue is proved daily, all over the world.* Chapters 4, 6 and 7

Once they start breeding they become different creatures. *There will certainly be some behavioural changes but much depends on how the stallion is trained and managed.* Chapters 6, 7, 10 and 11

Stallions are territorial and will defend their territory. *Horses are not territorial; what a stallion will defend is his personal space and the area immediately surrounding any mares he perceives as belonging to him.* Chapters 4, 5, 6, 7 and 11

Behavioural tendencies are genetically inherited. *There is certainly a genetic element to behaviour but we do not know to what extent it operates. Environmental influences and life experiences seem to play a much greater part in influencing behaviour.* Chapters 4, 8, 9 and 11

It is dangerous for a menstruating woman to be in the presence of a stallion. *There is no reason why this should be so and no convincing evidence to support it.* Chapter 2

Chapter 1

Myths, folk beliefs, and 'received wisdom'

It ain't so much the things we don't know that get us in trouble. It's the things we know that just ain't so.
– Artemus Ward

FEW domestic animals have been so misrepresented, misunderstood and mistreated than the entire male of the species *Equus caballus*. The idea of the proud, powerful, savage, untamed stallion seems to have etched itself deeply into the human psyche, particularly in those parts of the world where the prevailing culture promotes aggression as a means of obtaining and keeping power. This leads naturally to the perception that stallions are aggressive, dangerous and explosive, to be handled only by people with the skills necessary to dominate such a lethal animal.

This belief has become so widespread that many people who are otherwise quite competent in handling horses will have nothing to do with stallions, even where it is clear that the latter are good-tempered and well-behaved. For example, the (adult) daughter of a friend of ours will not approach our Arabian stallion, Nivalis, even though she has known him for years and has seen how quiet and well-behaved he is. On her visits to our yard she avoids going near Nivalis's stable if he happens to be in it, 'because he is a stallion'. Yet she has seen him take a mint from between my and my husband's lips without so much as touching me with his teeth, and she knows he adores petting and attention from family and strangers alike. But so strongly has the myth of the 'big, bad stallion, who will attack without warning' been ingrained in her mind that it simply overrides the evidence of her eyes.

Received wisdom and folk beliefs

These beliefs – and others – about stallions, form part of the 'received wisdom' – the body of information that is generally accepted as being true, even though it may not be – that constitutes equine lore. Much of this lore consists of beliefs that have seldom been questioned, because they have been generally accepted among horse people for a considerable amount of time, sometimes for generations, and sometimes even for hundreds of years.

In considering this equine lore, Dr Marthe Kiley-Worthington differentiates between what she calls 'folk knowledge' – that is, information that is well-known and which has been proven scientifically or by *critically assessed* experiences – and 'folk belief', which is what horse people believe (whether because of preconceived ideas or because of uncritically followed traditional practices), but which may not be correct. (Kiley-Worthington, Horse Watch: What it is to be Equine, 2005) Much of the lore concerning stallions comes under the heading of 'folk belief'.

Many of the people who perpetuate myths and half-truths about stallions are very experienced horsemen and women, often with years of experience in dealing with stallions, so in a logical world one might expect their testimony to be accurate and trustworthy. Unfortunately, even the most

The Natural Stallion

Nivalis will take a mint from between Brian's lips without even touching him with his teeth. Photo: Lesley Skipper

Many people have not had the privilege of seeing a stallion living with his family. Nivalis (right) with Tiff (Mikenah) and their colt foal Tariel. Photo: Lesley Skipper

knowledgeable and experienced of horsemen and women have their own conceptual baggage to hamper their understanding. For example, they may have been taught that horse society is organized as a dominance hierarchy, with the stallion at the top, and that to handle a stallion effectively you have to dominate him (see the first three myths in the list on page 14). Unless they have been privileged enough to see a free-ranging stallion living with his family, allowed to live without human interference, they are unlikely to see how misguided this idea is, and that no-one is the 'boss', let alone the stallion (see Chapter 5 for a fuller discussion of this). So, thinking that they have to show him who's boss, they behave towards the stallion in a way that causes him to confirm all the prejudices against him. This is a consequence of what is often referred to as a 'self-fulfilling prophecy'.

The 'self-fulfilling prophecy'

All of us tend to form certain expectations regarding other people; these expectations are usually coloured by what we have been told, or by prior experience with people who seem to resemble those about whom we are currently forming our ideas and expectations. These expectations influence our own behaviour towards the people concerned. Numerous studies have shown that if teachers are led to believe that children in a certain group are dull and those in another group bright, they will behave differently towards each group. The children in the group perceived to be bright will be given more encouragement and approval, will have more time spent on them and will be set more challenging tasks. Those perceived to be dull, on the other hand, will have less time spent on them, will be given less encouragement and approval, and will not have their abilities stretched because the teachers are convinced it would be a waste of time. Studies have shown that this is true regardless of the real abilities of the children concerned, *unless* teachers make a real effort to overcome prejudices and treat every child as having the ability to improve and perform well.

In everyday life, we may, for example, regard people who dress in a certain way or have numerous tattoos as threatening; our behaviour towards them (as expressed in our body-language or in the way we speak to them) may therefore become defensive and/or hostile. A natural response to such behaviour is for the other person to become threatening and/or aggressive: by communicating our fears we have actually provoked the very behaviour we fear. So our expectations have been proved correct and because of this, we will, in similar circumstances, tend to repeat our hostile and defensive behaviour – thus ensuring that our expectations continue to be met. In the same way, if someone is rude or unpleasant, we tend to react negatively. Similarly, if we expect someone to behave badly, we ourselves will very often behave in such a manner that our body language, tone of voice, choice of words etc. set up a reaction in the other person which provokes the very behaviour we expect. By creating the right conditions for this to happen, we bring about the very event we fear.

We then feel justified in our prior belief that this person was bound to behave badly. This might or might not have been true, but by making it almost inevitable we have prevented any possibility of an alternative. It might well be that if we approached this person in a positive or even neutral manner, we could defuse any tendencies for them to behave badly. This of course is by no means an infallible approach, because some people are unable to respond to positive approaches. However, it works often enough that we can adopt it as a working principle, and deal with those cases where it breaks down on an individual basis.

Exactly the same principles apply to our attitudes towards horses, who – with their exceptional sensitivity to body-language – respond to negative cues in the same way as humans do. So we can see how the behaviour of those trainers and handlers who believe the myths about stallions being dominant, and having to be dominated in turn, can result in their beliefs being constantly reaffirmed by the stallion's resulting negative behaviour. If you believe that every day with a stallion is going to be a fight to see who rules, it will be. If you believe you can never trust a stallion, then your own behaviour will reflect this, and lo and behold, you have an untrustworthy stallion.

Cultural perceptions

This attitude towards stallions may have its roots in particular cultures (a topic to which I shall return in Chapter 5). Marthe Kiley-Worthington comments that

> There may be problems in our everyday interpretation due to preconceived notions as a result of a particular cultural education . One of the most obvious examples of this is the development in the western United States of 'rodeo' breaking on which Sherpell (1986) remarks: 'The emphasis on gratuitous domination and cruelty has been aptly described as the modern equivalent of a public hanging.' This approach of treating other mammals either as robots without feelings, or brutalising them, is deeply ingrained in some human societies. Treating animals in brutalising ways transforms the individual animal into what he is perceived to be by, for example, heightening his fear and aggression. The result is that the individual animal responds aggressively, which is what is expected, and fulfils the preconceived notions of the human witnesses. This is not because the animals are 'red in tooth and claw, brutish and aggressive', but often because they are scared . (Kiley-Worthington, 2005)

Negative perceptions

In spite of the fact that so many people believe stallions to be innately vicious and dangerous, courts of law, relying on expert witness testimony, do not necessarily agree with this negative view. A case brought before the Superior Court of Pennsylvania in 2005 (Kinley v. Bierly, Superior Court of Pennsylvania 2005 PA Super 168 May 4, 2005) established that the fact that a horse is an uncastrated male will not, on its own, prove that the horse had dangerous propensities. A personal injury case was brought by a woman who had been bitten by a stallion while she was feeding her own horse nearby. The case failed, and the appellant appealed. The basis for her appeal was, as stated in the court record, that 'Stallions, as a "class" are generally known to have vicious propensities despite being legally characterized as a domestic animal.' After considering all the evidence and relevant case law, the court concluded that the fact that a horse is an uncastrated male will not on its own prove dangerous propensities. It cited an earlier case heard by the Pennsylvania Superior Court (*Commonwealth v. Brown*, 839 A.2d 433, 435, Pa. Super. 2003) where the court found that 'The tendency of a stallion to be spirited may be so well known as to be a matter of common knowledge, but the implication that everyone knows stallions are vicious and will bite simply is not true. In fact, Appellant's own expert witness conceded this fact in her report, admitting that not all stallions exhibit unpredictable and aggressive tendencies, but "the individual personality of the horse plays a large part" in whether a stallion is vicious and also that breeding and training are contributing factors.' The appellant in Kinley v. Bierly lost her appeal.

Unfortunately this eminently sensible judgement is not widely known, so that countless people remain convinced that stallions are inherently dangerous and not to be trusted. Regrettably, many of the negative ideas about stallions are reinforced, rather than diminished, by the teachings of some of those purporting to offer a more enlightened approach to horse training. Some of these trainers dwell on the worst aspects of stallion behaviour, telling horror stories about people being savaged and even killed by stallions.[1] By stressing the extreme negative side of stallion behaviour they continue to uphold the idea of stallions as innately aggressive and difficult.

Throughout the remainder of this book I will be challenging this perception, showing why it is faulty and how the training and management practices so often recommended to stallion owners can bring about the very behaviour they are meant to suppress, reinforcing all the worst prejudices about stallions.

Some readers may feel that in emphasizing the best side of stallion behaviour I have been guilty of viewing stallions through rose-tinted spectacles. I can assure them that this is not the case. I am as aware as anyone of the negative side of stallion behaviour, as I hope the rest of the book will show. However, I wanted to show that if we pay sufficient attention to a stallion's needs, and approach his training and management with a thorough understanding of the principles involved, we can largely eliminate the negative aspects and concentrate on the positive.

First of all, the next chapter will look at the related questions of why anyone should keep a male horse entire, and who is qualified to handle a stallion.

---

1 In February 2010 a man was killed by a stallion in Tennessee, USA, in a particularly horrific attack. This, and other incidents, will be discussed in Chapter 11, Dealing with problem behaviours

Chapter 2

Why keep a stallion?

Nothing is more misleading than an unchallenged false assumption.

– Desmond King-Hele

WHY keep a stallion? In a culture less prejudiced against stallions, one might counter this with another question, 'Why not?'

In virtually every culture that has depended on horses for long periods of its history, stallions have been accorded high status. There are certain exceptions: the Bedouin of Arabia, for example, rode only mares, reserving stallions purely for breeding and paying them very little attention except with regard to keeping the bloodlines pure. The Mongols, one of the major equestrian cultures, tended to ride geldings, as did many other nomad warrior peoples. In the West, however, and in some parts of the Near East such as Turkey, the stallion represented for many people the ultimate horse, the symbol of pride, strength and masculinity. Throughout much of history stallions were used for war. The Egyptians and Assyrians took stallions into battle, as did the Romans and indeed most European armies until comparatively recently in history.

For many military leaders, a stallion was the mount of choice. For example, the Emperor Napoleon Bonaparte preferred stallions; although he did occasionally ride mares (such as Marie and Desirée, both of them among the horses for whom he had a great deal of affection), his favourite charger was his grey Arabian Marengo (who may have actually been an Arabian stallion called Ali). Indeed, at one time stallions were the preferred sex of horses chosen for the French cavalry. Military legislation of 1803 decreed that the horses best suited for the cavalry were to be entire stallions; only those stallions with vices that could be not rehabilitated, or were dangerous, were to be castrated.[1]

The status of stallions in western cultures has led to some strange attitudes on the part of breeders. Whereas the Bedouin traced the breeding of their horses through the tail-female line, breeders in the West have traditionally placed more emphasis on the stallion's bloodlines. So, for example, accounts of how the Thoroughbred was created usually concentrate on the founders of the male bloodlines, the Byerly Turk, Godolphin Arabian, Darley Arabian etc., with scant attention being paid to the mares whose contribution to Thoroughbred breeding was equally as important as that of the stallions concerned.

Yet in the English-speaking cultures at least, this cult of the stallion has not resulted in greater familiarity with the nature and behaviour of entire male horses. Many horse owners and riders may never encounter a stallion in their entire equestrian career; the majority will have no experience

---

[1] A. Alexandrie, (1812) *Legislation Militaire* Paris: Chez Louis Caprido volume 3. Cited by Paul Dawson in *Au Galop!: Horses and Riders of Napoleon's Army,* Black Tent Publications, 2011

The Emperor Napoleon Bonaparte preferred stallions; here he is shown astride a stallion of his favourite breed, Arabian. From a print of *Napoleon at Wagram*, by Horace Vernet (Author's collection)

of handling stallions. This has traditionally been the preserve of stud grooms, since most stallions were (and still are) kept specifically for breeding. There have always been notable stallions who have made their mark as riding horses, mainly as chargers for military figures such as the Duke of Wellington, whose Thoroughbred Copenhagen carried him for fifteen hours on the day of the battle of Waterloo; British officers in India were also more likely to ride stallions. One of the best-known examples was the grey Arabian stallion Vonolel, who served as Lord Roberts's charger for 13 years, during which time he took part in the celebrated forced march of more than 300 miles from Kabul to Kandahar in August 1880. Vonolel was decorated with the Kabul Medal and the Kabul-Kandahar Star, and in 1897 he was ridden by Lord Roberts in Queen Victoria's Diamond Jubilee procession.

Arabian stallion Vonolel served as Lord Roberts's charger for thirteen years. The horse was decrated with the Kandahar Star and took part in Queen Victoria's Diamond Jubilee procession. *Field-Marshal Earl Roberts on his Charger 'Vonolel'* by Charles Wellington Furse (Tate Gallery)

However, as far as the majority of horsemen and women in the English-speaking countries have been concerned, most riding horses have been mares or geldings. This is in marked contrast to Hispanic cultures, where stallions are ridden as a matter of course and indeed are considered the only suitable horses for gentlemen to ride.

Gelding may not be an option

For some people, the castration of male horses may not be an option. For Muslims, for example, it is forbidden by Islamic law, as it is regarded as a mutilation. Many non-Muslims may also, for religious or philosophical reasons, recoil from the idea of gelding a male horse. They may feel, with some reason, that by castrating him one is taking away a large part of who a stallion *is*: he is being deprived not only of his ability to breed, but of a defining part of his personality. In many cultures, especially those of the Iberian Peninsula, a gelded horse has traditionally been seen as a lesser horse, one who has had some of his essential nature removed by castration.

Valid arguments for gelding

However, there are a number of valid arguments for gelding horses. One is to prevent indiscriminate breeding and the production of unwanted foals, although with good management this need not be a problem, as Chapter 7 will demonstrate. Another consideration is that nowadays increasing numbers of people become horse owners without any previous experience of horses. It would certainly not be either safe or fair to expect novices and children to ride and handle entire males, although in some cultures it is taken for granted that everyone who rides, whether novice or not, and regardless of age, will ride stallions. In Portugal, for example, few children will have access to the kind of ponies that English children learn to ride on; instead they will be put on their father's trained stallion. However, that is a culture geared to riding and handling stallions, where children in equestrian households will become familiar with them from their earliest years.

Children and stallions

Even so, there are a surprising number of English children whose early experiences of horses include an easy familiarity with at least one stallion. For example, the photographs on page 23 show a friend's seven-year-old daughter helping her father and my husband Brian to groom Nivalis, and later on sitting on his back (held firmly in place by Brian, since she is not wearing a hard hat).

Readers of a certain age may remember the White Horse Whisky television adverts. These showed a white horse (actually a grey Arabian stallion) galloping along a lake shore. That stallion, Roxan (who is also, incidentally, our own stallion Nivalis's grandfather), was described by his late owner, Pat Coward, as very much one of the family; her sons grew up literally playing about his feet. Mrs Coward's sons rode Roxan from an early age; the photographs below show her young son Jonathan riding Roxan bareback and standing on his back.

However, it is a completely different matter when neither the children concerned nor their parents have such early experience with stallions. I imagine that few parents, even those with some kind of equestrian background, would want to expose their children to the undoubted risks associated with handling and riding entire male horses.

Can we justify routine gelding?

In spite of these considerations, one may ask whether we can always justify the routine gelding of horses simply to make them more manageable. As Chapters 3 and 11 will show, gelding does not always have the desired effect. And, as I said in the Introduction, we must never lose sight of the fact that a stallion is still a horse, albeit with certain behavioural characteristics that in geldings may be less pronounced or even absent. As the rest of this book will show, when properly educated and

Chapter 2

Seven-year-old Chloe and her father help Brian groom Arabian stallion Nivalis. Photo: Lesley Skipper

Nivalis gives Chloe a ride: as she is not wearing a hat, she is being held firmly in place by Brian (partly out of shot on the other side of the horse). Photo: Lesley Skipper

Patricia Coward's young son Jonathan riding Arabian stallion Roxan bareback. Photos: courtesy of the late Mrs Coward

23

allowed to live a life that is as natural as possible in a domestic environment, stallions can become as tractable and easy to manage as any other horse.

Dr Marthe Kiley-Worthington, who for more than thirty years has been running an experimental stud and equine behaviour research centre, has strong views on the castration of horses as a matter of routine. As she points out, 'In the majority of cases, stallions are "difficult" because they are made so. Is it right that people should compensate for their own incompetence by surgery?' (Kiley-Worthington, 1987)

Where male horses are to be kept mainly for higher-level competition, there may be compelling reasons for *not* having them gelded. Many people believe that one of the reasons why performance horse breeding in the UK has lagged behind that of other European countries such as Germany, Belgium and the Netherlands is that so many of our top performance horses have been gelded and so we do not have the same resources of proven performance horses from which to select breeding stock. This situation is gradually changing, but attitudes towards stallions in competition have been slow to alter, both in the UK and in the other English-speaking countries.

With the possibilities raised by the successful cloning of performance horses some people may feel that this particular problem has been solved. However, cloning is still an extremely expensive option and the physiological problems experienced with other cloned species may also become a problem where horses are concerned, making cloning even more expensive in terms of viability. In any case, the ability to reproduce a horse's genome (that is, all the genetic information residing in an individual's DNA) is no guarantee that a resulting clone would have the performance ability of the genetic donor; environment, management and training undoubtedly play a huge part in determining a horse's athletic ability, not to mention his mental attitude to work.

The advantages of having a stallion

Even where the production of performance horses is not the priority, there are countless small-scale breeders who would like to have their own stallion. This would give them several advantages:

◊ They would not incur stud fees, thus reducing the cost of producing foals

◊ There would be no need to subject their mares to the stresses of being sent away to stud

◊ They would be able to oversee the whole mating process and manage it in their own way

Breeding apart, increasing numbers of people are attracted to the idea of keeping stallions for their own sake. They may have worked with, or ridden, stallions in various capacities and come to appreciate the extra qualities which give stallions that bit of extra 'edge' over geldings. Some people who have worked with stallions and colts for a long time may actually come to prefer them because they find entires easier to train. Many years ago our farrier remarked to me that he likes working with well-trained stallions more than with either mares or geldings. He made the point that once a stallion understands what is required of him, and provided he is treated fairly, he will co-operate readily.

The late Owen MacSwiney, Marquis of Mashanaglass, says in his book *Training from the Ground*:

> I shall never forget the outstanding stallion Romadour II, who stood for half
> an hour, half in, half out of his open box at the Westphalian National Stud,

> Warendorf, while I modelled his head and neck. It has to be pointed out that a very wide stable passage was in front of him and that fully occupied boxes of other stallions were to the right, the left and in front of him. He had simply been told to stand, and stand he did, his only movement during the whole session being to reach over and sniff at the model of himself on the modelling stand.
> (MacSwiney, 1987)

This willingness to co-operate, as well as the extra presence and muscular development that testosterone brings to stallions, is one of the reasons why some stunt trainers, such as Gerard Naprous, like to work with stallions. I have certainly found that the extra sharpness characteristic of so many stallions is a bonus when it comes to training, especially if that training is carried out using positive reinforcement (see Chapters 9 and 10). All our own horses respond well to training, but the stallion Nivalis is always extra keen to earn his rewards. The day before writing this, I was showing Nivalis off to a visitor, asking him to shake hands and perform a few other little party-pieces. At the end I asked him to 'stand up for the judge' and instantly he took up his 'show' pose – not the exaggerated stance of some show Arabians, but rather an alert posture with ears pricked and his neck slightly raised and extended in a graceful arch. He got his treat by way of a reward, and I gave him a scratch on the neck, clapped my hands and said 'OK' which he understands means we have finished. He relaxed his pose, but remained standing still as if waiting to be asked something else. So I brought a box into his stable for him to put his forefeet on, and I had scarcely set it down before he was offering to stand on it. I said 'Up!' and he immediately put both his forefeet on it. This willingness to offer a behaviour is characteristic of almost all horses trained with positive reinforcement, but it is especially so with stallions.

A closer relationship

Many people like stallions because they find they can develop a much closer relationship with them than they can with mares or geldings. In some cases this is because the stallions in question have been deprived of social contact with their own kind, and so develop a compensatory relationship with their human handlers. However, even where stallions are allowed to lead more natural lives, the bonds they forge with those who care for them may still be far stronger than humans might experience with other horses.

Of course, there are those people who want to keep a stallion for entirely the wrong reasons. They may feel that, because of the reputation stallions have for macho, aggressive behaviour, there is some kind of cachet attached to their ownership. Unfortunately, in some circles this is indeed the case, which leads to certain people acquiring a stallion as some kind of status symbol. This is never a good reason to keep any kind of animal, especially a sensitive, demanding equine.

It should go without saying that no-one should think of keeping an entire male horse unless they have the facilities to keep him securely while allowing him sufficient freedom to meet as many of his behavioural needs as possible. In the English-speaking countries many people do not have their own land and may have to keep their horse at a livery yard or other equestrian establishment. Many such establishments will not even consider taking a stallion because of the perceived risks and the difficulty of providing suitable, secure turnout. There is also the question of handling. As we shall see, a properly trained and managed stallion should be no more difficult to handle than any other horse; nevertheless, people handling entire male horses need certain qualities, one of the most essential of which is confidence. If equestrian establishment staff have no previous experience of

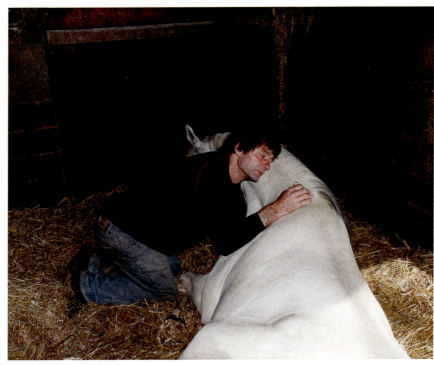

A good relationship: Brian and Nivalis enjoy a snooze together. Photo: Lesley Skipper

handling stallions and therefore lack confidence, then the safety of such staff may be compromised. Finally, there is the safety of other horses to consider. We will see in later chapters that companionship of one kind or another is essential for stallions if they are to be calm and content, and that in many cases it may be possible to keep them with geldings or even other stallions without any problems arising. Even so, it is understandable that many horse owners may be very reluctant to expose their horses to the possible risk of stallion aggression. They may also be anxious about the possibility of a stallion escaping and creating havoc among mares and geldings.

These fears are not always well-founded but, as we shall see, they cannot be dismissed or ignored. Concerns about the safety of staff and other horses may therefore, in very many cases, make it difficult if not impossible for horse owners without their own land to keep a stallion.

However, for people who do have their own land, then depending on individual circumstances and their level of knowledge and experience, keeping a stallion may be practical and even beneficial to all parties. In Chapter 7 we shall look at the kind of facilities needed; for now let us look at the qualities required by anyone thinking of keeping a stallion.

Who should keep a stallion?

Should only professionals keep or handle stallions?

Many people are of the opinion that only professionals should keep or handle stallions. Monty Roberts, for example, says that he is a firm believer that stallions should only be handled by trained professionals. 'It is my opinion,' he says, 'that all entire male horses that will potentially be handled by amateurs should be castrated.' He goes on to say, 'I have many strong reasons for making this recommendation, far too many to list here. Suffice to say that stallions should be castrated unless they are going to be controlled throughout their lives by these highly skilled individuals [i.e. trained professionals, L.S.].'[2]

This view is echoed by many other professionals. They have a point, yet this kind of advice implies that only professionals are competent to handle stallions. This assumes that professionals are necessarily more knowledgeable than amateurs, which is certainly not always the case. A professional is simply someone who earns his or her livelihood from some activity. We therefore tend to assume that a professional must be skilled or competent in order to be able to earn their living in this way. By contrast amateurs are often thought of as lacking expertise, yet this is not necessarily so. An amateur may be someone who engages in an activity or pursuit not for gain, but purely for the love of it: this is the literal meaning of the word *amateur*, from the Latin *amator*, a lover. They may have as much skill and expertise as any professional and an experienced amateur may be every bit as competent to handle a stallion as anyone else.

There are many people who handle stallions in the course of their professional activities who have a great deal of experience, yet who have little understanding of, or sympathy for, their charges. Their experience of stallions may be limited to what they have learned in the kind of environment where stallions have little if any opportunity to engage in natural behaviours. An alien observer whose experience of human male behaviour was limited to what they had seen in, say, a maximum security prison, would end up with a very distorted view of how human males behave and would learn very little about their behaviour in less restrictive surroundings.

In the same way, a professional stallion handler who has never seen how stallions behave in their natural family groups may have an equally distorted view of stallion behaviour. If they do not know or understand the role of the stallion in such a natural group, or if they have absorbed some of the more pernicious myths about stallions, they may misunderstand certain behaviours which they observe in their charges and may not know how to deal with such behaviours in an appropriate and non-punitive manner. In an article written for *Equine Behaviour*[3] in 2000, Lucy Rees describes the bizarre and dangerous behaviour of an Arabian stallion who had been rendered psychotic by the mishandling of so-called professionals. Commenting on the way the stallion had been treated, Rees pulls no punches :

> Professionals they call themselves: people who take an animal that others have spent a thousand years breeding to perfection, and systematically destroy his mind until there is nothing but fear, rage and dogmeat. They are professionals because they want paying for it. (Rees, 2000)

This is not to tar all professional handlers with the same brush; I am not saying that all such professionals lack the requisite knowledge or understanding, simply that their professional status is no guarantee that they have that knowledge and understanding.

It is not professional or amateur status that makes someone competent to handle stallions, but qualities that any sympathetic horseman or woman can develop. As a rule, however, stallions should not be handled by novices except under close supervision, for the simple reason that the novice will not yet have sufficient experience of equine behaviour in general to be able to anticipate problems and take steps to prevent them from happening – or to deal with them on the occasions when they do arise. But the experienced horseman or woman who knows how to handle horses calmly and

---

[2] See Roberts's website, www.montyroberts.com/ju_ask_monty_0805.html
[3] The magazine of the Equine Behaviour Forum

confidently, and with sympathy and understanding, can easily learn how to manage a stallion.

Women and stallions

Gender is, or should be, irrelevant. It used to be the case that handling stallions was not considered suitable for women, and even today there are still some people who feel that this is the case. Some (male) commentators periodically repeat the belief that women are too 'soft' with stallions, and spoil them with too much petting and allowing them to get away with too much (what the horse is being allowed to 'get away with' is often not specified). Yet when it comes to rehabilitating stallions made difficult or even dangerous by harsh treatment (usually, although not always, at the hands of men) some of the most spectacular successes have been achieved by women![4]

A persistent myth

One persistent myth that periodically resurfaces in the debate about who should handle stallions concerns the alleged reaction of stallions to menstruating women. This myth goes something like this: it is dangerous for a menstruating woman to be in the presence of a stallion because he can smell a woman's hormonal cycles and he may react to the woman as if she is a mare in oestrus. Presumably this would mean that a woman should not ride or handle a stallion either when she is menstruating or when she is ovulating, which would effectively restrict the times when it is 'safe' for her to be around stallions to around two weeks out of every four. This smacks of a not very subtle attempt to restrict what women do in an area of animal husbandry that has traditionally been the province of men. First of all, there is no supporting evidence that it is true; countless women of all ages have ridden and handled stallions for many years without experiencing any behavioural changes towards them on the part of the stallions at any particular time of the month. Second, there is no reason to think that human females smell the same as mares do during oestrus. Sometimes the myth as stated omits any mention of ovulation, focusing purely on the menstrual stage of the cycle. This is even less logical, because menstruation in human females does not equate to any stage in a mare's cycle when a stallion would find her receptive; it is not the same as being in oestrus. The only remotely likely cause of any behavioural change in a stallion at such a time could be the smell of blood, which might upset him. Yet although horses are commonly supposed to react to the smell of blood, and some do appear to do so, many others don't. For example, several weeks before I wrote this, my husband accidentally cut his arm quite badly at the stable yard. The wound bled profusely, but as he had to finish feeding and watering the horses, Brian simply bound up the wound as best he could and carried on. The wound continued to bleed, and before long the arm of his jacket was soaked in blood. Yet not one of the horses – including the two stallions – reacted in any way either to the sight or smell of the blood, even when it was literally right under their noses. So this myth about women and stallions should be consigned to the waste-bin – where it belongs.[5]

Confidence is necessary

A friend of mine had plenty of experience with all kinds of horses, but had had only a limited amount of contact with stallions. She was wary of our stallion Nivalis, even though she had ridden him and

---

4 For example, Lucy Rees's rehabilitation of the stallion mentioned above; further details of this are given in Chapter 11.
5 In his book *Talking with Horses* Henry Blake cites the lion tamer Alex Kerr. Kerr was once asked if he would allow his daughter to tame and train big cats, and he said no. Asked why, he said, 'Well, it is quite simple. To do it successfully she must think like a lion or a tiger, and if she thinks and acts like a lion or a tiger, the lion or tiger will look upon her as a lion or tiger, and that would mean that when she came into season, as human beings do just as animals do, the cat would know. And since the way a lion denotes affection is to pick the female up by the scruff of the neck, that is what he would do. And he would break her neck.'

lunged him under my husband's supervision. She was convinced that Nivalis disliked her, and he, reacting to her nervousness and uncertainty, became uncharacteristically nippy and awkward when being handled by her. I explained to her that what he disliked was her uncertain, fussy manner around him; that this made him in turn feel nervous, resulting in his awkwardness. To her credit she made a real effort to overcome her distrust of him, and as her confidence with him increased, his behaviour improved, making him easier to handle and so increasing my friend's confidence still further.

Of course not all stallions are as easy to manage as Nivalis; so much depends on how they have been brought up, trained and managed. But a sympathetic handler with the necessary knowledge and understanding should encounter few real difficulties, provided the stallion does not have any severe behavioural problems – in which case even an experienced stallion handler may need advice and assistance. (For a discussion of behavioural problems and how to deal with them, see Chapter 11.)

Women are perfectly capable of handling stallions: this big, immensely powerful Belgian Warmblood responded beautifully to Brian's niece Vicki. Photo: Lesley Skipper

What makes a competent stallion handler?

So what makes a competent stallion handler? Such a person needs to be

◊ Confident in their approach, without being aggressive. A confident handler will inspire confidence in the stallion, who will then be more inclined to trust his handler and to pay attention to them.

◊ Calm

◊ Patient.

◊ Consistent without being rigid.

◊ Willing to learn, to admit when they have been wrong, and to set aside considerations of personal pride and vanity. Egotistical posturing has no place in the successful management of any horse, let alone a stallion.

◊ Willing to adopt a flexible approach

(Blake, 1975) The same objections apply here as with horses; in any case, countless women have worked with, and trained, big cats, without the kind of disastrous results envisaged by Kerr. (for example *Diana L. Guerrero: see her article on training big cats at http://www.arkanimals.com/ark/ws_training_big_cats.html*)

◊ Sufficiently experienced with horses to be able to anticipate problems before they arise and to take steps to prevent them occurring.

◊ Able to 'read' and understand the subtle body postures that indicate a stallion's mood and imminent behaviour

◊ Able to set aside negative expectations and adopt a positive frame of mind (the 'self-fulfilling prophecy' works both ways: expect good behaviour and you are more likely to get it)

◊ Knowledgeable about what a stallion is and what his needs and priorities are.

◊ Able to apply the principles of learning correctly, in order to be able to train a stallion without the use of fear or coercion.

The latter point is especially important, because one of the commonest causes of problems with horses in general – not just stallions – is a failure to understand how animals learn, and how to motivate them to want to co-operate with humans. Too often this failure of understanding results in people resorting to coercion, which can be dangerous with any horse, and even more so with a stallion; Chapters 8 and 11 will show exactly why this is so.

The power of expectation should also never be underrated. In those cultures (for example, Portugal) where good stallion behaviour is expected and people adopt a relaxed[6] attitude around stallions, problems are far fewer than in those which adopt a negative attitude, with the constant expectation of things going wrong.[7]

Anyone, then, provided they are willing to acquire the necessary knowledge and understanding (and perhaps discarding a few preconceived ideas along the way!), can become a competent stallion handler. The knowledge they need is not arcane, and it does not depend on following any one method or 'system' of training and management. It can be readily acquired by anyone willing to learn and to accept ideas and information which, in some cases, may run counter to received wisdom. In the chapters that follow, we shall look at this information and these ideas, and see how they can improve our understanding of stallions and how to keep them happy, healthy and, above all, sane.

---

6 Being relaxed around stallions does not, of course, equate to being careless.
7 Anticipating problems is not at all the same as *expecting* them to occur.

Chapter 3

What is a stallion? Part I: Stallion physiology

Stallion *A horse, not under four years, capable of reproducing the species. An entire – ungelded horse.*

– Summerhays' Encyclopedia for Horsemen

A STALLION, as we know, is an entire male horse aged four years or over. That bald statement by itself tells us next to nothing about him. In this chapter we look at the physical characteristics of the stallion; Chapter 4 will cover one of the most neglected aspects of a stallion's life: his role in the social life of horses.

Sexual dimorphism

Many species show what scientists call *sexual dimorphism*, where the two sexes differ in appearance. One sex may be larger than the other, or the two sexes may differ in shape and colouring. These differences are common in various species of fish and birds; one of the most obvious examples is that of the peacock, whose gorgeous colouring and spectacular tail fan are in stark contrast with the drabber appearance of the peahen. In mammals the differences tend to be less dramatic; nevertheless, many species do show considerable difference in appearance between the sexes. For example, it is easy to distinguish lions from lionesses because of the lion's extravagant mane and bulkier torso.

Where horses are concerned it is not so easy to tell the sexes apart from a distance, because there is little external difference between the sexes other than the appearance and function of the exterior sex organs. As these are clearly absent from geldings, and male horses (whether entire or not) are by no means always larger than females of the same age and type, it can be difficult to determine the sex of a horse without closer examination. Even so, the experienced eye can sometimes identify stallions because of their greater muscular development and from their postural tonus.

Muscular development

What accounts for this muscular development? Although there are a number of factors at work here, one of the principal reasons for extra muscle bulk in stallions is the presence of testosterone. This is a male sex-hormone (androgen) which is also a naturally occurring *anabolic steroid* whose main function is to promote the growth and maintenance of bone and muscle tissue, as well as to enable the development of the male sex organs. It also plays a major role in libido and sexual responses. Production of testosterone in the testes is stimulated by LH (luteinizing hormone) secreted by the anterior pituitary gland. Although testosterone is produced mainly in the testes, it is also secreted in small amounts by the adrenal glands.

The penis

The muscles of the penis normally hold it up inside the sheath, which helps to protect it from damage. When these muscles relax the penis drops out of the sheath; in a healthy male horse (whether entire or gelded) this is usually a sign that the horse feels relaxed and at ease. The erect penis is produced by an increase in the blood pressure of the muscles of the penis, which when fully erect doubles in length and circumference. Following ejaculation the end of the penis inflates to about three times its resting size; this inflated end is often referred to as the 'rose', and the inflation itself is sometimes referred to as 'flowering' (or 'flare' in the US).

The sheath itself has to be roomy in order to accommodate the retracted penis, and sometimes when the horse is trotting it sucks in air, making a noise which is often colourfully described as 'oinking' (or sometimes 'gwooking'). Various explanations have been put forward for this, including dirt accumulated inside the sheath. However, systematic observation suggests that the main cause of 'oinking' is tension in the muscles surrounding the sheath; I have often heard it in stallions and geldings who are in a rather stressful situation, or who are finding some aspect of ridden or lunge work difficult, resulting in tension.

Certainly, an accumulation of dirt inside the sheath can cause problems. An oily, waxy substance called *smegma* is produced inside the sheath. It helps to keep the head of the penis lubricated, but it can build up to the extent that it causes the horse considerable discomfort, especially if the accumulations turn hard and lumpy. The sheath should be regularly washed out,[1] but nothing more than warm water should be used, otherwise the bacteria which normally live on the skin of the penis may be killed off, reducing or even eliminating protection against infections. Some stallions seem to find the procedure quite pleasant, but others may object to it. Washing the penis and sheath is discussed further in Chapter 10, Training Good Behaviours.

The testes

Each testicle is enclosed in a sac of tissue called the *vaginal tunic*. This is in turn attached to a powerful muscle which can pull the testis up into the groin area if the horse experiences fear, excitement (in some circumstances), or cold (try touching a stallion's testicles with cold hands – if he is the kind of stallion who will not take exception to this – and see what happens. Those testicles will immediately disappear up into the groin).

Castration

If people choose to keep a stallion, then – as discussed in Chapter 2 – one would like to think they have a good reason for doing so. However, problems may arise that conventional wisdom suggests will be solved by having the stallion gelded. Indeed, in popular equestrian literature (and even in some scientific literature), as well as in online forum discussions, gelding is often proposed not as a last resort, but almost as a cure-all.

Because castration involves the surgical removal of the testes, it results in a dramatic reduction in the amount of testosterone produced by the body, since the testes are the major source of that hormone. The general belief is that since testosterone is responsible for the traits which may cause perceived problem behaviour in entire males (for example aggression, the overpowering urge to

1 At least every couple of months or so; the penis should be washed after the stallion has covered a mare.

Chapter 3

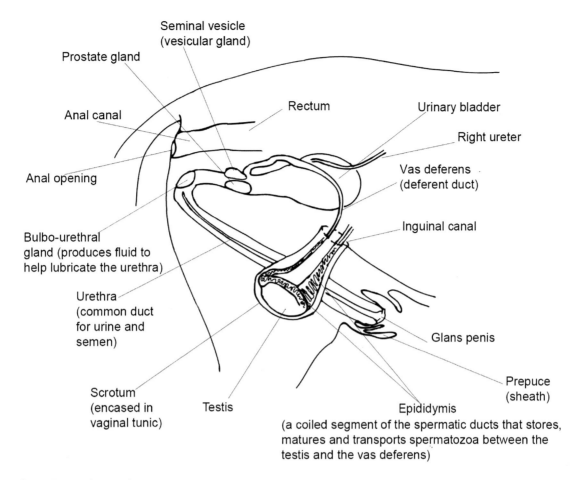

The male equid reproductive organs

find and mate with mares, inattention and so on), the removal of the main source of testosterone will cure, or at the very least reduce, that problem behaviour.

Is castration effective?

But is castration effective in eliminating these and other undesirable behaviours? Equestrian literature tends to give the impression that geldings lose almost every vestige of stallion behaviour (or, if gelded early in life, never develop such behaviour in the first place). At first the evidence might suggest that this is correct; after all, the majority of geldings do not pose the same kind of problems as many stallions do. However, things may not be all they seem on the surface.

Andy Beck of the White Horse Equine Ethology Project maintains (and personal observation, as well as research, convinces me that he is right) that castration cannot be relied upon to extinguish sexual behavior, although it may often do so.

> ...some geldings are able to maintain an erection and even to serve a mare, although there will be no issue. Nor is the uncertain behavior restricted to the physical; geldings kept with mares frequently become fixated to the point that it becomes impossible to remove them for work without incurring a level of separation anxiety that prevents concentration on the task at hand and can be very dangerous for both rider and horse. Yet there has been no diminution of the

sense of smell, so that when mares come into oestrus[2] the gelding is flooded with pheromone signals but lacks the capacity to act in accord with their reception.[3] The psychological impact is impossible to judge without almost certain anthropomorphosis, but only the brave or those determined not to admit the possibility would declare that there is none. (Beck, The Secret Life of Stallions, 2006)

Stallion-like geldings

Some research carried out into gelding behaviour suggests that at least 30 per cent of geldings retain a considerable part of their masculinity, while other researchers believe this figure may be as high as 50 per cent. Certainly my own experiences with geldings bear out the latter figure: of the geldings I have known and observed at least 60 per cent have shown some definite residual stallion characteristics. These range from aspects of stallion behaviour such as herding and protecting mares to actual copulation.

In 1985 a team of scientists from the School of Veterinary Medicine, University of California (Davis) carried out a survey of 140 horse owners in order to compare the effectiveness of castration carried out before puberty with that of castration carried out after puberty, on undesirable behaviour (specifically, sexual and aggressive behaviour). The survey found that out of 94 geldings castrated before puberty (i.e. before two years of age), 20 to 30 per cent continued to display stallion-like sexual behaviour and aggression toward horses, and 5 per cent were aggressive toward humans. It also found no significant difference between this level of problem behaviour, and that found in 46 geldings castrated after puberty (that is, at over 3 years of age). Overall the study revealed that as a means of eliminating objectionable behaviour towards humans, castration was effective in 60 to 70 per cent of cases, but it was only effective in eliminating aggression towards other horses in 40 per cent of cases.

In evaluating the effectiveness of gelding, the scientists carrying out the study looked at the behaviour of stallions before and after castration. Out of 18 stallions who had shown aggression towards humans before being gelded, six continued to be aggressive after being gelded. Out of those six, three were reported as being less aggressive. Out of 21 stallions who had been aggressive towards other horses before being gelded, 13 were still aggressive after being gelded; however, six of these were reported as being less aggressive.

The effectiveness of castration on sexual behaviour is more difficult to assess, because, as the authors of the paper in which these findings were presented point out,

> many male horses are not given an opportunity to express sexual interest toward mares in estrus after castration. In the survey, there were 30 stallions that copulated with mares before castration and also were observed in the presence of mares in estrus after castration. Of these horses, only 2 still copulated a year or later following castration and an additional 7 displayed some interest in the form of mounting, erection, or attempts to genitally investigate mares. (Line, *et al.* 1985)

---

2 Oestrus, the technical term for being in season, has its counterparts: anoestrus is often used as the opposite of oestrus, but some people prefer the term dioestrus for mares who are cycling but not in season, reserving the term anoestrus for mares who are not cycling and therefore are not in season.
3 Geldings flehm (see Chapter 4) less frequently than stallions do. Testosterone has been found to have effects on the olfactory bulb in rats; it enhances the response to oestrus. (Paredes, 1998)

As the authors go on to say, '…the probability of eliminating sexual behavior or aggression toward people in stallions was found to be between 60% and 70%, and the probability of eliminating aggression toward horses was about 40%.'

The authors also point out that 'It should be noted that the percentages we report were for those cases in which the owners reported an elimination of the behavior rather than just a reduction.' So whether these figures represent an acceptable reduction in objectionable behaviours depends on what is considered acceptable: some people might consider that any reduction in undesirable behaviour is better than none.

The findings reported from this survey suggest that the age at which a horse is gelded makes little difference to his behaviour as a gelding. However, it is very difficult to make a reliable assessment about this, as there are so many factors which affect stallion behaviour; furthermore, we have no way of knowing whether a colt castrated at a very young age, before any undesirable behaviours have emerged, might have developed those behaviours if he had not been gelded. Some mature stallions cease to show stallion-like behaviour a comparatively short while after castration; some take considerably longer (up to 18 months or more) to show any behaviour changes, and some never do. This suggests that certain aspects of stallion behaviour are only partially 'hard-wired' and require a degree of learning for them to become ingrained, and that once this learning takes place it may be difficult to eradicate.

In other words, there is no way to predict accurately what effect being gelded will have on a mature stallion.

Geldings often retain many stallion characteristics: Welsh Section B pony Dino was not gelded until he was four, and continued to behave in many ways like a stallion. Nevertheless, even though Dino could be a handful, he and his young rider, Abbie Nelson (shown here with Dino), developed a strong relationship which led to many successes in showjumping and dressage. Photo: Lesley Skipper

The castration process

The operation itself is relatively straightforward and, while all operations involve some risk, modern surgical techniques and post-operative care help to keep these risks to a minimum. It can be carried out at any time of the year, but in temperate climates such as that of the UK, spring and autumn are the preferred seasons for this operation, with spring being the usual option, before too many flies are around to cause irritation of the wound. Castration may be carried out with the horse in the standing position, or in a recumbent position with the horse lying on his side. The advantage of standing castration is that it can be done with a local anaesthetic rather than a general anaesthetic. The disadvantage is that the veterinary surgeon runs the risk of being kicked if the horse does not respond well to the initial sedation, but with modern sedatives this risk is comparatively low. In any case, the majority of vets (in the UK at least) appear to favour standing castration; not only is it less risky for the horse, but it is also a much simpler procedure which enables the vet to work without the assistance of another vet (recommended by British Equine Veterinary Association's guidelines in cases where a general anaesthetic is used). It also eliminates the need to have the horse 'cast', which in itself carries considerable risk, not only to the people handling the horse but to the horse himself.

There is almost always some swelling of the scrotum and sheath area after the operation, and until this goes down the horse should be exercised daily to help reduce the swelling (any abnormal bleeding – that is, anything other than the occasional drip – or swelling that does not reduce after several days – should of course be reported to the vet). Some horses take several days to get over the operation, while others seem to recover almost instantaneously. Our Warmblood gelding, for example, showed virtually no reaction to the operation; once the sedative had worn off, he went about his business, cavorting about in the field as if nothing had happened.

The right age for gelding

A horse may be gelded at any age provided the testes are of a reasonable size and have fully descended into the scrotum. However, many people believe that the longer they leave a horse entire before gelding him, the bigger he will grow. In fact, this is not the case. Testosterone affects both the growth of the long bones and the closure of the growth plates.[4] In horses who have been gelded at an early age, the dramatic reduction in testosterone production means that the long bones will continue to grow for longer than would be the case in a horse left entire, and the growth plates in the legs will close at a later date. Of course there could be other factors such as nutrition affecting the eventual height of a male horse; however, the effects of reduced testosterone on the growth of the long bones is indisputable, having been studied in a number of species, including humans. (There is a human genetic condition known as Klinefelter's syndrome, in which males have an extra female chromosome; low testosterone levels can result in excessive growth of the long bones of the arms and legs.)

Rigs: true or false?

When stallion behaviour is observed in a gelding, many people seem to assume automatically that the gelding in question must be a rig, and frequently the assumption is further made that such horses have been what is often called 'proud cut', in other words the vet has not removed all the testicular material when carrying out the castration. In fact, with modern surgical techniques this

---

4 Growth plates are areas of cartilage at both ends of the long bones. The cartilage cells divide and increase in number, eventually being converted to bone; this is how the long bones grow. When growth has ceased, the plates are completely replaced by bone; in other words, the growth plates are 'closed'.

is extremely unlikely to be the case; it is even less likely that the gelding is a true rig. The latter is a colloquial term for a horse, one or both of whose testicles have not descended into the scrotum. The correct term is *cryptorchid*, from the Greek roots *crypto-* (hidden) and *orchis* (testicle).

Crypdorchidism

The testes normally descend into the scrotum during the last months of gestation. However, occasionally one or both will fail to do so, being retained either in the abdomen (abdominal cryptorchidism) or the abdominal opening (inguinal cryptorchidism). Testes retained in the abdomen will never descend into the scrotum once the foal is more than a few weeks old, because they will have grown too big for the opening through which they need to pass. However, in cases of inguinal cryptorchidism the testes may sometimes develop normally (if later than usual) and descend into the scrotum when the horse is between the ages of two and three.

If both testicles fail to descend the horse is termed a *bilateral* cryptorchid; if only one testicle is retained in the inguinal canal then the horse is called a *monorchid*, or unilateral cryptorchid. In the latter case, the descended testicle may be larger than normal, will produce sperm, and (provided the sperm is viable) the horse will be fertile. In either case any sperm produced in the *undescended* testicle(s) will not be fertile; however the testes will continue to produce testosterone, which does of course affect behaviour.

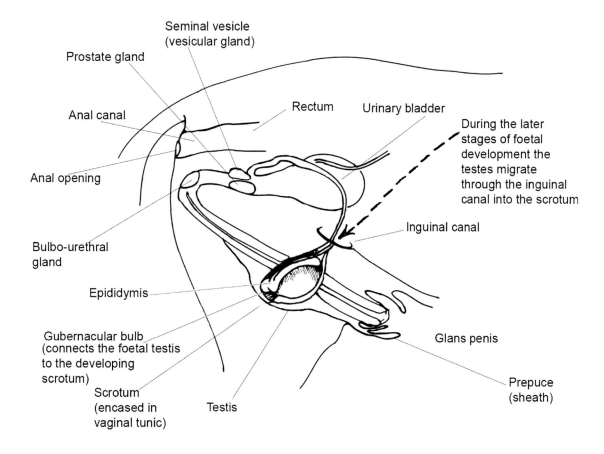

The testicles descend into the scrotum through the inguinal canal during the last months of gestation.

Cryptorchidism is caused by a number of factors, both genetic and hormonal, which are not yet fully understood. Whatever the causes, removal of the retained testes is generally advised because, quite apart from any behavioural issues which may arise, retained testicles are more prone to developing tumours than those which have descended normally. Until comparatively recently the surgery to remove retained testes required the opening up of the abdomen under a general anaesthetic (*laparotomy*). However, it is now possible in many cases to remove the testicle(s) via *laparoscopy*, which involves only a small incision enabling a tiny fibre-optic video camera to be inserted. This makes it easier for the veterinary surgeon to locate the retained testicle(s); the surgery can also be performed via the same incision. This procedure can be performed either under local anaesthetic with the horse sedated and in a standing position, or under general anaesthesia with the horse on his back. In either case it is much less traumatic and postoperative recovery is far quicker than with a laparotomy.

False rig

The term 'false rig' is often applied to true geldings who display some degree of stallion behaviour. This seems to echo the widespread belief that geldings should not behave like stallions, even though, as we have seen, this is not actually the case for a very large number of geldings. Even so, if a gelding's castration history is unknown and he is behaving like a stallion, some owners may wish to satisfy themselves that he is not a cryptorchid. This is a simple matter of having blood samples taken and tested for the presence of testosterone, since concentrations of hormones are usually lower in geldings than they are in cryptorchids. However, hormonal tests are not always accurate and the only way to be one hundred per cent certain would be through surgical exploration of the abdomen. As cryptorchids are fortunately not at all common, this would seem to be an extreme and unwarranted course of action in most cases, especially since, in the study referred to above (Line *et al.*), blood analysis revealed no difference in testosterone concentration between geldings who exhibited stallion-like behaviour, and those who did not. In summary, given what we know about the prevalence of stallion-like behaviour in geldings, and the fact that true rigs are uncommon, it is very unlikely that geldings behaving like stallions are in fact rigs. It is really far more likely that such behaviour is simply an aspect of normal gelding behaviour!

Castration may not be the answer

From all this, we can see that castration does not necessarily solve the kind of behavioural problems generally associated with stallions, which I shall look at in more detail in Chapter 11. If – as is generally supposed – stallion behaviour owes so much to testosterone, and the main source of testosterone – i.e. the testicles – is removed by castration, then why should so much of that behaviour persist *after* castration? As we saw earlier, testosterone is also produced by the adrenal glands, so it may be that some geldings who show this high level of residual stallion behaviour have over-active adrenal glands and/or are more sensitive to the effects of testosterone. However, there are usually other factors at work.

Testosterone alone does not cause behaviour

Hormones such as testosterone do not actually *cause* behaviour; they merely facilitate the occurrence of the behaviour under certain conditions. There may also be other hormones involved in the activation of certain behaviours. For example, testosterone alone is not responsible for aggressive behaviour in males; huge numbers of male animals of different species (including humans) do not routinely display aggressive behaviour, yet they have normal or even elevated levels of testosterone. Environmental and social factors play a great part in determining when – and to what extent – the behaviours normally associated with testosterone occur – as Chapter 11 will show.

So having a horse castrated should never be regarded as a first-step solution to problem behaviour in stallions. Nevertheless, there may be occasions when gelding may be the best solution for all concerned; we will consider this in Chapter 11.

Chapter 4

What is a stallion? Part II: The stallion's role in life

Wild horses look pathetic in captivity. I'm convinced they are in a state of depression. They have lost what they value most: their freedom and their family.

– *Ginger Kathrens,* Cloud: Wild Stallion of the Rockies

𝐿EAVING aside the uses to which humans have put him, what is a stallion's role in life? What makes him 'tick', so to speak?

Evolutionary and/or genetic explanations for just about everything became popular in the 1970s, and many scientists still follow this line of thinking, so we end up with silly statements to the effect that (for example) stallions perform certain behaviours in order to ensure the propagation (or survival) of their genes.[1] They don't do anything of the sort, of course; that is not why a stallion – or any other animal – performs any action. There is a monumental confusion here between process and outcome: propagating one's genes may be a long-term evolutionary *result*, but it certainly is not a *cause* of the behaviour, and it doesn't even begin to explain why the behaviour first arose, or how the animal feels when performing it. The most one could say about gene survival is that because animals who behave in certain ways are more likely to survive and produce offspring who (if the trait is inherited) also behave in a similar way, then the genes which influence that particular behaviour can be said to have 'survived'. Passing on one's genes is not, and cannot be (except for certain obsessive humans), any kind of motive: to believe otherwise is to put the cart well and truly before the horse. As philosopher Mary Midgley so eloquently puts it, '…if we are to understand the behavior of conscious beings, we must take their motives seriously and not try to reduce them to something else.' (Midgley, 1995)

Before we can begin to do this, we have to look at what stallions do in the wild state, without the interference from humans which affects their natural behaviour and prevents them from expressing the full range of that behaviour.

Unfortunately, this is where the kind of myths and received wisdom reviewed in Chapter 1 really get in the way of our understanding. There are so many distorted ideas and folk beliefs about what stallions do in the wild, and these have become so embedded in equine lore, that identifying and eradicating them is a mammoth task. This is not helped by the many trainers who help to perpetuate these folk beliefs. For example, Pat Parelli states that 'A stallion's job is to procreate and to fight for dominance. He lets nothing stand in his way. Stallions will even fight to the death for dominance.' (Parelli, www.parelli.com, Article 15: 'Stallions demand savvy')

---

[1] We should not forget that 'genes' are human constructs (simply names for specific lengths of DNA).

This is very misleading. First of all, although procreation is certainly one of the most powerful factors in the lives of animals, it takes up only a relatively small part of a stallion's life. Second, if stallions really let nothing stand in their way, bachelors attempting to steal mares or take over established bands would have a much higher success rate than is generally the case. As it is, such attempts are not frequent, and they are usually repelled by the band stallion, normally without any physical contact. Third, as we shall see in Chapter 5, 'dominance' refers to a relationship between two horses, not to some abstract quality or status. As wildlife ecologist Joel Berger points out in his book on the horses of the Granite Range,[2] 'The establishment of dominance in itself would seem to be an inadequate reason [for inter-male aggression] since no immediate benefit is conferred upon males that dominate in social interactions.' (Berger, 1986) The stallion's main role is to protect his family group, and he will indeed fight in order to do this if necessary. However, as we shall see, this does not happen nearly as often as many people like to believe, and the idea of stallions fighting to the death is therefore largely a figment of fiction; the few reliably documented cases have almost always taken place in highly unnatural conditions, for example where the stallions have been deliberately placed in a confined area and are thus unable to escape from each other. Most stallions will avoid physical conflict if at all possible, relying instead on ritual posturing to warn off intruders; actual combat is a last resort.

These and similar beliefs can mislead people into thinking about stallions in terms of aggression and dominance, whereas in fact they should be recognising the stallion's immense potential for co-operation – of which we shall see examples in this and later chapters.

Since comparatively few stallions in a domestic setting are kept in conditions which are even remotely comparable to what they would be in the wild, we must first of all look at what a stallion actually does in the wild.

This poses a further problem: what do we mean by 'in the wild'? In the context of equine behaviour, much reference is made to 'wild horses', but there are no truly wild horses now living. At one time the Mongolian 'wild horse', *Equus przewalskii*, was thought to be the ancestor of the domestic horse, *Equus caballus*. However, DNA analysis has shown that this is not the case, although both descend from a common ancestor. *Equus przewalskii* apart, All so-called 'wild' horses are actually either free-ranging horses (that is, horses who belong to someone but are allowed to roam freely) or feral horses: that is, domestic animals who have either escaped domesticity, or are the descendants of animals who have so escaped.

So how can we study the behaviour of wild horses when there aren't any? The answer is obvious when we think about it: we study the behaviour of feral horses! After all, they are not the remote ancestors of our modern domestic horses: they *are* our modern domestic horses. Observing how they behave when free from human interference can give us the key to understanding their behavioural needs and priorities.

However, not all feral populations will give us the same answers. While there are certain behaviour patterns common to all groups of horses, there are also many variations. These variations largely seem to depend on environmental factors such as climate, terrain, availability of food, group size (itself largely dependent on the foregoing factors) and so on. In addition, the horses in many feral populations may be periodically subjected to various types of human interference; for example they may be rounded up and culled, with a resulting disturbance of population balance and group stability, which affects their social behaviour, making it very difficult to determine how stable populations behave.

---

[2] *Wild Horses of the Great Basin*, University of Chicago Press, 1986

Nevertheless, long-term studies have been carried out on such stable populations, one of the most comprehensive of these being Joel Berger's five-year observation of the horses of the Granite Range of North West Nevada. Berger selected this area precisely because the horses hardly ever came into contact with humans, and because the area was not grazed by cattle, being populated mainly by mule deer, pronghorn mountain goats, elk and bighorn sheep, none of which interfered with the horses' grazing activities. This study resulted in a book already referred to: Berger's 1986 publication, *Wild Horses of the Great Basin* (University of Chicago Press), one of the most valuable sources of information about how horses organize their society when not interfered with by humans, and how they behave towards each other. Zoologist Telané Greyling has been studying the feral horses of the Namib Naukluft National Park for more than 16 years, and her findings are an extremely valuable source of information about feral populations.[3] Besides these, there are also shorter-term studies which, although they do not give us the same comprehensive range of information, are also very useful in analysing the behaviour of wild populations.

So how is horse society organized in the wild, and what is the stallion's true role within their society?

When James Feist and Dale McCullough carried out their detailed observations of groups of feral horses living on the Pryor Mountain Wild Horse Range in the western USA, and compared these with similar observations of other feral groups, they were struck by the extent to which the same social organization occurs within such bands. This is in spite of thousands of years of domestication, in which horses have commonly been kept in far from natural conditions, and selectively bred for certain behavioural characteristics. 'Despite this period of manipulation by man, once horses manage to escape and live in a wild or semi-wild state, the typical wild social organization emerges.' (Feist, 1976)

This 'typical wild social organization' is not, as is generally believed, the large, rather anonymous herd. The dictionary definition of 'herd' is 'a large group of mammals living and feeding together' (Collins English Dictionary). With occasional exceptions, feral horses left to their own devices do not usually come together in large groups. Instead they tend to form close-knit family groups usually referred to in the scientific literature as 'bands';[4] these seldom contain more than around ten members and usually fewer than that.

We can see a similar social structure in Przewalski's horses, as well as in plains and mountain zebras, who also live in small family groups. However in populations of Grevy's zebra the mares and stallions may form separate groups; in contrast to feral horses and other zebra species, they do not live together all the year round. Mountain zebra family groups do not generally join together to form large herds. There are times when small groups of plains zebras may come together into large herds, but the smaller family groups still remain discrete entities within the larger herd. Among feral horses, family bands have home ranges within which they move about; these ranges overlap with those of other bands and several family groups may often come quite close to each other, sometimes grazing as little as 100 metres apart. However, there is little interaction between such groups, which tend to remain separate, even when their ranges overlap.

So 'herd' is a term generally used by ethologists to describe an equine population in a defined area, consisting of discrete family bands which may or may not interact. It may thus be a useful term to describe a group of horses but we need to understand that it does not describe equine social organization all that accurately. The behaviour of horses kept in, say, a large, single-sex group will differ in many ways from that of horses forming a natural family group, especially if the former

---
3 Her MSc and PhD theses have not been published, but she has kindly made them available to me, together with much valuable information communicated privately.
4 In this book I use 'family bands' and 'family groups' interchangeably.

consists of horses who are for the most part comparative strangers to each other. We must keep this in mind, because all too often assumptions about equine behaviour are made from observations of non-related horses, brought together and kept in a restricted environment in circumstances that would never occur in the wild.

So the true basis of equine society is the family unit, or band. This consists of one, more unusually two, mature stallions, up to five mares (rarely more; the usual range is between two and seven, with four or five representing the median), and their immature offspring. In the extremely harsh environment of the Namib Desert a band may sometimes consist of as few as two members. All-male groups form bands of their own: these so-called 'bachelor bands' consist, on average, of around four sexually mature males who have left their family groups, although larger or smaller bands are occasionally seen. Occasionally bachelors have been seen to 'tag along' with a family band, possibly with the hope of supplanting the band stallion, but generally – with odd exceptions – these bachelors do not form part of the stable family group.

Horses in the Namib Naukluft Park: the true basis of equine society is the family band. Photo: Telané Greyling

The bachelor band.

As this is where the young stallion learns much of the behaviour that will later help him to hold a family group together, let's begin by looking at what a bachelor band consists of, and how bachelors behave within the band.

Between the ages of one and four years, young feral horses generally leave their family band – much like young adult humans leaving home to set up an independent existence. The onset of puberty seems to be a triggering factor in many cases; for example Berger (1986) found that 81 per cent of young females on the Granite Range left their family band following their first oestrus.

But what about the young males? There is a general belief that colts are kicked out of the family band by the stallion, but this is only true in some cases; Berger, for example, reported that stallion aggression towards young males was infrequent, only about 11 per cent of young dispersing males being driven out by the stallion. Berger's observations did suggest that prior exposure to bachelor stallions influenced the departure of young males from their family band: 76 per cent or more of the males who dispersed permanently from their family bands had engaged in social interactions with nearby bachelors. (Berger, 1986)

The Natural Stallion

Young males may leave at any time between the ages of one and five years, but it is most likely to occur when the colt is between two and three years of age. (Welsh, 1975) On leaving the family band they may seek out and visit bachelor bands, eventually joining one of them permanently; very rarely do they spend long in a solitary state. Such bachelor bands usually consist of two or three horses, but groups of eight or more have been recorded (e.g. Berger, 1977)

Berger (1986) observed that when young males first visited or joined a bachelor band, they were generally sniffed, nipped, bitten or chased much more than an established member of the group would have been. They might also be mounted by other members of the group (45 per cent of cases). Berger notes that

> My first impression early in the study of a horse that joined a bachelor group was that it was a female; the horse was mounted unsuccessfully a total of six times by three different bachelors in less than thirty-five minutes. Only several hours later did I discover that 'she' was a he. (Berger 1986)

Sue McDonnell and Samantha Murray of the University of Pennsylvania School of Veterinary Medicine carried out a study of bachelor pony stallions kept together in semi-feral conditions. They also report male-male mounting in the bachelor group they studied:

> Male-male mounting, sometimes with erection, was a relatively common occurrence among bachelors...Roughly half of the time, the target stallion appeared to present his rump, soliciting and tolerating the mount. In two such instances, anal insertion occurred and ejaculation was apparent. In three additional instances, ejaculation occurred with thrusting of the penis against the flank or perineum of the target stallion. The remaining mounts appeared to be unsolicited and occurred during sparring and chasing episodes. During these encounters, the mount was often sideways or even head-on across the back or shoulder of the target stallion. In these seemingly unsolicited mounts, erection, thrusting, insertion, and ejaculation were rare. (McDonnell and Murray, 1995)

Berger notes that such behaviour was not directed towards young males if they were at least three-and-a-half years old, although in the group studied by McDonnell and Murray the age of the recipient of this behaviour did not seem relevant. Homosexual mounting is common in some other species of hoofed mammals such as cattle; I have seen cows mount each other numerous times, and on one memorable occasion I saw a cow mount the bull who was supposed to be serving her (although of course this is not homosexual mounting). I have also seen colts attempt to mount geldings; as a yearling colt our senior stallion, Nivalis, once followed a gelding half-way across a field half-mounting him (the gelding was extraordinarily tolerant). One day when Nivalis and his entire son Rigel, then three years old, were out in the yard together, Rigel suddenly decided to mount Nivalis; the latter moved away very quickly but did not retaliate in any way. Rigel has also attempted to mount one of the geldings, without success (the gelding simply moved away). The meaning of this behaviour is obscure, although Feist and McCullough relate it to the establishment or reinforcing of dominance. (Feist, 1976)

Berger's observations are in contrast with those of Andy Beck of the White Horse Equine Ethology Project. He recorded the behaviour of group members towards a new arrival in a number of case studies, and gave his findings in an article for the French magazine *Planète Cheval Au Naturel* (April–May–June 2006):

> The new arrival is greeted with great interest, the whole group forming a tight cluster of bodies around him, and amongst this bustle each makes repeated contact to sample the newcomer's scent, paying special interest to the front 'armpits' and the sharing of breath – nostril to nostril. In as little as 15 minutes the group returns to grazing, with the newcomer in line-abreast, flanked on either side by the two highest status colts or stallions. In this format the two guide their charge about the grazing range in an inductive progress; facilitating the discovery of water, physical boundaries and other information essential to high speed escape should it become necessary. After only an hour the group is able to react in total unison to external stimuli and would, in the wild, be able to operate an escape manoeuvre with an excellent unity of purpose. (Beck, 2006)

Personal space

The 'tight cluster of bodies' described by Beck is especially interesting because of what it tells us about the relationships between bachelor stallions. One thing that humans and horses have in common is the need for *personal space*, the distance which separates members of the same species. Ethologists sometimes describe certain species as *contact* species, lacking individual distance, and *distance* species, maintaining a certain distance from others of the same species and avoiding bodily contact. Most mammals, including humans and horses, come somewhere between these two extremes, avoiding bodily contact with certain conspecifics (creatures of the same species) and inviting or allowing it with others. With horses, as with many other social animals including humans, personal space depends on relationships. If strangers enter a horse's personal space the horse will feel uncomfortable and possibly threatened; a close friend or relative would be allowed to get much closer. Based on my own observations I would suggest the following distances within which others are tolerated:

◊ Family and close friends: 0 to 2m

◊ Individuals who do not know each other well: 2 to 4m

◊ Strangers: 4m and over

These are approximate distances only and they may vary from individual to individual or even from group to group; Andy Beck, for example, gives the relative distances as

◊ The intimate zone – 0 > 50cm. (family and close friends)

◊ The casual or personal zone – 50cm > 1.25m. (individuals who do not know each other well)

◊ The social zone – 1.25m > 4m. (strangers)

The Natural Stallion

Some horses may need much more space, others will need less, and individuals who dislike each other, even though they know each other well, will need more space than those who get on well. In general, horses enjoy physical contact with individuals (including humans) whom they like, but invasion of their personal space by strangers is very stressful for them – just as it is for humans.

Andy Beck calls these different areas of social interaction 'zones of social interaction'. He made a particular study of them within groups of horses at the White Horse Equine Ethology Project. By recording the number of Zone 1 (intimate zone), Zone 2 (family and close friends) and Zone 3 interactions, Beck was able to identify which groups had the highest level of social integration. What makes this study very interesting from our point of view is the fact that the group showing the greatest level of integration was the bachelor group (seven colts and stallions), with all the observed interactions falling within Zone 1.

Relationships within the band

The bachelor band itself may be stable or unstable in terms of the length of time its members stay together, but relationships within the band appear to be very stable, and, as we have just seen, the members are generally well-integrated. In the study of bachelor and pony stallions referred to earlier, McDonnell and Murray found that in any one grouping, one stallion would assume the role of 'harem stallion'[5], vigilantly guarding an area within the pasture and the fence line facing nearby mare pastures. The remaining stallions interacted as a group, with behaviour similar to that described for bachelor bands among free-running equids. (McDonnell and Murray, 1995)

In a domestic situation, stallions may guard and patrol fence lines, as Nivalis is doing here. Photo: Lesley Skipper

They found that the bachelor stallions interacted almost continuously with other bachelor stallions, with most of their time spent in quiet side-by-side grazing and resting. These quiet interactions are similar to those of mares at pasture (McDonnell, unpublished observations, cited by McDonnell and Murray, 1995). The interactions included mutual grooming, usually as a pair but sometimes involving three or four participants. This is consistent with the close social integration of the bachelor group reported by Andy Beck.

---

5 The use of the term 'harem' has been criticized by some commentators as being 'anthropomorphic'; in this instance, using a term from human social history to describe a non-human social organization. However, although I personally tend not to use the word, I think it is actually quite appropriate. Although 'harem' tends to conjure up Eastern voluptuaries enjoying the favours of many women, in fact it is derived from the Arabic *harīm*, a sacred, inviolable place or sanctuary; in the domestic sense it was a sacrosanct place, where the women of the household were safe from disturbance or harm. In this sense it is quite apposite, since one of a stallion's main roles in life is to protect his mares.

However, interactions between bachelor stallions in McDonnell and Murray's study did include some aggressive behaviour, although this was limited to sparring, with serious aggression and play-fighting being seen much less frequently. 'Any one aggressive episode usually involved only 2 or 3 stallions, and typically did not disturb ongoing activities of the remaining bachelors.' (McDonnell and Murray, 1995). Bachelor behaviour in truly feral groups also includes regular fighting, both playful and serious (Feist and McCullough, 1976; Berger, 1986), although fighting seems to be of a milder nature than between mature breeding stallions. Feist and McCullough make the following observation:

> Mock fights' between immature ♂♂ or bachelor stallions...lacked the exaggeration in posturing, and biting and kicking were executed with much less intensity, seeming to be more symbolic gestures (intention movements) than attempts to deliver injury. (Feist, 1976)

Feral and domestic bachelors also go through faecal marking sequences (described later in this chapter, on pages 56–59).

In McDonnell and Murray's study, interactions of the harem stallion with the bachelors were limited to serious fighting (when a bachelor intruded on the area adjacent to the fence-line), chasing bachelors away from the fence-line, and occasional unprovoked attacks on the bachelor band. At this time the harem stallion would herd the bachelors together to an area of the pasture furthest from the fence line.

> Individual harem stallions varied with regard to their level of vigilance, tolerance, and aggressiveness in guarding the harem fence line area and keeping bachelors away. Unprovoked raids on bachelors occurred as frequently as every hour and lasted as long as 10 min for some harem stallions. For others, raids were as infrequent as once every 5 h and were as brief as 2 min. Five harem stallions did not perform unprovoked raids at regular intervals. (McDonnell and Murray, 1995)

An interesting observation made by McDonnell and Murray concerns the way in which, if the harem stallion was removed, a stallion from the bachelor band emerged to fill the vacant position.

> If we replaced to the pasture a former harem stallion, the former harem stallion typically displaced the incumbent harem stallion back to the bachelor band. Order of emergence from the bachelor band to fill harem position vacancies, while highly repeatable, was not strongly associated with bachelor age, height, weight, testosterone concentrations, ranked level of aggressive behavior, or ranked leader-follower behavior. (McDonnell and Murray, 1995)

It was therefore impossible to predict, from observed characteristics, which stallion would emerge to fill the vacant position of harem stallion.

Although colts do not generally join a bachelor band until after they have reached puberty, they usually remain sexually inactive[6] until such time as they manage to capture – and hold – mares of their own. And while bachelor bands may travel close to family bands, they do not

---

[6] With the exception of the homosexual activity described earlier, although this is probably not true sexual activity.

continuously challenge the family band stallion. When such challenges do occur, the established band stallion almost always manages to chase the intruder away. Joel Berger, for example, reports that 'Bachelors regularly approached bands, but they were almost always thwarted by stallions in their efforts to obtain mates.' (Berger, 1986) Generally speaking, it seems that bachelors are only likely to be successful in stealing mares from – or taking over – an established family band when the band stallion is old, sick or injured (or in some cases all three). (Berger, 1986)

Although Andy Beck speculates that bachelors might co-operate in attempts to steal mares (Beck 2006), this does not seem to be the case, at least among truly feral horses. For example, Feist and McCullough report that 'When a bachelor group approached a harem, it was always the dominant ♂ of the bachelor group that met and interacted with the stallion of the harem.'[7] (Encounters – and fights – with family band stallions are described later in this chapter.)

So it is not that easy for a bachelor to take over an established family group, although bachelors will of course try to steal mares if they get the chance. Telané Greyling says that among the Namib horses

> Bachelors, single or in groups, usually gave way to breeding groups at the water trough if the stallion confronted them. But they often drank simultaneously with a breeding group on opposite sides of the wall. The young bachelors often took chances trying to acquire mares approaching the water with their stallion behind, but they soon gave way to the older stallions. (Greyling 1994)

Bachelors will usually establish their own family group (if indeed they manage to do so – not all bachelors do, some remaining bachelors all their lives) by picking up young mares who have left their family group, or older mares who have strayed from their group and have not (for whatever reason) been retrieved by their stallion. Even so, encounters with band stallions – even when these are unsuccessful, as they will be most of the time – will teach them valuable lessons about interactions with band stallions, including the greeting rituals and fighting skills described later in this chapter.

We can see from this how the bachelor band teaches young stallions how to integrate socially with horses other than members of his own family, as well as preparing him, through mock-fighting, for the time when he may have to fight, either to gain mares of his own or to protect his family once he has established his own band.

What, then, is the stallion's role within the family band?

First and foremost, the stallion's 'job' (for want of a better word) is to protect his family. It is he who keeps the family group together, rounds up any strays, and confronts danger on their behalf. But does this mean that the stallion is effectively in charge of the family group, and if so, is this the same thing as being the group leader?

Leadership

Many people assume that every herd (or, to be more accurate, group) needs a leader, and that this leadership role must naturally fall to the stallion. Writing in the early 1970s, the distinguished veterinary surgeon R.H. Smythe said, '…one horse, almost invariably a stallion, places himself at the

---

[7] Feist and McCullough were able to construct a linear dominance hierarchy among the bachelors they observed; however some other observers (e.g. Berger, 1986, and Greyling, 1994) have been unable to do so. See Chapter 5.

front of a herd or drove of horses and stays there by virtue of general acceptance.' (Smythe, 1974) One can see here echoes of the earlier assumption (still prevalent in some circles) that the leader in any animal social organization must necessarily be male. But was Smythe (and the many others who made the same assumption) right? When further study of equine behaviour seemed to contradict this idea, a new myth arose: the leadership of a herd was no longer assumed to be a dominant stallion, but instead a dominant mare. 'In the case of herd hierarchies in general, the boss of the herd is far more normally a matriarchal mare rather than a stallion' (McBane, 1994) '...in the wild it is the dominant mare of the herd, and not the stallion, which makes all the decisions.' (Bayley and Maxwell, 1996). [8]

It may seem odd that I have called this idea a myth, yet in fact there are three myths here: that of the 'dominant stallion', that of the 'dominant mare', and – most pervasive of all – that of the leader, or 'boss' – the latter concepts expressed in rather rigid terms by R H Smythe, describing the supposed social order which ruled horses in the wild: 'When the "boss" stood still and listened, the others did likewise. When the "boss" decided it was an appropriate moment to make a rapid getaway, or even to make a leisurely move into some other neighbourhood, the others all followed without question. When the "boss" called a halt, all came to a standstill together.' (Smythe, 1974) More recently, other authors have stated that 'In equine society there is a leader: one horse which is the boss, and which the others respect and obey.' (Bayley and Maxwell, 1996). These statements are echoed throughout the equestrian literature, in books, magazines, in training sessions, on internet forums, and so on. All these ideas are part of 'received wisdom' about equine social organization; and none of them stands up to close examination.

Part of the problem is that people seldom define properly what they mean by 'leadership'. It is often conflated with 'dominance' – another woolly concept, which is too large a subject to deal with here; it has done so much damage to perceptions of what stallions are, and how we should relate to them, that I think it needs proper discussion, which is why I have given it a chapter to itself (Chapter 5). For now, let's look at how we can define leadership in a meaningful way.

We can do this in different ways, according to context. There is *social leadership*, which is concerned with the maintenance of harmony within the group, and its protection; Syme and Syme define the characteristics of this kind of leadership as 'the control of aggression between individuals within the group, and the protection of other members when the group is faced with threat or predation.' (Syme and Syme, 1979). As we shall see, this almost always falls to the stallion. There is also *spatial leadership*, which governs movement from place to place; a spatial leader decides when and where the group moves throughout its home range. So if the stallion normally takes care of group security, who decides group movements?

According to Feist and McCullough, spatial leadership 'can be expressed either by the taking of initiative by one animal with the others following, or by the active driving or herding of the group by a stallion.' (Feist and Mccullough, 1976)

Taking the initiative

In Feist and McCullough's study, leadership by initiative was recorded in 159 cases during movements from place to place, or going to and from water. Of these, 106 (66.7%) were led by the stallion, and 53 by a mare. Of the 53 cases in which a mare assumed leadership, seven were in response to the nearness of other harems, and nine were due to unnatural disturbances. In these 16 cases the stallion herded the group, directing its movements; in other words the mare led from the

---

8   In the light of more recent research regarding equine social organization, some of these authors may have changed their thinking about this; Susan McBane has certainly done so.

front, while the stallion drove from behind. 'Thus, in only 23.3% of the observed cases was the mare solely responsible for leadership.' (Feist and Mccullough, 1976).

Ebhardt (1954) reported that stallions were the common leaders among Icelandic pony bands. Hall (1972), studying the Pryor Mountain wild horse range, regarded the most consistent leaders to be dominant mares. Stephanie Tyler (1972) found that adult mares were the leaders in New Forest Ponies. However, Tyler herself acknowledged that her findings were skewed by the fact that there were very few stallions in the New Forest, and these were periodically moved around or removed altogether.

> From the small number of cases where stallions were associated with mare groups and because of the unstable nature of these relationships due to man, it was not possible to conclude whether the stallion as the dominant member of his group was the leader.(Tyler, 1972)

Welsh (1975) noted that among the Sable Island horses, the stallion might lead but was normally behind or lateral to the group in a 'satellite' position. However, if the group passed by another group the stallion would move to the leading position and then position himself beside the trail, placing himself between the other group and his family, until the former had passed by. Klingel (1964, 1967) reported that in plains zebras the oldest mares appeared to be the leaders in group movements, but the stallion was still the dominant animal. Klingel also recorded that among mountain and Hartmann's zebras leadership when moving *to* water was assumed by the stallion, but taken over by the dominant mare when moving *away* from water. Penzhorn (1979) says that zebra stallions mostly led when they approached water. This pattern was also occasionally observed by Feist and McCullough. Berger (1977) found that in walking *to* water stallions led on 32 occasions, mares on 24. In walking *away* from water, out of 52 observed walk patterns, stallions showed temporary leadership 15 times, mares 19. Telané Greyling notes that with regard to the horses of the Namib Naukluft

> The presence of a specific 'leading mare' in groups... was not evident in this population as no one mare consistently led in any of the groups. The order in which the groups trekked or moved around was not consistent either and changed continuously. No significant difference existed between mares or stallions leading a group to the water. Some stallions always walked behind and others always walked in front with exceptions in the presence of approaching stallions, thus it depended on the individual stallions. (Greyling, 1994)

Feist and McCullough describe how, when members of the group other than the stallion became excited or disturbed by something, they would whinny to attract the stallion's attention. If he did not see any cause for alarm, and remained calm, the rest of the group did likewise. They conclude that 'Both initiative leadership and herding behavior in the harem show that the stallions are the principal leaders and they direct most of the movements of the groups.' (Feist and McCullough, 1976). However, this is *not* the same as being the 'boss' or making all the decisions; as we shall see, equine society is much more flexible than the rather rigid model proposed by Smythe and other commentators.

Regardless of sex, can 'leadership' be assigned to a dominant individual? Thirty years ago, ethologists were warning us not to confuse leadership with dominance:

> An important distinction is to separate true leadership from forcing, and from being first; just because a horse forces others out of his way does not mean that he is the leader, nor is the first one in a walking group necessarily in charge. (Welsh, 1975)

This is borne out by the findings of various studies of feral horses. In his study of the Sable Island horses, D.A. Welsh says

> The leadership versus dominance question can be studied by observing who leads when going to the waterhole. Extensive observations in the summer of 1971 and 1972 show that all animals may lead the way but that lactating mares, especially those with recent foals, usually initiate movements to water and lead the way. *This does not reflect dominance.*[My italics, L.S.] (Welsh, 1975)

Joel Berger says that among the bands he observed in the Grand Canyon,

> No one horse served consistently as a leader during walking patterns to or from the spring…the origin of a leader for a walking pattern frequently was the individual that merely assumed the initiative and walked. When others followed, the lead horse continued, but when there were no followers, which often was the case, the horse soon stopped. (Berger, 1977)

Feist and McCullough remark that 'We were unable to determine a hierarchy among the mares of a group with regard to position in movements. However, observed leaders were usually older mares or mares with foals or yearlings.' (Feist and McCullough, 1976), while Berger, as in his comments quoted above, insists that 'At no time was complete leadership shown for any individual stallion or mare within a band.' (Berger, 1977)

Various observers have recorded that if a group was alarmed they would all gallop away alongside one another, with no obvious leader; Berger says that when terrain was flat, horses did follow each other, though different horses assumed leadership at different times.

We do not even know whether any horse, setting off, say, on the trail to a watering hole, specifically does so in order to influence the actions of the rest of the band. They may have no such motive; it could simply be the case that they decide to move and the others follow them, possibly because they know from experience that certain horses know where water or the best food can be found. The only member of a band who normally shows unambiguous 'active' leadership (in the sense of deliberately moving the band members around) is the band stallion, although on odd occasions mares have been seen to do this.

All we can really determine, then, is that with the exception of herding by the stallion, which combines spatial with social leadership, spatial leadership is not the property solely of either sex, but may at various times be assumed by mares or stallions, depending on context.

Social facilitation

It should be clear by now that the old idea of equine society is controlled by one animal, the alpha or 'boss' animal who directs all of the group's movements, is really hopelessly inaccurate, and in terms of explaining how horses co-operate with each other is not very helpful; Chapter 5 will show this even more clearly. But in the absence of such an animal, what social dynamic causes horses to move around as a group?

Do these horses of the Namib Naukluft Park have a specific 'leader'? Or do they simply follow the horse who seems to know where he or she needs to go? Photo: Telané Greyling

In his ground-breaking book *Dogs: A New Understanding of Canine Origin, Behavior, and Evolution*, Ray Coppinger points out that sled dogs run because the other dogs in the team run. (Coppinger, 2002) This is a phenomenon which ethologists call *social facilitation*; it can be observed in humans and most other social animals as well, and is the reason why certain types of advertising are particularly successful. If we see someone eating or drinking something which looks delicious, we may find ourselves wanting to eat or drink even if we are not particularly hungry or thirsty. In other words, the actions of others influence us to want to do the same. This is more likely to be the case if the actions in question are in some way internally rewarding, or if they serve to get the animal or human out of trouble, for example in escaping from danger which may be perceived by only one member of a group.

Social facilitation helps to explain why horses tend to follow others (and us). We can see this process at work when one horse in a group sets off to walk in a particular direction and the others follow. As we have already seen, this movement can be started by any member of a group; however, among feral horses, the rest of the group are more likely to follow if the horse initiating the movement is either the stallion or an older, more experienced mare. Among humans, this tendency to follow the movement of a group has been explained by the probability that those following assume that those initiating the movement have some information which causes them to start moving in a specific direction. It is quite possible that the same applies to horses; this would explain why, when the horse initiating the movement is a younger, less experienced member of the group, the rest may follow so far and then resume grazing; they may conclude that the initiator may not be worth following as he or she may be too inexperienced to have information worth acting on.

Nevertheless, as we have already seen, the group stallion does play a very prominent role in moving his family around in specific situations, specifically in his role of family protector.

Group co-ordination

In their excellent book *Equine Behaviour: Principles and Practice* (1999) Daniel Mills and Kathryn Nankervis describe the stallion as the group coordinator, and I think this is the most accurate way of describing what a stallion's true role is. This co-ordinating behaviour is most clearly seen when the stallion moves his family around by herding.

Herding behaviour

Driving (snaking)

How does a stallion move his family – either as a group or as individuals of that group? In order to do so, he most often adopts a threatening posture peculiar to stallions (although it has been, although rarely, seen in mares). The stallion lays back his ears and stretches his head and neck out. He then moves towards the other horse or horses, often moving his head from side to side in the motion frequently described as 'snaking'.[9] Feist and McCullough observe that among the Pryor Mountain range horses

> The strength of this signal was determined by how low the head and neck was, how vigorously the position was assumed, and how fast the stallion moved toward the other horses. If a stallion laid his ears back and stretched his head and neck horizontally but merely walked toward the horses, the group responded with the same speed of action. If the stallion laid his ears back, snapped his head down so that his chin almost touched the ground, and ran towards the horses, they responded rapidly. Often the stallion's head would move from side to side, producing a snake-like motion. The intensity of herding depended on the particular situation that evoked it and the differing temperament of individual stallions. Some stallions exercised close control over harems while others were more lax. (Feist, 1976)

This behaviour is interpreted by Feist and McCullough as a leadership or movement initiation behavior; Richard Miller, writing about the horses of Wyoming's Red Desert, disagrees. He interprets herding as an aggressive behavior 'because it was often non-directional and occurred in response to estrus in a female or as redirected aggression in response to aggression by another stallion. Females were often herded in circles or away from a stallion's band, rather than with the band and away from a disturbance.' (Miller, 1981) However, this does not automatically mean that the behavior is aggressive in intent. In the behavioural sciences, the term 'aggression' is usually used to describe behaviour that is intended to cause pain or harm. There is no evidence that herding

---

9   In the photograph on page 43, the horse at the rear of the group appears to be adopting a posture similar to snaking, although it is difficult to tell whether this is a true example of this behaviour.

behaviour on the part of stallions is intended in this way; rather it seems to be a way of ensuring that the horses being herded pay attention to the stallion and act quickly.

Protecting the family

When a stallion detects a threat, whether real or perceived, he will herd his family away from the danger. This danger most commonly consists of other horses, perhaps a lone bachelor, a band of bachelors, or one or more family bands.

Various studies of feral and semi-feral groups have shown that horses are not territorial in the sense of laying claim to specific areas. They defend their group and their personal space rather than a defined 'territory'; it is not uncommon for the geographic ranges of two or more groups to overlap considerably. However, in order to prevent discord (and lessen the chances of another stallion stealing mares), band stallions will often maintain a 'minimum distance' between bands.

When groups pass each other while moving along trails in the same direction, the group stallion may maintain spacing between the groups by positioning himself between his own family and the other group, as described on page 50 above. However, if another group is approaching from the opposite direction, the group stallion may herd his family off the trail altogether. (Feist, 1976; Greyling, 1994)

If a group is grazing and other horses approach, members of the group will usually stop feeding and gather behind the stallion. (Altmann, 1951; Welsh, 1975; Feist, 1976). As we saw earlier in this chapter, several family groups may often graze as little as 100 metres apart. Bachelors may also graze this close to family groups.

Initially, when different groups come into closer contact, the stallions of each group may approach each other, posture and threaten, and sometimes engage in mild fighting (pushing and kicking out). After such encounters the stallions return to their respective family groups and move them apart, usually maintaining a distance of at least 90 metres. (Feist, 1976) However, in many cases the stallions simply look at the other group or groups and no further interaction occurs. (Greyling, 1994)

Closer contact with other groups usually occurs at water holes. If a group is already present at a water hole, the group just arriving will wait until the first group has finished drinking and left. Feist and McCullough report that among the Pryor Mountain horses

> As many as five harems were observed near a water hole at the same time, each waiting until others had left before moving in to drink. On only one occasion (on an extremely hot day) was a harem observed to move into water while another group was still there. This resulted in considerable tension and threatening, but no fights. (Feist, 1976)

Telané Greyling says that among the Namib horses, half of all encounters at the water trough involve no direct interaction; in these cases the second group loafs around until the first group leaves the trough. Group stallions may engage in dungpile rituals (see pages 57–58 below) and posturing, in order to prevent another group coming closer; they may also engage in greeting rituals (see pages 58–59) and may even attack each other directly. This, however, only occurred in 10 per cent of cases and the fights lasted only a few seconds in each case. Greyling observes that stallions are only likely to engage in these brief fights when a stallion arrives at the trough wanting to drink immediately and finds it already occupied. (Greyling, 1994)

If a group stallion encounters a bachelor at the water trough, they may not interact at all, or they may engage in posturing, greeting and dungpile rituals. The group stallion may chase the bachelor away from the mares. (Greyling, 1994)

Other herding situations

As well as moving his mares and youngstock away from other groups, bringing the group closer together, or directing the movement of the group (e.g. to and from water) the group stallion may use herding behaviour to retrieve straying foals, or to gather mares (in some cases to retrieve mares who have strayed too far from the group, or to obtain an unattached mare). Established group stallions do not generally seek to increase the number of mares in their group by stealing them from other stallions. Welsh (1975) observes that among the Sable Island horses

> ...gains by herd stallions were always associated with some unusual circumstance or accident. Herd stallions usually took advantage of these situations but did not appear to look for them.

Stallions may also herd mares in an attempt to copulate. Many horse owners, even those who do not have stallions, will have observed herding behaviour in geldings (see page 34).

Stallions assisting with movement of mares

Andy Beck, who for many years has run an experimental stud farm (White Horse Equine Ethology Project) in New Zealand, describes how, during the early stages of the Project, he had to rely on the expertise of his stallion in moving their family group around:

> The group consisted of mares that had never been part of a natural harem group in any sense and, during the settling-in phase, it was sometimes necessary to remove mares that were having trouble adjusting to the new life style. Without the co-operation of the group stallion this would have been very difficult. Anyone who has had the opportunity to watch a stallion marshalling a harem group of mares will know just what a humbling experience it can be for handlers. We may think we're good at moving, or controlling the movement of horses, but stallions are supremely good. Not only did the Arabian stallion allow me to manage things so that social cohesion could be maintained but on many occasions he also appeared to be actively assisting. Paddock sizes and ground contour of the farm were such that it would have been either difficult or flatly impossible to coerce horses down to the yards for such operations as drenching against internal parasites or hoof trimming single handed. (Beck, 2005)

However, although as Andy Beck says, stallions are supremely good at moving other horses around, they are not *invariably* successful; there are times when things don't go the stallion's way. As Telané Greyling points out, among the Namib horses

> Although stallions were able to herd their mares away from other stallions or in specific directions, they were not domineering in any other way… In three cases mares with young foals exhibited kick threats and refused to obey the herding action of the stallions. (Greyling, 1994)

Encounters and fighting

Although fights between stallions can be severe, resulting in injuries to both parties, they are not actually all that common. Feist and McCullough remarked that among the Pryor Mountain horses, maintenance of spacing between groups was the most common cause of observed stallion fights (44 per cent). However, if at all possible stallions generally seem to avoid encounters with other stallions, preferring to adopt a strategy of mutual avoidance.

Paradoxically, though, stallions will sometimes leave their family group in order to investigate a potential rival; Berger (1986) noted that they would sometimes travel up to 400 m away from the family group in order to do so. Such encounters generally consisted of a brief interaction, including posturing and display, then the stallions would return to their respective groups. Why would a group stallion, whose greatest role is, after all, that of protector, leave his family unguarded in this way? Joel Berger believes that because there is little if any sexual dimorphism in horses (as mentioned in Chapter 3), it may be that stallions viewed strange horses as potential mates and approached them simply to investigate. Berger comments that

> The most striking characteristic of these interactions was the lack of clarity over the outcome. In 499 such cases between March and July 1982, a dominant (or 'winner') could be identified in less than 3.5% of the interactions. Nevertheless, it would be inappropriate to conclude that aggression was lacking in the remaining interband encounters or that these were not serious events. (Berger, 1986)

Sequence of events leading up to an encounter and possible fight.

Stallion encounters are highly ritualized, especially in the sequence of actions leading up to the encounter and any subsequent fighting.

The approach

As we have seen, most of the time stallions prefer to avoid each other, perhaps judging the danger of a fight ensuing to be not worth the trouble of meeting another stallion. However, when they do decide to 'exchange civilities' (or the reverse, as the case may be), they may first of all stand and stare at each other, occasionally pawing the ground. They may also call out to each other. They may then go through a ritual known as 'fecal marking'.

Such encounters frequently take place at or near a dung pile; Richard Miller notes that 25 per cent of all aggressive encounters between stallions in the Red Desert included the smelling or and/

or marking of fecal piles. He goes on to say that marking of piles occurred in 69 per cent of all encounters at established fecal piles. (Miller, 1981) Welsh (1975) notes that stallions apparently adjust the angle and speed of their approach so that they will meet near a pile. 'If not, they turn and prance parallel to each other towards a pile.' (Welsh, 1975)

Stallions meeting and greeting each other go through a series of rituals which may include striking out and pawing at the ground. Photo: Brian Skipper

Dungpile ritual (fecal marking)

Anyone who has spent any length of time with even one stallion will have seen him dung on top of another pile of dung if it has been left by another stallion; if it was left by a mare or gelding he will urinate on it instead. Lucy Rees describes this in a delightfully humorous way: 'A stallion discovering, or returning to, a dungpile sniffs it with deep concentration and then, with a great deal of flourish and braggadocio, steps over it with high, exaggerated paces to line himself up solemnly and add his contribution. Usually he turns round to smell the pile again afterwards, as if to satisfy himself that he has done it right.' (Rees, 1984)

Scent marking in many species is linked to the defence of territory; but as we have seen, horses are not territorial. Nevertheless stallions use dunging as a way of denoting their presence. Dunging by stallions, like urinating by male dogs, therefore seems to be a way of leaving a 'signature' – a kind of canine or equine *Kilroy was here!* By dunging (or urinating) on top of his family's dung piles, a stallion can make it clear to any other stallion investigating the dung piles that this is *his* family and no other's.

During Richard Miller's study of the Red Desert horses, he noted that pairs of males alternately marked the same piles up to eight times in succession, in what appeared to be competition between stallions to be the last to mark a pile. Miller says,

> I believe that fecal piles have a function in intraband and possibly interband stallion dominance in Red Desert feral horses because of 1) competition to

be the last stallion to mark a pile, 2) the dominant males' usually marking last and 3) the marking of the same pile by several stallions from one band on any one visit to the water hole. FEIST and MCCULLOUGH (1976), HALL and KIRKPATRICK (1975) and SALTER (1978) all reached similar conclusions working with feral horses in the Pryor Mountains and in Alberta. (Miller, 1981)

(When Miller talks about 'intraband stallion dominance' we must be aware that he is talking about bands with more than one stallion – a subject to which we will return later in this chapter.)

Watching a stallion marking dung piles in this way, one can see that only a small amount of dung suffices to mark the pile; nevertheless, it does seem to amount to an awful lot of dung for one stallion to produce on demand, so to speak. This conjures up a rather amusing picture of a stallion desperately trying to be last to mark a pile, only to be unable to produce enough dung for the purpose!

The approach and posturing

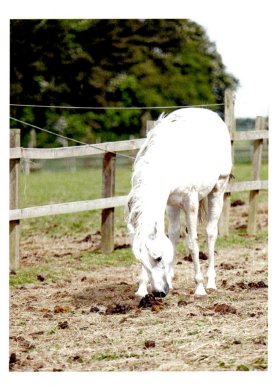

Having deposited a pile of dung… …**Nivalis turns round to sniff it.**

Photos: Lesley Skipper

Whether or not fecal marking takes place, the stallions will either part company and go their separate ways, or start to approach each other adopting an exaggerated posture, with head held high and neck arched, and moving in a high-stepping walk or a prancing trot.[10,11] The tail may also be held high and the stallions may toss their heads. Welsh says that when the stallions of Sable Island approached each other in this way, they frequently zig-zagged during their approach, enabling them to present to each other laterally throughout the approach. (Welsh, 1975) Presumably this is so that

---

10 Readers with a knowledge of the classical High School will recognize in these stallion displays the basis of certain High School movements such as the *passage* and *piaffe*.
11 Richard Miller says that among the Red Desert horses, arched neck threats were often the only aggressive behaviour seen in encounters between two stallions. (Miller, 1981)

they can clearly see the emphasized musculature of each other's neck and shoulders. The stallions may also prance parallel to each other. This may often be seen in domestic stallions separated by a fence; they will prance parallel to each other the length of the fence, then turn and repeat the exercise in the opposite direction. Feist and McCullough saw this parallel prance both during the initial stages of a fight and during intervals in the rest of the fight. (Feist, 1976)

If the stallions part company, there may be less zig-zagging and more head-tossing than on the approach, accompanied by very high stepping. David Welsh comments that 'This is thought to demonstrate to the mares that they have been defended.' (Welsh, 1975) This is a charming thought, echoed by Henry Blake in his book *Talking with Horses*. Describing how a stallion chases off a rival, Blake says, 'The stallion will then go to his mares and say *did you see that, girls, I murdered him*. He may do this by snorting and dancing round his mares, and he may also drive them away to safety.' (Blake, 1975)

Investigating

The stallions will then typically stop and begin to investigate each other. They may stop, facing each other, with their noses several inches apart. They will then stretch their necks forward and start sniffing at each other's nostrils; in some cases they move even closer and stand with their heads held high and their necks arched, while they smell each other's breath. At this point one or both of them may squeal and strike the ground with a forefoot.

The stallions will then proceed to move alongside each other, sniffing at each other's neck, withers, flank, genitals and rump. Welsh calls this position 'reverse-parallel' (Welsh, 1975). They may also groom each other around the withers and at the top of the loin area. Feist and McCullough noted that the ears were generally held forward while the stallions were smelling each other's noses and necks, but were usually laid back while smelling the rear of the body. (Feist, 1976) I have seen the ears held forward or back during the rear-body sniffing, but have always seen them held forward during the nostril-sniffing stage.

At this stage neither stallion has yet committed himself to fighting, and either or both may withdraw. Sometimes the contest may be limited to pushing and shoving.

Pushing, shoving and neck-wrestling

The stallions may then start pushing at each other's shoulders and lower neck; one or both of them may swing his head over the other's neck and engage in a type of neck-wrestling contest. They may strike the ground with a forefoot (usually the outside foot); this is often accompanied by a loud squeal. They may also swing their heads at each other's necks. Sometimes one of the stallions will rear up over his opponent's back in what appears to be an attempt to force the other to the ground. However, Feist and McCullough found that, among the Pryor Mountain horses they observed, the only time a stallion actually did fall was when both were rearing up and striking with their forefeet.

This is a comparatively mild form of fighting, which can in many respects be compared to the play-fighting of colts and young stallions with each other. Indeed, some commentators, notably Welsh, separate the foregoing behaviour patterns from real fights and consider them to be marking displays. (Welsh, 1975)

During close encounters stallions may push and shove at each other's neck and shoulders. Here Nivalis and his yearling son Tariel engage in some rough play which also involves some mild nipping. Many people mistake this rough play for aggression, but there is no serious intent behind it. It is this kind of rough play which helps to teach young male horses how to interact with others of the same sex. Photos: Lesley Skipper

Serious fights

Serious fights can and do occur, usually when a stallion feels his family is being directly threatened, for example by one or more bachelors trying to drive off part of the family group. On these occasions there may be little or no warning given by the family group stallion. He may simply charge at his opponent, ears back and mouth open ready to bite.

If his opponent does not turn and run (which many do), the stallion may then either try to bite his neck, or rear and attempt to kick his head or neck. If the other stallion engages in face-to-face combat, the result may be the rearing and violent striking with the forefeet so beloved of film-makers and writers of popular fiction. Together with the biting of necks, this can result in serious injuries, and many feral stallions bear scars on their necks, flanks and quarters as a result of bites. Berger, for example, found that among the horses of the Granite Range 96 per cent of the adult males in the population in any given year showed signs of bite-related wounds.

In order to avoid bites to the forelegs (which might incapacitate them and render them vulnerable to predation), stallions may drop to their knees during a fight. (Berger, 1986) This defensive posture may sometimes be seen in domestic horses; I have seen it in juvenile male horses confronted

Left: Tariel is in the process of dropping to his knees in order to protect his forelegs from bites, even though the big Warmblood gelding (Toska) is not really threatening him. Photo: Lesley Skipper

Above and below: Young stallion Rigel (left) play-fighting wth Toska. Photos: Lesley Skipper

by an adult male. I have an amusing instance of this on videotape: it shows a mature Arabian stallion being lunged, while the yearling gelding with whom the stallion was usually turned out stood by and watched. Every time the stallion passed by, the gelding would drop to his knees, almost as if he was bowing.[12] This indicates some degree of uncertainty on the gelding's part, yet as far as I know this stallion had never displayed any aggression towards the gelding. Indeed, as the latter matured into an adult, his owner would frequently take the pair of them out for a ride together, riding the stallion and leading the gelding; she reported to me that any boisterous behaviour was always on the part of the gelding, not the stallion.

Even more serious than bites are the potential injuries from hind-foot kicks. Although stallions will normally use their forefeet in fighting, they may sometimes turn away suddenly and kick out with both hind feet. A stallion on the receiving end of such a kick could easily be knocked off his feet, so most stallions attacked in this way will try their hardest to avoid these kicks. Commenting on this aspect of stallion fights, Feist and McCullough say that these efforts at avoidance

> ...gave many fights the appearance of consisting of active and passive phases. Broken jaws on skeletons recovered from the Range (3 out of 35) might well indicate the fate of a horse receiving a well-placed kick. (Feist, 1976)

Between December 1993 and July 1994 Telané Greyling observed 14 serious fights among the horses of the Namib Naukluft, of which only three involved preliminary rituals and or posturing. One fight was not settled, and seven ended or involved a chase where the 'winner' chased the other stallion. It was not clear what caused two of the fights; one involved two bachelor stallions fighting for a lost foal, three involved in-oestrous mares, and eight involved mares with young foals.

> One contest for possession of a mare and foal and two other mares lasted nearly a week. It involved at first three stallions, one with the mares, one in the middle and one outside, interaction consisted of dungpile rituals and posturing with chasing and kicking less often. Relatively more interaction occurred between the second and third stallion than between the second and first stallion. The second stallion supplanted the first stallion in a short aggressive fight to second position, although the dispute carried on the original stallion couldn't reclaim his mares. At last a fourth stallion herded the other two mares away while the three stallions fought for the mare and foal. All three stallions lost condition during the week and were left with a number of scars and superficial wounds.
>
> Two other battles lasted 20–45 minutes and involved a mare with a foal and 6–8 stallions. Both battles were preceded by 2 and 3 stallions only displaying towards each other with another stallion attacking the first or main stallion. This attack led to the start of the battle where any nearby stallions joined in the fight. The mare started to run blocking and protecting her foal while she kicked at any stallion too close to them. The stallions followed the mare biting and kicking among each other trying to fight their way to the position closest to the mare. Along the way the stallions fell out and stayed behind until only two were left of which the second one also backed off after a while. (Greyling, 1994)

---

12 This could lead some people to misinterpret this as a submissive gesture; however its use in serious fights – where a submissive gesture would be highly unlikely to succeed – precludes this interpretation.

In spite of all this, in many populations the majority of encounters between stallions consist entirely of threat displays (Miller, 1981; Hall and Kirkpatrick, 1975 (cited by Miller); Feist and McCullough, 1976 and Salter, 1978 (cited by Miller)). Berger, on the other hand, observed a much higher level of actual physical contact: for example, Miller recorded bites in only 10 per cent of stallion encounters, while Berger recorded bites in 82 per cent of such encounters (Miller, 1981; Berger, 1977). Berger suggested that the high levels of physical aggression noted in his 1977 study might be accounted for by drought stress (Berger, 1977).

Even when stallions do fight and inflict injuries on each other, these injuries are seldom immediately fatal. For example, of all the stallion fights observed during Joel Berger's five year study of the Granite Range horses, only three (about three per cent of all male deaths in any one year) resulted in the death of one of the combatants, and in each case the stallions did not die until some time afterwards.

Indeed, as Berger points out in his study of the Granite Range horses, more than 98 per cent of a stallion's time budget was spent in non-aggressive activities. So while stallions will undoubtedly fight – in some cases seriously – to protect their families (and, in some cases, to gain mares) it would be a great mistake to think that aggression and fighting are what define a stallion.

Playing

By no means all encounters with other stallions include threats or actual fighting. Joel Berger notes that out of 346 interactions recorded between stallions and bachelors whose genealogies were completely unknown, stallions initiated play fighting 34 times. They were more likely to do so if they were previously familiar with the bachelors. (Berger, 1986)

Acquiring mares

We have already seen that although stallions with an established family band may take the opportunity to acquire new mares when they get the chance, in contrast to bachelors, they do not go out of their way to do so. Family band stallions have enough to do just watching over their families and keeping them together, without going to look for more mares and creating problems by so doing. They may gather in mares who have left their own family group (although these are more likely to be acquired by bachelors), mares left behind while giving birth, wandering away from the group or waiting for their foals. Greyling (1994), for example, found that of the stallions acquiring new mares among the Namib Naukluft horses, only 33 per cent were stallions from established family groups; the rest were bachelors.

Family guy

This brings us to the least-known and least appreciated aspect of a stallion's role. Perhaps because stallions are so often observed on the periphery of the family group – as part of their duty as general 'look-out' – many people have simply assumed that apart from breeding activities, stallions take little part in family life. For example, in his book talking with horses, Henry Blake says that the stallion has a somewhat limited range of messages to deliver with his voice, simply because in his natural state he is concerned only with three things: sex, danger and food. (Blake, 1975) But more careful observation shows that this is far from being the case, and that one of the stallion's most important functions is that of the 'family guy' who not only acts to protect his family, but takes an active part in its day-to-day life.

This is nowhere more apparent than in the stallion's interactions with youngstock, particularly with foals. This may come as a surprise to many people, who may have read, or been told, that stallions cannot be trusted with foals as they are liable to attack and injure or even kill them (see the myths listed on page 14). This myth is so widespread that we need to look at it more carefully before going on to consider what stallions actually do within the family circle.

Are stallions likely to attack foals?

The belief that if a stallion is turned out with mares and foals he is likely to attack the foals has been fuelled by popular literature and some ill-informed comments in online media such as YouTube. For example, in March 2007 a video was posted showing a new-born foal struggling to stand. After investigating the foal a stallion picked it up and shook it by the neck, throwing the foal down. The foal died, its death captured on camera – a very distressing sight which naturally prompted shocked reactions to the video. There was much uninformed comment and speculation, some commentators remarking that this showed how aggressive horses really are and that stallions killing foals was a normal aspect of horse behaviour. But is this true? How common is it for stallions to attack and maim or kill foals?

Attacks on foals by stallions have occasionally been reported by breeders, but as Andy Beck points out, such attacks are poorly documented, for the obvious reason that 'no one is going to be particularly keen to make public what most would consider to be a fatality whose cause was bad management.' (Beck, 2005) Such attacks have, however, been properly documented in zoo populations of plains zebras, *Equus burchelli* (Pluháček and Bartoš, 2000; Pluháček and Bartoš, 2005) and Przewalski's horses, *Equus przewalskii* (Feh, 2008). Less well-documented (because relying to some extent on incomplete anecdotal evidence) are attacks by stallions on foals in groups of domestic horses in the Camargue area of southern France. In a review of these attacks, Patrick Duncan documents incidents reported by breeders in the Camargue area. (Duncan, 1982) In all the cases cited by Duncan (15 in all, between 1956 and approximately 1978), the foals were bitten by the stallion on the head, neck or back; at least, the breeders assumed that the stallion was the attacker, because not all the attacks were actually observed. In the cases that were observed, the stallion was seen to worry the foal, biting it, lifting it off the ground and shaking it; this is consistent with the behaviour of plains zebra and Przewalski stallions during such attacks, as well as that of the stallion in the video cited above.

In an unpublished thesis on mother-young relationhips and related behaviour in free-ranging Appaloosa horses, J.D. Blakeslee noted that the owner of the horses being studied had reported the killing of one new-born foal by a stallion. The mare and her new-born foal were brought into a pen by the owner for warmth, as the weather was quite cold. The foal slipped, fell down, and slid under the fence surrounding the pen. A stallion in the adjoining pen quickly ran over to the foal, bit it at the base of the neck and shook it, severing the spinal cord. Then the stallion mangled the foal with his feet. However, that was the only instance observed of a stallion killing a newborn foal (Blakeslee does not say over what time period this held true). The owner also reported two other instances of a stallion killing a foal; however, the circumstances were not the same, although we are not told what those circumstances were, other than that these two foals were older. Blakeslee does say, however, that all three foal killings occurred in small, fenced enclosures; none took place out in the pastures. (Blakeslee, 1974)

Stephanie Tyler reported the death of several foals in the New Forest which she believed were probably killed by stallions. One foal was seen being mauled by a stallion in 1966, and five young foals from the same part of one study area disappeared within two weeks of each other in 1968. One of these was found dead, with injuries on the neck suggesting that it had been attacked by a stallion. Other than that, Tyler gives no reasons why she believed the other foals had been killed by stallions. (Tyler, 1972)

Jan Pluháček and Ludek Bartoš documented nine attacks on foals by captive plains zebras in zoos in the Czech Republic (one at Prague and eight at Dvůr Králové) between 1974 and 1997. Two of the foals were female, the remainder male. The foals attacked were either new-born or between 10 and 33 days old.

Lee Boyd cited several cases of infanticide among Przewalski stallions in zoos; one stallion, who had just replaced his father as the harem stallion, killed three colts aged five to six months, and was also aggressive toward the two remaining foals.

Claudia Feh and Byamba Munkhtuya carried out a long-term study of Przewalski's horses, originating from eight different zoos and released into a 200 ha (later increased to 380 ha) pasture at Le Villaret in the Parc National des Cévennes, in southern France. From 1993 to 2003 Feh and Munkhtuya made systematic observations of the horses. During this time they witnessed five foals being attacked by stallions in the manner already noted earlier. Two foals survived due to the energetic interventions of their mothers; the mothers of the three other foals also tried to intervene, in one case helped by the half-sister of the mother. One foal died shortly after repeated attacks and two others were euthanized as they suffered from lethal wounds. (Feh and Munkhtuya, 2008)

What causes these attacks? Are they, as some commentators maintain, an inherent feature of equid social life? Or do they represent an aberration caused by stress of some kind?

One theory, which has overshadowed all other possibilities, is that infanticide gives a male an evolutionary advantage. According to this hypothesis, a male who has just taken over a group of females will kill the existing infants; this will bring the females into oestrus, enabling the male to mate with them and thus ensure the survival of his own genes rather than those of another male.

The 'evolutionary strategy' hypothesis was eagerly received when it was first put forward in the 1970s to explain infanticidal behaviour, first of all in primates, then in other species. This was partly because 'gene-survival' was then a very hot topic, but also no doubt because it seemed to explain some aspects of human infanticide: why *do* some fathers kill their children? If other species also kill their young, then maybe it's a genetic tendency!

Infanticide in lions has received particular attention, so that very many people now believe that male lions will invariably kill the cubs when they take over a pride. It is not such a big step from that belief to the assumption that if primates and lions routinely kill young that are not their own, then horses are likely to follow this pattern of behaviour. And from that, we go on to the next step: the belief that stallions are likely to be a threat to *all* foals, not just those that are not their own.

But more careful attention to detail has shown that all is not as it seems. Anne Innis Dagg of Waterloo University in Ontario examined the research on infanticide in lions and found that the data simply did not support the hypothesis that such infanticide has an evolutionary basis. She found that even though the researchers had appeared to follow proper scientific procedure in presenting their data, in fact they ignored or downplayed data that contradicted the hypothesis. Dagg wrote that

> The issue of infanticide by male lions as an evolutionary mechanism is a classic case of a satisfying hypothesis becoming accepted in the academic world and then in popular culture far beyond proper validation.

She goes on to say,

> It is lamentable that the infanticide by male lions hypothesis disproven here has been so widely accepted. It has been routinely cited since 1975 as fact and has promoted for other species the notion that infanticide must have an evolutionary purpose. (Dagg, 1998)

She points out that other researchers have noted that sometimes male lions kill a female lion, which is disadvantageous both to the female and the males involved, so why should it ever occur? Dagg provides the sensible reply: 'I think the answer is that not all animal behaviour is evolutionarily adaptive.'[13]

Dagg concludes that

> In reality, aggression is common among all lions; adult male and female lions as well as cubs are killed by both male and female adults at times of stress (such as lack of food or inter-group turmoil). Primary data show that the females much more than the males are responsible for cub deaths, both by killing non-pride cubs directly and by abandoning their own cubs to starvation. Moreover, even when males do kill cubs, this behaviour appears to be indiscriminate, with little evidence suggesting that it is directly linked to bringing females into estrus or to the 'takeover' of prides. (Dagg, 1998)

With regard to infanticide in primates, an extensive review of primate behavioural literature carried out by Thad Q. Bartlett, Robert W. Sussman and James M. Cheverud revealed that in fact there are very few verified cases of males killing a female's young and then mating with her to produce new offspring. They found that 'most cases of infanticide may simply be a genetically inconsequential epiphenomenon of tense, aggressive episodes' (Bartlett, 1993)

So do these findings help us to understand infanticide in horses? Following the general trend, commentators have generally sought to explain this behaviour in terms of evolutionary advantage (e.g. Duncan, 1982; Boyd, 1991). By killing unrelated foals, a stallion would gain evolutionary advantage (in the sense of leaving more offspring) in several ways: if only male foals were killed, the stallion would be eliminating possible future rivals; the fact that any female foals were unrelated to him would not exclude them as future mates; by killing young unrelated foals, a stallion could free mares from the physical stress of lactation, improving their chances of producing a foal by him the following year. (Boyd,1986) However, when Claudia Feh and Byamba Munkhtuya analysed the results of their 11-year study of Przewalski's horses at Le Villaret, they found that all of these hypotheses could be eliminated.

First of all, infanticide in this herd was not simply limited to takeovers. Although most infanticidal behaviour was directed against unrelated foals, 26 unrelated foals out of 35 (74 per cent) were *not* attacked following takeovers by the stallions present at birth. Infanticide did not result in earlier conception, and of the five cases reported in their study, in only one case was the infanticidal stallion the father of the mare's next foal. Moreover, Feh and Munkhtuya remark that

> mothers whose foals had been attacked avoided associating with the infanticidal stallion in the years after. Therefore, the evidence in support of the

---
13 A point made many times, over the years, by that giant among twentieth-century scientific thinkers, the late Stephen Jay Gould.

> classical sexual selection hypothesis was weak at most. (Feh and Munkhtuya, 2008)

They further observe that increases in population density and subsequent increase in grazing competition could not be a factor in this case, because as those factors increased, infanticidal attacks actually decreased, disappearing altogether after the first six years. And the hypothesis that killing male foals would eliminate future competition was weakened by the fact that two out of the five foals attacked were female; four out of the nine cases cited by Pluháček and Bartoš were also female.

There remains one possible explanation: social pathology as a result of disturbance of some kind. Patrick Duncan rejected this as a possibility in the case of the Camargue horses because, as he said, 'the fact that it has been observed in several herds makes this unlikely.' He goes on to say that 'Many owners claim that the frequency of this behaviour is higher in mature stallions which "become vicious towards foals", and state that they prefer to use sexually mature but sub-adult (2–4 years) horses for breeding for this reason.' (Duncan, 1982) Duncan does not say what he means by 'many owners'; we must assume that he means the five owners cited in his study. (However, the attacks were actually observed in only four of the cases cited by Duncan.) He concludes that 'It therefore seems more likely that infant killing is part of the behavioural repertoire of adult males, and that it has not been reported previously because of the widespread use of sub-adult stallions and the very loose surveillance of herds ranging extensive pastures.' (Duncan, 1982)

However, Duncan was basing his conclusion on a very small sample of behaviour. Furthermore, he misses one very significant point: the method of management usual in the Camargue area – at least at the time of the incidents cited in Duncan's study – was to keep all the males together, except in the spring and summer, when the stallions were released with the females. Generally, a different stallion was released each year. And if we look at the timing of the attacks on foals cited in Duncan's study, we can see that they all took place within two months of the release of the stallions with the mares. Most attacks took place within two to three weeks of the stallion's release, and six foals were killed immediately on the release of the stallion.

In the cases reported by Blakeslee, there is simply insufficient information on which to base a hypothesis about the reasons for the attacks, although it is interesting that the only attacks reported took place in small enclosures, never in open pastures. In the case of the New Forest foals which Tyler believed to have been killed by stallions, there is, again, insufficient information; the only point which may be relevant is the fact that – as with the Camargue stallions – there was a policy of removing and replacing stallions (in the case of the New Forest, every three years). No specific data are given regarding the ages of these foals.

After remarking that only zoo-bred stallions in the Le Villaret study committed infanticide, Feh and Munkhtuya go on to make some very pertinent observations:

> Interestingly, all witnessed records of male infanticide in equids concern stallions which have not grown up in socially natural herds, the main difference being that male foals born into a group are separated at a relatively early age from their father and sometimes their mother, before acting as reproductive stallions. Moreover, in all cases of witnessed infanticides, the reproductive partner of the infanticidal stallion, a pregnant mare, was always imposed by humans (Pluháček and Bartoš, 2000; Ryder and Massena, 1988; Kolter and Zimmermann, 1988; Zarkikh, 1999; Duncan, 1982). Infanticide by males in equids therefore seems clearly to contain an element of human 'disturbance' or intervention, even if

it may have gone unobserved in some populations due to its rarity. (Feh and Munkhtuya, 2008)

This is borne out by the fact that until recently no instances of infanticide had been observed in free-living equids, even though some of the studies have been long and very intensive. For example, Joel Berger's five-year study of the horses of the Great Basin reported not a single instance of infanticide, while Telané Greyling, who has been observing the horses of the Namib Naukluft park for 16 years, reports that in that time she has seen foals fatally injured by stallions accidentally (mostly being knocked over or stepped on) during interactions with mares, although this is not very common. However, she has never seen a stallion attacking a foal and/or killing it by biting, kicking or mauling. (Personal communication with the author). In their study of changes in herd stallions among the horses of Assateague Island, J.F. Kirkpatrick and J.V. Turner report that

> No incidents, during approximately 4100 h of direct observation over 6 years, have been recorded of herd stallions attempting to kill offspring (of either sex) from mares in their bands that were inseminated by other stallions. (Kirkpatrick and Turner, 1991)

In her beautiful and moving book *Cloud: Wild Stallion of the Rockies*, film-maker Ginger Kathrens describes a fatal attack on a foal. Kathrens had been observing the feral horses of the Arrowhead Mountains of southern Montana for several years, following the life of a colt whom she named Cloud, the subject of her book. One year, while she was observing a family band belonging to a stallion whom she named Boomer, Kathrens saw a new-born foal struggling to stand. The foal, a filly, continued the struggle for several hours; at one point Boomer walked up to the foal and bowed his head over her, softly touching her nose with his own. But the foal failed to rise, try as she might.

Then another band appeared with its stallion, a big dun called Looking Glass. The stallion stopped and stared at Boomer, who together with his own band, started to leave. One of the mares from Looking Glass's band noticed the foal and went over to investigate. She sniffed at the foal, who tried to stand, but immediately toppled over. Looking Glass approached and the mare backed away. Looking Glass sniffed the foal from a short distance away, then approached and put his nose on the foal's back and sniffed again. Then all of a sudden the stallion grabbed the foal with his teeth and lifted her, shaking her violently and repeatedly, and slamming her to the ground.

> The mares screamed and dashed in circles around the stallion, trying to stop his attack, but he paid no attention to them. Looking Glass gave the foal one last deadly shake, then, with his ears laid flat, he drove his mares away. (Kathrens, 2001)

Boomer then charged in, but too late. Strangely, Looking Glass stopped and walked some distance back to the foal's body, sniffed at it and walked away again.

This incident was caught on film, and is in fact the sequence that was posted on YouTube in 2007. It is sad and disturbing, and it is difficult even to guess why Looking Glass behaved as he did. None of the 'evolutionary advantage' explanations seems applicable here: Looking Glass did not take over Boomer's band (indeed he seems not to have been interested in Boomer's mares), so the fact that the foal was not his was irrelevant. Furthermore, the idea that he could have been eliminating a future rival also doesn't hold water, as the foal was a filly. And none of the cases previously recorded involved a stallion attacking a foal from a different band. The only point of similarity with previous cases (and with that described below), lies in the fact that the foal was a new-born. Perhaps Looking Glass was psychologically disturbed in some way; there is simply no way we can know. Ginger Kathrens comments,

> I could rationalize that Looking Glass did her a favour, saving her from a lingering death, for she was not destined to dance atop the Arrowheads with the other foals. Still, there was no avoiding the violence of this haunting and disturbing act. (Kathrens, 2001)

In a 2008 paper published in the journal *Biology Letters*, Meeghan Gray described an attempted infanticidal attack on a foal that was thwarted by the foal's dam. This attack has been said to be the first described in free-living horses, but the Looking Glass episode took place a number of years earlier. It was, however, the first such attack recorded in the scientific literature. It took place in April 2005, and was seen by observers taking part in a study being carried out on a feral horse population in the Virginia Mountain Range outside Reno, Nevada. At the time of the attack, the band in which the attack occurred consisted of two adult stallions, two adult mares, one juvenile male and one male foal. The foal who was attacked, a filly, was probably no more than an hour old when the attack took place; she had not yet attempted to stand up. I have quoted Gray's description of the attack here because it suggests a possible cause for this incident:

> The rest of the band, including the dominant band stallion (stallion A), were all resting near the mare and newborn foal. At 16.20, a stallion (stallion B) from a nearby band called out and approached the mare. She immediately gave a head threat towards stallion B. The foal attempted unsuccessfully to stand up. The band stallion (stallion A) lunged towards the mare and foal and immediately bit the foal on the neck several times. Stallion A subsequently picked the foal up by the shoulders twice and shook it around several times. The foal was dropped to the ground and subsequently bitten and kicked by the front legs of stallion A several times.
>
> The attack lasted approximately 1 min. During the attack, the mare defended her foal by charging, biting and kicking stallion A, which led to the end of the attack. After the attack, stallion A had several aggressive interactions with stallion B and continued to try to herd the mare away from the area. The mare continued to charge and head threat stallion A when he came near her and she remained in her position over the foal. Stallion B called out again, which led to another aggressive interaction between stallion A and the mare. While the foal appeared to be in shock, there was no visible major damage, but she suffered minor superficial wounds. The foal stood up at 17.39 and nursed at 17.47, and at that time the observations ended. The band was observed over the course of the next year and the foal successfully weaned. (Gray, 2009)

Gray follows earlier commentators in ascribing an evolutionary basis for this attack (the 'sexual selection' hypothesis mentioned earlier, and rejected by Feh and Munkhtuya). She points out that a) genetic analysis confirmed that the band stallion was not the sire. b) the band stallion had recently taken over the band, which he shared with another adult stallion. 'Owing to these factors,' she says, 'there was a high level of paternity uncertainty [on the part of the stallion] that may have influenced the decision to attack.' But how would a stallion know whether a foal was his or not? This is a subject which continues to puzzle ethologists. Some believe that some species such as primates detect paternity by the length of time they have consorted with the female, phenotypic matching (when an animal learns some aspect of its own outward appearance and later uses it as a comparison to identify its relatives) or the amount of time spent with the troop during the mating season. But these hypotheses remain controversial, and we do not know whether horses are able to connect the mating act with the birth of a foal eleven months later. Given that many humans have historically been unable to do this, it seems unlikely that horses would be able to do so.[14] Nevertheless, Gray concludes that uncertainty of paternity is believed to be a major cause in this case.

In her discussion, Gray says 'The attack was unmistakably an infanticide attempt as it was similar to other reported attacks in equids.' (Gray, 2009) Yet I wonder whether this really was an infanticide attempt. The attack seems to have been prompted by the approach of stallion B and the mare's response to him. Stallion A's attack, while unmistakably directed at the foal, could have been a case of redirected aggression of the kind described later in this chapter and in Chapter 11. This is also suggested by the fact that following the attack stallion A had further aggressive interactions with stallion B and continued to try to herd the mare away. I could construct a neat explanation as follows: stallion A wanted to get the mare away from stallion B, but as the foal had not yet stood up, the mare was unlikely to leave her. The stallion therefore attacked the foal to remove the mare's incentive to stay anywhere near stallion B; further evidence for this is the fact that he continued to try to herd the mare away even when she was defending the foal, and also the fact that when stallion B called out again there was another aggressive interaction between stallion A and the mare. Plausible? I think so. Likely? I don't know, but this explanation is at least as likely as any of the 'evolutionary advantage' hypotheses routinely put forward. It doesn't require any mysterious powers of paternity recognition on the part of the stallion, and it doesn't involve any convoluted theories about how a male might benefit by killing offspring that are not his.

But if it was a real infanticide attempt, the most likely explanation, which Gray ignores in favour of the 'sexual selection' hypothesis (even though she cites Feh and Munkhtuya) is the 'human interference' element. The Virginia Mountain Range horses are intensively managed by the Nevada Department of Agriculture; this management includes removals and contraception, suggesting a high level of interference and resulting stress to the horses. The horses of the Arrowhead Mountains in Montana, where Looking Glass's attack on the foal was recorded, are also subjected to intensive management, including periodic roundups. Could this kind of interference result in social pathology of the type described by Feh and Munkhtuya? And if so, why in these two populations and not others? Neither I nor anyone else as yet has the answer to those questions.

Regardless of what the explanation might be, I cannot see that there is any basis for Gray's assumption that infanticide plays a role in equid social structure (a view shared by Patrick Duncan). If this were the case, infanticide would surely be more widespread, rather than the rare event it actually is.

It is true that one sometimes comes across accounts of domestic stallions being aggressive to foals and occasionally killing them. But these accounts are difficult to evaluate, because precise details are seldom given regarding the exact nature of events and/or the stallion's previous history. In many cases the incidents are reported second- or even third-hand ('I know someone who knew someone whose stallion killed a foal' and so on), making it even more difficult to judge the truth of

---

14 Unlikely, but perhaps not impossible. We are only just beginning to learn what a horse's brain is capable of.

the matter.

All we can really say is that yes, stallions do sometimes attack foals and in some cases the foals die as a result. But this only makes it *possible* that such a thing will occur; it does not make it *probable*. And although there are no figures available to make a valid comparison, it might be just as likely (if not more so) for a foal to be attacked by a mare. For example, the National Foaling Bank in Shropshire, which provides help and advice on difficult foaling cases and rejected or orphaned foals, had 968 cases of mares savaging foals between 1965, when the Bank was set up, and 2007 (the last year for which statistics were published). And, unlike most of the stallions in the studies cited above, who did not normally continue attacking foals, mares who have savaged their foals will typically savage again. (McDonnell, 2001)

In spite of this, such attacks – whether by a mare or a stallion – are *very rare*. Most horses make good parents, and although we do not know for certain what makes some mares and stallions attack foals, the evidence suggests that human interference plays a large part. When we consider that most horses kept in a domestic setting are separated from their dams at a relatively early age, and in any case will rarely have the chance to grow up in a normal family group, it is hardly suprising that malajustments and, in some cases, social pathologies, can develop. Colts who are to be kept entire are typically separated from their conspecifics at a relatively early age – one of the factors identified by Feh and Munkhtuya in their study of infanticidal stallions. In most cases they will never have known their fathers, much less had any opportunity to learn from them; so they will never have any first-hand experience of how stallions normally relate to foals. Mares who have not grown up in a socially natural group may never have seen foals being born, or had first-hand experience of looking after foals, whereas in a natural group sisters and aunts (and even colts and young stallions) may regularly take on a 'baby-sitting' role. It is scarcely surprising, then, that a small number of horses of both sexes, possibly under the influence of stress, commit acts of savagery almost unknown in more natural social conditions.

The interesting thing is that, while many people believe it is not possible to keep stallions with mares and foals (even though stallions live with mares and foals in the wild, and have probably done so for millions of years[15]) because of the danger that the stallion may attack the foals, no one to my knowledge has suggested that mares and foals should be kept apart, even though some mares do savage foals. Perhaps this is because it is obvious that separating mares and foals at birth as a matter of course would be extremely unkind and highly detrimental to the wellbeing of both mare and foal. Few people stop to consider whether keeping stallions apart from mares and foals might also be detrimental.

The stallion as a father-figure

Ethologists have usually spent so much time focusing on agonistic behaviours[16] in horses – perhaps because these are so highly visible – that they have tended to neglect other, more benign, aspects of their behaviour, such as the stallion's role in caring for young stock. Andy Beck suggests that this neglect of the stallion's role in parenting may be a product of the concept of the father-figure as the bread-winner (or, as Beck points out, more precisely the 'meat-winner'. (Beck, 2006) And of course this role has no equivalent in grazing animals; one might say, tongue-in-cheek, that grass tends not to move around much, and so doesn't need catching! Nevertheless, there are many other parental

---
15 This prompts the thought that if stallions were likely to kill foals, the close-knit family structure which forms the basis of equine social organization would be unlikely to survive.
16 Agonistic behaviour is any form of behaviour associated with aggression, such as threat, attack, appeasement or flight.

roles that stallions can fill. Not the least of these is as a role-model, especially with regard to interactions with other horses, most notably non-family members.

In discussing this question Andy Beck invokes comparative psychology to highlight the analogy between human children growing up without a male role model, and that of young horses growing up – as most do in a domestic situation – without a comparable equine male role model. He says,

> ... there has been such a focus on the psycho-social problems of children growing up without any positive male paradigm that we are probably all aware to some degree of the research findings. Is there any compelling reason to believe that this should not also apply to horses, or that we should not bother to consider the consequences of male parental deprivation in species other than ourselves? Emphatically no! Yet the nature of such considerations is so subjective that proof can be hard to find - in fact, absolute proof is virtually impossible. But just because there is a difficulty does not mean the search has to be neglected. If there is no direct physical evidence that can be marshalled in support of the notion that stallions are an integral part of the social development of the young horse, then is there anecdotal evidence? And here the answer is a definite yes. (Beck, 2006)

Stallion interactions with foals

Beck reports that observations of the horses of his White Horse Equine Ethology Project have shown that stallions spend one-to-one time with the foals born into their family groups; he further remarks that 'it should be noted right away that there is no apparent difference in behavior towards biological progeny and foals born to mares introduced into a group when already pregnant.' (Beck, 2006) This is especially interesting in the light of the speculations cited earlier about stallions killing foals that are not their own. Similar observations have been made of stallions in other groups; for example, in an article for *Equine Behaviour*, the newsletter of the Equine Behaviour Forum, Diane Hicks described the behaviour of Houdini, a young stallion belonging to a group of Pottoka ponies brought together by Lucy Rees in the pre-Pyrenees region of Spain. Hicks noted that this was the stallion's first family group (she uses the term harem) and that the three mares with whom he was pastured had all been in foal when the group was formed; hence the foals were not his. Nevertheless, Hicks noted no aggression on Houdini's part toward the foal: quite the reverse, in fact. Observing Houdini for a period two hours, she noted no less than 49 affiliative behaviours on the part of Houdini during that time, which included mutual grooming with all three foals. Hicks goes on to say,

> The other thing that was becoming apparent was the foals' attachment to Houdini. They adored him. During observation periods we frequently noted that the colts were closer to Houdini than to their respective dams. (Hicks, 2008)

Members of the stallion care online list to which I belong have also reported similar attachments between stallions and foals. Our own senior stallion, Nivalis, loves to interact with his foals, whether out in the field or in the stable yard. If he is in his stable and one of the youngsters comes into the yard, he will make a very distinctive sound to call them over to him. This is similar to the nicker of a mare, but whereas the nicker is made principally through the nose, Nivalis's soft call comes mainly from the back of his throat. The foals readily go to him and greet him over the stable door, usually by nibbling at his neck, which he seems to enjoy, sometimes reciprocating but more usually just laying his nose against the foal's neck.

Stallions playing with foals

One of the principal ways in which stallions interact with their foals is in play. It is most likely to be colt foals who do this, rather than fillies, although I have seen Nivalis groom with one of his very young daughters over the stable door (but never out in the field). Play between stallions and foals has been reported by numerous members of the online stallion care list referred to earlier. It was also noted by Lee Boyd that Przewalski stallions at Topeka Zoo's Forbes Conservation/Propagation Center played with their colt foals, and that one stallion in particular was very tolerant of play behaviour directed at him by foals. Our own stallion, Nivalis, is very fond of playing with his foals, and is extraordinarily patient and tolerant. One of his foals, Tariel, was a very boisterous colt who would often grab hold of his father's headcollar and rive away at it as if trying to pull it off. Nivalis endured this rough treatment with great good humour, and never showed the slightest degree of aggression towards Tariel. Other stallion owners who turn their stallions out with mares and foals have reported a similar degree of tolerance on the part of their stallions.

Setting a social example

Earlier, I mentioned the stallion as a role-model with regard to interactions with other horses. It appears that this role-model can extend to interactions with humans, as well. From his observations of the experimental herd of the White Horse Equine Ethology Project, Andy Beck concludes that in this group at least, it is the stallion, rather than the mares, who inspires foals to trust humans:

> On occasions the work schedule allows for prolonged periods to be spent with the group, and very often, unless he is otherwise occupied with matters of oestrus, I'll spend some 'quality' socialising time with the stallion, as friends do. It soon became obvious that we would slowly be surrounded by a ring of foals – even those that had previously shown fear and refused contact with me. I needed only continue grooming the stallion, teasing knots out of his mane or removing insects from his coat, for the foals to press in closer and initiate contact with me. (Beck, The Secret Life of Stallions, 2006)

Diane Hicks, whose observations of Lucy Rees's herd of Pottoka ponies has already been mentioned, described how the band stallion, Houdini, encouraged foals to investigate the observers by his example:

> As we sat observing the herd he [Houdini] came over to investigate us…The mares were not interested in us but the foals, though more cautious, followed Houdini's lead and managed to tame themselves by using advance and retreat on us. At times this could disrupt the observation session for half an hour or more as the audience was captivated by the antics of the foals and in awe of the stallion who quickly found the benefit of humans for getting to that hard-to-reach itchy spot! (Hicks, 2008)

The Natural Stallion

It may be that the stallion is not deliberately trying to influence the foals; they may simply be following his example. But is this not how young animals (including humans) learn social behaviour – by following examples of their parents' behaviour? As Andy Beck comments,

> Clearly there is some particular behavioural mechanism involved here that is gender specific, not unlike the process whereby it is the human father from which children copy the paradigm for interaction with society at large. So, could it be that not only does traditional stallion management, in which most are kept isolated and deprived of any opportunity to enjoy family life, compromises the psychological and social development of stallions but also robs us of a most excellent natural tool in the socialization of the young horse to human handlers? (Beck, The Secret Life of Stallions, 2006)

Nivalis playing with his colt foal Tariel. Nivalis is extremely tolerant of his offspring's boisterous play. Photos: Lesley Skipper

Stallions sharing food with foals

In free-ranging conditions, or in the wild, horses' food is all around them, so there is no need for stallions to share food with their offspring. The do, however, allow foals to graze near to them. (Dobroruka, 1961; Boyd, 1991)[17] Przewalski stallions at Topeka Zoo's Forbes Conservation/Propagation Center and at the San Diego Wild Animal Park have been seen sharing grain with their offspring. Our stallion Nivalis has not been fed concentrate feed while out with foals, but if he is feeding from his manger slung over his stable door, he allows foals and youngstock to stick their noses in and share his food.

Protection of foals

Protection of the family group, which, as we have seen, is an important part of a stallion's life, naturally extends to protecting foals and retrieving them when they stray from the family group. (Feist, 1976, Berger, 1985; Berger, 1986). On one occasion Joel Berger and Rebecca Rudman saw a stallion chase two coyotes who had approached a group with three young foals. The stallion chased the coyotes with his head lowered for about 25 metres; a third coyote, who had watched the interaction nearby, also left.

If family groups are grazing close together, stallions may sometimes tolerate their foals playing with foals from other groups, provided they return to their own group when called. Feist and McCullough observed that when stallions wanted the foals to return, they would give a neigh, and the foals would return immediately to their group. The group stallion will also separate other members of the group from foals if the latter's mothers are unable to keep other horses away from the foal. Feist and McCullough noted that in these cases the mother would give a whinny and the stallion would move the other horse or horses away. Feist and McCullough remark that 'Such protectiveness is important since lost or orphaned foals are attacked by other horses.' (Feist, 1976) However, they give no evidence to support the statement that lost foals are likely to be attacked. Such foals may be chased away, quite aggressively, by horses from other groups, but this is not always the case; Telané Greyling, for example, reported no instances of aggression towards foals during the period December 1993 to July 1994. (Greyling, 1994) Welsh (1975) records a protracted series of encounters between different family groups, lasting several hours, during which one foal and his dam got separated from their group by one of the stallions. The foal ran back to what had been his own group and tried to suckle from one of the mares who had a foal. She rebuffed him initially but later adopted him and a few days later both foals were seen suckling.

Stallions adopting foals

There are numerous instances of lost foals being temporarily cared for, and in some cases adopted, by horses from other groups, and even by bachelor stallions. Greyling, for example, cites the case of a one-month-old colt who was separated from his mother; he was herded and accompanied by a bachelor stallion for a day until he found his mother again (Greyling, 1994). The two foals in Welsh's account, who were both suckling from the same mare, later left the group and were adopted by an old solitary bachelor (Welsh, 1975). Ginger Kathrens describes how a band stallion called Plenty Coups

---

17 I have also observed domestic stallions grazing very closely with foals

The Natural Stallion

adopted two orphaned foals from another band into his own family, after the foals' mother had been removed during a round-up and they were left behind (Kathrens, 2001).

Lee Boyd cites the case of a Przewalski stallion who took on part of the role of an orphaned foal's dam. The foal's mother died when it was only two-and-a-half months old; the stallion permitted the orphan to suckle his sheath over a period of several weeks. (Boyd, 1991) I have seen geldings behave in this manner towards foals, while Stephanie Tyler (1972) saw several New Forest foals sucking on the teats of older fillies, and one sucking on the sheath of a gelding.

The Przewalski stallion who allowed his foal to suckle his sheath was very tolerant of the foal. The orphan pushed in between his sire and other horses at the hayrack, or walked under the stallion's neck to get to the hayrack, interrupting the stallion's feeding. In each case, rather than take his annoyance out on the foal, the stallion leaned over the orphan and bit another horse – either an immature filly or an adult mare. On other occasions the stallion threatened other horses away from food (either hay or grain) but allowed the orphan to stay next to him and share the food. On one such occasion the orphaned foal bumped into the stallion, but instead of taking his annoyance out on the foal, the stallion instead threatened to kick a mare who was nearby. This was a clear case of redirected aggression;[18] Lee Boyd comments that 'The stallion was dominant to all members of the herd, so he could have threatened the foals. Instead he seemed to avoid aggression against them and redirected his aggression toward older herd members.' (Boyd, 1991)

One of the most touching accounts of a stallion adopting a foal comes from Andy Beck of the White Horse Equine Ethology Project in New Zealand. One of the project's colt foals became separated from his dam shortly after birth. By the time he was reunited with his mother, she refused to accept him. Although the foal was kept alive by bottle feeding, there were concerns about socialization. It is well-known that bottle-fed foals can become over-familiar with humans, and too boisterous for safety; they may establish a social preference for humans, and may later experience difficulties socializing with other horses. If at all possible it is better to find a foster mare whose own foal has died and persuade her to allow the orphan to suckle.[19] Unfortunately there was no such mare available, and the foal was too young to be accepted into the project's bachelor group. Eventually it was decided that the best option was to continue bottle-feeding the foal, but to find him a suitable equine companion. This meant removing another horse from the group so that a watch could be kept over the pair. After careful consideration, it was decided that the best candidate was an eight-year-old bachelor stallion, who was accustomed to being removed from the group for riding, training and to attend to visiting mares.

The stallion, named Risqué, and the foal, whom they named Eric, were introduced to each other with a low fence between them, but as there was no sign of intolerance on the part of the stallion, they were eventually put in together. The result was even better than hoped for. Andy Beck describes what happened:

> It is one thing to expect a stallion to show care for a foal born into the harem group of which he is monarch, but quite another to nurture a foal to which there is no direct biological tie. Yet this was exactly what happened. A somewhat ambiguous, or disinterested but tolerant, attitude might have been considered predictable, but a far more surprising and faithful level of surrogate father-

---

18 Redirected aggression is caused by frustration; for example if an animal feels aggressive towards another animal but is prevented from attacking it, the frustrated animal may instead attack a nearby animal that was not the cause of the aggression. In the above case the stallion appears to have felt a strong inhibition against attacking foals; he threatened nearby adults instead.
19 Since 1965, the National Foaling Bank has done sterling work in uniting orphaned foals with foster mares throughout the United Kingdom.

> hood resulted. The stallion first led and later accompanied the little colt up to the house for his milk feeds, and then returned with him, sometimes over half a kilometre, back to where the pair had been grazing. Just as mares will stand watch over their foals while they sleep, so too did the stallion – not going off to graze until the foal was awake again and ready to move. (Beck, 2006)

The colt thrived under the stallion's care, learning proper equine manners, and went on to become a well-adjusted young horse. As Andy Beck says of this unusual arrangement, 'if this challenge to the traditional status quo is possible what else might be?' (Beck, 2006)

Although our stallions have never been called upon to act as a foster-parent in this way, one of our geldings has voluntarily taken on the role of protector of foals and yearlings. This gelding, a pure-bred Arabian named Zareeba, has retained many stallion characteristics, one of which is this strong sense of protectiveness towards youngsters. Whenever a new foal has been introduced into the group, Zareeba has taken it on himself to assist the mother in protecting the foal from the inquisitive overtures of the other horses, by getting between them and the foal, until such time as he and the mother are satisfied that no harm will come to their charge.

Stallions and mares

Of course, stallion behaviour within a group consists of much more than protecting mares and looking after foals. Stallions also have close relationships with the mares in their family groups; we will look at stallion-mare relationships more closely in Chapters 6 and 7.

Incest

Among horses, as in many other species, there appear to be powerful inhibitions against mating with parents, offspring or siblings. Between 1979 and mid-1984, Joel Berger and his team spent more than 8,200 hours observing wild horses in the Granite Range of Nevada (the book which documents Berger's findings is *Wild Horses of the Great Basin*, already mentioned in this chapter and in Chapter 4). Of 32 young females that reached puberty during the period of the study 24 were observed to copulate. Five changed bands prior to puberty when they either accompanied their mothers to new bands or their natal bands were taken over by new stallions. This meant that five immature females reached puberty in bands with stallions who were not their true fathers.

> In none of the above cases did either true fathers or stepfathers mate, or even attempt to mate, with females that matured sexually within their bands despite ample opportunities to copulate with their pubescent true daughters or step-daughters prior to their emigration [from the family band]. In one instance, a pubescent female mated with an unfamiliar male while her father stood only 8 m away and ignored the copulation. On two other occasions, stallions stood less than 50 m away as their daughters mated with unfamiliar males. (Berger, 1987)

If the stallions had regarded their daughters (or stepdaughters) as potential mates, it is hardly conceivable that they would have stood by and let unfamiliar males mate with them. The fact that stepfathers did not mate with their stepdaughters suggests that it is familiarity which prevents stallions from mating with their own daughters. This is borne out by the fact that, as Berger and

Cunningham report, stallions encountering with true or stepdaughters later in life failed to differentiate sexually mature females with whom they had been familiar when the females were young.

> There were no indications of recognition between these fathers and daughters as the stallions courted their daughters in the same manner as they did unrelated mares, and neither sex refrained from subsequent copulations…it is not entirely clear which sex more actively promotes inbreeding avoidance. If it was the young females, they should offer stallions few opportunities for mating. The data support this idea since 100% of the young departed from natal bands when in estrus (although for unknown reasons 21% returned to natal bands after copulating). However, if stallions were responsible for inbreeding avoidance, they should refrain from copulating and not hinder breeding attempts by rival males with young familiar females. Our observations indicate that males avoided copulating even when they observed familiar young females mating. Thus, both sexes participated in the avoidance process. (Berger, 1987)

Dr Marthe Kiley-Worthington cites the case of her stallion Oberlix and his daughter Shemal, who lived together on and off for more than four years; because of the inhibitions against incest referred to above, they are not particularly attracted to each other sexually, but they remain close companions and friends (Kiley-Worthington, 2005). When he was still entire, my Arabian gelding Zareeba was still being turned out with his full sister Zarello when he was sexually mature. He was stabled next to Zarello, close enough to touch noses, but even when she was in season he showed no sign of being aroused, although he reacted normally to in-season mares whom he did not know.

Stallion alliances

One of the most intriguing examples of stallion behaviour found in feral groups is that of the two-stallion band. During his five year study of the horses of the Granite Range Joel Berger recorded no less than seventeen instances of this phenomenon. He dubbed these stallion relationships 'alliances', since the two stallions worked together to defend their group of mares from rivals. These were instances where – contrary to the general findings in Chapter 5 – being the dominant member in a relationship really did pay off. This was not only because the dominant stallion was able to sire more foals, but also because the subordinate stallion invariably did more to protect the group from rival males than the dominant stallion did. This meant that the dominant stallion was less likely to be injured in aggressive encounters than the subordinate. Nevertheless, both stallions would risk injury to aid each other; they would form defensive alliances to protect their group against intruders.

In most cases the subordinate stallion had either very limited access to the mares in the group, or none at all. Yet these stallions risked injury to defend the group, even though they derived little or no benefit from doing so. This probably explains why most such alliances were short-lived; only two in Berger's study exceeded seven months in duration, while the remaining two lasted two-and-a-half years and at least four years respectively.

Such multi-male bands may be more common than has generally been supposed. Other observers have noted similar alliances between stallions, notably Miller (1981), Linklater et al., 1999, and Feh (1999).

Claudia Feh, studying multi-male bands in Camargue horses, identified several different breeding strategies. In one-male family bands, the stallion had exclusive access to females. In multi-male bands reproductive access was shared, with the subordinate stallion managing to sire about a quarter of the foals. Finally there were what Feh calls 'sneak' matings by stallions living in all-male groups; these matings mainly occurred at night and no social bond existed between the partners (Claudia Feh, personal observation, cited in Feh,1999). She found that among the multi-male bands, some stallions formed alliances that could last a lifetime; these stallions were each other's closest associate and preferred grooming partner. Her findings were similar to Berger's in that both stallions might act to protect their group against intruders, or one might tend to the mares while the other confronted the rival. Feh also found, like Berger, that the subordinate stallion of each alliance pair fought off rivals more frequently than the dominant stallion.

Although this might seem like a very unequal partnership, in the case of the Camargue horses at least, the subordinate stallion was able to mate more frequently, and sire more foals, than the stallions who adopted a 'sneak' mating strategy. The dominant stallion also benefited, for obvious reasons: some of the burden of protecting his family was removed from him, and he was able to spend more time attending to his mares. Claudia Feh comments that

> Fights occurred all year round, and the subordinate stallion of each alliance pair fought outside competitors more than twice as often as the dominant. Forming short-term alliances before defending mares on their own may enhance long-term reproductive success for both partners. Other benefits to both partners include higher survivorship of their foals and increased access to proven reproductive mares. (Feh, 1999)

In his study of Red Desert feral horses, Richard Miller found a number of bands with two and sometimes three breeding stallions. He identified three separate breeding systems: 1) several stallions breeding with one mare within a band, 2) consort pair formation (i.e. a single stallion and mare in a long-term, stable relationship), and 3) the dominant stallion doing most or all of the breeding. Breeding systems varied between bands and within a band through time. Miller observes that

> In spite of the presence of several stallions during breeding in multiple male bands, only occasionally (10 of 67 fully recorded sequences) was there any aggression between stallions during breeding. A stallion would approach the breeding pair in an arched neck threat, and the breeding stallion would dismount to meet him. Most encounters ended as soon as the breeding male dismounted. On no occasion was a serious fight precipitated by breeding in multiple male bands. Often while one stallion copulated with a mare, another male would approach her and attempt to touch noses with her. The mare frequently turned in circles to avoid this contact. While the reason for this behavior is not clear, I do not believe that it was an aggressive act, but rather that it may have been an attempt by the second male to court the female. (Miller 1981)

He reported that these bands were larger than single-stallion bands; for example from 1977 to 1979 the average size of a multiple male band ranged from 9.3 to 9.6 horses, while single male bands averaged 5.8 to 6.8 horses. Multiple male bands also had a significantly more stable membership (Miller 1981).

Why did the Red Desert have so many multiple male bands, when the norm elsewhere is the single-male band? Miller points out that other authors have explained both large band size and multiple male bands as a response to specific resource distribution. He says that water holes and shelter are generally widely dispersed in the section of the Red Desert where his study was carried out; this, together with wide dispersal of forage in spring, during dry periods and after heavy snows, appears to be of primary importance in determining the home ranges and the distribution of horses.

> The distribution patterns of any one or all of these resources may in part explain the existence of large, multiple male bands in the Red Desert. Breeding advantages, patterns of resource distribution or pressure for large band size through competition for limited resources may have led to the high proportion of multiple male bands in Wyoming's Red Desert. (Miller, 1981)

Large and/or multiple male bands were apparently less affected by a severe winter, presumably because the size of the bands and the presence of more than one male guaranteed better access to limited resources (Miller 1981).

However, not all commentators agree on the advantages of multiple male bands. Studying seven multi-stallion and 12 single-stallion bands from the Kaimanawa feral horse population in New Zealand, Linklater *et al.* found that the number of aggressive interactions between stallions and mares in multi-stallion bands was significantly higher than in single stallion bands. They comment that

> Multistallion bands produced fewer surviving offspring per mare because the agonistic and competitive, not affiliative and coordinated, relationships between stallions imposed a reproductive cost on the mares. Consequently, our measures support Linklater's (1999) conclusion that cooperation is an inappropriate term for the relationship between stallions in multistallion bands... Mares that form stable relationships with other mares and a stallion have improved fecundity. We believe that the patterns of mare sociosexual behaviour and oestrus stimulate loyalty to mares and thus band stability, and are the proximate mechanism by which mares avoid detrimental levels of stallion harassment. We call the loyalty relationship between a stallion and mare a consort relationship. Ultimately the consort relationship functions to reduce intraspecific aggression and improve reproductive success. (Linklater *et al.*, 1999)

Claudia Feh produced a well-argued response to this (Feh, 2001). In this she points out that Linklater *et. al.* made several erroneous assumptions. They argued, for example, that harassment of mares by stallions is the origin of long-term male–female relationship in horses. But as Feh points out, if this hypothesis is correct, then mares should prefer to live in one-male groups. However, Linklater *et al.*'s own data on the dispersal of adult and young mares show that this is not the case. As Claudia Feh says,

> The evidence in favour of the hypothesis therefore seems weak. Equid mares may have other, or additional 'reasons' for forming long-term relationships with stallions than to avoid intraspecific harassment. One of these reasons may be

> protection from predators (Feh et al. 1994). All equid males forming long-term relationships with mares are known to defend all their band members actively against large and cooperatively hunting predators (Klingel 1972; Feh et al. 1994). In addition, phylogenetic inertia[20] may account for this behaviour in populations where predators are absent (Berger 1986).(Feh, 2001)

In addition, Linklater *et al.* maintained that co-operation is an inappropriate term for the relationship between stallions in multi-stallion bands (see above). However, as Feh says, multi-stallion groups and alliances are neither exclusively different nor the same. She disposes of the rest of the argument:

> Linklater et al. argued that long-term bonds between males and females evolved against harassment by stallions and that multimale groups are simply an artefact of selection for consort relationships. While this may be true for the Kaimanawa horses (it remains to be shown in the absence of data on the long-term relationships between stallions and their long-term reproductive success based on paternity) or other feral horses, they should not dismiss the existence of alliances in other populations where evidence is strong, especially as the evidence they present in support of their hypothesis is weak. The equid social system may simply be more flexible than previously thought. Territorial stallions have been observed in the typically nonterritorial feral horses (Rubenstein 1986) as have all-female groups (Hoffmann 1983). Sympatric[21] harems exist in feral donkeys where males are usually territorial and sexes segregate (McCort 1979).
>
> Multimale reproductive units are common in all seven equid species and may exist for several reasons. They do not imply special relationships between the individual members. In some multimale groups, stallions form alliances. Alliances are based on coalitions where the partners cooperate in the defence of their females against other males, as was shown by Berger (1986) and Feh (1999). Cooperative behaviour exists not only in feral horses, but also in plains zebras, *Equus burchelli* (Schilder 1990) and cooperative coalitions between related mares can be seen in Przewalski horses, *Equus przewalski* (personal observations). Alliances between stallions may be temporary or, in some cases, last for many years. (Feh, 2001)

The fact that such alliances exist at all tells us a great deal about the ability of stallions to co-operate with each other. In the next chapter we will be looking at relationships that can, in some respects, be the opposite of co-operative ones: dominance relationships, and the ways in which these have shaped human ideas about stallion behaviour and social relationships.

---

20 Phylogenetic inertia refers to the the nonadaptive retention of an ancestral trait. Even where predators are no longer a threat, horses will follow the same behavioural patterns their ancestors displayed in the presence of those predators. This explains why, in spite of several thousand years of domestication, domestic horses continue to behave like their wild counterparts.
21 Occupying the same or overlapping geographic areas without interbreeding.

Chapter 5

Dominance and the stallion

...for many of us primeval aggression and violent power have become synonymous with the very notion of this animal, resulting in a form of cultural monomania. And it is precisely this notion that is long overdue for serious challenge.

– Andy Beck, The Secret Life of Stallions

READERS might well be wondering why I have devoted a whole chapter (and a long one at that) to the subject of dominance and dominance hierarchies in horses. Unfortunately, the fact that so many trainers have latched onto theories of dominance, reinterpreted them and applied them in a simplistic way that has very little to do with how horses actually behave in social situations, means that unravelling fact from fiction has become an enormous task. It needs doing, though, because so much of what is routinely taught – and believed – about this subject affects the way people think about horses in general, and stallions in particular, not least the ways in which we relate to them and how we train them. So I ask you to forgive me, and stay the distance.

The idea that every animal society is based on a so-called 'dominance hierarchy' is so widespread that even people who know little if anything about animal behaviour frequently assert the truth of this idea with confidence. As Ronald Baenninger of Temple University's Department of Psychology in Philadelphia wrote in 1981,

> Dominance rank is one of those behavioral science concepts which have achieved the status of "common sense" in the popular mind. My undergraduate students, the readers of Sunday newspaper supplements, and cab drivers all seem to know about "pecking orders..."' (Baenninger, 1981)

Virtually all modern books on the training and management of horses, as well as countless articles and discussions in magazines and on internet websites and forums, stress that horses are herd animals, and that they have a well-defined social hierarchy. This is usually referred to as a 'pecking order'. The more thoughtful among us might wonder whether the use of such terms as 'pecking order' are really appropriate, since we are considering large grazing herbivores, and not a group of farmyard chickens. Nevertheless, this view of equine social organization is so widely accepted that few people question it. It is continually being reinforced in popular literature and on TV programmes (and sometimes in scientific literature, too), regardless of whether the evidence actually supports such a view.

Yet not everyone agrees. In an analysis of dominance, Dierendonck *et al.* remark that

'Often…dominance rank orders are constructed without prior investigations as to whether the concept of dominance is valid. This is the case for most of the studies of horse social organization.' (Dierendonck *et al.*, 1995) Dr Marthe Kiley-Worthington says, 'The organization of many mammalian societies described primarily in terms of a "dominance hierarchy" may be an unwarranted, and possibly an inaccurate over simplification which has not always been carefully assessed' (Kiley-Worthington, 1998) She goes on to remark that this dispute is not new, problems with the concept of 'dominance' in large herbivores having been pointed out a number of years ago (e.g. Kiley-Worthington, 1977, Syme and Syme 1979). Indeed, this problem is not confined to the behaviour of large herbivores, but applies to the study of all animal behaviour: ethologists and behavioural scientists are unable to agree even on such matters as how to define dominance, or how to measure it, let alone how to interpret their findings! (See Bernstein *et al.*, 1981 for a lengthy, complex and rather arcane discussion on this subject which, as we shall see, remains as obscure as ever, even after decades of debate.)

Nevertheless, the idea of dominance hierarchies forming the basis of equine society is so attractive to people (presumably because it is simple, tidy and – on the surface at least – does not require much thinking about) that even the suggestion that such an idea might not be correct – or might at least be a gross over-simplification – is often greeted with scorn and derision. How can so many authorities ('authorities' in this case being trainers, behavioural scientists and writers of books and articles on equine behaviour, management and training) be mistaken? Yet as the late Carl Sagan (himself no scientific slouch) put it,

> The character or beliefs of the scientist are irrelevant; all that matters is whether the evidence supports his contention. Arguments from authority simply do not count; too many authorities have been mistaken too often. (Sagan, 1974)

We have already seen in Chapter 4 that ideas about leadership in horses are confused and inaccurate, and that leadership – however it is defined – has nothing to do with any horse being the 'boss' or making all the decisions on behalf of the rest of the group. Yet when I try to explain this to people in the horse world, I am very often met with a polite (and sometimes not-so-polite) scepticism. I am frequently told about the mare who is definitely the 'boss' of her field, who orders all the other horses about, and so on, and so forth – almost everyone who keeps horses has a story to tell me about just such a mare. Or it may be a horse who is particularly 'dominant' – by which they usually mean pushy and determined to get his own way. I am sure these people – and the many others like them – are reporting what they see and experience as faithfully as they can. But the fact remains that the behaviour they have observed can be more easily explained in terms that have nothing to do with 'dominance' or 'pecking orders', and everything to do with learned behaviour and ways in which animals use the past behaviour of individuals to predict how those individuals will behave in a given situation.

Many trainers (some of whom have some strange, not to say bizarre, notions about equine behaviour) state unequivocally, not only that equine social organization is based on a 'pecking order',[1] but also that horses test their relationships with other horses by holding contests over valuable resources such as food, water, etc.; once a horse has established dominance over another horse (i.e. when the other horse concedes) in respect of each resource being contested, he will go on to challenge other individuals within the herd until he has established himself as either dominant or submissive in respect of every resource, in relation to every horse within the herd. In this way of

---

1 One trainer uses the term 'pecking order' no fewer than 21 times in the course of a 1500 word article!

thinking, horses have a responsibility to challenge those above them in the pecking order for leadership. In the words of one trainer, 'there is always a challenge going on between leaders and those being led.' (Russell, 1998)

I mean the above trainers no disrespect when I say that their statements appear to reflect the writers' own fantasies rather than any reality. I have searched the scientific literature and discussed this with people who, like me, have carried out systematic observations of groups of feral and/or domestic horses, and I can find nothing to support the claims made above. Moreover, the notion that horses hold contests among themselves for status reflects a failure to understand, first of all what a dominance relationship actually is, and further, what ethologists mean when they talk about 'rank' in social animals (in all fairness, sometimes even ethologists forget its true meaning). People who put forward this kind of idea are not describing what actually happens, but rather what they think *should* happen.

But before we can understand why this is so, we need first of all to understand the origins of concepts of 'dominance' and 'pecking orders', and what these terms actually mean.

One does not have to read too much of the scientific literature on animal behaviour and social organization to realize that many of the writers seem to have what almost amounts to an obsession with hierarchies and dominance. Why should this be? Prior to the twentieth century comparatively little had been done by way of studying animals in their natural habitat, and little was known about their social organization. But since the beginning of the twentieth century many wide-ranging studies in comparative psychology have been carried out. All kinds of animals were studied, and the idea of social dominance emerged as a result of observations of domestic chickens made by the Norwegian naturalist Thorleif Schjelderup-Ebbe in the early 1920s. He noted that aggression between any two birds within a flock was a one-way process: if one bird pecked another, the other bird would not respond in kind. Schjelderup-Ebbe therefore considered the aggressor to be the 'dominant' individual, and the one on the receiving end of the aggression was labelled the 'subordinate'. He believed that this overt aggression was the key to social organization in domestic fowl. 'Between any two birds,' he wrote in 1922, 'one individual *invariably* had precedence over the other' and further 'In this case Z is the despot, the superior being, the tyrant, he has the power and may use it as he pleases.' (Schjelderup-Ebbe, quoted by Syme & Syme, 1979) Because it was first documented among domestic fowl, this clearly defined hierarchy became known as a 'pecking order', which is how we ended up with a much-misused term, often conjured up indiscriminately to describe virtually any animal society where the writer believes a dominance hierarchy should operate, regardless of whether this is in fact the case.

The middle years of the twentieth century saw the rise of the new science of ethology – a branch of zoology that studies the behaviour of animals in their natural habitats. As studies of animal societies increased in number and scope, hierarchical organization was also found in many other species, and soon the phrase 'pecking order' was being used in a widespread, rather careless manner, to describe virtually any social arrangement where some kind of hierarchy was observed. Another popular phrase was 'dominance hierarchy'; so that – as I observed at the beginning of this chapter – one can scarcely pick up a book on animal behaviour without finding references to 'dominance hierarchies' of one kind or another.

It is important to realize that for many years almost all studies of animal behaviour were carried out in a captive environment, where human interference affected group size and gender distribution, and where highly unnatural conditions served to distort behaviour. It was not until ethologists started to observe animals in the wild, in their natural surroundings, that they began to realize that animal societies were far more complex than any simplistic model of 'dominance hierarchies' could predict.

Even so, much that was observed was 'shoehorned' into existing theories about hierarchies in animal societies; ethologists were still very much influenced by the pioneering work of earlier scientists such as Schjelderup-Ebbe, as well as that of one of the founders of the science of ethology – the very pro-Nazi Konrad Lorenz.[2]

There are very good reasons for this, and they have nothing to do with scientific objectivity. Scientists like to believe that their findings are based on objective research and observation. But scientists, like everyone else, are only human, and their conclusions are inevitably coloured by their world-view. In spite of dire warnings about the dangers of anthropomorphism (attributing human qualities to non-human animals), scientists have tended to base their interpretations of non-human societies on certain types of human society. As Jeffrey Masson and Susan McCarthy remark in their book *When Elephants Weep*,

> The notion of observing a group of animals engaged in mysterious interactions and extracting a tidy hierarchy which generates testable predictions has great appeal for scientists. Sometimes the idea that hierarchies are inevitable and prove certain things about humans is also part of the appeal. (Masson and McCarthy, 1996)

And as Alexandra Semyonova points out in her paper 'The social organization of the domestic dog'

> The dominance hierarchy model was developed in a period in which many human societies were struggling with authoritarian forms of government and the culture and ideologies that form of government propagated… Its spread continued in a post-war world in which a competitive market economy and its ideologies, based on a selective and flawed interpretation of Darwin's theory of natural selection, shaped a new generation of humans' perceptions of natural reality. A final factor is that the model was developed in a period in which there were very few women involved in scientific research. This means that a limited group of existential repertoires and paradigms was used as background in the search for explanations of observed animal behavior… It is also a widely investigated psychological fact that the first thing human males do when two or more of them have to share a physical space is investigate and order their relative power relations within the (fleeting) group. The conclusion that dogs are equally preoccupied with establishing 'dominance' in their social interactions is most likely a failure of imagination. Unable to conceive of any other way of organizing a group, scientists seem to have projected their own existential paradigm onto the animals they were observing.[3] (Semyonova, 2003)

And these biases are not confined to observations of dogs: they are found in studies of all animals, including, of course, horses. Later in the same paper, Semyonova remarks on yet another observer bias, 'namely the possible tendency to give more weight than is really justified to seemingly violent

---

[2] I mention Lorenz's support of Nazi ideals for a very good reason, which will become clear later in this chapter.
[3] In fact not all human societies have been organized on hierarchical lines. Nomadic hunter-gatherer societies, for example, have usually had non-hierarchical social structures. A group usually consisted of a small number of family units, comprising a band or clan.

encounters between observed animals, and thus the model's focus on what it calls aggression.' (Semyonova, 2003)

So the 'dominance hierarchy' model has persisted, in spite of the fact that it is all too easy, when studying animal societies, to find dominance hierarchies where they do not actually exist; such hierarchies may appear to be a feature of the society in question, when statistically they may in fact represent random patterns of behaviour. Very often, observers see what they expect to see, and ignore anything that does not fit their expectations. There have even been cases where observers have been so convinced that a hierarchy must exist that they have 'tweaked' their figures until a recognisable hierarchy emerges!

A factor not generally considered is that most of the major studies of dominance, which have shaped theories about its function in the social organization of non-human animals, have concentrated on birds or primates (especially the latter), and the results then applied to mammalian societies in general, often without regard to differences in habitat and lifestyle.

The 'alpha animal'

Another constantly misused concept which arose from early ethological studies of dominance hierarchies, and which is frequently invoked by trainers of dogs and horses alike, is that of the 'alpha' animal. This derives from methods used to determine dominance hierarchies in social animals. Ethologists using this method observe the number of aggressive interactions that take place within a specific period, then 'rank' the animals in order of the number of threats they have observed being made by each animal. The animal which has made the most threats is labelled the 'alpha' animal; the animal which made the next highest number of threats is classed as the 'beta' animal etc., all the way through the Greek alphabet to omega, if there are enough animals in the group to get that far. In some cases all aggressive acts between animals are recorded and individuals ranked in order so that each animal received threats from the smallest number of individuals below it; in other words, the animal that threatened the most was on top and that which threatened least on the bottom. It should be obvious that this is an extremely crude and unsatisfactory way of looking at animal societies, not least because it tells us virtually nothing about how the animals in question interact in different social contexts. Nevertheless, it has proved exceptionally enduring, perhaps because it is so simple, and people (being people) like to latch onto simple explanations.

Unfortunately, this liking for simplicity has got us into a terrible muddle when it comes to understanding what is going on in animal societies. Ethologists have a regrettable tendency to write about 'high (or low) ranking' animals; lay persons and writers of popular books and magazine articles on animal behaviour have then latched onto this phraseology and used it as if it describes some equivalent of class in human societies. We even read of sons or daughters 'inheriting' their mother's rank, when what is really being described is a simple 'ranking' in a hierarchy of aggression, as described above. As young animals will tend to take their lead from their parents, if (say) a mare tends to make a high number of threats towards other horses, then her daughters may well learn this behaviour from her. As Irwin S. Bernstein points out in his classic paper on the subject, 'Dominance per se and dominance ranks...cannot be genetically transmitted since they constitute relationships with other individuals rather than absolute attributes.' (Bernstein, 1981) 'Rank' in this context therefore means nothing more than this simple position in a hierarchy of aggression – and as I have said, this really tells us nothing useful about how horses relate to each other in different contexts.

In spite of this, the idea of the importance of the 'alpha' animal persists. For decades it has formed the core of much dog training theory, and as some of the ideas put forward by dog trainers are paralleled by those taught by some horse trainers, I think we need to take a look at how those ideas originated. So please bear with me as I digress into the realm of dogs and dog training.

Until comparatively recently, the assumption has been that since dogs are descended from wolves, their natural behaviour must parallel that of wolves. And, as wolves had a rigid social hierarchy, in which each wolf knew his place (submissive to those above him, aggressive to those beneath him) and which was controlled by the Alpha Wolf, the Supreme Leader, then it followed that this must also apply to domestic dogs. According to this theory, dogs would perceive the human family in which they lived as the equivalent of a dog pack. Owners were therefore exhorted to ensure that they achieved – and maintained – the 'alpha' status in the domestic 'pack', otherwise the dog would attempt to take control of the household. Rigid sets of 'pack rules' were laid down to establish and maintain this status, and much problematical behaviour in dogs was attributed to the owner's failure to achieve and hold 'alpha' status.

What most people don't realize is that this model of wolf society was to a large extent dreamed up by that charming but unrepentant Nazi Konrad Lorenz[4] – and of course the Nazis loved it. It was simply a projection of Nazi ideals onto an animal which had achieved cult status within the Nazi regime, because of its perceived wildness, nobility and ruthlessness.[5] If Lorenz's model was based on evidence, his politics would be irrelevant – but it was not. Lorenz's own field of study was birds, not wolves or dogs, and his views were strongly opposed by Rudolf Schenkel, who studied wolves in the Basel zoo for many years. But Lorenz was a very eminent scientist (and later, a Nobel prize-winner[6]), so he had clout in the scientific community – and his ideas prevailed for half a century.

However, theories about wolves were based on inadequate observations of wolves in captivity. More recent long-term studies of wolves in the wild (for example, David Mech's 13 years of summer observations of wolves on Ellesmere Island, Northwest Territories, Canada) have established that wolf packs consist of a family group: that is, the breeding pair and their offspring, and their behaviour is different in many key respects from that of the groups of mainly unrelated wolves generally observed in captivity. Hierarchy in such family groups is largely irrelevant (Mech, 1999; Mech, 2000).

As David Mech points out,

> The issue is not merely one of semantics or political correctness. It is one of biological correctness such that the term we use for breeding wolves accurately captures the biological and social role of the animals rather than perpetuate a faulty view. (Mech, 2008)

Furthermore Ray Coppinger, who has spent many years studying the behaviour of feral dogs as well as training working dogs for a number of different disciplines, has shown that the behaviour of feral dogs differs greatly from that of wolves, and that the whole concept of 'pack rules' is confused and confusing, not least for the dog (Coppinger 2002). Coppinger, who has also spent some time with wolves, is dismissive of the whole idea of using dominance to train either dogs or wolves.

---

[4] Lorenz's book *Man Meets Dog* (1954) was for a long time very influential in shaping ideas about the dog-human relationship.
[5] For a more detailed discussion of this, see Semyonova, 2009, Sax, 1997 and Sax, 2000. To be fair to Lorenz, the idea of the leader of a pack of dogs having despotic power had already been expressed, notably by Colonel Konrad Most, a police commissioner at the Royal Prussian Police Headquarters, in his book *Training dogs: a manual*, published in 1910. This may have been where some of Lorenz's ideas originated, although he does not specifically mention Most.
[6] 1973

'Imagine training a wolf by dominating it,' he says. 'Quick way to get killed.' (Petura, interview with Ray and Lorna Coppinger)

Towards the end of his life the late pet behaviour counsellor John Fisher, celebrated for his work with problem dogs, began to question much that had he had earlier accepted about 'pack rules', and eventually discarded this way of thinking. As he put it in one of his later books, '...if it's how you want to live with your dog I have news that is going to disappoint a lot of people who have striven to reach this Alpha status – it all means diddly squat to your dogs.' (Fisher, 1998)

Like Coppinger, Fisher pointed out the confusion that can arise in a dog's mind when owners attempt to apply the 'pack rules' cited above, especially when these 'rules' are applied too rigidly. Belatedly, more and more dog trainers are starting to realize that this pseudo-ethological approach is a rather hit-and-miss way of training dogs, and are looking instead to training programmes based on positive reinforcement – which we shall look at in Chapters 9 and 10.

In conclusion, then, as Alexandra Semyonova says, 'The idea about dogs living in a dominance hierarchy very like the Nazi Party, and that dogs spend the whole day thinking about power, is nothing more than Konrad Lorenz's fictional legacy to us.' (Semyonova, 2009)

What about horse trainers, though? It seems that, so far from passing out of favour, training based on the concept of the 'alpha horse' is actually becoming deeply entrenched, thanks largely to the rather uncritical acceptance of this and other ideas about equine society by many trainers, training organizations, authors and equestrian magazines, and hence of the equestrian public. The concepts behind the dog training theory outlined above have basically been reinvented and applied to horses. Some trainers insist that, in order to communicate with horses effectively, we must become the dominant, or alpha, horse of their herd, and that we must always maintain this position.

When trainers tell us that we must take the place of the dominant horse (however they define 'dominant'), it is often extraordinarily difficult to grasp exactly how they want us to do this. Part of the problem is that they do not define adequately what they mean by 'dominant'.

What is 'dominance'?

Observations of aggressive – or as animal behaviour scientists would put it, 'agonistic' – interactions between domestic horses, and also in feral horses living in natural groups, have led many observers to conclude that horses, too, are hierarchical, and that dominance plays a prominent part in their social organization. Most (although not all) of these observers have assumed, and described, dominance hierarchies; but they do not always make it clear how they have measured these hierarchies. When they do, the measurement has usually been based on the rather crude system described earlier in this chapter – that of counting threats and using the results to 'rank' the observed horses. The context of these threats – which would surely tell us how relevant they are to social organization – has rarely been recorded in detail. In some cases no observations have been recorded at all; the presence of a dominance hierarchy has simply been assumed. For example, in his M.A. thesis on the feral horses of Sable Island in Nova Scotia, D.A Welsh says,

> The detailed examination of intra-herd relationships and the subtleties of hierarchical structure are not necessary to understanding the ecology of the horses. It is important to know that one of the mares (mare in charge) is dominant over the others and is often responsible for important decisions about movement. All members of the herd are subordinate to the stallion-in-charge. (Welsh, 1975)

This sounds convincing, especially given that Welsh spent several years observing the Sable Island horses. But, as we have already seen in Chapter 4, the idea of one horse being 'in charge' does not stand up to closer examination, and he misunderstands the nature of 'dominance'.

So before we can see whether the idea of a 'dominance hierarchy' is really relevant to equine society, we must try to understand what is meant by dominance, and what its function is supposed to be.

At its simplest, dominance simply means exerting control. Parents do this with their children, just as mares and stallions do with their foals and other youngstock; both may therefore be said to be 'dominant' over their offspring. However, correctly speaking, 'dominance' describes the relationship between two individuals; one individual may be said to be 'dominant' over another, but since 'dominance' is a quality of a relationship and not a personality trait, it is nonsensical to use the term 'dominant' on its own to describe an individual, as so many people do (for example, they may talk about a 'dominant mare' or a 'dominant stallion'. Dominant over whom, and in what context(s)?

To an ethologist, a 'dominance relationship' is one in which one individual always responds submissively to another individual at the start of any aggressive encounter. A 'dominance hierarchy' is simply the order in which these dominance relationships arrange themselves; the idea is that this enables every individual to know his or her place within the society.

Sometimes the relationships are linear (often described as 'transitive'), e.g. A dominates B who in turn dominates C and so on. This is the classical 'pecking order' as described by Schjelderup-Ebbe. However, in many animal societies a perfectly linear order is the exception rather than the rule. Instead one might find that A dominates B and B dominates C, but C dominates A; this is known as a 'triangular' or 'intransitive' relationship.[7] Or, the hierarchy might be partly linear (e.g. A dominates B who dominates C who dominates D; D does not dominate E but E dominates A (but not B, C or D).

Some commentators insist that dominance relationships among horses are always linear, but this is not true. Some observers have found linear hierarchies, e.g. Grzimek, 1944, Tyler, 1972 (although the latter reports that when animals from different groups of the population were involved their rank order was complicated by various triangular relationships at any position in the hierarchy) and Rho *et al.*, 2004.

But others have found both linear hierarchies and triangular relationships: 'Horses form social hierarchies which are linear in small herds. In large herds complex triangular relationships…may occur.' (Houpt *et al.*, 1978). In fact, triangular relationships are found in smaller groups as well. For example, in her study of Przewalski's horses in Dutch semi-reserves, Claudia Feh found that no clear linear hierarchy existed in the harem group, which consisted of five horses (four mares and 1 stallion), and that a triangular relationship existed between two of the mares and the stallion. (Feh, 1988). In their study of Highland ponies and cows Clutton-Brock *et al.* found that

> …the study supported GARTLAN's (1968) emphasis on the complexity of social structure and the inadequacy of dominance in explaining many variations in social relationships. In neither group was the hierarchy fully linear, and there was no obvious explanation of the irregularities which occurred. (Clutton-Brock *et al.*, 1976)

---

[7] Higher order relationships of this kind may also occur, for example a square relationship: A→B→C→D→A. However, the triangular relationship is the most common type of intransitive relationship.

Montgomery found a triangular relationship among the group he studied (Montgomery, 1957). Schilder also found triangular relationships in his study of adult plains zebra stallions. (Schilder, 1988).

There are statistical problems with attempts to rank animals in linear hierarchies:

> It is a common practice to rank a group of animals in the closest possible order to a linear dominance hierarchy. It turns out that this method has a surprisingly high probability of producing a hierarchy in a group that actually has random dominance relationships. (Appleby, 1983)

Appleby goes on to say that '…no hierarchy in a group of less than 6 can have a statistically significant level of linearity.'

As Daniel Mills and Kathryn Nankervis point out,

> A common problem extending from dominance is the emphasis it puts on the ability of a single individual to gain overall control of everything. It is possible to construct a general hierarchy for a group of horses but it will not be as simple as the one described above [i.e. a linear hierarchy, L.S.]. We are most unlikely to find a single individual always winning every encounter if different individuals have different roles.[8] Even if we just use the trend in the relationship, triangular relationships become apparent. These structures may seem nice, but their importance to the horses living in the group is questionable. (Mills and Nankervis, 1999)

This is where ideas about dominance hierarchies start to break down; once we get beyond simple linear relationships, it all begins to get rather too complicated, so that even trained ethologists with a battery of notebooks and complex statistical programs are often at a loss to decipher the complexities they find. The neatly linear ranking system which supposedly tells us something about equine social organization disappears, making any system of ranking impossible except by ignoring – or treating as statistically insignificant – the non-linear relationships. Irwin S. Bernstein highlights this problem:

> The concept of a dominance rank hierarchy…requires transitivity. We cannot rank animals with triangular relationships; ordinal relationships are required to count the number of individuals above or below any referent individual and to assign rankings in a group. (Bernstein, 1981)

Yet many of the same scientists who expect horses to be able to work out such complex relationships then deny that horses have the kind of reasoning capacity that would enable them to do so!

Alexandra Semyonova points out the flaws in the use of statistical analysis in studying animal social organization:

> The use of statistical analysis to prove the existence of and unravel dominance hierarchies does not provide a solution to [the biases already described, L.S.]. These analyses begin based on definitions derived from the dominance hierarchy model, counting only behaviors that already fit the model, and are

---

8 See under **What role does dominance play?** on pages 94–99 for examples of differing contexts in which a horse might be dominant over another.

therefore unable to do anything but recirculate and affirm the model on which they are based. (Semyonova, 2003)

She goes on to say that

> ...superstition seems to play a role in the use of statistical analysis. Experimenters use statistics to assert that results obtained and conclusions drawn from observing a group of ten to forty animals have the same validity as a wide population study would. Even where the groups observed are larger, the animals are treated as static beings living in some permanent observable state. The statistical approach seems intended to sidestep instead of facing the complex problem of the individual learning histories of the organisms studied in order to draw broad conclusions from small group studies... A second superstition is that pulling data through a statistical program will, all by itself, solve the problem that the observer is inevitably interpreting what s/he sees...but scientists themselves have been too unaware that they, too, are animals whose behavior must be studied, and that they are subjects operating within a cognitive and social domain upon which the very questions they ask, their observations and their conclusions are dependent. The use of statistics is not adequate to solve this problem. In addition, though science is practiced with the aim of eliminating as much superstitious learning as it can from its models and belief systems, it is inevitable that some superstition always remains – though the content can shift with time. This has all had a huge effect on the way animal societies are studied, the models, which have been proposed, and the conclusions, which have been drawn throughout history. (Semyonova, 2003)

Problems with statistics apart, the methods used to construct dominance hierarchies in many studies of horses are themselves suspect. I have already commented on the crude methods often used to 'rank' horses; Dierendonck *et al.* go further:

> Several authors (GRZIMEK, 1944; HOUPT et al., 1978; SERENI & BOISSOU, 1978; ASA et al., 1979; HOUPT & WOLSKI, 1980; HOUPT & KEIPER, 1982) used the rivalry around limited and monopolisable resources to establish the dominance-subordination relationship by using (paired) feeding tests. In such tests a possible influence of other herd members is excluded. HOUPT *et al.* (1978) used paired feeding tests to show that in small herds (up to 9 animals) strictly linear hierarchies were found, while in larger herds (10–11 animals) also triangular relationships were formed. However, dominance relationships found in this way may differ from those found in a free roaming situation and during a longer period of observation. (Dierendonck et al., 1995)

The situation is further complicated by the fact that observers often use different behaviours to construct rank orders. They may use a mixture of offensive and defensive aggressive behaviours (e.g. Houpt and Wolski, 1980) whereas other observers treat offensive and defensive aggression separately (e.g. Wells and Rothschild (1978) Feh (1988) and Schilder

(1988). In addition, as Dierendonck *et al.* point out that avoidance behaviour has often been ignored, and that

> Since aggressive behaviours may well be used by lower ranking individuals against higher ranking ones, the use of aggressive behaviours only in investigating dominance may render an unclear or even invalid picture. This was the reason why in zebra stallions (SCHILDER, 1988) and wolves (VAN HOOFF & WENSING, 1987) aggressive behaviours could not be used to construct a rank order. (Dierendonck *et al.*, 1995)

As we shall see later in this chapter, the distinction between offensive and defensive aggressive behaviours is an important one, not least because it calls into question the idea that 'dominance hierarchies' serve to reduce aggression within a group.

Submission

Assuming that one horse accepts the dominance of another within their relationship, how does he or she show that acceptance? There is no equivalent in the equine behaviour repertoire of the kind of appeasement behaviour shown by animals of many other species. Even the 'foal-face', which every horse-owner who has had much to do with foals will have seen and which used to be regarded as appeasement, is now no longer seen as a gesture of submission. This gesture is often called 'snapping' in equine behaviour literature; the foal or young horse extends the neck and head and opens and closes the mouth without bringing the teeth or lips together. It is usually interpreted as being intended to prevent more mature horses from acting aggressively towards an immature horse; Zeeb, who first described it in 1959, called it *Unterlegenheitsgebärde* (gesture of inferiority) (Zeeb, 1959). However, there are several problems with this. First of all, in the majority of cases it does not actually do that; a number of studies (e.g. Tyler, 1972; Boyd, 1980; Crowell-Davis *et al.* 1985) have shown that it has little or no effect with regard to inhibiting aggression on the part of older horses. A three-year study carried out on the developmental behaviour of foals during their first 24 weeks of life showed that so far from preventing aggression, snapping sometimes triggered it; in addition, foals often approached older horses and snapped to them, initiating an encounter rather than simply reacting to one (Crowell-Davis *et al.*, 1985). I have seen a foal and a yearling snapping to each other, and I have read reports from several people who say they have observed mature stallions snapping to foals (for example, Isaac, 1997).

Crowell-Davis *et al.* concluded that snapping was ritualized nursing behaviour (i.e. the gesture was very similar to that of a foal suckling), and that it could occur as a displacement activity in situations where the foal is excited or subject to conflicting emotions. For example, he might be curious about other horses and want to seek them out, but lack the social skills to be able to approach them in an acceptable manner (much like a child whose manners with adults may be rather awkward). Similarly if they approach him he may not know how to deal with them – again like a child who lacks the confidence to talk to adults. In the case of the yearling and the foal snapping to each other, they may have both been unsure how to deal with the situation: the yearling had never seen another foal and the foal had never seen another yearling! The mature stallions observed snapping to foals are another matter; there may be something else altogether going on here. Perhaps, like the *Rossigkeitsgesicht* described in Chapter 6, it may serve as a signal that the animal performing the snapping will not harm the other; however, this is only conjecture. What is clear is that this is far from being the simple submissive gesture it is usually said to be.

As we shall see, the only behaviour which horses can use to signify submission is to move away – in other words, to avoid the dominant one. This has far-reaching implications for people who seek to use the dominant-submissive relationship in training horses – as Chapter 8 will show.

'Snapping': in the photograph on the left Tariel is snapping to his father, Nivalis. In the photographs below it is Tariel's full brother, Rigel, who is snapping to Nivalis. Photos: Lesley Skipper

Factors affecting position in the hierarchy

So what factors might affect a horse's position in a hierarchy? As Keiper and Sambraus point out, 'The determinants of social dominance in horses…remain obscure.' (Keiper and Sambraus, 1986). The authors of numerous studies have tried to find correlations between physical factors such as height, weight and age, but have found that either no such correlations exist (or are insignificant) or that they exist in some groups or not in others (Clutton-Brock *et al.*, 1976; Houpt *et al.*, 1978; Houpt and Keiper, 1982). The only consistent finding seems to be that adults are dominant over juveniles, which is exactly what we would expect to find. (See my comments re parents being dominant over their offspring on page 89.)

It should be obvious from all this that the whole concept of dominance and dominance hierarchies in equids is a mess, with observers and commentators unable to agree on what they are measuring or how they are measuring it, let alone how to interpret their findings. So what, in all this confusion, can we learn about the role of the stallion? Commentators have agonized over this question: why does the stallion usually appear to take a subordinate role in dominance relationships? The question itself reflects the old, fallacious assumption that females are naturally passive and subordinate; the answers seem to confirm only that equine social organization is far more complex and sophisticated than has generally been recognized. Nevertheless, they bear looking at.

Katherine Houpt and Ronald Keiper carried out a study of three groups of feral horses living on Assateague Island and three groups of domestic horses at Cornell University. The groups varied in size from six to 10 horses. The animals ranged in age from one to 15 years and consisted of at least one stallion and several mares. The results indicated that the stallion is usually not the most aggressive member of the group nor the one that has first access to food. (Houpt and Keiper, 1982). Berger (1977) noted that in one of four herds of horses in the Grand Canyon, the stallion was submissive to the mares of the herd. Feist and McCullough seem to contradict this; in their study of feral horses the Pryor Mountain Wild Horse Range they refer to the 'strong dominance of the stallion over the harem' (Feist and McCullough, 1976), but they do not say what they mean by this, or give any data in support. More recently Telané Greyling observes that among the feral horses of the Namib Naukluft Park, although stallions were able to herd their mares away from other stallions, they did not dominate them in any other way. (Greyling, 1994)

Possible explanations for the stallion's apparently submissive role include the lack of difference in body size:

> Although stallions are usually more heavily muscled than mares in the neck region, there is little sexual dimorphism in the sizes of hooves and teeth, the offensive weapons of horses. This lack of sexual dimorphism may explain why stallions are not always dominant. (Keiper & Sambraus, 1986)

This obviously assumes the use of physical force in establishing 'dominance' – but as we have already seen, body size and weight are either irrelevant or are not consistent factors. Another possible explanation put forward by Keiper and Sambraus relates to the stability of horse bands:

> mares tend to stay in the herds of their birth or enter a new band at a young age, whereas stallions disperse from their natal band, remain for several years in a bachelor band, and then must enter a band of mares in which the social order has been stabilized (Keiper & Sambraus, 1986)

But this is not necessarily the case. Houpt and Keiper point out that 'Stallions may acquire a herd by replacing a living stallion or a dead one, but more commonly they acquire mares that have left their parental band'. (Houpt and Keiper, 1982, citing Keiper, 1979).

It does not seem to occur to anyone that there might be an explanation that does not involve 'dominance': that apart from occasions when it is necessary for the stallion to move his mares away from real or perceived danger, there is simply no need for him to dominate his mares. What does he have to gain if he does? This raises the question of what purpose, if any, dominance relationships (and any hierarchies derived from them) might serve.

What role does dominance play?

If the social behaviour of a species does include dominance hierarchies, what purpose could they serve? Assumptions usually made are that such hierarchies give dominant animals priority of access to potential mates, food, water, territory, personal space etc. and serve to reduce levels of aggression within a group; the idea is that once dominance relationships are established, physical aggression is replaced by threat displays from which the subordinate animal retreats.

In addition, dominant animals are often assumed to be leaders, although as we have already seen, this does not apply to horses.

These ideas do apply to some extent in certain animal societies, although societies based on hierarchies of aggression are by no means as widespread as was once thought. But how – if at all – do they apply to equine society?

Access to potential mates

Let's consider the first point, access to potential mates. As we have seen, the basis of equine society is the family unit, or band, and colts generally leave the band when they become sexually mature. They are therefore rarely likely to challenge the stallion for the right to mate with mares within the family group. In any case, as Chapter 4 showed, there are powerful inhibitions against mating with parents, offspring or siblings. This 'weeding out' of sexually mature males does not leave much need for a stallion to exercise dominance within a group in order to gain priority of access to mates. The only real challenges to a stallion would therefore normally come from outside the family group, usually from bachelors seeking to supplant the band stallion, less often from a stallion belonging to an existing band.

According to Feist and McCullough, out of 82 observed encounters between stallions of different groups, 37 were the result of the nearness of other groups. 12 fights were caused by attempts on the part of a harem stallion to gain a mare from within another harem, while four other fights were part of attempts by stallions to recover mares that had become separated from the harem (in only one case was the mare not recovered). So from these limited data it would seem that the greater part of the aggression between stallions was the result of attempts to protect existing groups, rather than to gain access to mares from other groups, though clearly this did happen. This is consistent with other studies which have found that stallions appear to concentrate more on maintaining group cohesion and stability than on enlarging the size of their harems.

Berger (1977) found a direct relationship between harem size and what he called 'interband stallion rank' (a rather crude ranking of stallions in relation to stallions of other bands); however he also noted that when the number of foals was subtracted from the groups, there was negligible difference between the stallions in the middle rank. In any case, the number of stallions in this study (four in all) is hardly sufficient to give proof one way or the other.

Writing about male-to-male interactions, i.e. between stallions belonging to different bands, or between stallions and bachelors, Joel Berger notes that '… only when an individual chased the other away was it clear that one was dominant at that time over the other. In 96.5% of the interactions among males I was unable to assign dominance status.' (Berger, 1986)

So it would appear that stallions challenging or being challenged for access to potential mates are simply responding to a situation in which they either see an opportunity to acquire mates, or in which their family unit is being threatened.

So much for stallions and access to mates. But what about mares? Do they gain priority of access to the stallion through being dominant and, if so, how does this affect their reproductive success? To date no clear-cut correlation has been found between dominance and reproductive success. In fact throughout his five year study of the Granite Range horses Berger found that only one female in the entire Granite population retained her dominance status, and the number of foals she produced was neither better nor worse than the three other females with whom she associated for four years. Berger concludes that 'In Granite Range horses intraband dominance seems to be of little biological significance and had no effect on female reproductive success.' (Berger, 1986)

Access to food and water

Here again, we come up against assumptions which are not borne out by the evidence. For example, Paul McGreevy says, 'most hierarchies are established in relation to food resources' (McGreevy, 1996)

He further says that 'Free-ranging horses are usually familiar with the seasonal disappearance of food sources, and it is at times of relative paucity that rank can mean the difference between surviving and perishing. The horse that demands access to the best of what food is available is less likely to suffer illness and is also the least likely to be lethargic when escaping a potential predator.' (McGreevy, 1996)

As with the other assumptions examined so far, we must ask, what evidence is there that this is really the case?

The study of the Tour du Valat herd of Camargue horses made by Wells and Rothschild gives no real evidence of dominance affecting access to food and water. The authors content themselves with the observation that 'Headthreats ... are given to subordinate individuals in more general situations such as grazing, seeking shelter and maintaining individual distance.'. However they give no data from this study which would support this statement. (Wells and Rothschild, 1979)

In his 1977 study, Berger makes no mention of dominance in relation to feeding; while Clutton-Brock *et al.* in their study of Highland ponies merely state that 'Apart from increasing the frequency of interaction, the provision of food had little effect on the social structure of the group.' (Clutton-Brock *et al.*, 1976)

Feist and McCullough record no correlation between dominance and access to food; with regard to drinking they observe that 'Threats were used at the water holes to gain drinking space, although for the most part group members were tolerant of each other in this circumstance.' They also note that 'As each horse finished drinking it would wait for the rest of the group to finish when all moved away together.' (Feist and McCullough, 1976) As all thus had the same amount of opportunity to drink (because the rest of the group would wait for them), a dominance hierarchy would not seem to confer any benefit here.

In the context of competition for scarce resources, it is interesting to note that during Stephanie Tyler's celebrated study of New Forest ponies, hay was supplied to the ponies in winter to provide competition, so that large numbers of threats could be recorded in a short time – far more than would be observed during 'normal grazing, when *competition was negligible* [my italics].' (Tyler, 1972) How does this lack of competition fit in with the picture of rank as a matter of life and death?

The same lack of competitiveness dogged Grzimek when he conducted his early experiments in determining rank in horses. As Syme and Syme comment, 'Observing insufficient aggressive behaviour in a non-competitive situation he then recorded the response of 29 young stallions to restricted food in a bucket and eventually obtained enough data for an hierarchy. Even in this competitive setting the horses were extremely tolerant of each other and possible situational variation in dominance relationships was noted.' (Syme & Syme, 1979)

For some species food comes in discrete 'packages' (e.g. fruit among apes and monkeys), so one might expect challenges for access to food to be common. However horses' food is all around them, in the form of forage (grass, herbs, and less commonly shrubs and the leaves of trees) and is therefore freely available to all. Berger reported that 'Mares were not often aggressive to those with whom they were familiar...even in early spring when food was most limited and new vegetative growth had not yet begun, few feeding displacements occurred.' (Berger, 1986) This applied regardless of whether the foraging was good or poor and these findings reflect those of other studies, i.e. that food shortages rarely increased antagonism among band members. So left to their own devices, horses do not commonly challenge others over food; it is we who create artificial situations (limited access to grazing; concentrate feed in buckets; insufficient personal space etc.) in which competition occurs.

Berger noted some jostling at water holes when water was frozen in winter or when it had partially dried up in summer, but in the main aggression between the mares in a band occurred when individuals approached too close to a new-born foal. This is similar to findings reported by Telané Greyling from her observations of the feral horses of the Namib Naukluft Park. Greyling concludes that 'Dominance in the Namib population...seemed to be of little importance. No dominance hierarchies could be determined for the mares in groups or individuals in bachelor groups.' (Greyling, 1994)

Reduction of aggression

So what role, if any, do dominance hierarchies play? Do they, as is often claimed, serve to reduce aggression? They may do so in some species, but it is debatable whether this is the case where horses are concerned. Some other species use highly ritualized displays whereby a subordinate indicates acknowledgement of the status of another in order to deflect possible aggression. Dierendonck and Schilder note that horses and zebras do not appear to use these formal dominance signals. The only ritualized behaviour shown by horses is the 'foal-face' which, as we saw earlier in this chapter, may be simply a displacement activity rather than showing submission, and displays such as posturing, urinating or defecating on dung piles etc. But the latter behaviour applies exclusively to encounters between adult stallions, not to general relationships within a group. As Dierendonck and Schilder remark

> ...the behaviour which reflects best the dominance relationship between two horses is avoidance...This means that if subordinate non-juvenile horses get involved in a conflict with a higher ranking horse, they can only give ground or defend themselves, but are unable to present a display (with the possible exclusion of tooth-clapping[9]) by which they acknowledge the dominance status of the other, thereby possibly reducing its aggression.

---

9 By this they mean the 'foal-face' described on pages 92–93

The Natural Stallion

Above: Horses of the Namib Naukluft: Telané Greyling was unable to determine dominance hierarchies either for mares in family groups or in bachelor groups. Photo: Telané Greyling

Below left: Nivalis and Tiff (Mikenah) sharing a bucket of feed. **Below right:** Nivalis and Tiff share a pile of hay. It has been impossible to determine a consistent dominance relationship beteeen the two of them in relation to food as they are so tolerant of each other. Photos: Lesley Skipper

So the only way horses can avoid aggression on the part of another horse is either to move away (which may not always be possible) or to retaliate – which, as we shall see, they often do – far more often than the literature on dominance in horses generally suggests.[10] This is hardly compatible with the idea of a dominance hierarchy which serves to reduce aggression.

The only way a horse can avoid aggression on the part of another horse is either to move away or to retaliate. Photo: Lesley Skipper

Furthermore, a dominance hierarchy could only reduce aggression if, once the hierarchy had been established, every animal within it not only knew their place but actually kept to it. This does not necessarily happen. For example, Joel Berger reports that the same females were rarely the consistently dominant members of their bands. He says

> Dominance relationships changed regularly and most often over periods that spanned a few days to several weeks. Because feeding displacements were rare and dominance changed among individuals, it was difficult if not impossible to assign a 'dominant female' status for intraband hierarchies. In fact the only periods when females consistently dominated others in their bands were after the births of their foals. (Berger, 1986)

This is echoed by the findings of Feist and McCullough, who say that 'No consistent dominance hierarchy was observed among individual mares of a harem.' (Feist, 1976)

Yet in the popular literature we come up against more muddled thinking. We are told that it is every horse's responsibility to try to climb to the top of the rank ladder – as if they were so many human social climbers. But if, as a number of trainers insist, there is always a challenge going on between leaders and those being led, how can the dominance hierarchy serve to minimize aggression? In such a case there would be continual conflict among the members of the group, which makes nonsense of the idea of a dominance hierarchy acting to reduce aggression. And by the end of this chapter it will be clear that feral groups, and well-integrated domestic groups, do not spend their time in perpetual conflict.

---

10 See the summary of Dr Marthe Kiley-Worthington's findings on pages 100–101

Identifying hierarchies

We may, if we feel we really must, identify hierarchies of aggression in groups of horses in a domestic setting. I can easily do so with regard to our own horses, by the simple (and very crude) test of making them go hungry, then presenting them with a bucket of feed and seeing who ends up with the bucket. This is how dominance hierarchies have largely been determined in groups of domestic horses. The scientists carrying out such tests are using a species' behaviour in extreme situations which in the case of horses, would never be encountered in the wild, and then applying their findings to predict that species' normal behaviour. But everyday life is not lived at such extreme levels, so why should behaviour at those levels be cited as the norm?

Determining such a hierarchy could certainly help us to decide who is turned out with whom in order to avoid conflict over food (supplied in buckets or troughs, or as discrete piles of hay) or water. However, it does nothing to inform us how a group of horses actually relate to each other socially in different contexts. A different situation could well see either a partial or complete reorganization of the hierarchy. For example, in the days before our stallion Nivalis fully realized what being a stallion meant, he was usually turned out with the rest of our horses. Now one horse, Kruger can be (not to mince words) a bit of a bully and Nivalis would regularly step in to protect his dam Roxzella from Kruger's bullying tactics. On one occasion Roxzella was drinking from the large water container in the field. Kruger came barrelling up to her, intent on driving her away from the water. Nivalis promptly stepped between them, his whole posture saying something like, 'Stop right there and there'll be no trouble. Come any closer and I'll pulverize you.' Kruger, who is a whole hand taller than Nivalis and powerfully built into the bargain, did indeed 'stop right there'; in fact, he actually went into reverse, so clear was the message Nivalis was sending out. Nivalis simply stood by until his mother had finished drinking, then quietly moved away, without giving Kruger another glance. So we would be unwise to rely on simple 'dominance hierarchies' derived from one context to predict how horses will behave socially in other situations.

There is, however, an alternative to the 'dominance' model, which has largely been ignored by commentators on equine social behaviour.

Tit-for-tat

In the mid-1990s Dr Marthe Kiley-Worthington carried out a comprehensive, systematic survey of behaviour patterns among her own domestic group. She identified two aspects of this group's social organization which add far more to our understanding of horses than the usual rather rigid concepts of 'dominance': these are the 'tit-for-tat' response, which she likens to Charles Kingsley's famous maxim 'Be-done-by-as-you-did', and the opposite, which encourages co-operation: 'Do-as-you-would-be-done-by'.

Commenting on the findings of her study, Dr Kiley-Worthington says, '… the amount of behaviour related to cementing bonds and deflating potential splitting of the group, that is "sticking behaviour" [i.e. cohesive behaviour, L.S.] was 73% and behaviour related to "splitting" was only 26%. Every individual showed over 60% "sticking" behaviour.' (Kiley-Worthington, 2005) Aggression was responded to mainly with avoidance or ignoring, but in 25 er cent of cases the response was aggression (Be-done-by-as-you-did). So it emerges from this study that the predominant friendly actions (Do-as-you-would-be-done-by) are what help to keep the group together.

Group cohesion

This is important, because as Dr Kiley-Worthington points out, for a prey species such as the horse, group cohesion is necessary for survival. The more experienced members of the group will have essential ecological knowledge, such as how to avoid areas inhabited by predators, where the best feeding sites are, what plants are safe to eat, how to find water at different times of the year (including how to dig for water if necessary, as feral groups have been observed doing), the location of sites offering shelter in bad weather, etc. Social disharmony resulting from aggression among group members could severely hamper the transmission of such ecological knowledge.

Dr Kiley-Worthington concludes that instead of trying to explain this equine society in terms of a rather vague 'dominance hierarchy' based on competition (which in free-ranging equine societies has in any case little relevance), we should consider other organising features. She proposes that the equine society in her study should be considered more as a unit of co-operative individuals. 'The majority of the behaviour, and the majority of the individuals in this society behaved to encourage cohesion of the group and deflate potentially inflammatory/dispersive situations' (Kiley-Worthington, 1998)

Dr Kiley-Worthington does not claim that this is a definitive study of equine social organization; rather, that it could be used as a basis from which to explore the latter in terms of a somewhat more subtle, complex organization than the rather crude 'dominance hierarchy' so often assumed. She maintains that '...the relationships between horses are just as complex as between people, and to describe them in simple terms, such as "dominance hierarchy" is inadequate and pointless.' (Kiley-Worthington, 1987)

Chapter 8 will consider how we, as humans, relate to stallions, and take a critical look at the ways in which some of the issues raised in this chapter have been incorporated into ideas about the training and management of stallions. Before then, however, Chapters 6 and 7 will look at the courtship and mating behaviour of stallions, and ways in which we can keep them healthy and happy.

In the meantime, we will (with some relief!) leave the subject of dominance with a quote from Stuart A. Altmann of the Allee Laboratory of Animal Behavior, University of Chicago. In his commentary on Bernstein's paper on dominance (Altmann, 1981), he says:

> Dominance relationships are an *invention*, not a discovery. Asymmetry, transitivity, linearity, and the like are not rules that animals must obey but regularities for the scientist to discern. Dominance relationships are an epiphenomenon of agonistic interactions. As such, they have causes but not consequences. In sharp contrast to the agonistic *interactions* on which they are based, dominance relationships can have no influence, no effects, no functions, and no adaptive significance. They are not social agents, and to treat them as if they were is to indulge in reification[11]... Do dominance relationships exist? Yes, in the mind and notebook of the human observer. Like the Cheshire cat's grin, they are an abstraction, a discerned pattern. With few exceptions, however, there is *nothing* in the agonistic behavior of animals that implicates an ability to make such abstractions. Are dominance relationships important? They surely are, but to the investigators, not to their subjects.

---

11 Treating an abstract concept as if it is an actual *thing* rather than an idea or a description.

Chapter 6

Mating behaviour

He looks upon his love and neighs unto her;
She answers him as if she knew his mind:
Being proud, as females are, to see him woo her,
She puts on outward strangeness, seems unkind,
Spurns at his love and scorns the heat he feels,
Beating his kind embracements with her heels.

– William Shakespeare, Venus and Adonis

MANY people who have never been privileged to watch mares and stallions interacting freely, and have only ever seen mating carried out in-hand, may believe that for horses the mating act is something rather mechanical, a matter of instinct rather than involving any emotional input. However, this is far from being the case.

Under natural conditions – that is, when allowed to associate freely with each other – mares and stallions interact continually, and not only when the mare is in season (oestrus).(Bristol, 1982; Feist, 1976; McDonnell and Bristol, unpublished observations 1987–1988 (cited by McDonnell, 2000); McDonnell, unpublished observations, 1994 to present (cited by McDonnell, 2000); Kiley-Worthington, 1997, 2005; Skipper, personal observations) Much of the time these interactions are quiet and subtle, and may consist of little more than the stallion and mare grazing very close together, moving around together, touching noses, shoulders or flanks, with occasional bouts of mutual grooming; sometimes one or the other will rest his or her head across the other's back or rump. The stallion may periodically sniff at the mare's anal or perineal area, and may investigate urine and faeces; all of this will help him to determine whether the mare is about to come into season.

When the mare is actually in season, the frequency of these interactions increases dramatically. Under natural or nearly natural conditions courtship is quite a lengthy process. The experienced stallion will be able to tell from a mare's body language, as well as her scent, whether she is receptive and will make advances to her – or, in the initial stages of courtship, accept her advances – accordingly.

Mares take the initiative

Sometimes, especially in older books on horse behaviour, we may come across statements such as 'the stallion [performs a certain behaviour] in order to signal his intention to copulate'. This makes it sound as if the mare has no say in the matter; it is a very outdated relic of a time when females were assumed to be passive partners in the mating process. Nothing could be further from the truth; in most species females play a very active role in mating, and this is no less true of horses. Indeed, observations of free-running mares and stallions show that it is usually the mare who initiates sexual interaction with the stallion. Sue McDonnell, who has studied sexual behaviour in both pasture-breeding horses and semi-feral groups, has found that during the early stages of oestrus, it is the mare who approaches the stallion, rather than the other way round, although stallion approaches to the mare increase later during the oestrus period. 'Nonetheless,' says Sue McDonnell, 'almost 88%. of stallion and mare precopulatory interactions that lead to successful copulation are initiated by the mare approaching the stallion as opposed to the stallion approaching the mare.'(McDonnell and Bristol, unpublished observations 1987–1988;McDonnell, unpublished observations 1994 to present; cited by McDonnell, 2000) My personal observations of our own mares' interactions with our stallions, as well as those of visiting mares, bear this out; the mares will typically seek out the stallion before he even begins to show an interest in them. It seems that although olfactory stimulation plays a significant role in the stallion's sexual response, it is the mare's behaviour that appears to be the primary stimulus. (Klingel, 1969; Tyler, 1972; Ginther, 1979; Pickett *et al.*, 1979, all cited by Bristol, 1982) In our own small yard, mares are often brought in from the field by the simple expedient of opening the field and yard gates and allowing them to wander freely into the yard. They will usually go straight into their allotted stables, but when one of them is just coming into season she will go over to the senior stallion, if he is in (the younger stallion is typically ignored as he is not yet recognized as a potential mate, even though he makes all the right noises and tries to attract their attention with soft nickers, as stallions do) and interact with him over the stable door. They will sniff at each other's nostrils; the stallion will grunt and occasionally squeal; the mare may also squeal, lift her tail, urinate and evert the clitoris ('wink'). She may also kick out behind, and both mare and stallion may strike out with their forefeet. Depending on what stage in her oestrus cycle the mare has reached, it may be very difficult to pry her away from the stallion's stable door; some mares will simply 'plant' themselves and refuse to move (I have found the best remedy for this is to pull the mare's head round, taking care not to be rough; this puts her off-balance, and she will usually move her feet to regain her balance. This is the point at which I can move her away from the stallion.)

Out in the field, mares will approach the stallion in the same way. Typically they will sidle up to him and present their rump, lifting the tail and 'winking', with or without urinating (the mares I have observed tend not to urinate until a couple of days into oestrus, but of course individual mares may differ in their oestrus behaviour).

Exceptions to this may include either mares who have had bad experiences at stud, and so have come to fear a stallion, or maiden mares who have never had any previous contact with stallions, and so do not know how to interact with them. I deal with these later in this chapter.

Olfactory stimuli

Dungpile investigation

Apart from the mare's behaviour, stallions are able to detect the onset of oestrus by olfactory investigation. They may do this by sniffing the mare's head, neck, shoulder, flank, tail, and perineal area, but usually they will start by investigating the mare's droppings and urine. We have already seen, in Chapter 4, how stallions investigate the droppings of other horses. Even stallions who have been shut in a stable for several days may, on being let out into a field, make the investigation of dungpiles their priority, rather than the mad dash around so characteristic of cooped-up horses on first being let out. It can be quite amusing to watch a stallion trot solemnly from one pile to another, only moving on when he has thoroughly investigated. These investigations can be lengthy and very thorough, and some stallions sniff so intensively that their nostrils vibrate, producing a low-level 'buzzing' sound (the author's personal observation).

[Interestingly, this preoccupation with sniffing dungpiles may be put to good use in the management of stallions. I have used the fresh dung of a favourite mare to entice a stallion into an unfamiliar stable, or into a horsebox, that he was otherwise reluctant to enter. On one occasion, our senior stallion was recovering from a severe bout of colic. Although he was recovering well, the memory of the pain and discomfort he had endured made him reluctant to pass dung. I led him out into the field to a place where I knew there was a fresh pile of dung, and let him sniff at it. Within seconds, as if in response to some automatic trigger, he had – without any sign of discomfort – passed a respectable amount of dung, positioning it neatly on top of the existing pile.]

Flehmen

If he smells something unusual or interesting, the stallion may raise his head and curl his upper lip, almost as if he is laughing.[1] This is the gesture known as *flehmen* and it involves a structure in the nose called the *vomeronasal* or Jacobson's organ. This is a sensory receptor enclosed in a cartilage capsule opening into the base of the nasal cavity. The vomeronasal organ, which is found in many mammals, is split into two parts, divided by the nasal septum (the structure which divides the nose into two nasal passages). Each vomeronasal organ consists of a mucous membrane tube or duct enclosed for much of its length within a capsule of cartilage. Its main purpose is to detect the chemicals known as *pheromones*, which trigger behavioural responses in members of the same species.

The stallion may bring his nose very close to the source of the smell, sniffing very intensely and often vibrating the nostrils as described under **Dungpile investigation** above. Sometimes he may sniff with each nostril in turn. His upper lip may twitch, or it may curl up as shown in the photographs on page 106. Usually the lip-curl is accompanied by raising and extending the head and neck. A clear fluid drips from both nostrils, sometimes after sniffing and almost always after, or during, lip-curl. The observations made by Flora Lindsay and Francis Burton suggest that because the lip-curl effectively closes off part of the nasal apertures, this restricts and directs the flow of air towards the vomeronasal ducts. (Lindsay and Burton, 1983)

Horses of both sexes (and geldings) and all ages may display flehmen in response to interesting, unusual or unfamiliar smells. In a study carried out by Sharon Crowell-Davis and Katharine Houpt, a mare was observed performing flehmen in the absence of any obvious stimulus; however, she was downwind from two stallions and two mares that were probably in oestrus (Crowell-Davis and Houpt, 1985). Marinier *et al.* (1988) found that stallions were significantly more responsive than either mares or geldings to urine, vaginal secretions and faecal samples. They did not find any significant differences in stallion responses to the odour of urine/vaginal secretions of a oestrus mare from responses when she was not in season. Katharine Houpt points out that stallions may show the flehmen response more often in the presence of an oestrus mare because mares in oestrus urinate more often, but that stallions show no preference for or more flehmen in response to oestrous than nonoestrous urine. 'Because mares give so many visual and auditory cues that they are in estrus, the stallion does not have to depend upon olfaction.' (Houpt, 1984)

---

1 Popular TV programmes featuring humorous video clips sometimes show this gesture in horses and interpret it as 'laughing'.

However, Lindsay and Burton (1983) found a distinct difference in the responses of both horse and donkey stallions to the urine of oestrus and dioestrus mares.

> Two extremes of response intensity were observed; a minimal response in which sniffing might or might not be followed by lip twitch and nasal secretion and a maximal response, where each investigation commenced with sniffing and was followed by lower lip movement, upper lip-curl, jaw, tongue, head and neck movements and nasal secretion. A minimal or weak response was most often observed when urine from dioestrous mares was presented, whereas a maximal vigorous response was commonly associated with investigation of urine from a mare in oestrus. (Lindsay and Burton, 1983)

Francis Burton, co-author of the 1983 study of flehmen in horse and donkey stallions, makes this additional observation:

> Based on what I saw in the 1981/82 study and subsequent occasional observations of behaviour where no mare was present to offer additional cues, I am 100% sure that stallions are able to tell the difference between urine from oestrus and dioestrus mares. Responses of horse stallions may be less markedly different compared to those of donkey stallions in terms of the frequency of showing flehmen after sniffing urine from mares of different status (one donkey vs many horses), but it is a consistent observation that horse stallions are more interested when they encounter traces of oestrus urine – and they are much more likely to become aroused if allowed to continue investigating it – than with dioestrus urine. (Burton, personal communication)

My own observations tend to support Dr Burton's view. For many years we have been using the stallion's response to the urine of mares (in the absence of the mares themselves) out in the field, as a guide to when one or more of them might be coming into season. Having found that our own predictions based on the dates of the last oestrus were somewhat less than accurate in many cases, we began using the stallion's responses as a back-up. He has never been wrong.

In any case, it would be very surprising if stallions could not readily tell the difference between urine from oestrus and dioestrus mares. The former is thicker and yellower than normal urine, and pretty pungent;[2] if humans can tell the difference then I am very certain stallions can!

Approaching the mare

Once the stallion's interest has been engaged, he will let the mare know that he is interested by prancing up to her with his neck arched and his tail raised. If the mare is not yet fully in season, her response may contain an element of aggression, squealing and kicking out as described above under **Mares take the initiative.** The mare may also clamp her tail down, while the stallion may also strike out with a forefoot, and typically takes little nips at the mare's neck and shoulder. As courtship

---

[2] The response of a (non-horsy) friend to the smell of an oestrus mare's urine was unequivocal: 'Cor, that stinks!'

The Natural Stallion

Rigel sniffs intently at a pile of dung. Photo: Lesley Skipper

Above left: Nivalis sniffs at a patch of urine. Above right: he raises his head and curls his upper lip, directing the scent flow towards the vomeronasal organ. Right: Rigel flehming, showing the degree to which the upper lip curls. Photos: Lesley Skipper

progresses, the stallion will nuzzle, sniff and lick at the mare's head, neck and shoulders, working his way down her body to the flank, tail and anal/perineal area.

During the various stages of courtship the mare may show alternating patterns of attraction and interest, then suddenly reject the stallion just as he is about to initiate mating. If the stallion persists with his courtship and teasing activities, the mare will eventually accept him. Sue McDonnell, who has spent many years observing mare-stallion interactions, emphasizes that even at this stage, the mare plays the primary role:

> Even when the stallion's persistence leads to eventual tolerance of mounting, it clearly appears that the behavior of the mare more than the stallion initiates interactions and determines the time of actual mating. The mare's active role continues during copulation. Her movement and postures facilitate insertion and appear to accommodate the stallion during thrusting. (McDonnell 2000)

During courtship the stallion may sniff the mare's perineal/anal area. Nivalis with Tiff. Photo: Lesley Skipper

Sue McDonnell has pointed out that the head-to-head approach typically adopted by the mare and stallion, which allows this pre-copulatory interaction (which is much more intense than the interaction typical of mares and 'teaser' stallions) appears to be more stimulating to both mare and stallion than if the stallion immediately turns his attention to the mare's hindquarters (as is usually the case in in-hand matings).

> Simple movement by the mare, forward and back a step or two, or in a quick turn from head-to-head to hips-to-head can also be a strong positive stimulus for most stallions. Allowing or encouraging the mare to turn her head back toward her abdomen or to naturally flex her foreleg on the side near the stallion (the natural mounting invitation) will likely increase the stallion's sexual interest. (McDonnell, 2000)

If the mare is fully in season she will display the usual pre-copulatory behaviours, such as lifting the tail, 'winking' straddling and urinating, and squatting, often while backing up towards the stallion's head. At this stage the stallion will frequently mount without achieving erection. According to Sue McDonnell, this is true for both novice and experienced stallions.

> The ratio of two mounts without erection to each mount with erection remains quite constant between equid species (McDonnell, unpublished personal observations of zebra, donkeys, Przewalski, horses, and ponies, 1982 to present). Mounting without erection, then, must be considered to be a normal element of

The Natural Stallion

Above left: Nivalis and Tiff greet each other face-to-face. Above right: Nivalis nuzzles at Tiff's head. Centre left: Nivalis nibbles at Tiff's withers. Centre right: Tiff rejectes Nivalis's initial approach. Bottom left: Face-to-face again: Tiff signals hear readiness by squatting and urinating (the blue bandage, meant to bind up Tiff's tail so the hairs do not get caught on the stallion's penis, has come undone). Bottom right: Although Tiff is now accepting Nivalis, he is mounting without erection, possibly to test Tiff's receptivity. Photos: Lesley Skipper

the precopulatory interactive sequence, just as vocalization, sniffing, nuzzling, nipping, or flehmen response. It appears to be a test and/or inducer of the solid estrous stance of the mare. (McDonnell, 2000)

Rossigkeitsgesicht

There is one behaviour which seems to indicate that the mare is ready to mate, which has received little attention in the literature on equine behaviour. This is the facial expression known only by its German name, *Rossigkeitsgesicht*. The most accurate translation would be 'horsing face' (*Rossig* = horsing = the old term for 'in season'; *-keit* = the equivalent of the English suffix -ness, i.e. a state of being, in this case, 'being in season', and *Gesicht* = face).

It is a peculiar expression, which at first sight resembles the foal-face ('snapping') described in Chapter 5 (page 92). It was first described by O. Antonius (Antonius, 1937). Klingel, who observed the expression in young zebra mares during copulation and when stallions approached them, said that the ears were held downwards and backwards, the corners of the mouth were drawn up and that the mares opened and closed ('chewed') with slightly exposed teeth and open lips. (Klingel, 1969) Stephanie Tyler, who observed that young pony mares frequently snapped during their first oestrous periods when stallions sniffed, licked or nibbled them and during copulation, said that Klingel's description seemed very similar to that of the pony mares she had observed, and also seemed identical to the snapping displayed by foals. (Tyler, 1972)

According to Antonius, the expression only occurs in zebras, asses and half-asses. (Antonius, 1937) However, it is seen in horses, albeit infrequently. G.A. Woods and K.A Houpt described what they called an 'abnormal facial gesture' in a 24-year-old mare, who exhibited what seems to resemble 'snapping' when she first noticed the stallion or heard his neighs. After describing the mare's behaviour during oestrus (flexing her limbs, clamping her tail and opening and closing her mouth when a stallion approached) they say,

> It is hypothesized that the mare's expression, the snapping of foals and the facial expression of donkeys and zebras [in oestrus] are the same expression – one that indicates that the animal is in an approach-avoidance situation. In this case, the mare may have been both fearful of, and attracted to, stallions. (Woods and Houpt, 1986)

It is true that the *Rossigkeitsgesicht* is uncommon in horses; while researching this book I asked a number of breeders if they had ever seen it. I only received one positive reply, from a lady who operates a stallion station in Florida. She told me that in a career with horses spanning more than thirty years, she had only observed it in one mare. However, she said, it is common in donkey jennets, and indeed it is often the only way to tell that they are in season. I have personally seen the *Rossigkeitsgesicht* in three mares, including one who was initially very difficult at stud. When we bred her to our own stallion, Nivalis[3] we made a point of introducing her to him over a period of time, as described later in this chapter. When I first saw her display the *Rossigkeitsgesicht* I simply

---

3 She was actually his very first mare.

knew that she was ready for him, although I could not have said why. Sure enough, she was as receptive as any mare could have been, and stood beautifully for the stallion, without any fuss whatsoever.

I did wonder at the time what the significance of the expression could be. It would be easy to say that she was showing submission – except that there has never been anything submissive about this mare. It could have been a kind of displacement activity – a sign of ambivalence about the stallion – but again, she never showed any other signs of having mixed feelings about him – and she never displayed the expression other than when absolutely ready to accept the stallion. The same has applied to the other two mares in whom I've observed the expression. In the contexts in which I've seen it, it seems to be just one of the signals a mare uses to let the stallion know she's ready – perhaps a reassurance that she won't kick him. I only know that on the few occasions when we have seen it, it's been a very accurate indication of when the mare is ready for the stallion, and that is precisely how it has been used by staff in zoos to manage breeding activity in zebras.

Mounting and copulation

Young and inexperienced stallions may initially try to mount over the mare's withers or middle back, shuffling round to the rear. This may sometimes be due to over-excitement, but it is more likely to be caused by the young stallion's lack of experience in determining whether the mare is really going to accept him. It may be a way of testing whether she will do so while the stallion is out of the way of a potentially disabling kick. Once he is in position, the stallion clasps the mare's body with his forelegs, resting his head near her withers. Sometimes the stallion may grip the mare's mane with his teeth; this is especially likely to be the case where the mare is so tall or her barrel so round that the stallion feels unbalanced and needs something to hang on to. This seems to be the source of the widespread belief that stallions will bite mares during mating, but well-behaved stallions, especially those who have been properly introduced to mares and allowed to court them properly, will not actually bite the mare (unlike donkey stallions, for whom biting is the norm).

Nivalis and Rosie: once he is in position, the stallion clasps the mare's body with his forelegs, resting his head near her withers. Photo: Lesley Skipper

Although courtship may be extended, the mating act itself is very brief, typically taking less than twenty seconds. During ejaculation the stallion's tail may flip up and down ('flagging') and his head may droop onto the mare's withers. Sometimes the stallion seems to collapse onto the mare's back; if he and the mare are left to their own devices, it is often not so much the case that the stallion dismounts, as that the mare moves forward from under him.

Among free-ranging mares and stallions, it sometimes happens that another mare will interfere with the mating process, although generally speaking breeders who pasture their mares and stallions together do not report that this causes significant problems; the horses usually manage to sort things out for themselves without too much fuss. Interference may also occur from the mare's own offspring – perhaps wondering what is going on and fearing that 'mum' might be in danger. We have seen this with our own foals; both mare and stallion were extremely tolerant of the foal's interference and did not react to it.

Foals sometimes interfere with their parents' mating activities. Here Tariel appears to be trying to intervene, but both Nivalis and Tiff ignore him. Photo: Lesley Skipper

The stallion typically recovers quickly, and may be ready to mate again within several minutes. For example, James Feist observed a stallion mate twice with the same mare in seven minutes; Stephanie Tyler saw a New Forest stallion copulate with two mares (three times each) within a period of two hours; Kownacki and co-workers observed a stallion copulate with the same mare three times within an hour (McDonnell, 1986). I have observed similar frequencies with our own stallions when breeding at liberty. Some stallion owners express concern that such frequent mating will have an adverse effect on fertility. In fact the opposite seem to be the case. For example, Sue McDonnell comments that

> Breeding rates as high as 18 per, day have been recorded in several different studies. Reported first-cycle pregnancy rates of free-running or pastured populations typically are well above the 75% level considered to be excellent for in-hand domestic breeding systems. (McDonnell, 1986)

This is borne out by further studies (Bristol, 1982, 1987; Henry *et al.*, 1991; McDonnell and Bristol, unpublished 1987–1988; McDonnell, unpublished observations with semi-feral ponies 1994 to present, cited by McDonnell, 2000)
Some breeders are understandably concerned that such high frequency of copulation may injure the mare. However, none of the different studies cited above reports injuries to mares as a result of frequent mating, and I have been unable to find any evidence that mares actually do suffer as a result of repeated matings. Indeed, it has been my experience that it is usually the mare who initiates the repeated matings, not the stallion, which would be unlikely to be the case if the mare was suffering

The Natural Stallion

discomfort as a result. In fact the only injuries I have seen were to the stallion, where the mare was slightly taller than he, making him clasp her body more tightly in order to maintain balance. In these cases the insides of the stallion's forelegs were rubbed raw by the resulting friction. However the discomfort was not sufficient to put him off, and the rawness subsided within a day or so.

[In this context it is interesting to see how, if a stallion is running out with a mare who is taller than he is, if the ground is sloping the stallion will often guide the mare to a position where she is facing downhill, so he can mount her more easily. We have also done this with in-hand matings where the mare is bigger than the stallion.]

Nivalis and Tiff: if a stallion is running out with a mare who is taller than he is, if the ground is sloping he will often guide the mare to a position where she is facing downhill, so he can mount her more easily. Photo: Lesley Skipper

Horses know how to be horses

I have to say that I find it rather amusing that so many people seem to think that unless mares and stallions are shown what to do (by us humans, of course), they will not be able to mate successfully. This is in spite of the fact that a truly wild setting there are no humans around to give a helping hand, and that mares and stallions have been getting on with the business of sex for millions of years; they really do not need us to show them how it is done! In fact, even the most sexually inexperienced of mares and stallions will quickly work it out for themselves. I have known countless instances where colts and stallions with no experience whatsoever have broken through fences and managed to cover mares successfully – and the mares have not necessarily been experienced either! One example comes readily to mind, even though it happened twenty years ago. At that time our stables had not yet been built, so we were keeping our horses at livery. My Arabian gelding, Zareeba, then aged two, had recently been gelded, and at the yard owner's insistence was turned out with a mixed group of mares and geldings. Going to check on Zareeba in the field, I found him happily mounting a mare, who was standing quite peacefully for him. As he was no longer fertile, and there had been no fuss, no harm was done; but it does show how well horses are able to sort these things out for themselves. Of course, with another mare, things might have been different: the mare might have objected and kicked out at Zareeba. This might indeed have happened, but I was not around to see it if it did; and I could see no signs of him having been kicked or otherwise injured.

In the wild, it would be unlikely (although not impossible) that a two-year-old colt would manage to mate with a mare; most young stallions do not get the opportunity until they are four or five, or even older. However, when the opportunity is there, young stallions will naturally take advantage of it. In 2009, when our young stallion Rigel was three years old, we had to leave him out in the stallion paddock all night with his half-sister, Imzadi, with whom he normally goes out when she is not in season. This was because we were having some work done in the stable yard which necessitated the use of machinery in the yard until late in the evening; Rigel's sire Nivalis, the only other horse stabled up at that time, was not at all bothered by the machinery, but Rigel had not yet been fully habituated to that kind of thing, and would have become quite stressed if left in. So we turned him out with Imzadi in the belief that, as they normally get on very well, everything would be fine. So it was, except that we had miscalculated when she was due to come into season. Within minutes of turning them out together, we saw Rigel teasing and then mounting Imzadi, who alternately encouraged and rejected him, eventually standing for him without fuss. We could not see whether he had actually managed to achieve intromission, although there were a few occasions when he seemed to have done so. It was too late to make alternative arrangements; we simply left them to get on with it, deciding to deal with any consequences as and when they arose. As it happened, Imzadi was not in foal; but it was interesting to see how easily she and Rigel sorted things out between them, even though neither of them had any prior sexual experience. Rigel sustained a few kicks to his chest, but apart from a few scrapes he was otherwise uninjured; Imzadi had no injuries at all, and both of them seemed quite relaxed when we retrieved them from the paddock the next day.

However, this is not an ideal way to introduce a young stallion to stud duties. The best way – other than through in-hand mating – is to turn him out with an older, experienced mare, preferably one who has had previous experience of running out with a stallion.

Is pasture breeding always best?

This is rather like the question, 'Is breast-feeding always best for [human] babies?'. The answer is: it all depends on circumstances. In an ideal world, all breeding stallions would be allowed to run free with the mares they cover, but in the real world, this is not always possible even if the people managing the stallion would like it to be. When you are standing a stallion worth millions of pounds (or dollars), the possibility of injury to him may be too great to take any chances. And setting aside the question of the stallion's monetary value, there may be other considerations. Some stallions may have developed behavioural problems too severe to risk turning him out with a mare. I do believe (as I hope Chapter 11 will show) that most such problems can be cured (or at least alleviated) with time and correct training and management; however, many breeders may understandably decide that it is simply not worth risking injury to mare and stallion by turning them out together.

There is also the matter of visiting mares. If such mares are accustomed to pasture breeding, there should be few problems; however, many (perhaps most) mares will not be so accustomed. If the stallion is good with his mares (and if he has been properly educated in such matters, there is no reason why he should not be) then most mares will soon grow used to going out with him and will start to respond to his advances. However, many mare owners may not want to take the risk of injury to their mares, while the stallion owner accepting mares for covering may also be reluctant to expose such mares to injury. It would be disingenuous of me to pretend that accidents never happen, or that mares and stallions are never injured in the course of pasture breeding. This can and does occur, and even though serious injury (other than a few minor scrapes and bruises) may not be common, the risk does still exist.

The risk is compounded by the fact that so few mares and stallions are accustomed to associating freely with members of the opposite sex. On pages 112–113 I mention the problems that can arise when stallions are kept isolated from other horses; but what about mares? This brings us to the problem of maiden mares, and how to deal with them.

Maiden mares

Maiden mares can be difficult – so much so that some smaller studs, perhaps with minimal help available, will not accept them. This is an unfortunate consequence of modern management practices.

Very few mares are raised in anything like a natural family group, so many will never have seen stallions in their lives, let alone had the chance to observe their behaviour and learn how to interact with them, until they go to stud. It must be a very frightening experience for a maiden mare to be suddenly taken away from her normal surroundings, whisked off to a strange place where she knows no-one, either equine or human, then subjected to all kinds of invasive procedures prior to being suddenly introduced to the stallion who is to cover her. Even a quiet, well-mannered stallion can be a daunting sight as he rears up to mount a mare; a noisy, rough-mannered stallion must be absolutely terrifying to a mare completely unused to such behaviour. No wonder some mares have to be twitched or hobbled before they will stand to accept the stallion. Forced copulations do occasionally occur in natural environments, but these are exceptional and in such a situation the mare often has at least some chance of getting away. The mare restrained by twitches, hobbles or severe bridles has little such chance – although some mares do break away, a situation which is both frightening and dangerous for the handler. (I give an example of this on pages 116–117)

On the other hand, maiden mares who have grown up with stallions around – such as our mares Roxzella, Tiff and Imzadi – are less likely to be frightened by the sight and sound of a stallion and to accept him without fuss. On page 113 I described what happened when Imzadi was turned out overnight with our young stallion, Rigel. Imzadi was a maiden mare, but because she had been around stallions all her life, even though she had never mated with one, she was not at all intimidated or frightened by Rigel's rather noisy overtures to her.

Imzadi (right) was not at all intimidated by Rigel's rather boisterous advances. Photo: Lesley Skipper

Nevertheless, unless she has had that kind of upbringing, I do not believe it is a good idea to turn a maiden mare out with a stallion, especially if she is a visiting mare. Some mares, even experienced ones (although this is less likely), can give the stallion all the right signals, then change their mind at the last moment. If the mare does this several times, the stallion may become annoyed, and chase the mare. I have seen this happen on several occasions, and while it did not result in any injury other than a few cuts and bruises, it was very stressful for all concerned, and there is always the risk of real injury in a situation like this. So regrettably, unless the mare is yours, she is familiar with stallions and you have had her long enough to have some idea of how she might react on being turned out with a stallion, I would always advocate (initially at least) in-hand service for maiden mares. This is unfortunate, because it does not necessarily give the mare the best introduction to the mating process, but it may be the lesser of two evils. The same applies to visiting mares, unless your stallion is very experienced in natural breeding and is very good running out with mares, and of course the mare owner is willing to accept all the risks involved.

This may sound as though I am contradicting my contention that mares and stallions do best when allowed to mate naturally, but it is not that; it is simply a recognition that management practices may make it difficult, in some cases, for that natural mating to occur without an unacceptable degree of risk. This is a sad reflection on the way we keep and manage mares and stallions, but until attitudes change across the horse world, it is likely to continue.

Chases do sometimes ensue; here Nivalis is chasing Tiff, but because they are so familiar with each other such chases are of very brief duration and usually only for a few yards. Tariel (right) seems more concerned than either of his parents. Photo: Lesley Skipper

The down-side of too much control

Although it is understandable that commercial studs like to keep as tight a control over the mating process as possible, the kind of over-control that is all too common is not beneficial, and may even be injurious, to both mare and stallion.

Typically, stallions and mares are allowed little if any contact before mating (the mare will often have been teased by a special 'teaser' stallion, to test her readiness to mate). The stallion is usually brought to the mare, who will often be restrained in one or more ways. As Sue McDonnell points out, 'Typical methods of restraint, for example a lip or ear twitch, or a foreleg lifted, evoke head, ear, tail, leg, and whole body postures that are visibly different from the receptive estrous posture of the mare.' (McDonnell, 2000) This may make the stallion reluctant to approach the mare, as he is not receiving the signals which would give him confidence that the mare will accept him. He may also not be allowed any contact with the mare's head and neck, instead being directed straight to the mare's hindquarters, so he will be unable to perform any of the normal pre-copulatory teasing activities.

The mare who is restrained cannot play the active role in the mating process that she would naturally assume when running with the stallion. She cannot indicate to the stallion that she is not ready; and even if she is ready, the very fact that she is restrained may create resistance through fear. During the stallion's vigorous thrusts, mares will usually move forward a little; mares who are restrained are usually actively prevented from doing this, which may cause them considerable discomfort.

In addition, because of concerns about the safety of personnel handling the mare and stallion, and so that the whole procedure may be carried out as quickly as possible, the mating process itself may rushed, with the stallion being made to dismount rather than allowing the mare to walk out from under him as she would naturally do. The stallion must therefore raise his forehand even higher and back away; he then drops his forehand abruptly. Sue McDonnell points out that

> For some stallions, particularly older and or lame stallions, dismounting appears to represent an aversive or difficult experience, particularly when rushed or when landing abruptly on a hard surface. Stallions may hyperextend a foreleg or lose their footing when rushed to dismount. After even only a few such experiences, some stallions appear to anticipate the negative experience and become reluctant to mount or to ejaculate. Some may also begin to dismount during ejaculation. (McDonnell, 2000)

Many stallions adapt to this truncated mating experience very well, in spite of the lack of the kind of stimuli which would normally precede mating. Some, however, do not, and may need much more contact and interaction with mares before they can breed efficiently. But what about the mares concerned? Given the lack of the kind of prolonged pre-copulatory contact with the stallion that natural mating rituals require, is it surprising that so many mares, even after considerable breeding experience, are resistant and difficult to handle?

Safety first

Obviously, the safety of the mare and stallion handlers is of paramount importance. Covering in hand is a potentially dangerous activity for handlers, particularly for the person handling the mare. This is especially the case where the covering is carried out in a confined space. We have always covered mares out in the open, away from distracting influences such as other horses, certainly, but in an enclosure large enough to give the handlers sufficient space to get out of the way quickly if things go awry. Hard hats and gloves should always be worn. Some years ago, when we still covered mares in hand, I was holding a mare ready to be covered while my husband managed the stallion. All was going well when the mare – who up until then had been enthusiastic enough – changed her mind at the last moment. She pulled away violently, tearing the lead rope out of my hands, knocked me over and ran straight over me. Fortunately my husband managed to hang on to the stallion, or I might have been in real trouble. As it was, I sustained only some minor bruising to my legs and some rather painful rope burns to the palms of my hands. It could have been much worse: the fact that I was wearing a hard hat definitely prevented a nasty head injury, as I later found that the hat was dented where the mare had caught it with her hoof. Had I been wearing gloves I could also have avoided the rope burns.

Preparation is the key

In-hand covering can be made much easier and less stressful if the mare and stallion have been introduced to each other well before the time comes for the mare to be covered. If they are given a chance to get to know each other, even over a stable door (with precautions taken as described later, in Chapter 7, under **Introducing stallions to each other**), the stallion is less likely to become over-excited at the sight of a strange mare, and the mare is less likely to be alarmed by the stallion's noisy attentions. The ideal would be to let them live next to each other for several months, but this is hardly going to be practical for stud owners who accept outside mares; most mare owners would be unwilling to pay for the mare's keep for such an extended period of time. Even so, in the interests of both mare and stallion, it might be worthwhile reducing the keep fee (whether for grass keep or full keep) in order to persuade mare owners to leave their mares at the stud for longer periods than usual, in order to allow the mare to settle in and be introduced to the stallion properly.[4]

This prior introduction period helps the actual covering by allowing things to proceed at a much more leisurely pace than is normally the case. There should be an atmosphere of calm, and nothing should be rushed. Allowing the mare and stallion more time to interact lets them give each other the right signals, and makes it much more likely that the covering will proceed without fuss – and hopefully with the desired result.

Adjusting handling practices to take account of what the stallion[5] prefers, rather than what is convenient for the handler, provides what Sue McDonnell calls '…gentle, respectful accommodation of the stallion's needs or limitations' which can, as she points out, 'resolve or avoid most problems.' (McDonnell, 2000)

Introducing the stallion to pasture breeding

If an inexperienced stallion is to run with mares, it is best if he is first turned out with an older, experienced mare who can teach him manners and the proper way to approach and court mares; the same applies to a stallion who has previously only covered mares in-hand. One of the main reasons why stallion-owners insist on in-hand service is the risk of injury to the stallion if the mare kicks him. This caution is understandable, yet provided mares are unshod (as they should be, on the hind feet at least) serious injuries are not common. Most stallions quickly learn to keep out of range of a full kick, while a kick at close range is unlikely to cause real damage as there is insufficient power behind it. A few days ago I watched Imzadi lash out at Rigel; she caught him several times but the only injuries were very minor scrapes and bruises. It is surely a risk worth taking for the sake of giving both mare and stallion a chance to perform the mating behaviours that are so important to them.

The Duke of Newcastle

More than three hundred and fifty years ago William Cavendish, Duke of Newcastle – one of the most celebrated of the great Classical Masters of horsemanship – was expressing much the same views as those given above. In his book *A General System of Horsemanship* (first published in French,

---
4   Of course, stallion owners who cover only their own mares will be able to prolong the introduction period for as long as they wish.
5   And, of course, the mare's preferences.

The Natural Stallion

in Antwerp, in 1658 as *La Methode Nouvelle et Invention Extraordinaire de Dresser les Chevaux*), the Duke, writing about breeding management practices, says

> With regard to covering a mare, I disapprove of its being in hand, or by confining the creature, since it is then rather a compulsion than a natural inclination; for every natural action of this kind ought to be performed with freedom and love, and not by violence or constraint. (Newcastle, 2000)

He goes on to say – and I think what he says regarding covering a mare in hand beforehand is excellent advice – that

> You ought therefore at this season[6] to put all your mares together into an inclosure well fenced, where there is plenty of grass during the time the stallion is with them, and they are hot: then let your stallion run with them, first taking off his hind-shoes, that he may not hurt the mares by a kick, leaving his fore-shoes on. Let him cover one mare twice in hand at first, to render him more gentle; then take off his bridle, and let him have the liberty of running among the rest, which will make him so familiar with them by degrees, that they will be fond of his caresses, so that no mare will be cover'd before she is inclined. When he has served them all, he will try them again one after the other, and cover all those that are willing to receive him. The horse is sensible that he has finished his performance, by the mare's refusal of his caresses, and then begins to kick against the fence that he may be gone: therefore it is proper to remove him at this time, and send your mares into a fresh pasture.

Imzadi hoists her hindquarters to let Rigel know she is not interested; he raises his head to avoid a possible kick, although Imzadi is too close to be able to kick high enough to catch him. A kick to the chest area at this range would be unlikely to do any real damage. Mares running out with stallions should alays be unshod, or at the very least have any hind shoes removed. Photo: Lesley Skipper

---

6   The Duke cites June as being the best month, so that the mares will foal the following May – one of the best times of year for foaling in England.

Celibacy

Do stallions get frustrated?

Many people feel it is unfair to keep a stallion entire if he is not intended for breeding, because he will become sexually frustrated. However, many feral horses never breed, even when they belong to a multi-stallion band. The same applies to any number of stallions kept as school horses in establishments such as the Spanish Riding School,[7] yet there is no real evidence that such horses suffer psychologically; in the absence of mares, the libido of most stallions seems to become naturally dormant, with an associated decrease in the amount of testosterone they produce. In their study of bachelor and harem stallion behaviour, Sue McDonnell and Samantha Murray found that when bachelors emerged from the main group to take on the role of harem stallion (as described in Chapter 4), their testosterone levels rose sharply, but after they returned to the bachelor band testosterone levels decreased sharply again. From the results of their study, they conclude that

> Our findings suggest that group-housed domestic stallions may have testosterone concentrations similar to those of bachelor stallions in this model. For most months of the year, testosterone concentrations with harem status were higher than published norms for stabled breeding stallions...It is possible, therefore, that inter-male effects may be involved in behaviour-related subfertility seen in some domestic breeding stallions or in the generally lower behavioral vigor and apparent fertility of stabled stallions compared to pasture-bred stallions. Pasture-bred horses, for example, typically exhibit very high levels of fertility and greater sexual behavior endurance than stabled hand-bred stallions (Bristol, 1982, 1987). Increased testosterone concentrations with harem status and/ or suppression due to stabling stallions together may play a role in this phenomenon. (McDonnell and Murray, 1995)

Sue McDonnell further notes that 'Both in research animals and in clinical cases, we have found that simply moving a stallion to a barn with mares can increase libido, testosterone levels, testicular volume, and sperm production efficiency.' (McDonnell, 2000)

Spontaneous erection and masturbation

Stallion owners often express concern because they have seen their stallion masturbating, which stallions (and geldings) do by swinging the erect penis until it strikes their bellies. This is nothing to be concerned about. It is not a sign of frustration; almost all stallions of all ages masturbate, even when they are covering several mares a day; even geldings do it, and it has been seen in foals as little as one day old.

> These erections occur at the rate of about one 3-min episode every 90 min. Ejaculation is rare – less than 0.01% of episodes. The frequency of spontaneous erection and masturbation is the same for domestic horse stallions regardless of breed, type of housing, type and level of work, sociosexual environment, breeding status, androgen levels, libido, or fertility. Similar periodic erections

---
7 Although the best stallions from the school may take up stud duties for a period; see Chapter 12.

> are common to all mammals studied, including humans. This phenomenon appears to be normal behavior. (McDonnell, 2000)

Contrary to popular belief, it does not affect fertility, as little or no sperm is ejaculated. So it is pointless to try to stop a stallion masturbating; it is perfectly normal stallion behaviour.

Likes and dislikes

According to Henry Blake, '…it is unusual for anything except sexual attraction to be involved in the mating of horses.' (Blake, 1975) But if we watch their behaviour, I think we must conclude that horses can and do form very strong bonds of affection with their mates. Strictly controlled breeding conditions are the rule in a domestic setting, and mares and stallions are usually given little or no choice in the matter of a mate. The fact that they will mate with each other– and that stallions can be taught to mount a dummy 'mare' for artificial insemination purposes – in spite of this, is often taken as proof that instinct alone is at work, and that they are incapable of emotional involvement at such times (though I do not think any species which exhibits such a predilection for sexual 'toys', such as inflatable rubber dolls, has any right to pass judgement in this matter). But regardless of this, mares and stallions can still display very strong likes and dislikes in the matter of potential mates – and they can make these preferences known in no uncertain manner. Countless breeders have stories to tell of how mares or stallions have fallen in love with specific members of the opposite sex, and will not look at another. One of our own Arabian mares, Roxzella, ran out with a stallion for several years. Their relations were perfectly amicable, but Roxzella positively refused to have anything to do with the stallion sexually. Nor, when she was sent away to stud, did the stud staff have any greater success in persuading her to accept a very handsome Thoroughbred as a mate. Eventually she went to another Arabian, and this time she decided that this was the one for her. The result was Nivalis. A former stud manager recalls how one mare she had in her care was equally determined not to succumb to any stallion presented to her. After endless rejections, they turned her out with a stallion who ran with his mares. The manager went into the field one day to find this mare, who previously would not entertain a stallion anywhere near her, standing with her head over the stallion's back, blissfully happy and relaxed.

Given the choice (which few are), stallions too can be extremely discriminating in the choice of a mate. The refusal of stallions to mate with mares with whom they have grown up, even where they are not related, may be a natural inhibition that safeguards against close inbreeding (see under **Incest** in Chapter 3). But in many cases, one cannot discount the possibility of simple personal dislike. Some stallions show preferences – or dislikes – for mares, on account of their colour. Lady Anne Blunt, of the famous Crabbet Arabian Stud, recounted how her grey stallion Azrek only became excited by mares of the same colour as himself. Colonel Alois Podhajsky, director of the Spanish Riding School in Vienna for over 20 years, recounted how some of the stallions of the school displayed a preference for horses of a different colour. This preference was particularly strong in a stallion called Siglavy Neapolitano.[8] This stallion did not at all care for the white[9] Lipizzaner mares, and simply refused to look at them. He was, however, strongly attracted to the brown Nonius mares used on the same farm to produce a half-breed strain. At that time there were few Lipizzaners of the Siglavy line and it was considered important to produce pure-bred foals by Siglavy Neapolitano. So

---

8 Lipizzaner stallions are normally named for the sire line – in this case Siglavy – and for the dam. So a stallion of the Siglavy line whose dam was called Mantua would be named Siglavy Mantua. However at the time of which Podhajsky was writing, the second part of the name was not that of the dam but of her sire, in this case Neapolitano.
9 Strictly speaking, grey.

the stud manager tried everything he could think of to persuade the stallion to accept Lipizzaner mares, even going so far as to dye one of the mares with a substance used to camouflage grey horses during the First World War. But Siglavy Neapolitano was having none of this, and his aversion to the Lipizzaner mares intensified. Finally the stud director chose a young and beautiful Nonius mare in oestrus and had her walked up and down in front of the stallion. His interest was immediately aroused, but the Nonius mare was quickly switched for a Lipizzaner mare, whom Siglavy Neapolitano, in the throes of desire, finally accepted as a substitute. As Podhajsky remarks, 'What a strange role for the poor Nonius mare to earn her oats as a "come-on"!' (Podhajsky, 1997)

This widely reported phenomenon is usually explained in terms of the stallion being reminded of his dam's colour; and in some cases this may be so. But it does not explain our own senior stallion's preference for bay mares, since his mother is grey – as he is himself. But Nivalis was born bay, and only very gradually turned grey. It seems that in his case, he associates bay mares with his own colour. Another stallion whom I know, who is bay, dislikes bay mares and prefers chestnuts. Other stallions can show all kinds of preferences in mares, some of them apparently eccentric, but clearly of great importance to the horses concerned.

It is not true, either, that horses only take an interest in each other sexually at certain times of the year. Dr Marthe Kiley-Worthington has experimented with a system of running a vasectomized stallion with mares, thus allowing them a more natural lifestyle without the complications of too many foals.

> One of the interesting consequences is that the mares appear to encourage sex and copulation from the stallion, and in some cases this has continued throughout the year. Interestingly enough it looks as if the mares are happy to have sex with him when they have been separated and returned and even when, according to their cycling, they should not be in season. Whether they are having sex at other times than just when in season remains to be confirmed. (Kiley-Worthington, 1997)

There is some evidence that this does occur; I have heard numerous reports of mares allowing stallions to serve them when they are not in season. One of our own mares will still solicit the stallion for sex even when she is in foal; the late Dr June Alexander, who bred both Arabians and Welsh Cobs at her Okeden Stud, told me of a mare she had who would willingly stand for the stallion only a matter of hours before foaling. These may be far from isolated instances; there have been relatively few observations made to see whether stallions and mares who run together do copulate other than just when the mare is in season. Certainly, there are numerous instances among other species where copulation takes places outside the female's 'season', and not just among primates. Female cats who have been spayed will sometimes have sexual relations with tomcats, if they like them enough; this has occurred with several of my own cats. There may be many other such examples throughout the animal world, but so widely has it been assumed that sex is a purely seasonal matter that little investigation has been carried out.

Regarding her experimental group, Dr Kiley-Worthington continues:

> … what is very clear is that sex is frequent and appears to be extremely important to both the stallion and the mares. After all why should it not be as important to them as it is to humans? Perhaps more so, if they are such emotional creatures. (Kiley-Worthington, 1997)

Chapter 7

Keeping a stallion happy

A contented stallion, gentle in his strength and brilliant in his pride, is a joy both to watch and to be with.

– Lucy Rees, The Horse's Mind

HOW do we keep a stallion happy? Some people might argue that 'happiness' is a human concept, and that it is anthropomorphic to attribute it to animals of any non-human species. And it is true that even for humans happiness is a rather fuzzy concept. But I believe that horses can feel something that is at least very close to how humans feel when they are happy. Perhaps 'contented' would be a better term.

A contented stallion can demonstrate his state of mind in many ways. He will be more relaxed, easier to handle and to teach, than if he were discontented and continually frustrated.[1]

Mismanagement

By now it should, I hope, be clear that the restricted, isolated lifestyle to which all too many stallions are condemned is very remote from the kind of rich social environment a stallion would enjoy in a wild or free-ranging situation. Harsh training methods, management practices which echo the belief that stallions cannot associate safely with other horses, and punitive corrective action to combat the problem behaviours which almost inevitably occur – all of these spell misery for the stallion condemned to such a lifestyle. As Chapter 11 will show, the inability to perform certain social behaviours appears to be at the root of much self-mutilation behaviour – like so-called 'stable vices', this is a sure indication of severe distress.

There is ample evidence from experiments on a variety of animals, that living in a restricted environment of the kind that all too many stallions are forced to endure, has long-term effects on the central nervous system's ability to cope with external stimuli, making it more sensitive and reactive. For example, one author[2] states that

> When stimulus variation is restricted, central regulation of threshold sensitivities will function to lower sensory thresholds. Thus, the organism becomes increasingly sensitized to stimulation in an attempt to restore balance. (Schultz, 1965).

---

[1] I do not mean this in a sexual sense, but in the sense of being unable to perform natural social behaviours.
[2] For a review of the literature on sensory deprivation in animals, see Temple Grandin's dissertation *Dendritic Growth in Somatosensory Region of Brain Cortex in Pigs Residing in a Simple or a Complex Environment*. (University of Illinois, 1989)

A contented stallion, gentle in his strength and brilliant in his pride, is a joy both to watch and to be with: Arabian stallion Hlayyil Ramadan at the Jordanian Royal Stud, Amman. Photo: courtesy of H.R.H. Princess Alia bint al Hussain al Salah of Jordan; photograph by Reindert Jansen.

It is easy to see that if stallions are deprived of social contact in the mistaken belief that such contact will be dangerous, the resulting lack of social stimulus will lower the threshold at which the stallion becomes aroused by the close presence of other horses. This is yet another example of the self-fulfilling prophecy. The practice of isolating colts at weaning is greatly to blame for many of the problems encountered with mature stallions. Colts isolated in this manner will never learn how to approach a mare without being rebuffed, as their mothers will normally reject any sexual advances; after weaning – which will very often be both abrupt and too early – they are prevented from coming into contact with any other horses until it is time for them to cover mares. Having no idea how to approach a mare, they will usually be far too excited and may become aggressive to both the mare and the handlers. They are then subjected to all kinds of restraint, including severe bits and/or chains pulled tight over their noses or round their gums. This tends to worsen their behaviour, not improve it.

Such stallions may not only have problems when they come to cover mares, but also they will never have learned appropriate behaviour with adult male horses, whether entire or gelded. This lack of social contact then makes it difficult to introduce them to other adult males, or to take them to places where they may encounter other horses – thus ensuring that expectations about stallion behaviour continue to be met.

Good behaviour

In countries where it is the general rule to ride a stallion, good stallion behaviour is taken for granted. In Spain and Portugal, for instance, no one thinks anything of riding stallions in company, stabling them side by side or tethering them next to each other. Because these entires are not segregated from other horses, they do not regard them as threats in the same way as stallions kept apart may well do.

The difference between the behaviour of stallions accustomed to working in the presence of others, and those who are not, is quite remarkable. The former are usually calm and well-behaved, whereas the latter may become so excited as to be virtually unmanageable (of course there are many degrees of arousal in between). The famous white stallions of the Spanish Riding School in Vienna work together every day, sometimes in very close formation. They are continually in each other's company, and while jealousies and rivalries do of course arise, so do lasting friendships and attachments. As a result they are calm in each other's presence. This calmness was well-illustrated one night in November 1992 when fire broke out in part of the Hofburg Palace complex in Vienna, very near to the famous Winter Riding School where the stallions are trained and give their performances. The Hofburg also houses the Stallburg, where the stallions are stabled. The fire made it necessary to evacuate the horses, and video recordings taken that night show the stallions crowding out into the streets of Vienna. Yet there was no fuss; some bystanders, many of whom may have had little if any experience with horses, even pitched in to help hold the stallions and lead them away to safety.

Plenty of turnout

It may seem superfluous these days to point out the difference adequate turnout can make to any horse's mental and physical wellbeing, not just a stallion's; yet surprisingly, this is sometimes not appreciated, even by people with many years of experience of keeping horses of different breeds and all sexes. For example, some such owners feel that it is better to keep stallions stabled up all year round, because that way they do not injure themselves galloping excitedly round fields and paddock, with the risk of injury that brings.[3] The answer is obvious: if you only turn a stallion out once in a while (or even every few days) then of *course* he is going to gallop round excitedly! On the other hand, horses turned out 24/7 (or even a considerable part of each day) are usually far too laid-back to spend time galloping around. We have found that wintering as many of our horses out as possible means that the ground is less cut up than it would be if they were only out for brief spells, precisely because the horses hardly if ever gallop about.

There is an argument that if stallions are given work that is sufficiently varied and interesting, this will compensate them for the lack of turnout. This may be true for some stallions, and of course there are some situations where turnout is impossible because of the environment (for example at the Spanish Riding School, which is situated in the heart of Vienna, a very busy city).[4] However, for most stallions – indeed for most horses, regardless of sex – it is very far from being adequate. A recent study entitled 'Could Work Be a Source of Behavioural Disorders? A Study in Horses' by Martine Hausberger *et al.* was published in a peer-reviewed online journal in 2009. Hausberger and her colleagues studied 76 horses at one of the world's most renowned equestrian academies,[5] and found an alarming prevalence of some of the stereotypical behaviour described in Chapter 11. These horses were all kept in the same conditions, only differing by the type of work they did.

---

3 This is also the reason often given to explain why many valuable dressage horses are not turned out.
4 One big compensation for the stallions at the Spanish Riding School is that they spend almost all of their time in the company of other horses.
5 Not the Spanish Riding School

> Observations in their box of 76 horses all living in the same conditions, belonging to one breed and one sex, revealed that the prevalence and types of stereotypies performed strongly depended upon the type of work they were used for. The stereotypies observed involved mostly mouth movements and head tossing/nodding. Work constraints probably added to unfavourable living conditions, favouring the emergence of chronic abnormal behaviours. This is especially remarkable as the 23 hours spent in the box were influenced by the one hour work performed every day. To our knowledge, this is the first evidence of potential effects of work stressors on the emergence of abnormal behaviours in an animal species. It raises an important line of thought on the chronic impact of the work situation on the daily life of individuals. (Hausberger *et al.*, 2009)

Another study was recently carried out by researchers at the School of Animal and Veterinary Sciences, Charles Sturt University, New South Wales in Australia, to see whether different locomotor activities are equally effective at meeting the stabled horse's need for exercise and whether they weaken or reduce unwanted behaviour. The researchers found that although exercise significantly reduced the amount of unwanted behaviour, the amount of exercise, per se, that horses receive is not the critical factor. 'Instead,' said one of the researchers, Dr Raf Freire, 'the ability of horses to show free-movement – gallop, buck, roll, and interact with other horses – is probably the most important factor for horses' well-being.' (Freire *et al.*, 2009)

I do not think, therefore, that we should assume that work alone is sufficient to keep horses happy; this applies especially to stallions, with their extra degree of emotionality and reactivity. I am not suggesting that 24/7 turnout is the be-all and end-all; that is an ideal which simply may not be practical for many people and, depending on local conditions and on the preferences of individual horses, not necessarily *always* in the horse's best interest. I do however believe that we should strive, as far as possible, to allow stallions as much turnout and freedom as possible. Just like humans, they need time to relax away from a work environment; for horses, this means freedom to run, jump about if they want to, have a good roll, amble about grazing, hang out with friends if possible, or just loaf around enjoying the fresh air. If we can give our stallions that much, we will have gone some way towards keeping them happy and contented.[6]

Social contact

In spite of dire warnings about letting stallions interact with other horses, many people do manage to allow their stallions to enjoy social contact with other horses. There are many ways in which this can be done, ranging from full integration into family or bachelor groups, to allowing contact in restricted circumstances, such as over a fence or a stable door. The latter is far from ideal, but it is better than nothing!

So what kind of social life is most likely to result in a calm, contented stallion? Research carried out by Andy Beck provides some clues.

After identifying the zones of interaction described on page 46, Andy went on to observe the interactions of horses within these zones in several distinct groups:

Group 1 included a two-year-old colt, a yearling colt and three mares. This group was well-integrated socially, with low levels of stress and aggression.

---
6 See also the Conclusion, under the Five Freedoms (page 265).

Group 2 consisted of a stallion, four mares and two foals. The stallion was the uniting force in this group, and Beck's analysis of the group's interactions indicated that if the stallion were removed, the group would become dysfunctional as a result.

Group 3, a mixed group of mares and fillies, was well-integrated enough to function reasonably well, although some of the youngsters did not receive as much support from the older members of the group as would be considered ideal.

Group 4 consisted of seven geldings. This group displayed a high level of aggression and lack of co-operation. Andy Beck comments,

> Considering the lack of energy expended on sexual behaviour, it might be expected that the need for supplementary feeding, given an appropriate grazing availability and quality, would be lower than that of harem groups. This has not been found to be the case, in fact the reverse seems true. The group was observed over a period of several weeks for a minimum of two hours per session and the mapping carried out in order to assess whether changes in group content might create a lower level of stress in the environment.[7]

Group 5, consisting of 8 mares, showed a high level of integration.

Group 6, a bachelor group of seven stallions, showed total integration – a result which may surprise those people who think that stallions can never live together peacefully.

So in the absence of mares, it may be that integration into a bachelor group could provide a stallion with the kind of social integration that would keep him contented and socially fulfilled. However, many stallion owners are not in a position to create a bachelor group, even if they had sufficient confidence in their stallions' behaviour to do so. The best solution – and perhaps the most practical – is to allow the stallion to live with one or more mares and foals in a proper family group. This would enable him to fulfil his role as protector of the family while enjoying the company of his mares and progeny – without, of course, any sexually mature colts to cause any upsets.

However, before thinking about such a solution, a few basic safety measures must first of all be thought out and put into place.

Turning stallions out with other horses: safety measures

The turn-out enclosure should be as big as possible, so that in the event of aggression (whether on the part of the stallion or not – it is not always the stallion who becomes aggressive!) the horses can get away from each other to a safe distance, beyond which they are unlikely to be pursued. There is no hard-and-fast way of determining this, even in the wild.

Our senior stallion, Nivalis, is generally tolerant towards the geldings, except for a large Warmblood gelding named Toska, who used to be Nivalis's playmate when they were young colts together, but for whom he developed an intense hatred after he had covered Toska's dam, evidently resenting the close relationship Toska still had with the mare whom Nivalis now considered to be *his*. This feeling was exacerbated when Nivalis saw my husband, Brian (with whom Nivalis has a

---

[7] Beck split this group into three smaller groups at supplementary feeding times, and this proved successful in terms of greater ease of management.

Chapter 7

Nivalis is generally tolerant of geldings. Gelding Zareeba (left) and stallion (Nivalis, right) greeting each other amicably over the stable door. Photo: Lesley Skipper

very close relationship) starting to work with Toska in preparation for the latter's ridden career. One day, Nivalis and Toska were out together in the field behind the stable block. Kiri, Toska's dam, was looking out into the field over the half-door of her stable, which opens into the field. Toska went over to see her, and Nivalis immediately shot over to them, chasing Toska away. Toska galloped off up the field, and when he was about 100 yards away, Nivalis broke off the pursuit, returning to Kiri. He kept looking over to where Toska, looking bemused, was standing; if Toska made the slightest move in Kiri's direction Nivalis would trot out into the field a short distance away from Kiri and stare at Toska, just as a stallion would in the wild. In this way he kept Toska pinned at the far side of the field until we intervened and took both of them in (separately, of course).

The distances in this case were not very great – from Kiri's back door to where Toska halted being, as I said above, about 100 yards – and Nivalis made no attempt to chase Toska any further away. However, each case is different, and what one stallion might consider an adequate distance might not be sufficient for another. So the more space you can provide, the better.

The turnout area should also be free of any man-made obstacles, such as farm machinery or equipment, jumps, etc. If at all possible, sharp angles in fencing should be rounded off, to prevent horses from getting trapped in corners; this could be done by stretching electrified tape across them (see Appendix I: Safety, for ideas about suitable fencing). There should be some means of letting horses out into a secure area in the event of severe aggression and/or relentless chasing. One summer we had let Nivalis out in the stallion paddock, while Toska was out in the field farthest from the stable. However, Toska managed to break the fence down and came wandering into the field adjoining Nivalis's paddock. Fortunately the electric fence was on, but even so, when Toska came ambling over to see Nivalis,[8] the latter went charging over to the fence, and the two immediately started running up and down the fence line. To Toska, it appeared to be no more than fun, as he showed no signs at all of any aggressive intent; however for Nivalis it was obviously not fun at all, but deadly serious. There was no point in trying to catch Nivalis, so my friend (who was helping

---

8 We have never quite worked out whether he does this deliberately to 'wind up' Nivalis, or whether he simply wants to try to regain the friendship of his former companion. Either way, he does seem to go out of his way to annoy Nivalis.

out that day) managed to distract Toska and lure him away out of sight, while I opened the paddock gate for Nivalis to come through (which I knew he would, in order to see where Toska had gone). I was able to catch hold of him once he was through the gate and into the secure area just outside the stable yard, and lead him back into the yard and the safety of his stable.

On another occasion, a well-grown Thoroughbred colt belonging to the people next door escaped from his nearby field, broke through into one of ours, and set off in pursuit of Nivalis's mother Roxzella, although she was not in season and would most likely have rejected him even if she had been. Nivalis and my gelding Zareeba, who were both in the field with her, galloped after them, and the result was a terrifying wall-of-death chase. Although fast horses of their type, neither Nivalis nor Zareeba, at 15 hh and 14.3hh respectively, was any match for a large Thoroughbred hell-bent on having his wicked way with a mare. Roxzella herself – more long-striding than her son or her boyfriend Zareeba – only just kept ahead of the would-be ravisher. Fortunately my husband managed somehow to chase Nivalis and Zareeba into the adjoining field and shut the gate on them before any serious damage was done; by the time the colt caught up with Roxzella he was too worn out to do anything about it, and Brian was able to catch him quite easily and restore him to his home.

Having sorted out the safety aspect, how do we go about introducing the stallion to a family group?

The family group

In Chapter 6, we looked at introducing mares and stallions to each other. Assuming the stallion has learned how to behave with mares, how do we go about introducing him to foals? If he has already been accustomed to going out, or living with, mares and foals, there should be little difficulty in that respect. But what of the stallion who has never been out with foals? As we saw in Chapter 4, there is a persistent belief that stallions will attack foals, and although it is unlikely that a stallion will do so, concerns regarding that possibility cannot be dismissed out of hand. Even if the stallion does not show any aggression towards the foal(s), there is a possibility that a mare with a new-born or very young foal will be aggressive to the stallion.

So before simply turning a stallion out with one or more mares and foals, it would be wise, if possible, to put him in a stable where he can see, and ideally interact with, at least one mare and her foal for several days before being turned out with them. If stabling them next to each other is not practical, then turning them out in an adjoining paddock or other fenced-off area is the next best solution. Most stallions (and many geldings) are fascinated by foals, but as always treat each horse as an individual and never make assumptions about what may or may not happen. Observe the stallion's reactions to the foal closely over the next few days, and if all seems to be well, try introducing the stallion to the paddock containing the mare and foal. Keep the turnout sessions short (if you train your stallion to accept being separated from his mares as described in Chapter 10 you should have little difficulty in removing him from the paddock). When all the parties seem to be settled and happy to interact, you can start to leave them out together for longer and longer periods.

We have found that properly socialized stallions love to interact with foals. Nivalis has a way of calling to them that is actually very like the soft nicker of a mare – if anything even softer – and the foals invariably respond. I described on page 73 Nivalis's great good humour when his sons play roughly with him, and never once have I seen him become even slightly aggressive with a foal or any other youngster. Many other stallion owners have reported similar observations regarding their own stallions.

Chapter 7

A contented family group: Tariel, Tiff and Nivalis. Photo: Lesley Skipper

Initially Tiff kept between Nivalis and her foal Tariel (here shown at a week old) but before long they were interacting freely.

Running out with mares

It may not always be possible to keep stallions in family groups, but an effective compromise is to ensure they have at least one mare living with them permanently. The use of synthetic hormones to suppress ovulation in the mare is an option if you have a mare and a stallion whom you would like to run together but do not want the complication of too many foals; however, this is an expensive option. One alternative is to let them run together but simply remove the mare when she shows signs of coming into season; this is what we do with both our stallions. The stallion should not object to being separated from her for a few days if he has been properly managed and knows she

129

The Natural Stallion

will eventually be returned to him (see below). Another alternative is to let him live with a barren mare (i.e. one who is unable to conceive, as opposed to one who is simply not in foal).

Tiff and Nivalis grazing together in harmony.
Photo: Lesley Skipper

Separating stallions and mares

One concern for people thinking of turning a stallion and one or more mares out together is the difficulty that may potentially arise of separating them once they are used to being together. I have heard stories about people being attacked when they have tried to separate a stallion from his mares out in the field, and this kind of thing is one of the reasons why so many people are reluctant to consider turning a stallion out with mares. It is understandable that a stallion will not want to be separated from his mares, but it is not inevitable that problems will arise. Neither of our stallions has caused any difficulties in this respect, because they know that eventually they and the mares will be reunited.[9] This is the key to managing this situation: the stallion must be confident that no harm will come to his mare(s) and that eventually he will be reunited with them. It is not just the fact that the mares have been removed that upsets the stallion, but the fact that when they are taken away from him he cannot protect them.

In this context, Marthe Kiley-Worthington relates what happened when she took one of her stallions to a show together with some mares with whom he lived. This stallion was normally very well-behaved and could be ridden out with his own and strange mares, whether in season or not. However, at this show, when his mares went off to different classes, he made a terrible fuss.

> What made him behave so atrociously in a ridden horse class was not his mares going away, which is mildly upsetting but something he was very used to, but them going off with other horses without him being able to do anything about it! (Kiley-Worthington, 1987)

There may be no issue at all if the stallion is turned out with just one mare who is visiting for stud purposes. In most such instances there will not have been time for the mare and stallion to form

---

9 In fact, the younger stallion, Rigel, will come running to the gate when called, and will readily follow us into the yard regardless of whether his mare is with him, before or behind him, or at the other end of the field!

On being called, Rigel comes galloping towards the field gate, even though it means leaving Imzadi (right). Because he knows he will soon be reunited with her, he is not concerned about being separated from her.
Photo: Lesley Skipper

a real bond, so although the stallion may be slightly upset at being separated from the mare, he is unlikely to make a real fuss. This issue is dealt with in more detail in Chapter 10.

Keeping stallions with other stallions

In spite of the findings of people like Sue McDonnell and Andy Beck, to many people, the idea of keeping stallions together in close contact, let alone turning mature stallions out with each other, is horrifying. Surely the stallions will try to kill each other! If we think about how non-breeding stallions in the wild form bachelor groups, and how they behave within those bachelor groups, we can see that in the absence of mares, there is really no reason why they should attack each other. Certainly, if the stallions concerned have poor social skills (almost invariably caused by the practice of separating them at an early age), the situation can be fraught with potential problems. For some stallions, turning them out with other stallions might never be an option. But for many others, being kept with – and if possible, turned out with, another stallion might not only be practical but actually very beneficial to both.

The downside of keeping stallions together

One possible disadvantage of keeping stallions together (even keeping them stabled in a separate stallion yard away from mares, as is common practice in many large studs) is that if the stallions in question are to be bred from, keeping them together and separate from mares could actually decrease their libido, as described in Chapter 6. However, if they are all regularly exposed to mares, this need not be a problem, as it seems to be the proximity of mares (or lack thereof) that either stimulates the hormones that increase libido, or alternatively suppresses the production of those hormones (thus decreasing the libido).

Introducing stallions to each other.

The safest and easiest way to do this is by allowing the stallions to have a gradually increasing amount of contact with each other in a controlled environment. Perhaps the most successful way of doing this is to start by keeping the stallions stabled next to each other in such a way that they can safely interact with each other. This works best in an American barn type set-up, but the kind of stabling

The Natural Stallion

Two stallions and a gelding: Arabian stallion Pharis (left), Arabian gelding Merlin (centre) and Arabian stallion Balthasar (right). Photo: Lyn Debnam

common in the UK and in some other parts of Europe can be adapted without too much disruption. There are several ways of doing this.

Barred partitions

One method is to construct barred partitions above a certain height, with kicking-boards below. The bars need to be constructed so that a horse cannot get his feet trapped in them in the event of kicking out, yet wide enough to allow him to touch noses with his companion. A similar arrangement was used in an experiment carried out at the University of Lincoln to determine whether the use of mirrors in stables reduced weaving (it did). Some of the horses taking part in this experiment were housed in stables modified with barred partitions, separating the weaver from a non-weaver stabled in the next box. Such partitions were just as effective in reducing weaving as the mirrors were. (Mills and Davenport, 2002)

I once visited a very well-run stud farm where the stallions were housed in stables with a similar arrangement: they could see and touch each other but could not bite or kick each other. All four of the stallions housed like this seemed very content, and there appeared to be no squabbling between them. It should go without saying that all stables should have adequate kicking-boards.

It may be easiest (and safest, as well as cheaper) to use plastic piping instead of metal bars. If you are planning to construct such a barrier it would be a good idea to obtain samples of different gauges of plastic piping, so that you can test them for rigidity – you do not want bars that are bent out of shape very quickly, but some degree of 'give' would be advisable – another advantage over metal bars.

Removing part of the dividing wall

Alternatively, you could arrange for part of the dividing wall between the two stables to be removed so that the two horses can see and touch each other, as in the situation described above. With a small opening there is always the risk of the horses bumping their heads if they move suddenly (for example, if one of them nips the other, as even the best of friends will do on occasion). You could make the opening tall enough to prevent this; you would in any case need to ensure that the lower part of the opening was high enough to prevent the horses attempting to climb through and possibly injuring themselves in the process.

Some people have found it possible to lower the dividing wall across its whole width to as little as four or even three feet, but this would be safe only with stallions who have come to know and tolerate each other well; I would certainly not recommend it when first introducing stallions to each other.

Movable partitioning

Perhaps the best solution would be one which includes movable partitioning of some kind. We introduced a variation of this many years ago, when we first set up the stable in which our senior stallion Nivalis has lived (when not out in the field) ever since he was nine months old. Wanting to let him continue to interact with other horses even when in the stable, we set up a movable anti-weave grid in his stable, which has two doors, one opening into the stable yard, the other into our grassed-over riding arena. The anti-weave grid was set up on the bottom half of the door leading to the arena. It consists of a metal grid (quite heavy) with a removable v-shaped centre portion, the whole grid dropping into two metal slots fastened to the outside of the bottom door (see the photograph on page 203). I always have to explain to visitors that the purpose of this is not to prevent weaving (which it doesn't do in any case – see Chapter 11) because Nivalis has never displayed any stereotypical actions; rather its purpose is to allow him not only to see what is going on, but also to interact with other horses who might be out in the arena (or with the mare Tiff who, when she is not with Nivalis, lives in a partially-open barn close to the latter's stable) without any risk of him either rearing up over the door or trying to jump out.[10] It might be possible to construct something similar to go on an internal dividing wall; it would be partially or wholly removable, enabling an increase of interaction when the two stallions appeared to be accepting each other.

Another method is to introduce the two over a stable door. This has the advantage that the stallion (or gelding) on the outside can be quickly moved out of the way if the situation gets too intense. However, it has the great disadvantage that if one or the other half-rears (which is not uncommon during stallion interactions, even friendly ones) he could hit his head on the door-frame. This happened to Nivalis once when he got away from my husband in the yard.[11] He immediately went over to see the only horse whom he appears to really hate – Toska, the big Warmblood gelding described earlier in this chapter. On this occasion Nivalis half-reared, at the same time attempting to bite Toska. He hit his head on the door-frame, and appeared to be stunned for several minutes afterwards. There was no permanent damage done, and Nivalis soon recovered, but the door-frame suffered considerably. If Nivalis had hit his nose, instead of the more densely bony part of his head, he might have done some real damage. It was also fortunate that the door-frame was made of wood; if there had been a concrete lintel (which may be the case in some stables built of brick or breeze-block) Nivalis could have fractured his skull and even died as a result.

Perhaps because of this experience, he is much more circumspect when interacting with his son Rigel over the stable door. We allow this because, although their play can be pretty rough, it never involves half-rearing, and they both seem to know when to back off. However, if you do choose to let stallions get to know each other over the stable door, be prepared for something like this to happen – perhaps keeping the one outside on a long line (so that you don't have to get too close, and possibly in the way of any rough play), ready to pull him away if he looks like rearing in a way that might be dangerous to him. Otherwise, unless things get really out of hand, I would try to interfere as little as possible. Learning what is and is not acceptable to the other – and the consequences of stepping over the mark – is part of what being a horse – not just a stallion – is all about. Stallions who – like Rigel and his brother, the gelding Tariel – have had the advantage of growing up with their father as a male role-model, will already have most of the social skills necessary to interact with other

---

10 He has never shown any inclination to do either, but one never knows.
11 This happened before we taught him the *Stand!* control cue described in Chapter 8 (page 156).

stallions; those who have not had such advantages will naturally take longer to learn the manners and ground-rules that govern stallion behaviour.

Whichever method you choose, be prepared for some very noisy encounters! There will be lots of squealing and maybe grunting (although probably not as much as there would be in an encounter with an oestrus mare), and they will almost certainly strike out, just as they would if encountering each other in the wild. This does not seem to be an attempt to actually strike the other stallion; it appears more akin to pawing (see Chapter 11). If you are concerned about the stallions injuring a foot by striking the stable door, hang (or nail) some thick matting on both sides of the door to absorb most of the impact.

Gradually introducing stallions – or stallions and geldings – to each other in this way, even if they never actually go out together, will help to increase their social skills. This will help them to adjust more easily to other situations where they may encounter geldings or other stallions – such as at shows, or when being ridden out, for example. It will also mean that if they manage to escape from a field into a situation where contact with other horses is inevitable, such contact will not come as such a surprise to them that sensory overload makes them create havoc.

We have had an example of this comparatively recently. Our young stallion Rigel is an escape artist – if there is a weakness in a fence, he will find it, and being an especially sociable horse he will go looking for company. As a result of this we have had to re-work the fencing round the stallion paddock; I will say more about this in Appendix I: Safety, where I talk about fencing and what may be best for stallion enclosures. Before we managed to do that, however, Rigel decided one day that he would go and visit the horses in the next field. Having broken through the dividing fence, he went in search of the playmate of his early years – the big Warmblood gelding referred to on pages 126–27. We saw him running about quite happily among the other horses; because he was used to being with them, or interacting with them over the fence, there was no fuss, even though there were mares in the same field. My husband was able to capture him quite easily and return him to the stallion paddock – after mending the fence, of course.

Naturally, there is no guarantee that other stallions, no matter how well-socialized they may be, would react in the same way, especially if there were mares around, as in this case. I would certainly not advise any relaxation of the kind of safety measures described in Appendix I. However, it does show that, at the very least, a stallion who is accustomed to interacting with other horses is less likely to explode and/or become aggressive when confronted with other horses at close quarters.

Turning stallions out together

The next logical progression would be turning stallions out together. I must emphasize that, as I said earlier, this may *not* always be an option, and it would be foolhardy to think that every stallion can be socialized to the extent that it *does* become an option. Some stallions may have behavioural problems, caused by social isolation, that are too deeply ingrained for such a huge adjustment to be practical. However, for many stallions it *is* possible, even if a considerable degree of social adjustment is necessary before it can be done. How can you tell which stallions will respond to such socialization? The answer is that you can't. So much depends on the stallion's early upbringing and what interaction he has been allowed to have with other horses, as well as on the temperament of individual horses (although this is of course something that is, to a large extent, dependent on environmental influences). It also depends on the chosen companion(s) and how well they interact with other horses. I know, for example, that while Nivalis can quite happily be turned out with the gelding Zareeba, with whom he has had a good relationship since foalhood, it would be utterly disastrous to turn him out with the big Warmblood gelding, Toska, whom he has always hated. It would also be possible to turn him out with his entire son Rigel, as long as there were no mares close by; this also applies when turning out stallions and geldings together.[12]

So having allowed them to interact in a safe, controlled environment, and assuming they have responded well to each other, how does one then go about turning stallions out together?

The first step might be to allow them to interact over the fence. If they are used to doing this over a stable door, or over an internal partition wall, there are unlikely to be any problems; however, it might be as well, to be on the safe side, for two people to be on hand to make sure things do not get out of hand. Have both stallions on a long line (such as a lunge line) ready to pull one away if necessary. Allow them to interact just as they would over the stable door. If there is any increase in aggression in this different environment, separate them just enough for safety while still allowing them to touch noses over the fence. If they seem to be settling, then the next step could be to turn them out in adjoining paddocks (if this is practicable), with at least one strand of electrified rope or tape as described in Appendix I. If you are concerned about them striking out and catching a foot on the fence, consider running a strand of tape/wire along the bottom rail of the fence on both sides.

Finally, if they are getting on well over the fence, you could try actually turning them out together. The turnout area should be prepared as described on page 127; make sure that in the event of a serious chase, the gate can be opened quickly to allow one stallion to run through, and closed again equally quickly to prevent the other from following him. In any event, keep a close eye on them and make the turnout sessions together short until they are settled and appear to be getting on well. Even then, monitor their behaviour towards each other as changes in behaviour can be unexpected and not always predictable.

Ultimately, it is up to you whether you want to risk turning two or more stallions out together. Some stallions may never accept each other; others may become best of friends in a very short space of time. There is simply no way to predict, ahead of the event, which will be the case. You can only take things step by step, monitoring behaviour closely at each step and proceeding with caution.

Lusitano stallions Tigre (left) and Quinito (right) interacting from the safety of adjoining paddocks. Photo: Rachael Johnson

---

12 We have not yet tried turning them out together in the field, although they have been together in the yard, because at the time of writing (summer 2010) Nivalis is still recovering from a life-threatening bout of acute laminitis which occurred in 2009. His recovery, at one time seriously in doubt, is now almost complete but his turnout has had to be very closely monitored. Attempting to turn him out with Rigel (with whom he interacts daily over the stable door, as described above), might result in too much running about on hard ground to be good for his feet.

The Natural Stallion

Stallions with geldings

It might seem odd that I have mentioned turning stallions out together before turning a stallion out with one or more geldings. One might reasonably think that it would be easier to get a stallion to accept a gelding rather than another stallion. The problem is that geldings, as 'artificial' creatures, don't really fit into any normal equine social structure. They don't behave like mares, but neither (with, as we have seen, a few exceptions) do they behave totally like stallions. Some stallions accept geldings well and get along with them fine; others can't tolerate them at all. If you are thinking of turning your stallion out with one or more geldings, take exactly the same precautions as you would when introducing stallions to each other.

Companionship of another species

If no suitable equine companionship can be found, an animal companion of another species is often welcomed. The late Lady Wentworth, breeder of some of the finest Arabian horses of the twentieth century, recalled one stallion who was very fond of a stable cat which used to sleep in his manger. At feed times, the stallion would very gently take the cat in his teeth by the scruff of its neck, and equally gently deposit it on the floor. He never hurt the cat, which would sleep on his back. (Wentworth, 1962). But while many accounts exist of horses making friends with cats, goats, sheep and various other animals, there seem to be relatively few examples of friendships between horses and dogs. This may be because dogs are among the horse's natural predators, and this tends to make horses very wary of them. Even so, while some of our horses have remained either indifferent or actively hostile to our dogs, others have responded to them in a friendly manner. Not so the senior stallion Nivalis; he hates dogs, and chases them from his paddock if one strays in there. We have now run

Above right: Mr Summerhays's Arabian stallion Jaleel and his cat. Above right: Arabian stallion with cat. From: *The Authentic Arabian Horse*, **by Lady Wentworth.**

136

a strand of electrified wire along the bottom rail of the fence to discourage dogs from entering the paddock, for fear that if he caught one, Nivalis would kill it.

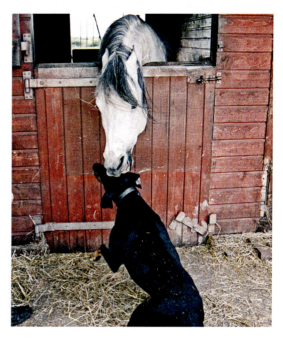

Nivalis hates dogs and would try to kill one if it got into his paddock. Here he is trying to get at our old Doberman x Rottweiler, Max. Photo: Lesley Skipper

Some stallions like sheep and goats; others may attack them, so be careful if you are trying this. Even where stallions get on well with their non-specific companions, accidents can happen, so care needs to be taken in the selection of a companion, and the pair needs to be monitored for any changes in behaviour towards each other. This is true whether the horse is a stallion, a gelding or a mare, but obviously special care needs to be taken in the case of a stallion.

When Sylvia Loch lived in Suffolk, her Lusitano-Arab stallion Palomo Linares[13] used to be turned out with a pair of sheep, Toffee and Treacle, whom Sylvia had had since they were weanlings. Sylvia observes that sheep make excellent companions for equines, as they have a very calming influence, and the sheep and Palomo had always got on peacefully. Then, one day, quite without warning, Palomo turned on Toffee, the ram. He grabbed hold of Toffee, tossed him in the air (and Toffee weighed around 76 kg, or 168 lb) and savaged him. It took the vet three hours to stitch his lacerations. Toffee survived, but he had almost died, and it was never quite clear what had made Palomo turn on him.[14] I did wonder whether it had something to do with Palomo's previous history: some years before Sylvia acquired him, he had been a bullfighting horse in Portugal.[15] Rams often make little 'charges' and butting motions with their heads. Could Toffee have possibly been doing something like this, and could Palomo have been reminded of the actions of a fighting bull, and simply been responding to this? Of course the sheep was many times smaller than a fighting bull, but the action alone might have been enough to trigger a defensive attack on the part of the stallion. I have discussed this with Sylvia, and she too thinks it is a distinct possibility.

However, although there are risks involved in turning stallions out with other species, the benefits to the horse far outweigh these. While such attacks are certainly *possible*, that does not mean they are *probable*. We have to apply the same criteria as we did when considering turning stallions out with mares and foals.

---

13 Profiled in Chapter 12
14 As I point out in Chapter 11, horses (like other animals) do not do things 'for no reason'. There is always a reason, even if it is not immediately obvious what it is.
15 I explain more about the mounted bullfight in Chapter 12.

The Natural Stallion

Mental stimulation

Companionship apart, stallions do best if they are provided with adequate mental stimulation. Their extra emotional 'edge' and mental sharpness means that they thrive on such stimulation, and without it may well develop behavioural problems. An excellent way of providing such mental stimulation is to teach them different things. Free-shaping, using the horse's spontaneously offered behaviour,[16] is a wonderful way to do this. For example, when Nivalis was about four, we were keeping bales of straw in a barn at the back of his stable. We used to bring the straw bales into the yard through Nivalis's stable; one day my husband was bringing bales through while Nivalis was inside. Brian put the bale on the floor while he shut the back door; Nivalis, intrigued, started pawing at it. Brian, seeing the possibility of teaching him something new, waited until Nivalis actually placed his hoof on the bale rather than just pawing at it, and the instant he did so, Brian gave him an Extra-Strong mint, which he loves. This reinforced the behaviour (as described in Chapter 9), and soon Nivalis was putting both front feet on the bale. Each time his did this, he got a mint, until eventually he was happy to stand with both front feet on the bale. Brian then paired the behaviour with the word 'Up!' so that if we want Nivalis to stand with his front feet on a bale, all we have to do is say 'Up!'. We now have only to put a bale of straw on the ground near Nivalis for him to offer to stand on it. (Using bales of straw for this exercise is *not* recommended, however, as the front feet can easily get caught in the baling twine if it is not absolutely taut. If you are going to try this, it would be

Nivalis will freely offer to stand with his forefeet on a bale of straw, or a box, because it's fun for him and he gets well rewarded. A solid pedestal or box is better for this kind of exercise. Photo: Lesley Skipper

---

16 See Chapter 9 under **Shaping, selective reinforcement and variable schedules.** Free shaping is simply a variant of this which initially makes use of behaviour offered spontaneously, without any prompting.

better to construct a proper, sturdy wooden pedestal that will take the horse's weight and not skid around.)

Many people feel that this kind of thing is demeaning to the horse. However, I doubt whether that is how the horse sees the matter, especially if the work is amply rewarded. Such exercises (call them 'tricks' if you will; the horse doesn't care what you call them) are not only a wonderful way of educating the horse to think about what he is doing, but also of developing the *handler's* patience and strength of character. So is liberty work, described in a book called *Classical Circus Equitation*, by Henrik Jan Lijsen (J A Allen, 1993). This excellent book, now sadly out of print,[17] takes the reader through liberty work, High School (at its best, no different in principle from the classical High School of the *manège*), quadrilles, and vaulting. Liberty work, properly done, is invaluable in giving sharp horses such as stallions something to think about. They can develop such power of concentration that they forget all about whatever normally distracts them, or about 'acting up' in order to gain attention. Indeed, this was how we started to prepare Nivalis, as a youngster, for shows and develop his attention to the handler.

As with any aspect of their training, one must be careful not to ask too much of them, or to make the training sessions too long; but if it is done in a relaxed way, they will not feel pressurized, and most will learn amazingly quickly. Effectively they 'learn to learn'; as a result of education, they actually become more intelligent. There are benefits, too, for the handler. Working with a horse in this intimate way can help to strengthen the bond that should always exist between the horse and his trainer. As Lijsen says, 'There is no better way of getting to know animals than by training them. It leads to mutual understanding, a fine appreciation of animal reaction – and, you will find, it greatly improves your patience. One soon discovers that humans, too, can make mistakes.' (Lijsen, 1993)

Many of the exercises set out by Alexandra Kurland in her excellent book on clicker-training (see Chapter 9)[18] are as good as (if not better than) Lijsen's for stimulating the horse's mind, and her book is easier to come by. I recommend both; the principles on which this kind of work is based are described in Chapter 9.

In-hand work

This type of work from the ground is not at all well-known outside Spain, Portugal and academies of equitation such as the Spanish Riding School. This is a pity, as it is an excellent way of relaxing the horse, softening his back and gaining his attention. At the Spanish Riding School and in Spain, in-hand work is carried out with the horse wearing a cavesson, whereas in Portugal a simple snaffle bridle is generally used.

The trainer walks by the horse's side, holding the inside rein close to the bit, with the outside rein held over the horse's neck. The horse is asked to walk on, halt, rein back, or perform a shoulder-in; these movements can be carried out either in a straight line (for example, along a fence or other boundary) or in a circle around the trainer.

The trainer can encourage the horse to bend while being worked in-hand by pressing the horse's side at approximately the same point where the rider's leg would touch him. This stimulates the intercostal nerves in exactly the same way as the rider's leg would in a ridden horse, causing the horse to incurve his side away from the pressure, at the same time raising his back. If he is then gently worked in shoulder-in, the joints of his hind legs will bend and consequently become looser and more active. I give some of the kind of exercises that can be carried out in this kind of work in my book *Exercise School for Horse and Rider* (New Holland Publishing, 2008)

---

17 Second-hand copies may be available online via various Internet outlets such as Amazon, Abe Books, Alibris etc.
18 Kurland, Alexandra: Clicker Training For Your Horse, Ringpress, 2001

The Natural Stallion

Portuguese trainer Pedro Neves takes Lusitano stallion Audaz through some classical in-hand exercises at the Classical Riding Club's 15th Anniversary event at Myerscough, Lancashire, in July 2010. These exercises help to relax the horse, soften and raise his back and gain his attention. Photos: Lesley Skipper

I would stress, however, that you should not attempt serious in-hand work, especially with a stallion, without first of all studying someone who really knows what they are doing. There are several good books on in-hand training; see the Bibliography for more details and Appendix II for some useful contacts, including the Classical Riding Club.

Ridden work

As we saw in Chapter 2, stallions are ridden as a matter of course in the Iberian Peninsula and the Spanish-speaking countries in other parts of the world, as well as in some other countries where male horses are not gelded (for example, in many Muslim countries, although in Saudi Arabia mares are still the first choice for ridden horses). Until comparatively recently, it was not common to see stallions ridden in the English-speaking countries; the exceptions were racehorses and certain top-level competition horses, as well as horses of certain breeds such as Arabians and Iberian horses such as Andalusians[19] and Lusitanos.

Over the past few decades, however, this has started to change, and we are now starting to see more stallions of other breeds ridden, and not just in competition. More and more people are beginning to realize that a well-adjusted, properly trained stallion can be a delightful companion out on a ride. Of course the rider must be competent and able to retain control of the stallion should he become excited or upset by other horses (or sometimes animals of other species); this naturally applies to riding all horses, not just stallions, but is especially important where the latter are concerned, because of the possible consequences if the stallion got loose among other horses. It also applies even if the stallion is being ridden at home, in an enclosed area; being generally sharper and more emotional than geldings,[20] stallions may be more easily upset than the latter. However, a competent rider who is sensitive to the signals a horse is giving and who can remain calm if things go wrong should find a stallion no more difficult to manage than any other horse. Of all the things one can do with a horse, there are few to compare with the sheer pleasure of riding through the countryside, across fields or through woods, or even just down a quiet bridle path, with a horse with whom one has the kind of close relationship that so many stallions can offer.

Brian and Nivalis out for a relaxing hack around the fields. Photos: Lesley Skipper

---

19 Now more correctly known as Pure Bred Spanish horses (*Pura Raza Española*, or PRE)
20 And some mares; people tend to forget that mares are also entire horses!

It should go without saying that ridden stallions should be properly schooled. Unfortunately many people are put off by the idea of schooling, regarding it as a chore rather than as something necessary for the horse's wellbeing under saddle. Dressage has become very popular, yet because it is usually thought of in the context of competitive dressage, it is not generally realized that dressage is actually nothing more or less than the education of the horse under saddle: that is, schooling! All the movements required in dressage tests are actually schooling movements, and that is how they should be seen, rather than simply as something horse and rider have to perform in order to take part in a competition.

It is essential to make the schooling sessions as interesting and as varied as possible, and the school movements can be used to do this as well as to develop the horse's muscles and make him more supple and responsive . These movements and how to ride them are described in a number of excellent books: *Dressage in Lightness*, by Sylvia Loch (J.A. Allen, 2000); my own *Exercise School for Horse and Rider*, already mentioned on page 142; and *Riding Revelations: Classical Training from the Beginning* by Anne Wilson (Black Tent Publications, 2009)

As classical trainer Erik F. Herbermann has observed, 'Contrary to popular belief, horses do not get bored with basic work. If the rider demands exact responses, paying close attention to detail and quality, neither horse nor rider will have time to get bored, rather, a true sense of accomplishment will be gained.' (Herbermann, 1989)

Going out for a walk

Even if, for whatever reason, ridden work is not practicable, a stallion's interest – and therefore his mind – can be engaged by taking him out for walks in-hand. All the usual safety precautions should be taken: wear a hat and gloves, just as you would for lungeing (in the photographs on page 226, as well as on this page, my husband is shown taking Nivalis out for a walk minus hat and gloves; this is not ideal but as he knows Nivalis so well and has a very close relationship with him, and as Nivalis is so well-behaved, Brian felt confident about not wearing a hat. Needless to say, he would never ride without a hat.). Perhaps even more so than any other horses, stallions appreciate – and benefit from – the opportunity to see and investigate new sights and hear new sounds, or to re-experience familiar ones away from home. The more they are given the chance to do so, the better-behaved they will be when confronted with different situations, such as they would experience at shows. Many stallions are never allowed to get out and about and indulge their curiosity; then their owners take

Going out for a walk: Brian and Nivalis. Stallions appreciate – and benefit from – the opportunity to see and investigate new sights and hear new sounds, or to re-experience familiar ones away from home. Photo: Lesley Skipper

them to a show, without any kind of preparation, and wonder why the stallion is so explosive and unmanageable!

Going to shows

Provided the experience is not too stressful for them, and they are not under too much pressure to perform, I have found that most horses enjoy going to shows. They are intensely curious creatures, and none more so than stallions, who, as we have seen, would typically be the first members of the group to investigate new phenomena in wild or free-ranging conditions. Ideally they should be taken to shows early in life (although this should not be overdone; two or three shows a season is enough) to accustom them to the sights and sounds of a showground. Some young colts can become very boisterous at shows; they become over-stimulated by all the mind-blowing activity around them. It is pointless to punish a colt for this, as Chapter 9 will show; the way to deal with it is to introduce some activity which engages the horse's mind. This has to be done beforehand, because as we shall see in Chapter 8, it is difficult if not impossible for an animal to learn in a stressful situation. Nivalis was a very boisterous foal and yearling; we found that liberty work, as mentioned on page 139, helped to gain his attention and focus his mind on the trainer. The verbal cues he learned during this work (as well as the 'stand!' cue which I go on to mention in the next chapter) were later used to settle him down at shows. That, together with repeated exposure to the show environment, made him calm and responsive in the showring.

Mental stimulation, plenty of outlet for his energy, exposure to potentially exciting sights, sounds and activities, and above all a fulfilling social life will all help to ensure that you have a stallion who will be calm, relaxed and responsive – and a delightful companion with whom you can share some of the best moments a human can have with a horse.

Two Lusitano stallions at the Lusitano Breed Society of Great Britain's annual breed show, 2009: Rachael Johnson with Quinito and Rui Campeão with Tigre (both stallions owned by Rachael Johnson). Photo: courtesy of Rachael Johnson.

Chapter 8

What kind of relationship do we want with a stallion?

When you are incoherent in your notions about an animal you are working with, things do not go so well with the animal.

– Vicki Hearne

What kind of relationship do we want with a stallion? And how do we achieve it?

HAVING looked at how stallions relate to other horses, and how they may relate to animals of other species, we must also consider what kind of relationship we, as humans, want to have with them. Do we want a relationship based on mutual trust and understanding, or do we simply want to impose our will on them without regard to their thoughts and feelings about the matter?

Many people believe that the latter type of relationship is the only kind we should – or can – have with any horse, not just a stallion. Such people may express their views by sayings something like, 'My horses don't fart unless I give them permission to!' They insist on having absolute control at all times, and refuse to consider any excuse for what they call misbehaviour – that is, any step out of line, no matter what the reason. Any such infringement of this rule is regarded as showing 'disrespect', and such infringements are to be dealt with severely, especially if the horse in question is a stallion. So we have Dr James McCall advising us that you should 'Draw the line and when he steps over it, knock the dickens out of him.' (McCall, 2001)

As we have seen, many people – including Dr McCall – feel that stallions are inherently untrustworthy ('never trust a stallion'), so for anyone sharing this point of view, a relationship based on mutual trust is not something that can realistically be achieved. If we cannot trust a stallion (and I most emphatically do *not* believe that this is the case), how then can we relate to him – or indeed to any horse?

Dominance-based training

Because so many people believe that horses, especially stallions, are innately aggressive, they may end up believing that certain behaviours directed towards humans are aggressive, and that the way to prevent or combat these is by adopting a similarly aggressive attitude. This belief is fuelled, and in many cases caused, by the idea that horses will always try to dominate us if we do not first of all establish (and then maintain) our dominance over *them*. Underlying this is the assumption that horses are not only constantly challenging each other for social status, but that they will also challenge *us* in the same way. So we have Dr McCall stating that 'A stallion only respects the person who is more dominant than he. That is a law of nature.' 'Every day can be a fight with a stallion to see who rules.' 'Stallions play mind games with humans in order to gain dominance' (McCall, 2001) As I said in Chapter 1, the first two statements are examples of the 'self-fulfilling prophecy', while the third is extremely unlikely; I have seen no evidence that horses play 'mind games' with each other, let alone with humans.[1] Yet such beliefs are widespread. So we have influential trainers like Pat Parelli making statements such as 'If more people knew how to relate to their horse as a dominant horse would, there would be a lot more happy horses and happy people' (Parelli, www.parelli.com, Article 12, 'Become a natural horseman without strings attached'). But what does he mean by this? It is not immediately obvious why it would make anyone happy, let alone the horse. But some of the faulty ideas about the nature of dominance in horses, described in Chapter 5, give us a clue.

Becoming 'alpha'

We have already seen in Chapter 5 how widespread (one might almost say universal) these ideas have become, and the way in which many trainers have latched onto theories of dominance, reinterpreted them and applied them in a simplistic way to their theories of training. These theories often include the belief that the way to relate to horses is to emulate their behaviour towards each other – by which they mean the behaviour of a dominant horse towards a subordinate. In this way, we are told, we can not only gain acceptance as a member of the 'herd', but also achieve the status of the 'alpha' horse.

This echoes – and is probably derived from – the belief that dogs perceive their owners as members of the family 'pack', and that the said owner must achieve 'alpha' status in the pack. That idea was preposterous when it was proposed in respect of dogs (recall Ray Coppinger's remark about attempting to train a wolf by dominating it: 'Quick way to get killed'), and it is just as preposterous when applied to horses.

A flawed approach

First of all, we do not have the necessary physical equipment to emulate horses. Equines signal their mood in ways that humans cannot hope to duplicate. Apart from the more obvious displays, such as threat postures, their body language is often subtle, consisting of small, almost imperceptible movements of the ears or facial muscles. The ears in particular can indicate, by their position, many subtle variations in mood. Human ears, small and fixed, cannot. Horses undoubtedly possess, in an astonishing degree, the ability to read our body language, but they can only relate it to what they have already learned about us. They will not automatically assume, for example, that the human approaching them waving their arms (or a piece of equipment) is doing so in order to assert his (or her) dominant status. All they will see is something vaguely alarming which they might do well to avoid.

The second flaw in this argument is that relating to a horse as a dominant horse would, even if it were possible, restrict us to an exceedingly narrow range of interactions with our horses – as the rest of this chapter will show.

When we bring together these two ideas – that of emulating the horse's behaviour and that of making ourselves the equivalent of the hypothetical 'alpha horse' – we create a huge potential for disaster, especially where stallions are concerned. First of all, there are two fallacies involved: that

---

[1] While I am the first to admit that horses' mental capacities are almost certainly far greater than is generally supposed, playing 'mind games' requires a sophistication of thought which it is unlikely they possess (especially given that many *humans* are mentally too unsophisticated to play such games).

of the Supreme Leader, or herd 'boss' (or 'alpha' horse, if you will) and that of the Supreme Leader as Dominant Horse No.1.

As Chapters 3 and 4 established, there is no 'Supreme Leader', and the description of an animal as 'dominant' refers to a relationship between two animals. Labels such as 'more dominant' or 'most dominant' are therefore nonsense, because in a dominance relationship only one animal can be dominant at a time. And, as we have also seen, dominance status within a relationship is not fixed and can change with context and time. Perhaps it is a dimly felt recognition of this that makes some trainers insist that horses challenge each other horse within a group for each resource available to the group, but again, this has more to do with their own beliefs than any observed reality.

So all we can realistically have, then, is a dominance relationship between horse and handler. But is this either necessary or desirable? Many trainers believe that it is, and indeed some base their whole training program around this concept. They appear to believe that unless we establish a dominance relationship with our horses, we are inviting them to walk all over us, which will inevitably result in injury to us. There seems to be a strongly-held belief that without the establishment of such a relationship, horses would inevitably become aggressive and bite and kick humans. The fact that countless people who have never established such a dominance relationship manage to have well-mannered horses who are safe to be around, and who never bite or kick them, seems to escape them. One of the biggest problems with this approach, however, is how to establish a dominance relationship.

The use of threats

As I pointed out in Chapter 5, it is often extraordinarily difficult to grasp exactly how trainers want us to do this. We have seen that dominance is established by one horse threatening another; the horse being threatened either moves away or retaliates. So it would seem that in order to establish oneself as the 'dominant', threats of some kind are involved. But what kind of threats? Lacking a horse's physical equipment, we cannot lay our ears back or thrust our head out and threaten to bite, as a horse would – at least, not convincingly! I once tried making a bite-threat to our senior stallion, just to see what his reaction would be; he simply looked at me (possibly wondering what this mad human was up to), then continued placidly eating his hay.

We can threaten to kick, but as two-legged creatures our feeble efforts are unlikely to impress horses any more than my attempt at a 'bite-threat' did. We can 'stand square' and make ourselves look bigger, as many animals do, and in fact such an action (especially if used in conjunction with a raised hand) can work wonders in stopping an unruly horse from approaching too close for comfort (see Chapter 11 for more about this). But we are not talking specifically about unruly horses at this juncture; we are considering how to make ourselves 'dominant' in order to establish a relationship with the horse. So what else can we do? We can twirl (or waggle) a rope at the horse to prevent him from encroaching on our personal space; most horses will step back in order to avoid the rope. But all that really achieves is to make the horse step back (and there are better ways of doing this, as Chapters 9 and 10 will show). What then can we do to establish our 'dominance'?

This is where things really start to come unstuck. We can threaten all we like; we can twirl or waggle ropes to our heart's content, we can wave our arms about in a threatening way, we can hit the horse with the end of a rope, or with a stick, or our hands (I have seen all of these done with varying levels of skill and to varying effect), and all we can teach him is a) to be at the very least wary of us, and most probably afraid of us, and b) to move away from us. There are undoubtedly some trainers who are very skilled at moving horses around using such techniques, but that is still all they

Chapter 8

Above left: as Rigel approaches, Brian stands square and raises his arms. Above right: Rigel halts, his attention focused on Brian. He will not approach any closer until invited to do so. This is nothing to do with dominance or 'respect'; it is learned behaviour. See Chapter 11 for more about teaching colts and stallions to be polite around humans.

are doing: moving the horse around. They would no doubt argue that that is what a dominant horse does; he or she moves other horses around. But in fact, as we have seen, it is only the band stallion (and, very occasionally, a mare) who moves other horses around, and then only in response to specific situations such as the proximity of other horses or threats from other stallions or potential predators. Horses don't waste precious energy moving other horses around just for the sake of it. And they certainly don't move other horses around in order to teach them anything except 'Get out of my way!' or 'Move, because danger threatens!'. So given this, and the fact that dominant horses are *not* the leaders, what does acting like a dominant horse actually achieve?

Respect, disrespect and faulty reasoning

Proponents of this approach claim that it teaches a horse respect. 'Respect' and 'disrespect' are words that crop up continually in the training vocabulary. If a horse moves too close to you without your permission, he is not 'respecting your personal space'. (What about humans moving too close to horses without *their* permission? Is that then 'disrespect'? Perhaps it is.) Alternatively, he is being 'dominant'. If he does not pay attention during a training session, he is exhibiting 'disrespect'. If he throws his head up to avoid being hit in the face with the end of a rope, he is being 'disrespectful'. If he does not move back the instant you ask him to, he is showing a lack of 'respect' (or being 'dominant'; take your pick). In fact, it seems that virtually anything a horse might do in the course of a training session can be interpreted as either showing a lack of respect for the trainer, or as the horse being 'dominant'.[2]

I have heard such explanations given as justification for some truly brutal acts on the part of trainers: horses being repeatedly hit on the head, beaten with sticks, kicked, punched, and generally physically and mentally abused; one observer reports that during one training session she saw a filly being punched hard in the nose for not backing up quickly enough (Arab Horse Society News,

---

2 Part of the mythology of dominance states that in the wild, a horse who shows disrespect to higher-ranking horses is expelled from the herd, and that such a horse is only allowed back into the herd when he has shown proper respect and submission. I can find absolutely nothing in either the scientific literature or in any systematic observations, including my own, to back up this assertion. I have found no evidence to support the idea that horses have any concept of this kind of 'respect'.

147

2006). One excuse is that this is how horses treat each other, so the trainer is only doing what one horse would do to another anyway.

Of course, it would be ridiculous and unfair to suggest that all trainers who use dominance-based methods resort to such brutality; there are plenty of such trainers who get good results without using unduly aversive methods. But trainers – and there are all too many of them – who *do* use physical force and intimidation display a monumental failure to understand either equine behaviour or the learning process itself. In the case of the filly who was not backing up quickly enough, the punch on the nose was effectively punishing[3] her for what she was already doing – i.e., backing up. It could never teach her specifically that backing up more quickly was what the trainer wanted, although she probably did move more quickly, simply to get out of the way. And as far as the 'equine behaviour' defence goes, the excuse that horses bite and kick each other 'all the time' (as some apologists put it) is based on faulty reasoning, as well as on a very distorted view of equine society. When horses do kick and bite each other it is in response to specific situations, using rules of conduct that all understand. It does not mean that they understand roughly equivalent behaviour coming from humans. And as we saw in Chapters 3 and 4, in feral and free-ranging horses such behaviour is minimal, except among rival stallions; it is only in horses kept in restricted environments, in unbalanced groups, that we see kicking and biting to any significant degree.

The brutal approach

Some of the techniques used by trainers in what are often referred to as 'dominance reduction' programs for dogs are, thankfully, not available to trainers of horses. It would be very difficult, if not impossible, for example, to get hold of a horse by the scruff of the neck or by the jowls (as some trainers have been advising dog owners to do for decades) and give him a good shake, or (heaven forbid!) half strangle him in order to show 'who's boss'.[4] I was about to cite the infamous 'alpha roll' (where the owner rolls the dog over on his back and pins him down to force 'submission') as another example of something we can't do with horses; but of course we can. I would like to be able to say that the very dangerous practice of casting a horse on the ground to make him submit is no longer carried out, but there is some evidence that it is. In the 1990s Nicholas Evans reputedly consulted a horse trainer about the training methods used to rehabilitate a traumatized horse for his book *The Horse Whisperer*. At the end of his rehabilitation program the 'horse whisperer' of the title forces the horse to lie down by means of ropes. When the horse's owner protests, the trainer's assistant tells her, 'He's got to lie down.' (Evans, 1995) No explanation is given regarding why this was either a necessary or even a desirable outcome; presumably Evans and/or his adviser felt readers would understand, even though their reasoning is far from obvious to anyone not well-versed in the whole dominance myth.[5]

Natural horsemanship practitioner John Lyons was strongly critical of this sequence in the film that was subsequently made of the book, arguing that the risk of injury to both horse and human in such a method is considerable. Monty Roberts, inaccurately supposed by some to have been the inspiration for the trainer in the book, has also condemned this practice on a number of occasions, saying that he would never cast a horse like this and that he would not recommend it to anyone else either. Unfortunately there are some people who have such bizarre ideas about natural horse behaviour that they not only recommend it, but they also go one stage further.

---
3 Although if she did not then *stop* backing up in response to the punch on the nose, the trainer's action was not punishment: it was simply abuse. See under Punishment in the next chapter.
4 Alexandra Semyonova gives a chilling example of this in her book *100 Silliest Things People Say About Dogs*.
5 It is actually a form of 'flooding' leading to learned helplessness; see Chapter 9 and page 150 in this chapter.

In 2003 a query was posted on TheHorse.com, a website which features news and veterinary-approved articles on equine health care from *The Horse* magazine. The enquirer explained that she and her boyfriend had been talking to an old-time horseman about their two-year-old colt. This man described what to do with tough stallions to get them to 'settle down and submit'. He said that the best way was to tie the horse up and flip them over onto the ground so that they are unable to get away. Then, he said, 'you get into them pretty bad' – by which he meant beat the horse up – until they give in from exhaustion; then you (and this obviously applies to men!) stand over them and urinate on them. He said that this works because this is what stallions do to each other in the wild – one would beat the other up and then urinate on him as the ultimate humiliation.

I wish I could say I was making this up, but Dr Sue McDonnell – who dispenses much excellent and sensible advice on TheHorse.com – confirmed that although the immobilization and beating is a sad old-timer technique, she had never heard of a method that included the urination, until a few years prior to the query, when she had met someone who had a similarly shocking method. Fortunately Dr McDonnell was able to reassure the enquirer that while stallions certainly fight, urination on a defeated rival is *not* part of their behavioural repertoire. Speaking of the advice given by the 'old-time horseman' advice, she said, 'In my opinion, this is the act of a desperate and poorly informed "wannabe" horseman.' (McDonnell, 2003) Sadly, there are all too many such 'wannabes' out there, and while their 'advice' may not always be as bizarre and extreme as this man's, it can often be distressingly brutal, inhumane and unethical.

Creating conflict

In any case, as I observed earlier horses do not threaten other horses (or bite, kick or shove each other around) in order to teach them anything except 'Go away!' (or, as it may be, 'Stop that!'). And remember that, lacking formal displays by which they can acknowledge the dominance of another, horses can only move away (which is not very useful if we want them to stay with us so that we can train them) or, alternatively, defend themselves. So if a trainer is holding a horse by means of a rope or any other method of restraint, the horse is thereby deprived of the *only means he has* of acknowledging the human's dominance – assuming, of course, that that is how he would interpret it anyway – which is by no means certain. As Abigail Hogg points out in her book, *The Horse Behaviour Handbook*, the fact that horses move away from threats by other horses does not necessarily imply that by moving away they have accepted the other horse's authority over them – it just means they have got out of the way. (Hogg, 2003)

The conflict created by such an approach is also illustrated by Abigail Hogg:

> We act aggressively and exert dominance *while keeping the animal with us*. The horse, whose first action is to move away from aggression and who understands that this is what is required of him by the situation, is actually being punished while at the same time being deprived of the ability to carry out the correct course of action. (Hogg, 2003)

The only other course of action open to the horse is to retaliate. That more horses do not do so in such a situation is a tribute to the patience and forbearance of horses, most of whom seem to do their best to make sense of what the trainer is asking of them. However, some horses do retaliate, and the consequences can be severe, especially when the horse is a stallion. I have personally witnessed attacks on handlers by stallions driven to despair by the relentless attempts of their handlers to 'dominate' them; fortunately in these cases the handlers were not severely injured, but there have been many other cases where the handlers were not so fortunate, and some of them have even been killed.

Some horses panic when faced with such conflict. The commentator who described the filly being punched on the nose says that on another occasion, during a training session using the same principles, a panicked horse dragged the trainer several hundred yards across a field on the end of a long rope after he had failed to send the horse into a trailer of which he or she was afraid. (Arab Horse Society News, 2006)

Learned helplessness

The use of methods which create conflict may induce in certain horses a state of what is known as 'learned helplessness'. This term was introduced by the psychologist Martin Seligman in the 1970s. Seligman demonstrated that animals placed in an experimental position in which they cannot avoid something unpleasant (such as an electric shock) no matter what they do, will later generalize their experiences in situations where they are powerless to situations in which they *could* act to avoid unpleasantness or even life-threatening situations, but they fail to do so. In other words, they have been trained to be helpless.

Seligman's theories have not gone unchallenged, especially as other experiments have shown that learned helplessness may be a temporary state, which resolves itself after a comparatively short period of time (sometimes as little as forty-eight hours). Some other researchers believe that learned helplessness is produced by some form of debilitation induced by stress, and that it is a short-term physiological imbalance that is self-correcting with the passage of time.

Even so, it is easy to see how the concept of learned helplessness can apply to certain horses subjected to the kind of situation described above, where the trainer employs aggressive body language or physical punishment but gives the horse no opportunity to move right away (for example because he is held on a rope or confined in a pen, round or otherwise; or restrained by a rope round a foreleg, or even cast on the ground – surely, from the horse's point of view, a truly terrifying situation to be in). Such horses could well fall into – and remain in – a state of learned helplessness, especially if they learn from such experiences that there is nothing they can do to avoid the situation. This would mean that their natural flight responses would be suppressed, resulting in a horse that to all outward appearances is exceptionally obedient, but which is in fact in a state of induced helplessness. Indeed, we can see this in all too many horses trained by such methods; they appear 'shut down' even to the inexperienced but perceptive eye.

The 'shut-down' horse

Unfortunately, it seems that such shut-down horses are what an increasing number of people want. They are led to believe that if only they follow such-and such a training method, they will end up with a totally 'bomb proof' horse. This has often resulted in unrealistic expectations on the part of students of these methods. Many of them end up believing that, unless their horse behaves perfectly at all times, they have somehow failed. We certainly want our horses to have good manners and to be calm and confident, so that they do not continually spook at imaginary monsters in the hedge, or panic whenever anything unusual happens. But reactivity is so much a part of the horse's psychological make-up that the only way we could overcome it completely would be to suppress every aspect of behaviour that makes a horse a horse and not some other mammal. Attempts to create the 'super-obedient' horse can, as we have seen, result in the use of oppressive methods which create superficially obedient horses existing in a state of perpetual anxiety, unable to relax for fear of making a mistake; they may perform mechanically, with all spontaneity trained out of them.

It is also a potentially dangerous and possibly unethical way of dealing with problem behaviours. There is a widespread failure to investigate the causes of such behaviours; too often, trainers (and their pupils) attribute them to the above-mentioned lack of 'respect' for the handler, or to the horse being, or attempting to be, 'dominant'. I have heard these explanations for almost every type of 'problem' behaviour (which is frequently not a problem to the horse, only to the handler), including head-tossing (which, depending on the context, may have a variety of causes, all of them physical). Any trainer worth his or her salt will *first of all* make sure that any behavioural problems are not being caused by some physical factor such as pain – by far the commonest cause of such problems. Fear, learned behaviour in response to a specific situation, stress created by inadequate/inappropriate management, and so on – these are all possible causes of problem behaviour, which will be dealt with in Chapter 11. Ignoring these possibilities in favour of explanations such as 'disrespect' or 'dominance' not only shows a lack of real understanding of equine behaviour, but it may also compromise the horse's welfare.

The dangers of suppression

The danger inherent in this approach should be obvious: a behaviour that is merely suppressed, no matter how this is done,[6] may resurface at any time if the pressures of keeping it suppressed are great enough – and only the horse knows when this point has been reached, making the reoccurrence unpredictable. Furthermore, whoever is handling the horse may have developed a false sense of security through the belief that the horse's behaviour is now 'cured', and so may be totally unprepared for this sudden resurgence of the problem. Alternatively, the original behaviour may be replaced by another, equally (or even more) undesirable behaviour; this phenomenon has often been observed when punishment is used to try to cure a problem.

These warnings are especially relevant when one is dealing with a stallion, who – because of his natural role as defender of his family group and the increased vigilance this requires – is more likely to be reactive and ready to engage in either flight or, if that proves impossible, to fight. The latter is a very real possibility, as the examples given earlier in this chapter show. And, because they tend to be more emotional than either mares or geldings, the likelihood of suppressed behaviour resurfacing in stallions is correspondingly higher.

Please note that I am not saying there is *never* a place for either punishment or 'getting tough' with a horse – even a stallion. Horses need to learn boundaries, and there may be occasions – especially with bumptious colts – where the proverbial 'short, sharp shock' is appropriate. I explain in Chapters 9 and 11 how and when these might be appropriate. But such an approach must never become a method in itself, or indeed, any more than a temporary response until you can work out a permanent solution. Otherwise it simply becomes another form of coercion and even brutality, especially when (as is, unfortunately, so often the case) it is accompanied by poor timing and a failure to understand how punishment works.

The effects of stress on the ability to learn

This can result in acute stress, which not only has an adverse effect on the horse's wellbeing, but also affects his ability to learn. It has been established beyond doubt that stress inhibits the learning process. It makes concentrating on a task difficult and sometimes impossible. If the stressor is

---

6 Behaviour suppression can also be achieved not just by dominance-based training, but also by the misuse of positive reinforcement, although this is not so common. For more about this, see the next chapter.

strong enough, the brain can seem to 'freeze', as if all its attention is concentrated on whatever is causing the stress. From my schooldays I have a vivid memory of a classroom situation in which a teacher of whom I was afraid came and stood behind me, looking over my shoulder as I attempted to write the answer to a question which I should have found easy. Stressed by the presence of the teacher behind me, I couldn't write a thing; I couldn't even think. The fear of 'getting it wrong' paralysed my thought processes. Imagine what it must be like, then, for a horse who – no matter how clever he may be – has to work much harder to understand what a human wants than I did to understand what my teacher wanted. Expecting a horse to learn when under stress is simply unfair and, to my mind, unethical.

And the effects of stress on the ability to learn may be far greater than was previously believed. Researchers have found that acute short-term stress can impair brain-cell communication in areas associated with learning and memory. Brain cells (neurons, which are actually found throughout the central nervous system, not just the brain) communicate with each other via junctions known as *synapses*. These synapses are situated on branchlike structures protruding from neurons, called *dendritic spines*, and it is at the synapses that learning and memory take place. Acute stress activates a hormone known as CRH (corticotrophin-releasing hormone), a *neurotransmitter*[7] activated by acute stress. The release of CRH in the brain's principal learning and memory centre, the hippocampus, causes the dendritic spines to disintegrate, limiting the ability of the synapses to collect and store memories, or even preventing such collection altogether. In this way, the ability to learn and to remember is severely compromised. (Chen, 2008). No matter what training approach we use, then, we must use it in a way that minimizes stress, otherwise the horse may learn slowly, or not at all.

Meaning well is not enough

I am sure that most of the people who opt to use dominance-based methods of training are sincere in their belief that this is the most – if not the only – effective way to manage horses, especially with regard to staying safe around them. They want to do well by their horse(s) and believe that such methods are not detrimental to the horse. Unfortunately, believing something, however sincerely, does not make it so, and their beliefs, no matter how well-meant they may be, are irrelevant to the horse; it is the effect of our actions on the horse that matter to him, not the intent behind them. If these actions are not informed by a thorough understanding of the learning processes that are universal to all animals, no matter what their species may be, then the results may end up being disastrous, for both horse and handler.

Responding through learning

The belief that horses behave in certain ways because they are trying to establish their 'dominance' over us (in the social sense, not simply in the sense of being in control) is seriously flawed, as the evidence set out in this chapter and in Chapter 5 shows. Having looked at how horses actually do organize their social lives, we can see that it is extremely unlikely that they see that organization in terms of social status. It is equally unlikely that they spend any of their time plotting to increase their social status in respect of the humans who train and care for them. Instead, they develop behavioural responses to conspecifics, humans, and events by means of the learning processes which are universal to all animals (and which will be covered in more detail in Chapter 9).

For example, consider the horse (and of course this applies to many stallions) who is kept stabled for most of the time. Say he has been kept cooped up in his stable for 23 hours, and the time comes

---

7 Neurotransmitters are chemical substances which relay signals between neurons.

for him to be let out in the field for an hour. The halter is put on, and the lead-rope clipped onto it. The door is opened, and the handler proceeds to lead the horse out. He is excited – perhaps over-excited – to be out of his stable. In his excitement, he barges out of the stable and either bowls his handler over or drags her along at the end of the lead-rope. He is out! He has learned, in that one session (for as we shall see, horses are excellent one-time learners) that if he barges through the door and pushes his handler aside, he will be let out. Now suppose the handler does not know how to prevent him from doing this again; he repeats the behaviour the next time he is taken out of his stable, and the next time...and before long, his bargy behaviour becomes established.

Is this horse being 'dominant'? No – except in the very specific sense of having controlled the situation. He is not establishing his social status over the handler, he is simply doing what he has learned to do in order to achieve something he finds rewarding – freedom! But the handler now has a problem: she cannot take the horse out of his stable without him barging and possibly knocking her flying; not, we all agree, a happy state of affairs. So the handler consults a trainer who, she is assured, knows all about dealing with problem horses. This trainer looks at the problem (which is actually the handler's, not the horse's – *he* doesn't have a problem with his behaviour) and shakes his head: this is a dominant, disrespectful horse, who will end up killing someone if his behaviour isn't corrected. So the trainer proceeds to 'correct' the horse using aggressive techniques to establish his status as the 'alpha horse'. This might, as I said earlier, produce a horse who appears compliant, thus enabling the trainer to proclaim the success of his techniques. However, it might not.

Our hypothetical horse, on being threatened by this puny human, might feel as though his life is in danger; he could well resort to defensive actions such as running away, kicking, biting, striking out or charging at his handler. Sometimes the threatening actions of the trainer take the horse so much by surprise that he becomes deceptively docile, only for his defensive behaviours to erupt once the trainer is replaced by his normal handler (or indeed, anyone else).

But what else could the handler have done to prevent the horse's behaviour from becoming dangerous? I am often asked this by people who only know punitive methods of dealing with such behaviour. The answer is: plenty! The long-term solution would be to allow the horse more freedom to run around, to play with conspecifics (or other field-companions) so that he does not become stressed by confinement[8] or over-excited at the idea of being taken out of his stable. In the short-term, the handler (or any trainer brought in to solve the problem) could wait until the horse had been out in the field long enough for his high spirits to wear off, then bring him in and, in an atmosphere of calm and quiet, use positive reinforcement (defined in the next chapter) to teach the horse first of all to stand calmly in his stable while his halter and lead-rope are put on, then to stand calmly while the handler opens the door, and then to walk quietly beside her to wherever his turn-out area might be. Provided the handler understands how essential good timing is, and knows how to break the learning sessions down into easy steps, this whole process is very easy, non-confrontational, pleasant for both horse and handler, and produces no unwanted side-effects such as the defensive behaviour so often provoked by training based on the 'dominance model'. The horse is not rushed; he is allowed to understand, and learn what the handler wants him to do, without conflict and without any pressure.

Establishing a bond

Ironically, there *are* aspects of equine social behaviour that we can use to establish a bond with horses. When we groom a horse, we are (whether deliberately or not) imitating the actions of an equine grooming partner – except that we may not wish the horse being groomed to reciprocate,

8   See Chapter 11 for more information about management-related stress and its effects on the horse.

The Natural Stallion

as another horse would! And in fact most horses do learn to inhibit this natural response, whether because they are discouraged from responding, or whether they recognize that there *is* a difference (the actions of a brush may not feel anything like the actions of a conspecific's teeth and lips, for example). However, in some Middle Eastern countries the *sā'is*[9] would traditionally groom a horse with his (or her – among the Bedouin it was often the women who cared for the horses) fingers. This seems to emulate the actions of another horse much more closely than grooming with a brush, and horses groomed in this way will often respond by trying to groom the groomer.[10]

Both our stallions can be groomed in this manner, and both are very polite about it. They have been taught that while gentle (or even quite vigorous) nibbling is tolerated, anything too rough will result in the loss of their grooming partner (me – or my husband), who will simply move away. This incidentally proves that allowing stallions to nibble will *not* automatically result in a habit of savage biting. I have been allowing mutual grooming with our senior stallion, Nivalis, for all of his 16 years, and not once has he even nipped me in the course of such a grooming session. In fact, he is so gentle with his lips that a neck massage from him is a real treat (see the photograph on page 155). Of course, you have to have established a real bond with your stallion, together with rules of acceptable behaviour, before you can safely do this; not all stallions are as gentle as Nivalis. (His son, four years old at the time of writing, has not yet learned to be quite so gentle, but he is getting there.) With some stallions you may never be able to do this, and with some you would be foolish even to try; much depends on their individual characters and previous experiences. It is, however, a very effective way of strengthening the bond between horse and handler. It is really quite touching when a horse asks you to groom him in this way.

Left: Brian and Nivalis enjoy a mutual scratch.

Right: Nivalis's expression leaves us in no doubt that he is enjoying this scratch on a hard-to reach spot.

Photos: Lesley Skipper

Some trainers believe that if we allow horses to make the first move and initiate bodily contact with us, we are allowing them to dominate us. This evidently stems from the belief that when two horses indulge in mutual grooming, it is always the dominant horse of the pair who initiates the

---
9 The Arabic word for the person who takes care of a horse.
10 This is not a case of the horse treating the human like another horse; the 'reciprocal grooming' response seems to be a reflex response to being groomed. If the horse being groomed like this cannot reach the groomer, he will often 'groom' nearby objects such as the stable door, a wall, his manger, etc.

This was the first time Nivalis had had anyone on his back. Joanne is scratching his withers, and Nivalis is responding by 'massaging' Brian's neck. Photo: Lesley Skipper

grooming. Is this true? In my experience it is not; much depends on the context and (as always) on the individual horses concerned. There is also the conflicting belief that mutual grooming is principally a way of reducing or avoiding aggression, so it will be the subordinate who initiates the grooming sessions; this shows how confused and confusing the whole issue really is. Many years ago I used to worry about this, and almost stopped initiating mutual grooming sessions with my horse. Thank goodness I did not, or I would have missed one of the most rewarding experiences one can have with a horse. In fact, in most feral bands, virtually any horse may initiate grooming with any other horse and this is what I have found with regard to our own horses.

Nivalis is often allowed to roam around the yard freely when we are working there; he can socialize with any horses who happen to be in, nibble at hay, or interact with us as we work. Sometimes, when he wants a scratch, he will come up to me and 'ask' to be groomed: he sidles up to me, as he would to another horse, positioning himself so that I am presented with whatever part of his anatomy needs scratching. Note that this is *learned* behaviour; he is not thinking of me as another horse, because a) I don't look or smell right, and b) I don't have the same physical equipment as another horse; for example, I can't use my teeth in the way another horse would (in the interest of science, I tried, once, to groom another horse with my teeth; all I got was a mouthful of loose hair). If we had not already established our mutual grooming routine, Nivalis would have no way of knowing that I understand from his actions a) that he wants a scratch, and b) that I understand where he wants scratching.

Interacting within personal space

Many people will no doubt think that we are asking for trouble, encouraging a stallion to interact so freely, invading my personal space uninvited. But they would be missing the point. If we look back to Chapter 4, we can see that horses admit close friends into the inner area of their personal space. This requires that they have first established their relationship with each other – I don't mean in the sense of establishing a dominance relationship, because, as we have also seen, horses generally avoid the dominant animal in such a relationship. I mean that they know each other well enough to predict how the other will behave, and this knowledge enables them to interact at close quarters without the fear that one of them will behave badly towards the other. This is the kind of relationship we have established with our stallions, especially Nivalis.[11] It is easy enough to teach a horse not

---

11 His son, Rigel (stable name Jas) has not quite reached the same level as his father in this respect. Being at the time of writing just four years old, he is still, as we say, 'young and daft'. But he is so easy to manage that this is not as much of an issue as it might be with another horse, and in the meantime his education progresses at a rate that suits his stage of development.

The Natural Stallion

to invade a human's personal space uninvited, using the kind of control cues described below. See Chapter 11, pages 235-236 for more about this.

Nivalis scratching his leg on Brian's foot. Many people would be horrified by the idea of allowing a stallion the freedom to do this. However, we can give Nivalis this kind of freedom because we have established the kind of relationship with him that allows a high degree of mutual trust. Photo: Lesley Skipper

Control cues and formal/informal contexts

We – that is, my husband and I – have trained Nivalis to respond instantly to certain cues. If he starts to become unacceptably boisterous, whether in his stable or outside, we only have to say, 'Nivalis – stand!' and he does – stock-still. He is so good at this that we can ask him to stand in his stable, leave the door open, and go away – and he will keep standing there until we give the release, which is to clap our hands and say, 'Ok!' It would be easy to abuse this by making him stand for long periods of time, so we never ask him to stand for more than a minute or so. But it has been an invaluable means of control in difficult situations – for example, during veterinary procedures, on the rare occasions when we cover mares in-hand, and during potentially dangerous situations, such as occurred once when he was being lunged (not by me or my husband). During the course of the lunge session Nivalis became upset by some horses galloping about in the field next door. The person lunging, startled by Nivalis's reaction, let go of the lunge line. Frightened, Nivalis ran across the *manège* with the lunge-line wrapped round his legs. I yelled, 'Nivalis – stand!'[12] and he stopped immediately, standing still (though still frightened) while I untangled the lunge-line from his legs.

Having control cues like this (and there are many others one can devise) to fall back on in this way means that one can be fairly relaxed in situations which do not actually require such absolute control. Dr Ian Dunbar, renowned for his work with dogs, uses what he calls 'formal names' and 'formal obedience commands' for situations which *do* require such a degree of control. So, for example, in a relaxed situation, Dunbar might say to one of his dogs, 'Hugey, come 'ere' – which the dog may obey or not, as it is a suggestion, not a command. But where absolute compliance is essential, Dunbar would say, 'Hugo Louis, come!' and calmly insist that the dog complies. (Dunbar, 2010) Reading the excellent article in which he describes this, I suddenly realized that that this was, in effect, what we had been doing with our horses for years, except that I had never formalized it in my mind in quite that way. So I might say, 'Come on, Niv' if I want Nivalis to come up to me in his stable, in the yard, or in the field (for a scratch, a bit of mutual grooming, or just to spend time together). However, in a situation where I need control, I would say in a firm tone of voice,

---

12 Care needs to be taken when using a control cue in this manner. If my yelling at Nivalis had upset him (it didn't) he might start to associate the use of the cue (or his name) with something unpleasant. It would then cease to be effective. See Chapter 9, **The poisoned cue.**

'Nivalis – come!'. (In exactly the same way we might say to our Border Collie x GSD Jasper, 'Here, Jasp' or, 'Jasper – come!' depending on the context.) Horses and dogs are both perfectly capable of understanding – and responding to – the different forms of address in different contexts. Being able to differentiate in this manner releases horses (and dogs) and their handlers from the straitjacket imposed by insisting on absolute obedience at all times. Of course one must be consistent in the use of different forms of address – but that applies to *any* cues or commands used in training animals. And allowing such freedom is certainly not being permissive – on the contrary, it relies on ground rules for behaviour having been established from the start.

If simply asked to 'stand', Nivalis will continue standing in his stable, even with the door wide open as in this photograph, until given the release. We have to take care not to abuse this by asking him to stand for too long, or without a purpose. Photo: Lesley Skipper

Respect and disrespect

Note that I have not said anything about respect forming part of this relationship. 'Respect', like its antithesis, *dis*respect, has been used so indiscriminately (and frequently *mis*-used) in the context of training and managing horses that it is now virtually meaningless, a buzz-word trotted out without regard to whether it is actually appropriate or not. There are several dictionary definitions of 'respect', but the only one truly relevant to our relationship with horses is 'polite or kind regard' (Collins English Dictionary, definition (5)). We can be polite with our horses – and teach them to be polite with us – without invoking concepts of dominance or absolute submission.

A narrow range of options

One of the most detrimental effects of this obsession with dominance is that by focusing on a very narrow range of options it deprives us of many excellent training tools. As Mark Twain is reputed to have said, 'When all you have is a hammer, all problems start to look like nails.' This leaves us with

The Natural Stallion

nothing to fall back on when efforts fail (as they surely will, at some point). It is at this stage that so many people, frustrated by their lack of progress, start to punish the horse for not understanding.[13]

The risks of aversive training techniques

This is a subject covered in the next chapter, but here I want to reiterate several points about the kind of aversive techniques that dominance-based training commonly involves. Such techniques carry with them the very strong risk that

- ◊ The horse will be confused about which behaviour is required

- ◊ The training will inhibit specific behaviours, but fail to address the underlying cause(s), increasing the chances of further problems occurring

- ◊ It will create fear and anxiety, preventing the horse from learning effectively, or even at all

- ◊ The horse will associate other, unrelated but coincidentally present or occurring events, people, other horses or surroundings with the fear and anxiety provoked by the training, causing problematic behaviour in connection with those other factors in the future

- ◊ The horse will respond aggressively, or find new ways to resist

- ◊ Physical injury to the horse and/or handler may occur

Letting go

Letting go of ideas of dominance forces us to think hard about what we are actually teaching our horses, and how the learning process works. Instead of relying on woolly ideas about equine society, we can start to use the principles of learning – outlined in the next chapter – to be absolutely clear what we want to achieve with our horses and how we can achieve it without the use of force or any undue stress to the horse.

---

13 Devotees of the training philosophy described in this chapter tend to protest that this does not happen, even when confronted by evidence caught on video. This denial is an effect of the 'cognitive dissonance' described in the Conclusion.

Chapter 8

Brian demonstrates the high degree of trust he has in Nivalis. Please DON'T try this: it entails considerable risks, even with good-natured, well-trained horse. Brian is fully aware of the risks and chose to take them in order to show what is possible when you have the kind of relationship he has with Nivalis. Photos: Lesley Skipper

CHAPTER 9

Training principles

In nature there are neither rewards nor punishments – there are consequences.
– Robert Greene Ingersoll, Lectures & Essays

By now, it should be clear that if we want to establish a good relationship with a stallion, and to be able to train and manage him safely and in such a way that he is not only easy to manage but regards his handler as someone whose company he enjoys, and with whom he is eager to co-operate, we have to look at scientifically proven principles and learn how to employ them correctly.

It was not until the nineteenth and twentieth centuries that the different components of learning were established scientifically. Nevertheless, there have always been horse trainers who have had an instinctive understanding of learning processes, even if they were not able to define how these worked. However, for every such trainer there are many others who create problems because they do not have sufficient understanding. Yet an understanding of how animals learn is essential if we are to avoid problems with the training and management of stallions. People who take the trouble to learn about, and understand, those principles, will find that the process of training and managing their stallions becomes much easier and more pleasant – for horses and trainers alike.

Alpha intelligence?

There is one idea which I should like to dispose of before going any further. The obsession with dominance has led a number of people astray when it comes to assessing a horse's 'trainability'. Just as many people assume that the horse at the top of a dominance hierarchy is going to be the leader, there is also a tendency to assume that dominance equates to intelligence. One trainer asserts that 'The dominant horse is the most intelligent, and as a result they are usually quick learners.' (Hudson, 2004) There is no definition of 'intelligent' given here, but however one defines intelligence, is there any truth in this writer's assertion? Scientific studies carried out so far have found no correlation between social dominance and learning ability (Mader and Price, 1980). I do not think it is at all helpful to make prior assumptions about intelligence and learning ability; any assessment of trainability must be based on knowledge of the individual horse and not on unexamined dogma.

A huge amount of research into learning processes, carried on throughout the 20th century and continuing into the twenty-first, has revealed that all animals – not just horses – learn in the same ways. The strengths of some species may lie in different areas of learning than others, but essentially the processes are the same. Different modes of learning have been identified, all of which are important to everyone concerned with the care and training of horses.

Imprinting

The earliest form of learning that newly-born foals encounter is *imprinting*.[1] This is how animals learn their species identity. It is nature's way of ensuring that a duck knows he is a duck, a goat that she is a goat, and a horse that he is a horse. The image of the mother is 'imprinted' on the baby's brain, so that it knows who she is and will not try to follow either another individual of the same species, or an animal of a different species, which in some cases could be fatal. In his delightful book *King Solomon's Ring* Konrad Lorenz gives some hilarious descriptions of birds who, having imprinted on him, proceeded to treat him as another bird and would try to feed him worms and other choice morsels.

At one time ethologists thought that the imprinting process was irreversible but, although this may be true of some species of birds, it is not so with many other birds and mammals. However, there is a period during which the imprinting must take place or it will not happen at all: this is often referred to as the 'sensitive period';[2] in horses it appears to start during the second hour following birth and may last for up to twenty-four hours, although the length of time involved is not known precisely. (Waring, 1983)

Learning about the environment

Having learned who his mother is and how to move around without falling over, the foal must then learn all kinds of things about his environment. We absorb all kinds of information about our surroundings and the people we associate with; so do horses.

> We all know that the horse manages to remember routes and particularly the way home. The feral equine *knows* about his home area and where he is in it and much about this has not been conditioned learning; it has been the absorption of information without conditioning. This has been called "silent learning". (Kiley-Worthington, 1997)

Horses are particularly good at this kind of learning, which is also called latent learning. There is no apparent reinforcement going on; such learning just 'happens'.

Insight learning

Horses are not so good, however, at what is called 'insight' learning, which bypasses normal 'trial and error' learning: sudden realization of the answer to a problem. Humans are great solvers of the kind of problems that require insight, partly because of our manipulative ability; horses in the wild would have little need to tackle this kind of problem. Their talents lie elsewhere, and we should not judge them as lacking intelligence because of that. However as Lucy Rees points out, some horses, particularly bright youngsters, sometimes do show insight on being given new cues for the first time. Such horses may readily make the connection between the cue and the required response –

---

1 In the 1990s an American veterinary surgeon, Dr Robert Miller, devised a technique which he believed mirrored the imprinting process. According to Miller, if a foal is intensively handled during the first few hours after birth this will make later handling easy and render the horse more trainable. This technique has been heavily criticized and in any case is not true imprinting; see my book *Let Horses Be Horses*, Chapter 9, for more about this.
2 In some older ethological literature this is referred to as the 'critical period'

much depends on how calm the horse is, and how attentive he is to his handler or trainer. (Rees, The Horse's Mind, 1984)

Social learning

Clearly, horses learn from their environment, but do they learn from each other? There is a great deal of controversy about whether horses do learn by direct observation. Relatively few studies have been made of this type of learning; two of these (Baer et al.,1983, and Baker and Crawford, 1986) concluded that horses allowed to watch a 'demonstrator' horse perform a task did not learn the task any more quickly than horses which did not watch the demonstrator. A group at the University of Bristol veterinary school designed an experiment to investigate this type of learning (called *social learning*), which tested the ability of two groups of horses to learn from a 'demonstrator' horse always to choose a certain coloured bucket to eat from, rather than a different one. The test group, which was allowed to watch the demonstrator horse, learned to approach the buckets much more quickly than the control group, which was not allowed to watch the demonstrator. However their choice of buckets was random, as was the control group's. So although they had learned from the demonstrator horse how to enhance their foraging skills, they had not learned to discriminate between the buckets. Paul McGreevy, who was involved in this experiment, believes that it was possible the experiment was not designed well enough to allow what he calls 'discriminative social learning'; he believes that one day a demonstration system that is more 'user friendly' for the observer horses may well show more positive results. (McGreevy, 1996) And in fact Marthe Kiley-Worthington has demonstrated, albeit not in a strictly controlled experiment, that horses can learn from observing each other (Kiley-Worthington, 2005).

One-trial learning

One ability horses do possess in a high degree is that of 'one-trial learning' – that is, they can learn after only one experience.[3] This is a particularly valuable trait for a prey animal to possess; after all, a predator can make mistakes in hunting and live to hunt again, but a wild horse would need to learn fast which animals and places to avoid, and how to escape from danger, otherwise he or she might simply be dead. Second chances, while they may be forthcoming, cannot be relied upon.

This can work for us, who seek to train horses, or it can work against us. The horse can learn bad things just as easily as he can learn desirable things; one careless error may affect a horse, in some cases for the rest of his life, in others, certainly for a very long time.

Habituation

Horses, like other animals, have to learn what elements in their environment are worthy of their fear, and what may be safely ignored – in other words, they grow accustomed, or *habituated* to things which would otherwise cause constant alarm. Habituation can be an extremely useful tool in training horses; by gradually introducing a horse to scary objects such as rustling bags, washing flapping on clothes lines, bicycles, tractors with the engine running etc. we can get him accustomed to the idea that they are not so scary after all and eventually he will ignore them. If this process is carried out too quickly the reverse may occur and the horse, instead of getting used to scary objects,

---

[3] Not all horses will respond in the same way; for example, some horses may learn to fear travelling in a horsebox after only one bad experience, while others might not be so affected, or might only come to fear travelling after several bad experiences. As always, much depends on the character of the individual horse.

sees them as an object of even greater fear; this is known as *sensitization*. Care must therefore be taken not to rush the habituation process.

Flooding

The technique known as *flooding*, mentioned in the previous chapter, is sometimes used in the treatment of human phobias; it involves exposing the person to whatever their phobia is centred on, without possibility of escape, until they become habituated to it. An example might be making someone suffering from a phobia about spiders hold a large spider in their hand, or submit to having spiders crawl all over them, until they become de-sensitized and no longer fear spiders. This technique can be successful in some cases but appears to work mainly with people who were not very anxious about their phobia in the first place. With others, if the anxiety level is too high, the subject may either terminate the session or simply 'switch off'. This means that the phobia is not cured, it is just being temporarily 'shelved' and may break out anew in a sufficiently frightening situation. It therefore carries its fair share of risks when used on humans and these risks are compounded with animals, as they cannot tell us just how anxious they really are in the first place. Flooding can therefore actually increase the degree of fear, sometimes to the point where the animal collapses. Because of these dangers it is not generally recommended in the training of animals, although some trainers do make use of it; some 'natural horsemanship' techniques are akin to flooding (for example, some f the techniques mentioned in Chapter 8).[4] Gradual desensitization to potentially frightening objects and situations, as described in Chapters 10 and 11, is preferable by far.

Disconnected brains?

Horses may appear not to connect something they have seen, say, on their left, with the same object when they pass it again on their right. Many people believe that the two halves of the equine brain are imperfectly connected, and that the two sides of a horse's brain do not communicate effectively. So, we are told, we have to teach the horse everything twice, once for each side. In fact, there is no physiological reason why the two halves should not communicate just as well as they do in human brains. Indeed, experiments carried out by Dr Evelyn Hanggi in the USA have shown that horses can certainly transfer information efficiently from one side of the brain to the other (Hanggi, 1999). The apparent disconnection between left and right may have more to do with the way horses see things than with anything else. Because their range of binocular vision is limited in comparison with ours, it may well be that they do not immediately make the connection between an object seen from one side, and later from the other (try looking at a reversed image of a familiar scene, and you too may experience an initial lack of recognition). Or it could be that they did not pay sufficient attention to it in the first place.

In addition horses, like humans, are usually right- or left- 'handed': that is, they are more supple on one side than the other. So in ridden work it is one-sidedness, not an imperfectly joined brain, that prevents them from performing equally well on both reins.

Conditioning

Every time we interact with a horse, whether we are aware of it or not, we are training him. Suppose a horse is anticipating his feed, and in his excitement he bangs on his door. Wanting him to stop, his

---

4 See also Chapter 9 of *Let Horses Be Horses*, where I talk about flooding in the context of 'imprint' training. See also Chapter 10, **Teaching a foal to accept a headcollar.**

owner rushes over to give him his feed. Unknowingly, she has just trained him to do the opposite of what she wants: in other words, to bang on his door. If the horse never receives feed again while banging on the door, the door banging may eventually stop; however, if the owner repeatedly rushes over to feed the horse when he bangs on the door, he will continue to bang, as it has got him what he wanted. The feed has *reinforced* the action which preceded it, i.e. banging on the door.

This is the process known as *conditioning*, and as this example shows, it can occur even when we don't want it to. Many behavioural problems are actually created in this way, because the people handling the horse in question have not been aware of the effects of their own actions. Learning theory revolves around the process of conditioning, and it represents the single most powerful tool we have in the training and management of animals (and other humans).

Classical conditioning

There are two types of conditioning: *classical* and *operant*. The most famous example of classical conditioning comes from experiments carried out by the Russian physiologist I.P. Pavlov with dogs. Pavlov trained the dogs to associate being fed with the ringing of a bell; eventually the sound of the bell alone was sufficient to make the dogs salivate in anticipation. Many humans will have developed a dislike of certain places, sights, sounds or smells because they are associated with some unpleasant experience. In the same way horses may come to associate certain places or objects with something alarming. For example, a horse who has happily gone past a gateway for years may have a frightening experience there – perhaps a dog rushes out barking, or a plastic bag in the hedge flaps and gives the horse a fright. The horse subsequently refuses to approach that gateway, even though whatever frightened him may no longer be there; he has been 'conditioned' to fear it. Understanding this helps to explain a great deal of equine behaviour.

Operant conditioning

Operant conditioning is based on *consequences*; it occurs when the subject performs a behaviour (i.e. *operates* within the environment) in response to a cue or *stimulus*, which has a certain consequence; the nature of that consequence increases the probability that the subject will repeat the behaviour which led to the consequence. This is known as a *reinforcer*. In the example above, the consequence was that the horse got fed when he banged on the door; the feed was therefore the reinforcer for the behaviour.

Reinforcers

Reinforcers can be *positive* or *negative*. In positive reinforcement, the reinforcer consists of something the subject wants or likes; in the case of horses this might be a food treat, a scratch or a rub, or indeed anything else that particular horse would find rewarding. Negative reinforcement consists of the removal of something the subject wants to avoid. With horses this commonly consists of pressure of some kind. This could be something unpleasant, such as strong pressure on the bit, or it could be very mild pressure, such as a light touch of the rider's leg. Another example might be asking the horse to step back by means of backward pressure on the headcollar. Immediately the horse complies the pressure is released; this is the reinforcer.

A stimulus or cue such as the pressure referred to above is often referred to as an *aversive* stimulus. This is unfortunate, because it immediately conjures up something unpleasant, whereas an aversive stimulus might actually be something very mild, as in the example just given. I think that for this reason it is not a good description (although scientifically it may be an accurate one) and so I use the term stimulus (or cue, if the latter is more appropriate) on its own.

Many people believe that the removal of the stimulus or cue constitutes a reward, but this is not the case, as we shall see later in this chapter. It is far better to think of negative reinforcement in terms of taking something away – hence the term 'negative'.

Timing is essential

With either type of reinforcement, correct timing is essential or the horse may learn the wrong thing, or even nothing at all. For example, if the horse steps back and you reward him once he has stood still again, you have actually reinforced standing still, not stepping back. The reinforcer must be given as the action takes place or the horse will not make the connection. The same applies to negative reinforcement: if we don't release pressure on the bit, or the headcollar or whatever at the right time, the horse won't understand exactly what action produced the release. This is not because horses are stupid but because we don't speak the same language – a point I return to in the next part of this chapter, which deals with *punishment*.

Punishment

I want to start with punishment, because humans seem to find it a great deal easier to administer than reward. It's certainly a lot easier than thinking hard about whether punishment is actually appropriate.

First of all, what do we actually mean by punishment? At its simplest, it is an action which (in theory at least) reduces the likelihood of a behaviour being repeated. So if little Billy kicks a football in spite of being told not to, and breaks a window, we may punish him as a way of letting him know that his actions are unacceptable and that if he repeats them he will have to face the consequences.

This is really what it is all about: actions and consequences. The American lawyer and orator Robert G. Ingersoll said, 'In nature there are neither rewards nor punishments; there are consequences.' I think this is a very useful way of looking at our subject. If Billy breaks a window, certain consequences will follow. He may be deprived of something he really wants (e.g. his toys might be taken away from him); or he may be given something he really doesn't want (for example a smack, although that could be frowned upon these days; or he might be made to do something he doesn't want to do). The first consequence is properly called negative punishment (-P) because something is being taken away; the second is called positive punishment (+P) because something is being added.

Taking punishment for granted

The use of punishment is so much a part of our western culture that we tend to take it for granted, e.g. punishing schoolchildren for not doing their homework, punishing workers for being late for work, etc. Very often it does not occur to us that there might be a better and more effective way of getting children to do their homework, or encouraging workers to arrive on time. So we continue to use punishment, even when it does not bring about any kind of improvement, simply because we do not know the alternatives.

The same applies to the training and management of horses. The horse bites? He must be punished. He misbehaves in the show ring? Punishment will stop him (or will it?). He stops at a jump? Give him a whack! And so on. People who apply such thinking are not, for the most part, either cruel or unkind. Indeed, I know many people who are otherwise extremely kind and gentle with their horses, who do not hesitate to use punishment when it is required. And, as we shall see in Chapter 11, punishment *is* sometimes necessary. But as a way of training horses to do something (as opposed to *stopping* them from doing something) it is singularly ineffective.

Punishment is difficult to administer effectively

Even though punishment does have its place, it is extremely difficult to administer effectively. It must occur either while the unwanted behaviour is occurring, or within a couple of seconds, or the animal simply cannot make the connection between the punishment and the behaviour being punished. As I said above, this is not because they are stupid but because we have no way of telling horses directly exactly what they are being punished for. Imagine you are a worker being punished for doing something wrong, by someone using a foreign language you don't understand, without having any idea what you have done wrong. Would you be stupid for not understanding, or would there simply be a breakdown of communications?

Few of us would care to think that we have been harsh or unkind to our horses. But all too many people use punishment inappropriately, not because they are cruel or unkind but because they have simply not understood the principles of learning. For many people punishment and coercion are the only training tools they possess, which severely limits their options, especially when problems are encountered. Sadly, the inappropriate use of punishment is at the root of all too many behavioural and training problems. Examples of this inappropriate use could include:

◊ Punishing a horse for showing a reaction based on fear

◊ Punishing a horse for behaviour that is natural and appropriate to horses, e.g. punishing a stallion for 'dropping' or calling out to other horses

◊ Using punishment unjustly, e.g. when the horse is already complying with the handler's request

◊ Punishing a horse for not understanding what is required of him

◊ Punishing a horse after the event, e.g. smacking a horse *after* he has jumped a fence (so effectively punishing him for jumping the fence)

◊ Punishing a horse, not because he has done anything wrong but because the rider/handler/trainer is in a bad mood or is indulging in a temper tantrum (e.g. because of a poor result in the showring).

We must always bear in mind that our intentions when administering punishment – or any other form of conditioner – are irrelevant; it is the effect on the *subject* that matters. If a horse is unjustly punished he is very likely to become sour and possibly rebellious; this is the cause of a great deal of problem behaviour, especially in stallions. Indeed, punishing a horse in the circumstances outlined above – no matter what the rider's or trainer's intentions may be – is not in fact punishment at all; it is simply abuse.

Inappropriate use of punishment

Inappropriate and/or mistimed use of punishment can cause major problems. Punishment is often used inappropriately because the person using it assumes that the horse should understand that he has done something wrong. One of the commonest examples of this can be seen at almost any jumping competition. The horse or pony refuses a fence; the rider presents the horse at the fence again, and gives him a whack with a crop. He may or may not jump the fence the second time around; but what is he actually learning from this? The rider may believe that he or she is teaching the horse to 'jump the fence, or else'. Leaving aside for the moment the question of whether such coercion is morally right, does the horse think the same way as the rider? If he refuses to jump a fence because he is afraid, should he be punished for that? Even if he wants to please the rider, how can he know that it is important to her for him to jump the fence? And if the rider whacks him, what action is being punished? How can the horse make the connection between not jumping the fence and being hit with the stick, especially as the two events are not connected in time? All he is really learning is that if he approaches a fence, he is likely to be hit with a stick. It does not take too much imagination to see what the result is liable to be. If this scenario is repeated too often, the horse may become increasingly reluctant to jump, and in extreme cases may start refusing even to enter the jumping ring.

A failure of horsemanship

This example represents a failure of horsemanship. The rider has made no attempt to assess the reason(s) for the horse's refusal to jump; instead, (s)he has resorted immediately to punishment. Yet there might be many reasons why, at that particular time, the horse refused the fence. Fear is the commonest reason; fences can be far more daunting to horses than many riders realize. The horse may have misjudged the take-off, and decided against it at the last moment. The rider may be giving him conflicting signals, such as driving with the legs and hanging onto the reins – like driving with the hand-brake on. Or the horse may sense that the rider is not really committed to the jump, and be uncertain as to her intentions. These are only a few of the possible reasons for a refusal; is punishment an appropriate and reasonable response to any of them? If we think it is, then we are no better than the old-fashioned school teachers who use to beat children for being left-handed, dyslexic, short-sighted, or any other deficiency that a little thought would have shown them was scarcely the child's fault.

Distorted thinking

An extreme example of inappropriate punishment which also smacks of such distorted thinking is to deprive a horse of his dinner as a punishment for some transgression. The people who do this kind of thing are not necessarily cruel or stupid (although their actions are); they are simply treating the horse like a child sent to bed without any supper as a punishment. They are assuming that the horse (like a child) will understand what he is being punished for. But why should he? Once again, how can he make the connection between whatever he has done to merit the punishment, and being deprived of his dinner?

The limitations of punishment

One of the biggest problems with punishment is that, while it can be used (with varying degrees of effectiveness) to teach a horse what *not* to do, it is really pretty useless as a means of showing him what we *do* want him to do. We can certainly use the method of rewarding a correct response and punishing an incorrect response, which is what seems to be recommended in many books and articles on training. But this is a very cumbersome and time-consuming, hit-and-miss way of working,[5] and it cannot be very pleasant for the horse, as he is bound to make many mistakes at the beginning. Punishing an animal for making a mistake is not only grossly unjust; it can lead to the state of 'learned helplessness' described in Chapter 8. If, for example, a horse makes many mistakes and is punished for them, he may feel that he will be punished no matter what happens, and simply stop doing anything at all.

What about the horse who doesn't do quite what we asked (or thought we were asking)? In his book *The Nature of Horses*, Stephen Budiansky says, '...every rider can think of times when he let his horse get away with something he shouldn't have (break into a canter when he should still have been trotting, cut across the ring, take a few steps after being brought to a halt).' (Budiansky, 1997) But is this necessarily disobedience? What exactly is the horse 'getting away with'? The horse might misinterpret the rider's aids, especially if they are not clear enough. If he breaks into a canter because he thought that's what we were asking for, would it be just to punish him for that? If we think it is, and we give him a whack, he might decide (especially if this is repeated) that cantering simply isn't worth getting whacked for, and stop cantering altogether.

If the horse hasn't understood what the rider wants, why should he be punished for not understanding, especially if – as is so often the case – his trainer is not making it clear what is being expected of him? Say for example the rider is asking a green horse to canter under saddle. If she is proceeding logically, the horse will already have been taught the verbal command 'canter!' on the lunge, so – in theory – when the rider gives the aids for canter and at the same time says 'canter!' the horse should understand what she wants. Perhaps he does, but is too unbalanced to comply. Or perhaps the rider is unbalanced, and making it difficult for the horse to go to canter. Would punishment be appropriate, or would it simply be like caning a child for not understanding something beyond his ability to comprehend? Nowadays most of us don't treat our children like that, so why should we punish horses for something that isn't their fault?

In any case, even if he does understand what is wanted, how can the horse possibly be expected to obey every single time? A horse may, for instance, break into a canter because he lost his balance in the trot. Indeed, loss of balance is one of the commonest causes of so-called 'disobedience', including bucking – observe how often horses, galloping around in the field or cavorting about in play, lose their balance and give a great buck to try to restore their equilibrium. If the horse loses his balance under the weight of the rider, which commonly happens, is he to be punished for this? Is no account to be taken of the many other factors which might prevent the horse from carrying out the rider's wishes? And what sort of rider could possibly insist on such unconditional obedience?

---

5 It may also render the training more difficult or even ineffective; see page 179 under **The poisoned cue**.

Avoiding injustice

As the former Director of the Spanish Riding School, the late Colonel Alois Podhajsky, put it, 'In most cases insubordination is caused by the horse's fear of his rider, by the fact that he does not understand what is required of him, or is unable to execute an exercise for which he is not prepared.' (Podhajsky, 1967) Elsewhere, this wise man – who successfully re-trained many extremely 'difficult' horses, says, 'Whenever difficulties appear the first thing the rider must do is ask himself: does the horse not want to execute my demands, does he not understand what I want, or is he physically unable to carry them out? The rider's conscience must find the answer. If there is any doubt it is much better to assume that the horse is unable to carry out the commands and leave it at that, which is much wiser than obtaining the exercise by force. An omission is never of such bad consequence as an injustice.' (Podhajsky, 1997)

As we have just seen, appropriate and effective punishment can be extremely difficult to administer properly. Let's think about the example of little Billy breaking the window with his football. Regardless of whether we use +P or –P, the consequence must be something that has a chance of affecting Billy's future behaviour. If it is too mild, he may find the thrill of kicking a football near the house worth the risk of subsequent punishment if he breaks another window. In fact, this is one of the biggest problems with punishment: the consequence must be such that it acts as a real deterrent, otherwise the punishment is either ineffective or it may even act to increase, rather than decrease, the objectionable behaviour. This means that any punishment administered must not only be given at exactly the right time, it must also be of sufficient intensity to act as a deterrent. As Chapter 11 will show, this can be extremely difficult to judge, as some behaviours – however inconvenient they may be to us – are simply too rewarding to the horse to be deterred without extremely severe punishment, which may be effective, but which may also result in the emergence of other, equally undesirable behaviours, as well as creating health and welfare problems.

There are a number of reasons why we should avoid punishment as far as possible, and instead seek other solutions to problem behaviour:

◊ Punishment has been shown, through monitoring of neurochemical changes, to increase fear and anxiety.

◊ Even if the punishment stops the undesirable behaviour, the associated fear and anxiety may interfere with the learning process sufficiently to prevent the animal from learning new, more desirable behaviours.

◊ It may result in the animal regarding the person administering the punishment as a threat, ruining any chances of a trusting relationship developing between the two.

◊ Because punishment increases fear and anxiety, it may lead directly to aggression. If aggression is already present, it may serve to increase that aggression.

◊ Punishment can only tell an animal what *not* to do; it cannot indicate what the desired behaviour is, because there are far too many possibilities to choose from. If an animal is then punished for every wrong choice, he may simply stop doing anything at all.

Behaviour analyst Murray Sidman has written at length about the damaging side effects of coercion and punishment, which extend far beyond the circumstances in which they are used. However, this does not mean that we must never use punishment. There may be situations – for example if a horse is behaving aggressively and we do not have enough information to know what is causing the aggression – where we need to take action in order to avoid injury. As Dr Sidman points out, in such situations '…common sense tells us that we have to use whatever effective means are at hand.' But as he goes on to say, the occasional emergency 'may justify punishment as a treatment of last resort, but never as the treatment of choice. To use punishment occasionally as an act of desperation is not the same as advocating the use of punishment as a principle of behaviour management.' (Sidman, 2000)

Naturally, we want our horses to be well-behaved, and we need to teach them what is acceptable to us and what is not. But the use of punishment is so fraught with dangers that unless we are very skilled in its use and know exactly when and how to use it and when it is inappropriate, we run the risk, not only of damaging our relationship with our horses, but of creating far more problems than the punishment solves. Most of us like to think that we would be able to use punishment appropriately and correctly, but sadly, the examples given in this chapter show that this is frequently not the case. The use of punishment is so widespread, and so often indiscriminate – almost like a knee-jerk reaction – that before we even think about using it we need to find a more intelligent – and effective – way to prevent behaviour we don't want, and encourage behaviour we do want. Only when we truly understand, and can use, the principles of learning, should we consider ourselves fit to administer punishment. The next part of this chapter looks at the alternatives to punishment, and learn how they work and when their use is appropriate.

Negative reinforcement (-R)

It helps us to understand negative reinforcement if we use examples that we can easily relate to. Suppose you are in a crowd of people with a friend who knows in which direction you need to go, but you do not. There is a lot of noise and you cannot hear what the friend is saying when she tells you to turn left. So she puts her hand on your shoulder and gently steers you in the direction you need to go. You do not want to resist the pressure of your friend's hand, so you turn away from the pressure. The instant you start to move in the right direction, the friend removes her hand. When the pressure is removed, that reinforces the turn (if she kept on pressing, you might get annoyed, because you would not know where she wanted you to go and might even end up going round in circles). Without even thinking about it too much, you have moved in the right direction. That is an example of negative reinforcement; as we can see, the reinforcement consists of taking something away. In this instance the thing to be avoided is the pressure of your friend's hand (and note that this does not have to be something unpleasant, although it could be if your friend used too much pressure); when it is removed, that is the reinforcer.

We can see from this that much of what we do with horses consists of negative reinforcement. The horse moves away from the pressure of the rider's leg, yields to the pressure of the bit, or steps sideways in order to re-balance himself in response to a change in the rider's weight distribution. In good riding this use of negative reinforcement will be as mild as possible and used in conjunction with frequent rewards.

Negative reinforcement is often confused with punishment, even by otherwise knowledgeable people who really ought to know better. It makes things simpler if we remember that negative reinforcement acts to *increase* the probability that a behaviour will be repeated, while punishment acts to *decrease* that probability.

Some books and magazine articles have given the impression that all negative reinforcement is bad and virtually synonymous with punishment. This is not true; negative reinforcement can be extremely mild and, judiciously used, can be an excellent training tool. However, like all training tools it can be misused and in excess it can easily become just another form of coercion. Many of the training methods described as 'natural' rely heavily on negative reinforcement, which is often referred to as 'pressure-and-release'; for example, the trainer who waggles a rope to get the horse to step back, or flicks a rope at the horse's hindquarters to get him to move. This is fine as long as the people using these methods understand this and know when to release pressure and how to avoid using it to excess. I have seen some trainers use such methods very mildly and with such superb timing that the technique is not only very effective but causes the horse little if any stress. But over-use of negative reinforcement could induce in certain horses the 'learned helplessness' referred to in Chapter 8 and earlier in this chapter. Even if it does not go that far, negative reinforcement techniques which use too much pressure, especially combined with poor timing, will almost certainly result in the horse becoming over-stressed and anxious. Because of their extra 'edge' and increased reactivity, stallions, especially those of sensitive breeds such as Arabs, Iberians and Thoroughbreds, are especially likely to react badly to an excessive use of heavy-handed negative reinforcement.

Using negative reinforcement on the ground

Suppose we want to teach the horse to step back. There are several ways of doing this. Perhaps the commonest, unthinking method is to approach the horse waving our arms and shouting, 'Get back!' The sensitive horse may well shoot away; very few horses will stand still while people wave arms in their faces. Some horses might think that such shouting and arm-waving is a prelude to a physical attack, and as a result they could become nervous and possibly defensive whenever people approach them. They might also develop a degree of head-shyness; I have seen this happen with a number of horses subjected to this treatment. A less sensitive horse might ignore the shouting and arm-waving completely, which leaves the arm-waver with very little to fall back on, short of actual physical assault, to make the horse move back.

Another common approach, which often meets with a degree of success, is to physically push the horse in the chest until he moves back. Again, this may work with more sensitive horses, and if paired with the exclamation 'Back!' may result in a horse who steps back as soon as he hears the command 'Back!' However, it is not so successful with the horse who simply doesn't feel like stepping back; some horses you could push and shove all day and they would not move (many Warmbloods are like this, but such horses can be found in all breeds). It also smacks of physical assault, albeit of a very mild nature, and some horses may take exception to this.

One method used by some trainers to get horses to back up from the ground, which I have already mentioned, consists of waving or twirling a long line at them. This is effective because no horse likes having things waved or waggled in his face. However, although this technique has its place, and can be very effective if used properly, in its more extreme forms it is not exactly a pleasant experience for the horse. At the same time as the horse is stepping away from the waggling line, he is also raising his head to avoid the line, which acts to hollow his back. Horses *can* back up with a raised head and hollowed back, but the process is difficult and may actually be painful for them, and they may become pre-disposed to head-shyness as a result of trying to avoid the line.

All the above methods rely on *avoidance*; if the action the horse wants to avoid ceases as soon as the horse backs up, then the horse's behaviour (i.e. backing up) has been reinforced. They are all examples of -R. As we have seen, this can either be quite unpleasant for the horse, or it can be relatively benign. An example of benign -R is a method which I have already mentioned earlier in this chapter; it involves taking hold of the horse's headcollar (or a rope attached to the centre ring of the headcollar) and exerting mild pressure on either the headcollar or the rope; the horse steps back to avoid the pressure, which is instantly released. Although there is certainly a degree of pressure involved, most horses accept this method quite readily, and it does not seem to have any of the unpleasant side-effects so easily associated with the other methods mentioned.

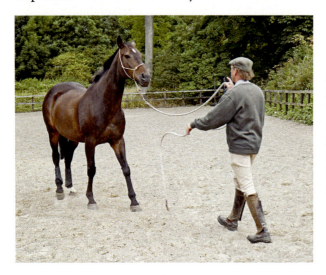

Benign use of -R: the trainer is asking the horse to move back by simultaneously raising his hand, moving the line lightly, and walking towards the horse. Once the horse steps back, the trainer releass this mild pressure. I would like to see the horse's head a little lower, but in general this is a good example of the technique. Photo: Lesley Skipper

However, some other methods commonly used by the new wave of trainers may not always be so benign. This is not to say that the intention behind them is not good; it is the use of such methods without an understanding of how they really work that can create problems. This includes certain techniques for gaining control of the horse's feet; the idea is that by controlling the feet we gain control of the whole horse. There is much truth in this, but anyone using such methods needs to take care that they are not sending out conflicting messages to the horse. As we saw in Chapter 8, if we adopt an aggressive attitude (and this might mean nothing more than mildly aggressive body language), we are telling the horse to go away while at the same time preventing him from doing so (e.g. because we have hold of him on the end of a rope). This can create serious conflict and, depending on how the technique is used, can even introduce an element of punishment. This does not mean that we should never use such methods. With some horses, especially bumptious young colts who – perhaps because they have been isolated from normal equine society – have never learned appropriate behaviour and how to respect personal space, the technique of (for example) swinging a rope to induce the horse to move away and keep his distance can be very useful; I give examples of this in Chapter 11. However, such techniques should be used very carefully, and with due regard to the temperament of the horse in question, especially with stallions; used indiscriminately, such techniques could – by introducing the elements of conflict and punishment already referred to – render a timid horse neurotic or a bolder one dangerous.

Criticisms have been levelled at the use of round pens in training, and for similar reasons; if the horse feels under too much pressure in the round pen, he may well react explosively. Responsible trainers apply only mild pressure and know when to back off; it is the less responsible trainers who have given rise to criticism of round pen techniques. In any case, the round pen is merely a training tool, not a technique or method in itself; and like all tools, it can be used well or badly.

Chapter 9

Using negative reinforcement under saddle

The moment we sit on the horse's back we are influencing him with our own body, whether we like it or not. The very act of sitting on a horse's back is a form of negative reinforcement, as even the least sensitive of horses cannot avoid reacting in some way to the presence of the rider in the saddle. If the horse feels even slightly unbalanced by the rider, he will move so as to regain his balance. If he succeeds, again his action will have been reinforced. There is not room here to go into detail about how the rider's body affects the horse, so for a fuller explanation of this, see my books *Let Horses Be Horses* (J.A. Allen, 2005) *Understanding Horse Behaviour* (New Holland Publishing, 2007) and *Exercise School for Horse and Rider* (New Holland Publishing, 2008).

When the horse moves away from the pressure of the rider's leg, the release of pressure acts as the (negative) reinforcer. Photo: Lesley Skipper

Well used, mild -R can provide the horse with clear, unambiguous indications of what we want. Used oppressively, it can sour a horse, create stress and lead to behavioural problems. Whether the -R is benign or oppressive depends on how it is used, the individual trainer's approach and on the sensitivity of the horse.

One of the problems with negative reinforcement is that it gives the horse no incentive to do more than is necessary to avoid whatever aversive stimulus is being applied. Research has shown that positive reinforcement is more effective in encouraging horses to comply willingly and even to offer desired behaviours spontaneously (Innes and McBride, 2007).

We will now look at positive reinforcement and how it can transform our working relationships with horses.

Positive reinforcement (+R)

What do we mean by 'positive reinforcement'? I am often told by people that they don't use positive reinforcement because 'feeding treats leads to nipping' or, increasingly, something like, 'My trainer says he doesn't use positive reinforcement because it isn't natural – after all, horses don't give each other "treats" or "presents", so they don't understand food rewards.' However, to think like this is to misunderstand the whole nature of positive reinforcement. It's not about giving 'treats', although these can be powerful reinforcers. It's about reinforcing a desired behaviour by adding something that the subject likes and wants.

People are often confused by the use of the term 'reward', which is commonly used in referring to positive reinforcement. Some people refer to the cessation of an aid in riding, or the release of pressure, as a 'reward'. For example, rather a lot of trainers maintain that it is the pain caused by pressure on the bit which causes a horse to stop, and that release of the pressure (i.e. removal of the unpleasant sensation caused by the bit) constitutes the horse's reward. Personally I regard this is a pretty cockeyed way of looking at things; circumstances would have to be very bad for anyone, let alone a horse, to feel in any way 'rewarded' merely by the removal of something unpleasant. An analogy might be with a certain style of management very common today. In the kind of workplace culture I have in mind, employees are not praised for their efforts; instead, their 'reward' for extra effort is to have the threat of dismissal removed – until next time. What kind of morale does this result in? That's right: lousy.

The problem with this way of thinking is that it doesn't actually provide much of an incentive to the horse to do as we wish. Some horses might indeed stop as a result of pressure on the bit, but there are far better ways of getting a horse to halt. Some sensitive horses might breathe a sigh of relief as the rider stops using the leg; others might simply not care very much one way or the other. Where does one go from there? If the horse is 'switched off' to the stimulus, then how is removing it going to make very much difference?

Of course, you might argue that this is a question of applying the stimulus correctly rather than changing tactics. Certainly I would agree that no matter what methods of training you use, if the horse is mentally switched off, getting through to him will be difficult if not impossible, and may require an exceptional degree of skill from the handler and/or trainer. Regrettably, one sees all too many horses who have retreated into themselves in this manner, especially in competitive dressage; they may perform adequately, even brilliantly from a purely technical point of view, yet all spark of life is lacking, and they go through their routines like zombies. They may behave like zombies in an out of the stable, too. And most of these horses have been trained using extreme negative reinforcement.

So the bottom line is: any animal, human or non-human, might feel a sense of relief at the removal of something they wanted to avoid, but would they feel particularly rewarded?

Or might they respond better to something that resulted in positive gain for them, i.e. something they liked and/or wanted? For a horse this could be a food reward, a scratch, a stroke, or whatever else the horse likes.

Sometimes people confuse this with a *bribe*, and talk as though it is somehow immoral to offer one to a horse. But is a salary a bribe or a reward for work done? Would you work for no pay? It would depend on whether you found your work sufficiently rewarding in itself, and also whether you could support yourself without a salary. However, most people want and demand payment for work done. But of course horses don't need a salary, so is rewarding them the equivalent of a bribe?

Bribery

Bribery is something which people use in an attempt to reinforce behaviour which has not yet occurred – and behaviour that has not happened cannot be reinforced, simply because it hasn't happened yet! This is not to say that we cannot or should not use something very like bribery on occasion; we can use food, for example, as a *lure* or an *incentive*, to elicit a specific behaviour (such as walking forward). The main problem with this is that the lure can be very distracting, as the animal (whether a horse or a dog or whatever) is not concentrating on the behaviour but on the food; this distraction may make it much more difficult for him to understand what you want.

Does feeding treats cause nipping?

So positive reinforcement and bribery are not the same thing. But what about the idea that feeding treats causes nipping? Well, it can do, but only if treats are fed indiscriminately. If they are given only as a reward for desired behaviour, or at certain very specific times (such as when saying goodnight) horses soon learn that treats will be forthcoming on these occasions only. The *Bereiters* (riders) of the Spanish Riding School have special pockets for sugar lumps in the tailcoats of their uniforms; they have been feeding the Lipizzaner stallions rewards of sugar for generations without any problems.[6]

Do horses understand rewards?

Finally, what about the idea that horses do not understand rewards? This suggests that the people who put forward such ideas haven't thought the matter through properly and also that they don't really understand the nature of reinforcements. There are plenty of examples of positive reinforcement in equine society. Say one horse (A) wants to groom with another (B). He approaches B using body language which suggests he wants to groom. If B feels like reciprocating, he will stop whatever he is doing and allow A to indicate where on his body he wants to be groomed. The fact that B responds in this way is a reinforcer: A's approach to B in that specific manner has been successful so in future he will be able to approach B in the same manner and hopefully start a mutual grooming session. Of course, it may not be as straightforward as this: A also has to learn to read B's body language to see if he is likely to be in the mood to groom. Nevertheless, the fact that his approach has been successful encourages him to try again: in other words it has been reinforced. Another example might be the foal who wants to take milk while his dam is walking. The foal nips in front of her and blocks her movement; she stops, and he moves to the udder and starts suckling. His blocking movement has succeeded: he has got his milk, and this reinforces the behaviour which led to it. And this is surely positive reinforcement.

For anything to be a positive reinforcer it has to be something the subject a) likes, and b) wants at that particular time. A piece of carrot (for example) would not be reinforcing if the horse did not like carrots! Similarly a horse who has just eaten may not respond to food rewards, and a horse who dislikes being stroked or scratched would not appreciate a stroke or a scratch as a reinforcer. In deciding what to use as a reinforcer each horse's preferences must be taken into account, as well as the circumstances.

Like negative reinforcement, a positive reinforcer must be given immediately the horse complies. Sometimes – for instance when the horse is on the lunge – this is not possible, because the trainer is not close enough to the horse. So we can pair the reinforcer with a verbal marker, such as 'Good!' (short words are best): as we give the reinforcer, we say, 'Good!' (or whatever) and the horse comes to understand that the marker means that a reward will be forthcoming. Even better is a marker such as a clicker, which is quicker than a verbal marker and more accurate in indicating exactly what the horse has done correctly. Advocates of clicker-training sometimes give the impression that it is a miracle cure-all, but it is not. It is simply a training tool, and like all tools it can be used well or badly.

The great advantage of positive reinforcement is that horses trained mainly by this means tend to offer desirable behaviours willingly and spontaneously. If they also know that offering the wrong behaviour (such as cantering when the rider wanted trot) will not have any negative consequences, but that offering the right behaviour means something good for them, they will tend to try much harder than if their only reward is relief from something they want to avoid.

Is positive reinforcement always good?

So does this mean that positive reinforcement is always good, or that it should *always* be used in preference to negative reinforcement? No. Horses trained by positive reinforcement can still be put

---

6 It used to be the case that if one of the *Bereiters* fell off in the course of training, he had to buy sugar lumps for the stallions. In 2006 I asked *Ober-Bereiter* Johann Riegler about this; he laughed and said that nowadays they have to buy a round of drinks.

under an unacceptable degree of stress if the trainer does not give a clear indication of what he or she wants. And it is possible to abuse positive reinforcement by using it to overcome a horse's reluctance to perform an action. We may congratulate ourselves on having trained our horse to do whatever we want by means of a humane method, only to find that his reluctance to perform was caused by pain or discomfort, or that he was not yet physically ready to perform that particular movement. This does not mean that the principle is wrong, it just means that we have not made proper use of it.

And there are some situation where we cannot avoid using negative reinforcement: for example, in ridden work, as explained in the section on negative reinforcement. So there is a place for both positive and negative reinforcement in the training of horses. But before we can use either effectively, we must first understand how they work.

Getting the timing right

Whatever type of reinforcement we are using, it is essential to remember two very important things. First, for behaviour to be reinforced we must introduce the reinforcement the very instant the desired behaviour is occurring, or the animal has no means of knowing exactly what action we are approving. Second, behaviour that is not occurring cannot be reinforced. We either have to wait for the behaviour we want to reinforce to occur naturally, or we have to create conditions in which it can occur. If we are using +R we pair a specific behaviour as it is occurring with a reinforcer; the behaviour might be something like stepping back if the subject is a horse, or sitting in the case of a dog. When the desired response occurs we give the reward. If we are using -R, we introduce something the animal wants to avoid; with a horse this might be pressure on a head collar to make him move back, with a dog it could be pushing his hind end down to make him sit. As soon as we get the desired response we remove the pressure. In both cases – whether we use +R or -R – we have *reinforced* the desired behaviour. What we can then do is introduce a cue or signal at the same time as we reinforce the behaviour. In the examples given, this might be 'Back!' or 'Sit!' respectively, but it can (and usually will) be something that, in itself, is initially meaningless to the animal. (For example, a horse does not understand that 'Walk on!' means just that, until we teach him to associate the phrase with the act of walking on.) The actual words used do not matter as long as we use them consistently; we tend to use words that mean to us what we want them to mean to the animal because it is easier for us to relate words to actions in this way. We could say 'Back!' or 'Sit!' at the same time as we reinforce the behaviour. This pairing of a reinforcer with a cue or signal enables us to ask for a specific behaviour without either having to wait for it to occur naturally or inducing it by some means. So if we have paired 'Back!' with either a reward or, say, pressure on the headcollar, the horse knows that we want him to step back, just as 'Sit!' tells the dog we want him to sit.

Conditioned reinforcement

We can then take this a step further. It may be that, because of the nature of what we are doing, we cannot give the reinforcer in time for it to coincide with the exact behaviour we want to reinforce. Say we are lungeing a horse and want to reinforce breaking into canter. We cannot get to the horse to give him a reward, so what do we do? We pair some kind of signal, which could be a verbal one such as 'Good!', or a click using a clicker box (see the photographs on page 178), or anything else that can be clearly heard or seen, with the reinforcer. This enables the animal to understand that 'Good!' (or a click, or whatever) means that a reward is forthcoming, and that it was for performing *that* specific action and not some other. This is called *conditioned reinforcement*. The timing of the conditioned reinforcer has to be just right but correctly used it is a very powerful training tool indeed.

Above left: Brian asks Nivalis to come to him. Because Brian is not next to the horse, he cannot give the reinforcer directly the moment Nivalis moves towards him. By using a 'marker' (in this case the verbal marker 'Good!' he can indicate when the horse has done the right thing. Nivalis knows that this means he will get a mint. **Above right:** Nivalis gets his mint. Photo: Lesley Skipper

Clicker-training

Conditioned reinforcement forms the basis of clicker-training, which is now becoming more and more widely used in horse training. I must confess that when I first learned about clicker-training I disliked the idea, feeling that it smacked of mindless teaching by rote. Now that I know more about it I freely admit that I was wrong and in fact I had been using a verbal equivalent of the click for many years without even thinking about the fact that it was basically the same thing! The click is only a *marker*, used to tell the horse that he has done something correctly as described above. It is useful because it is a clear, discrete sound which enables very precise timing of the conditioned reinforcer. Anyone wanting to learn more about clicker-training should start by reading the books by Karen Pryor, Ben Hart and Alexandra Kurland listed in the bibliography, before attempting it for themselves.

Target training

In clicker-training the horse may be introduced to the marker by being taught to touch a target, which can then be moved around to encourage different behaviours. However, targets can be used regardless of whether one uses the clicker or some other marker. The target can be anything you choose, as long as it is large enough for the horse to see properly: Alexandra Kurland often uses a small plastic cone. If you hold the target close enough to the horse's nose (without actually pushing it at him), eventually he will touch it, either because he is curious or simply because it is positioned so that at some point he is bound to touch it. The instant this happens, click (if you are using a clicker) or say 'Good' or use whatever other marker you choose, and give your horse a tiny amount of food (grain, pieces of carrot or whatever the horse likes). Eventually he will work out that every time he touches the target he gets some food; he will also learn to associate the marker (clicker, voice or whatever) with the food. Soon he will be deliberately touching the target, because he knows that this is the way to get something he enjoys. Once he is confirmed in this behaviour you can start moving the target around. Do this in very small steps (a principle which we apply to any training situation); for example if you want the horse to touch the target while it is on the ground, you do not simply lower it to the ground or the horse will become confused and discouraged. Instead, lower it a little at a time – just a few centimetres – and eventually you will find that the horse will readily reach out to touch it when it is on the ground.

When you are satisfied that the horse will touch the target whenever it is presented (i.e. because this behaviour is now confirmed as part of his repertoire), you can introduce the cue. You present the target and say, 'Touch!'. The horse knows that the presence of the target means you want him to touch it, and if you say 'Touch!' every time you present the target, the horse will soon associate the cue with seeking out and touching the target. Most horses respond to this willingly and enthusiastically. You can then use the target to move the horse around without laying a finger on him – which gives him a choice and ensures that he is complying of his own free will, without any element of coercion.

An example of this is teaching the horse to move back. Using +R on its own, or a combination of +R and target training, we can use a method that is actually pleasant for the horse as well as being physically comfortable. We can wait until the horse steps back of his own accord and then reinforce the behaviour as it occurs (+R). Alternatively, we may set up a situation in which we can elicit the behaviour we want. Before trying the following exercise you will need to make sure that your horse has been taught to touch a target as described above and has been confirmed in his response to being asked to do so.

Hold the target (which, as previously explained, can be anything you choose) fairly close to his chest, high enough so that he cannot simply bend his neck and touch it; make sure he knows it is there. Say 'Touch!' and you will find that in order to touch the target he has to step back. The instant he takes the first step, reinforce his action with a small amount of food, a scratch or whatever he likes. Once he is confirmed in stepping back you can introduce the cue; this will typically be 'Back!' When he is stepping back consistently as soon as you say 'Back!' you can build on this as described below under *shaping* and get him to take progressively more steps backwards; you do not reward him until he takes another step back, and so on until eventually you only have to say 'Back!' and he automatically takes the required number of steps backwards. This is only one method of teaching a horse to step back, but I have used it with colts and stallions and found it extremely effective. (For more about how you can use target-training, see Alexandra Kurland's *Clicker Training for Your Horse*, Ringpress ed. 2001.)

Above left: a simple clicker. Above right: a slightly more sophisticated clicker; the rate of click is adjustable.

Shaping, selective reinforcement and variable schedules

If we are using +R it may seem as if we will have to go on rewarding a behaviour or the animal will simply stop producing it. However, this is not the case. It is only in the very early stages of learning that constant reinforcement is needed. Say we want to teach a horse to 'shake hands'. Nivalis was taught to 'shake hands' by Brian, reinforcing a slight raising of the leg when it occurred naturally.[7] Once Nivalis was raising his leg for him on request, Brian moved on to only reinforcing when Nivalis raised it higher. Gradually Brian was able to get him to raise his leg to a level where Brian could 'shake hands' with him, by only reinforcing when he raised the leg a little higher than before. This process is called *shaping* and that of selectively reinforcing some responses and ignoring others is called a *selective* schedule of reinforcement. Now it is ingrained in Nivalis's behavioural repertoire, we have no need to reinforce it every time he does it for us; if we only reward him for it now and then he is more motivated to produce the behaviour for us ('This time I might get a reward') than if we rewarded him every time. This is called a *variable* schedule of reinforcement. If this sounds odd, think about some of the strange things humans do to gain a reward. The example most often used is that of the slot machine: the occasional win makes gamblers keep on playing, in the hope that they will win again and, like the roulette table, it can be seriously addictive. (For more about schedules of reinforcement and why they have such a powerful effect, see the books identified in the Bibliography as offering excellent guides to the principles of learning, set out in a way the lay person can easily understand).

Extinction

If a behaviour is not reinforced to the point where it becomes ingrained, or not reinforced at all, it will cease completely; hence it is said to have become *extinct*. However, the use of extinction to modify behaviour, while a very powerful tool, is also full of pitfalls. For that reason it will be described more fully in Chapter 11.

The poisoned cue

One very important reason why it is not a good idea to combine reward and punishment is the danger that it will render cues ineffective. Suppose (for example) you want to teach your horse to lift his hoof for inspection on request. You teach him the cue 'Lift!' using +R, but if the horse does not comply, you whack him on the shoulder while saying 'Lift!'. Now he associates the cue with being whacked on the shoulder; instead of being associated with the positive reinforcer, the cue now becomes ambiguous or even aversive. It has effectively been 'poisoned'. This can happen accidentally (for example, if something aversive happens while you are giving the cue, such as a sudden noise which startles the horse) and there is not much you can do about that. You can, however, avoid the use of punishment; if the horse doesn't offer the correct behaviour, simply ignore the incorrect behaviour and try again.

A cue may also be poisoned if the supposed reinforcer is something the horse doesn't actually care for. For example, if you attempt to reinforce a behaviour by patting the horse, and the horse doesn't like to be patted (many do not; most prefer a stroke or a scratch), the effect will be the same as that described above. This is why it is important to find out what the horse does like.

If a cue does become poisoned, you need to start all over again, and re-train the behaviour using a new cue.

---

7 This is an example of 'free shaping'.

The Natural Stallion

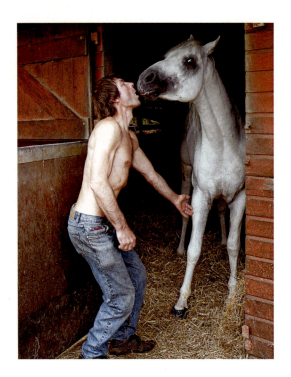
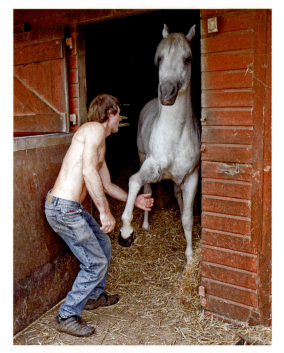
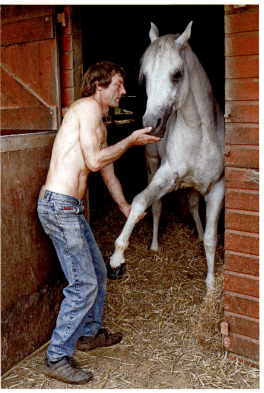

Shaping: teaching a horse to 'shake hands'.

Above left: As Nivalis starts to lift his right leg, Brian gives him a mint (in the case, from his mouth!). **Above right:** Nivalis lifts the right leg a little higher. **Below right:** having lifted his leg to where Brian wanted it to be, Nivalis gets another reinforcing mint. Photos: Lesley Skipper

Putting it into practice

Having looked at the principles of learning theory, we can now see how it can be put into practice. We have learned that

◊ A specific behaviour must actually be occurring for it to be reinforced.

◊ We cannot reinforce something that has not happened.

◊ A reinforcer must be given at the correct time or the wrong behaviour may be reinforced

◊ Punishment is not a very effective training tool: it can only be used to tell the horse what *not* to do; it can never tell him what he *should* be doing.

◊ It is not a good idea to combine reward and punishment, whatever training manuals may say. The cue or stimulus may become poisoned, making it necessary to re-train the behaviour.

Alternatives to coercive methods of training are not a 'soft' option – neither sentimental nor impractical, but a necessity if we are to train and manage effectively and reduce or eliminate (and preferably prevent) behavioural problems. Ultimately only the horses themselves can tell us what is acceptable to them and what is not. As they cannot tell us directly, their distress manifests itself in behaviour; it is up to us to learn to read this behaviour and recognize signs that all is not well with the horse concerned.

CHAPTER 10

Training good behaviours

The intelligence of the horse increases rapidly with education. An intelligent master or trainer can make an intelligent horse. It is a stupid trainer that makes the so-called stupid horse.

– Colonel R. S. Timmis, DSO, ca. 1915

The best possible start

IF you are fortunate enough to bring a stallion up from foalhood to adulthood, you have a wonderful opportunity to ensure that his training and management reflect his needs, and not just human convenience, as well as influencing his behaviour in ways that will make him easier to train and handle.

Nature or nurture?

Temperament, defined as 'an individual's character, disposition, and tendencies as revealed in his reactions' (Collins English Dictionary), is certainly very important in a stallion, but how much of a stallion's good (or bad) temperament is due to nature, and how much to nurture?

The answer: there is simply no way to tell. Temperament, character (the combination of traits and qualities distinguishing the individual nature of a person or thing) and personality (the sum total of all the behavioural and mental characteristics by means of which an individual is recognized as being unique) are not (despite what many popular books and magazine articles suggest) determined solely by genetic inheritance. People who believe this fall into the trap of thinking of traits of temperament or personality as *things*, rather than concepts which help us to understand why individuals think and behave as they do. To describe someone (whether human or equine) as having, say, a *bold* temperament is not like saying they have red (or chestnut) hair; a bold temperament is not an observable, measurable trait, it is a description.

An animal (and this includes humans) may have certain general *tendencies* or qualities which are inborn, but an animal's temperament, as well as its overall personality, is shaped by a very complex interaction of internal and external influences. *Personality* (including temperament) is therefore the sum of those qualities with which the animal was born, together with its lifetime experiences. The innate qualities can be affected, shaped, developed or suppressed by those experiences; this is why, from the moment they are born, the ways in which horses are handled can have such a profound effect on their later development.

Bringing up stallions from foalhood is a wonderful opportunity to shape their future development. Left: the author with Nivalis, aged five months. Photo: Joanne Husband. Right: Joanne with Nivalis, aged six months. Below left: Brian with Rigel, aged one week. Below right: Brian with Rigel, aged nine months. Photos: Lesley Skipper

We cannot know, for example, how many of the world's greatest horses would have achieved what they did had they been raised and trained in different circumstances. I do not mean to imply that such horses were not exceptional in themselves, but beyond doubt their abilities were nurtured and allowed expression by the conditions of their upbringing, training and the manner in which they were ridden.

So a stallion may inherit (and, by definition, pass on to his progeny – although the dam may contribute as much, if not more – after all she is the earliest influence on a foal) certain tendencies which may affect the way he reacts to situations and external stimuli. But his life experiences will have an enormous impact on his general behaviour.

Consistency is the key

All animals, including humans, want life to be predictable. If they know which actions produce specific results, they will be able to avoid unpleasant consequences and achieve pleasant ones. Uncertainty breeds anxiety, which inhibits learning and may result in behavioural problems. So consistency in the trainer's behaviour is essential. All too often people will reward a behaviour one day, and punish it the next. Horses *can* learn that a certain behaviour is acceptable in one context but not in another, but they have to be trained specifically to do this (recall the control cues and formal/informal contexts mentioned in Chapter 8). For example, many horses, especially Arabians, love to rub their heads on humans. This is *not*, as some people maintain, showing 'disrespect' or an attempt at dominance (any more than a child asking for a hug is showing disrespect or trying to 'dominate' her mother); it is simply what horses do when they want to get rid of loose or sweaty hair from their heads. Many people dislike it when their horses try to do this; I can quite understand that, as a horse rubbing his head on a human can easily send the latter flying, and even if that does not happen, a horse's head is very bony and can readily bruise a human. Personally I don't mind it; it shows that my horses have confidence in their relationship with me and so are not afraid to initiate such behaviour. However, I don't particularly want a horse's head rubbing on me whenever I go in the stable, so I put the behaviour 'on cue'; when the horse rubs his head on me I say, 'head rub!' and reinforce the action with a treat; once this is confirmed, I only give the cue 'head rub!' when it's OK for the horse to rub his head on me. And I brace myself against something solid, so I will not be knocked over. In this way I can teach my horses that there is a time when head-rubbing is acceptable, and times when it is not.

In the same way, by being consistent in our use of tack we can teach a stallion that the time to be interested in mares is when he is wearing the halter (or bridle) in which he covers mares (or goes out with them), and not when he is wearing an ordinary halter or riding bridle.

Before you start

Before you even start training, decide what you want to achieve, then break it down into small, manageable 'chunks'. Remember that the horse doesn't know what you want; you have to make it clear to him each step of the way. This is where the idea of 'shaping' comes into play. An example of breaking lessons down into manageable chunks is given on page 185, where I describe re-training a foal to accept the halter after an accident.

Conditions must be right

Before we can even think about training, we must first of all ensure that the conditions are right for learning. As Chapter 8 showed, stress inhibits learning – and sometimes prevents it altogether. So if you are intending to train a stallion, first of all you must both be *calm*. Don't attempt to train in conditions which are likely to upset the horse.

The exception to this is when you are teaching a stallion to accept a situation which he may find upsetting (see, for example, under **Training a stallion to accept separation from mares**). This kind of training is largely a matter of habituation, and a considerable part of it consists of getting the horse to remain calm in that situation. That is not the same as training him for a specific behaviour (for example, standing still; leading; moving away etc.). For those kinds of situations, a calm atmosphere is essential.

Breaking it all down into easy steps

It is easy to become impatient and try to achieve too much all at once. Too many horses develop behavioural problems because their training has been rushed, and they have been asked to learn too many things at once.

The example given below refers to an incident in the training of a colt foal, but the steps taken to correct the problem that arose can be applied to any horse and in many other situations. It is the principles behind those steps that are important, rather than their context.

Teaching a foal to accept a headcollar

Our Arabian colt foal Tariel had become accustomed to a headcollar and was calm and compliant when being led. One day he was being led when suddenly he was startled by something and jerked his head sharply to one side. The headcollar twisted, causing the lead rope to flip up. The clip of the lead rope caught on Tariel's eyelid; fortunately, the eye itself was not damaged and the eyelid suffered only a minor cut. However, this unpleasant experience made him refuse to have anything to do with attempts to reintroduce the headcollar; it had conditioned him to fear it as a source of pain and discomfort.

At this stage many people would have forced a headcollar on him. However, attempts to do so would not only have confirmed his fears, but also they might well have caused him to panic and injure himself in the process. A different approach was called for. Over a period of a week or more my husband fed the foal with one hand, at the same time bringing the other hand, holding the headcollar, closer to the foal's head and neck. To begin with Tariel was inclined to move away from the headcollar as soon as it approached him. Brian had to sense the point at which the foal was about to withdraw, and remove the headcollar before he did so. In this way Tariel did not simply grab a mouthful of food and then move away, as he might otherwise have done. He gradually accepted having the headcollar near his head for longer spells; as he was being fed at the same time, this distracted him and introduced something pleasant into what could otherwise have been a rather fraught situation.

After a couple of weeks of doing this every day, and making a little progress every time, Brian was eventually able to persuade Tariel to put his nose through the noseband of the headcollar. He was happy to do so if Brian held some food so that the foal had to put his nose through the noseband in order to get to the food (I must emphasize that at no time was he deprived of food). The next step was to get him to accept having the strap over his neck and eventually over the top of his head. All this was done very gradually over a period of three weeks. It had to be done very slowly and calmly so as not to upset or startle the foal. At the same time Brian had to be sure to remove the headcollar the instant he sensed that the foal was about to back away. Finally the time came to see if he would accept having the strap fastened.

For safety and ease of fastening, an extension was attached to the headcollar strap and fastened to the cheek-piece on the other side. This extension consisted of two parts which joined together by means of two pieces of Velcro. If Tariel tolerated having the strap brought over his head to join the cheek-piece on the other side, the strap could be fastened by means of the Velcro – quick, easy and safe. If he struggled, or caught the headcollar on anything, the Velcro would come apart and he would not be injured.

In the event, the foal allowed Brian, assisted by me, to fasten the Velcro without fuss. Once he was aware that the headcollar was on, he leaped around the stable for a minute or so, shaking his head to try to get rid of it.[1] However, he soon calmed down and within minutes appeared to have accepted the headcollar as something which was not particularly pleasant but which was evidently not going to harm him. He wore it for the rest of that day without mishap, and it was left on that night. Although he managed to get rid of it during the night, he accepted having it put on again the next day, and even allowed Brian to make adjustments to the fit. After a few more days of getting accustomed to it, he was quite happy to have it put on and taken off, and was even starting to allow himself to be led. Again, this was done gradually; with Brian holding the headcollar very gently, I

---

1 This could be described as a mild, benign form of flooding. It differs, however, from the usual forms of flooding in that if the foal (who seemed more irritated than alarmed) did panic, the Velcro ensured that the headcollar would come apart easily and he would be able to escape from it.

The Natural Stallion

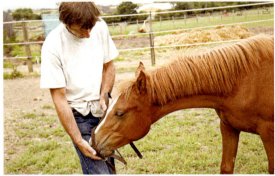

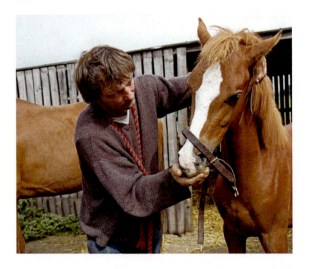

Teaching a foal to overcome his fear of the headcollar.

Top left: Brian shows Tariel the headcollar.
Top right: Tariel sniffs it.
Centre left: Tariel puts his nose just inside the noseband to take a treat.
Centre right: He allows Brian to slip the headcollar little higher up his nose.
Above left: after a couple of weeks Brian can slip his hand up Tariel's neck without the foal pulling away
Above right: Brian slips the head strap over the top of Tariel's neck
Right: Brian holds the head strap in place so that I can fasten the headcollar with Velcro (not shown)

Photos: Lesley Skipper

asked the foal to walk forward (which he had been taught to do at an early age, in response to the voice). The instant he complied, even if only to take one step forward, Brian released the headcollar and rewarded the foal with some food. In this way the behaviour of moving forward while someone held the headcollar was gradually built up until he was allowing himself to be led freely.

Although this process took several weeks, it achieved the desired result without any further trauma to the foal. There was absolutely no coercion involved; if he showed signs of backing off, so did the handler (as previously explained, this was done before the foal actually did back away, so that he was not accidentally rewarded for doing so).

Don't expect instant results

Forget all about achieving a specific result within a specific time-frame. As Colonel Alois Podhajsky used to say, 'I have time.' This should be a horse' trainer's mantra.

Teaching the stallion to accept separation from mares

This is really a form of habituation. First teach the stallion a control cue as described in Chapter 8 so that you can ask him to stand quietly. Next practise taking the stallion out for brief spells, leaving the mare(s) in the field or paddock. At this stage, don't take him too far away; let him see that his mares are still safe and not being seduced by a strange stallion. Once he is calm, standing still and paying attention, give him a treat or a scratch or a rub – whatever he likes – then let him back out into the field. Repeat this, spreading the lessons out over a number of days, gradually moving him farther and farther away, until you can move him out of sight of the mares altogether.

If you have a stallion who does make a lot of fuss, one way to deal with this – if you have the facilities – is to put him in a separate enclosure (a round pen would be ideal; failing that, section off a part of his paddock or field with electrified tape or rope – see Appendix I) before you take any of the mares out. The important thing is for him to realize that they will come back, so they should only be taken out for a short spell initially, then brought back again as soon as the stallion has settled down (he should of course be rewarded for any sign that he is accepting their absence). The length of time they are out of the paddock can then be gradually increased.

Washing the sheath and penis

This is one of those jobs that few people enjoy but which have to be done from time to time if you have male horses, to get rid of all the crusty 'bits' of smegma that can accumulate within the sheath and on the penis itself. As I mentioned in Chapter 2, only water should be used for this. Many horses enjoy the procedure, sometimes going so far as to relax the penis, making the job much easier. However, others dislike the whole business and have to be taught progressively to tolerate it. The following is taken from 'Stallion sexual behaviour' by Sue McDonnell, Chapter 4 of *Equine Breeding Management and Artificial Insemination*. (Saunders (Elsevier) 1999). I have reproduced it here in full (with permission) because it would be difficult to improve on as an example of how to introduce a stallion to having his penis washed.[2] This is the procedure used at the University of Pennsylvania School of Veterinary Medicine's clinic:

1. The handler of the stallion positions the stallion to stand under control, for example, parallel to a padded wall. The stallion handler stands on the near side almost in front of the stallion, but

---

2 The inside of the sheath should be washed out at the same time as a matter of course.

out of the way of a strike.

2. The washing technician approaches at the shoulder of the stallion, running the back of the left hand along the neck, shoulder and abdomen of the horse until standing with the left shoulder of the technician touching the side of the stallion. The erect penis is firmly grasped with the left hand midway along the shaft; it is gently directed toward the handler.[3]

3. If the stallion moves away, the technician should attempt to move with the horse, without flinching or otherwise reacting. The stallion needs to learn two things: (a) the procedure is not going to hurt him (it actually quickly appears pleasant to most stallions), and (b) nothing the stallion does will avoid the procedure. In other words, his movement does not stop the washing of the penis.

4. If the stallion kicks, explosive punishment should be avoided. Gentle discouragement and continuation of the job so that the stallion gets to know that it can be pleasant and that it leads to the opportunity to breed is usually the best strategy for all but the most dangerously resistant stallions.

5. If the stallion should thrust forward or the glans penis should flower from the stimulation, no discipline is necessary. Gently deflecting the penis downward toward the back legs naturally reduces the tumescence. Cooler wash water is less likely to stimulate thrusting or flowering. It is useful for most handlers to appreciate that the horse is not misbehaving, just responding positively to this unnatural procedure.

6. All that is necessary to adequately cleanse the penis is gentle massage along the shaft to loosen flakey debris, with warm water splashed from a cup or towel onto the penis. Up and down stroking motion abrades the surface and is unnecessary.

7. Some horses resent having hot water splashed on their hind legs or abdomen and scrotum. With experience technicians can effectively deliver a vigorous splash of water to the penis without hitting the belly or legs.

8. The glans penis is deflected with the thumb to rinse out the fossa and any smegma 'bean.'

9. The base of the penis is an area with heavy smegma accumulation that cannot be effectively cleansed. It is often best left undisturbed.

10. Care should be exercised to allow water run-off to flow toward the base rather than the glans penis, which was just cleaned.

11. The penis is dried by wrapping and blotting with a clean cloth or paper towel from glans to base direction. This keeps the glans cleanest. Rubbing abrades the delicate tissues and is unnecessary.

12. Nondisposable fabrics are generally too abrasive. Air-drying for a minute or two is also adequate.

---

[3] Author's note: some stallions will not readily 'drop' to allow this part of the procedure; in that case warm water should be used to wash out the sheath as thoroughly as possible. In many cases this will actually encourage the stallion to relax the penis; when he does so this should be positively reinforced as described in Chapter 9..

Common mistakes

Ditzing with the head of the horse during washing of the penis
Startling the stallion by simply grasping the penis without warning
Too light or too rough handling of the penis
Abrading the penis by vigorous rubbing of the shaft
Splashing water on the belly, scrotum, or hind legs
Reacting each time the horse flinches or lifts a leg, teaching him that he can control human behaviour (McDonnell, 1999)

Teaching stallions to ignore oestrus mares

A stallion whose only experience of oestrus mares is in a breeding context will initially find it difficult to ignore them in other contexts. As always, time and patience are the keys. First of all you must ensure that you can get your stallion's attention, as described in Chapter 8 and earlier in this chapter. Bear in mind that he is not a machine, and to begin with he may not be as attentive as he would be in less exciting circumstances. This is to be expected, and must not be punished. The last thing you want is to get into a fight with him!

Put the oestrus mare in a secure area where the stallion can see her. Having initially got his attention, lead him (if necessary in a bridle; whether you use a bridle or a halter of some kind, make sure it is not one in which he normally covers mares) to a point where he becomes aware of the mare. The moment he becomes distracted and starts to shout out to her and/or pull away from you, ask him to do something. Turn him away, back him up, ask him for shoulder-in in hand (safer than asking him to circle as he is less likely to crowd you in his excitement) or any other exercise you can think of to engage his mind and body. Don't ask for perfection; he will probably be too distracted at this stage to produce more than a sketchy movement. This doesn't matter; all you are aiming for here is that his attention is focused on *you*, not the mare. As soon as he become calm again, reinforce the calmness with whatever kind of reward he likes, as suggested in Chapter 9 (if you use food rewards, I suggest you carry out this exercise when the stallion is hungry). If he remains calm enough, just let him stand and look at the mare. If the area is grassed so much the better; if he stays calm enough to drop his head and graze, let him; he is well on the way to understanding what you want of him. Again, don't ask for absolute calmness and obedience just yet; at this stage you want an approximation, however small, of the behaviour you eventually want. If his attention wanders again, repeat the exercise until he is calm once more, and reward. Eventually he will get the message that a) just because the mare is in oestrus doesn't mean he has to do something about it, and b) when he does encounter an oestrus mare, if he behaves himself there will be something pleasant in it for him (rewards, relaxation), but if he doesn't he will have to work.

How long do you make the training session? This depends very much on the individual stallion, but I would be prepared to set aside a considerable part of the day. Normally I would keep training sessions short, but in this case part of the training consists of habituation, so the stallion needs to be around the mare for the lesson to 'stick'. Once he shows more interest in paying attention to you, or in eating grass, than the mare, spend a few minutes making a fuss of him, then end the session. Repeat the lesson on successive days – and perhaps over the course of several oestrus periods – until he is reliably calm in the presence of the oestrus mare. You can gradually move him closer and closer to her until he accepts that without fuss; if at any time he gets distracted, simply repeat the exercises until he is calm again.

Indeed, calmness is the key: no matter what the stallion does, *you* must remain calm – as in every situation when dealing with stallions. If you think the stallion may become too upset for you to handle, enlist a competent assistant. If you have gone through the preliminary training suggested earlier in this chapter, however, you will already have instilled in your stallion the basics of good behaviour, which can be transferred to virtually any learning situation.

A stallion who can remain calm in the presence of oestrus mares – surely the most distracting situation a stallion can find himself in, in a domestic setting – will easily be able to learn to remain calm in the presence of non-oestrus mares, geldings, and other stallions. He will also be able to transfer that good behaviour to being ridden in the presence of other horses of whatever sex, and regardless of whether a mare is oestrus or dioestrus. Exactly the same principles apply: the stallion learns that the distracting presence does not mean that good behaviour is not required, and once that good behaviour becomes part of his repertoire he will be able to call upon it even in exciting situations, for example at shows, where he may have to contend with the close proximity of horses of both sexes as well as geldings.

Even comparatively young, inexperienced stallions can learn to behave themselves in such a situation. When Nivalis was a youngster, we took him, together with his dam, to our county show. By that time he had covered a mare, so he knew what that aspect of life was about; however, having been accustomed to going to shows since he was a foal, he already knew what kind of behaviour was expected of him. In a large mixed class[4] he stood calmly, sandwiched between a mare and a gelding, and allowed the judge to examine him closely without turning a hair.

---

4 Arabian breed shows are among the few where mixed classes are allowed.

CHAPTER 11

Dealing with problem behaviours

Speak roughly to your little boy
And beat him when he sneezes:
He only does it to annoy
Because he knows it teases.

– Lewis Carroll, Alice's Adventures in Wonderland

[**PLEASE NOTE:** The suggestions made in this chapter are just that – suggestions and approaches based on the science of learning and behaviour. There is no guarantee that any of them will solve your horse's particular problem, because every horse is an individual, and problems must be solved by taking into account everything about an individual: past history and management (if known); veterinary history; current management regime; how the horse is handled now or has been handled in the past – and, of course, the individual horse's character and temperament. If you do not have extensive experience in dealing with equine behaviour problems and your stallion is exhibiting behaviour which may be dangerous or injurious, please consult someone who does have the necessary experience. See Appendix II for some suggestions.]

What counts as a behavioural problem?

$\mathcal{A}$T its simplest, a 'problem' behaviour is one which affects the health of the horse, whether physical or mental, and/or creates difficulties with management and training.

All mammals are born with the potential to develop a wide range of behaviours. Some of these behaviours are species-specific, while others may be found in many different species. Some behaviours are innate, while others must be learned. Certain behaviours are essential to survival, while others may only emerge in very specific situations. And, finally, there are some behaviours which are so extreme and bizarre that we wonder whether the animal's brain has been affected by some disease or injury.

Temperament and behavioural problems

It can be tempting to see behavioural problems as the result of a stallion's individual temperament, and to attribute this to genetic inheritance. However, as Chapter 10 showed, temperament (and therefore personality) is shaped by a very complex interaction of inborn tendencies and life experiences. When behavioural problems arise, dealing with them effectively, humanely and ethically means that we cannot simply attribute them to a faulty temperament, or say, as some people do, that a stallion is 'mean', 'bad-tempered', or – to use a term common in the US – 'rank'. We have to look more carefully at the behaviour and try to determine the cause before we even think about 'curing' or modifying it.

As Dr Marthe Kiley-Worthington points, 'In the majority of cases, stallions are "difficult" because they are made so.' (Kiley-Worthington, 1987) Having seen how 'killer' stallions can be reformed by sympathetic handling and management, and how poor management and handling can turn an easy-going, good-tempered stallion into a savage monster, I can only concur with Dr Kiley-Worthington's view. I must re-state my earlier conclusions: that many of the problems associated with stallions are actually created by the beliefs and expectations of the people handling and managing them (the so-called 'self-fulfilling prophecy' referred to in Chapter 1).

Castration is not necessarily the answer

Along with the idea that behavioural problems can be attributed to a faulty temperament, is the pervasive idea, referred to in Chapter 3, that such problems can be solved by castration, which may not necessarily be the case.[1] As we saw in that chapter, Andy Beck of the White Horse Equine Ethology Project believes – and the evidence supports him – that castration is not necessarily effective in extinguishing sexual behaviour. Andy also has strong views on castration as a 'cure' for behavioural problems:

> ... far from being the panacea that many believe it is, the outcome of this most intrusive of all management techniques is as uncertain as it is irreversible. Where there is an established history of anti-social or psychologically dysfunctional behavior, the operation will have achieved nothing, except to create real discomfort and perhaps confusion. The notion that the excision of a body part will somehow heal behavioural dysfunction resulting from an extended period of inappropriate treatment is so without any logical foundation that it should amaze us that there are so many people willing to believe it. (Beck, The Secret Life of Stallions, 2006)

In a similar vein Dr Marthe Kiley-Worthington, having pointed out that the majority of 'difficult' stallions are difficult because they are made so, goes on to ask, 'Is it right that people should compensate for their own incompetence by surgery?' (Kiley-Worthington, 1987)

However, there may be some situations where castration does offer the horse the best chance of a decent life. I refer to those cases where, for one reason or another, a stallion can no longer be kept entire without severely compromising his welfare (for example, because his owner is ill or has died and there is no-one with the necessary experience to look after an entire male horse; or because the owner has had to move the horse to a livery yard which does not accept stallions, and so on). As we have seen, there is no guarantee that castration will solve any behavioural problems, but where the horse's behaviour is not in itself a problem (only the fact that he *is* entire) then castration may be the kindest option for him.

---

[1] In their book *Canine and Feline behavioural therapy*, (Lea and Febiger, 1985), B.L. and L.A. Hart showed that about 50 per cent of dogs neutered because of excessive aggression towards other dogs continue to attack dogs after castration.(cited by Dierendonck *et al.*, 1995)

Taking responsibility

Whether we like it or not, ethical and humane considerations mean that we must accept the fact that in many cases we (or a previous owner or trainer) may be responsible for a stallion's difficult or dangerous behaviour. Having said that, many behavioural problems may have at their root some physical cause. Anyone seeking to find the cause of problem behaviour should *first of all* try to determine whether there is some physical condition that is causing the stallion to behave in the way that is causing problems. This involves working with a veterinary surgeon to try to eliminate physical causes. Bear in mind that many veterinary surgeons may have little specialist knowledge of equine behaviour. This is entirely understandable; vets have to learn about the anatomy and physiology of so many different species that learning about their behaviour as well would take many years and be an impossible burden for student vets to bear. Some vets, especially those who go on to specialize in horses and other large animals once they have qualified and gone into practice, do take the trouble to learn more about equine behaviour; in some cases they may believe they know more than they actually do. So you may have to exercise considerable tact in dealing with your vet regarding behavioural issues.[2]

Diagnosing the problem

The first step in dealing with any problem is defining what the problem actually is. The best way to start is to make detailed notes over a period of time. This requires time and considerable self-discipline, but it is necessary in order to get a full picture of what is going on. Keep a notebook handy so that you can record the following details:

1. What does the stallion do (or not do)? Avoid trying to interpret the behaviour, or attempting to guess what the horse is thinking or feeling. State, in simple terms, what he actually does.

2. Where is he when he does it? If it occurs in more than one location, specify where.

3. How often does he do it?

4. When did it start?

5. What was the stallion doing when the behaviour first occurred?

6. How intense is the behaviour?

7. Did it start off being mild, and then get worse, or has it always been at the same intensity?

8. What does it seem to achieve (i.e. what is the immediate consequence of the behaviour)?

9. Can the behaviour be triggered by something you do? If so, what?

10. Who else is around at the time? List any humans or other animals, including other horses, who are present when the stallion performs the behaviour

---

2 I remember some years ago being lectured about stallion behaviour by a young Australian vet who had evidently swallowed some of the sillier ideas about stallions and dominance. I smiled politely, and let him continue – arguing would not have changed his mind, or convinced him that I actually knew more than he did.

11. What – if anything – happened just before the behaviour?

12. How did you – or anyone else – react to the stallion's behaviour? Did you do anything to correct it?

13. If you did something to correct the behaviour, what did you do?

It will also be very helpful if you can video the behaviour as it occurs, although this may be difficult if the behaviour is unpredictable. However, if the behaviour can be triggered at will, then (always taking safety considerations into account if the behaviour is potentially dangerous) it may be worth doing this in order to take a video and thereby have as full a record as possible.

The answers to these questions will help you (and your vet, or anyone else you may call upon for help – see Appendix II) to diagnose the probable cause of the behaviour, and devise a solution.

Physical or behavioural?

Even after carrying out a thorough review of the stallion's behaviour, it may still be difficult to determine whether or not the behaviour has a physical cause. Sometimes even veterinary surgeons are unable to find anything wrong even after a battery of tests have been carried out. However, there may be some clues which will help. Dr Sue McDonnell, who is a certified animal behaviour scientist with many years' experience of stallions, suggests that the form of the behaviour can give clues about its cause. 'For example, if the behavior is more dramatic, unusual, or intense than necessary to achieve a perceived goal, then the cause is probably physical.' (McDonnell, 2005)

Dealing with the problem

Once we have diagnosed the problem, how do we deal with it? Obviously, this depends on whether the cause is physical, behavioural, or a combination of the two; if physical causes are a factor then these must be dealt with before any attempt is made to deal with the behavioural aspect.

Behaviour modification

There are various principles that we can use in modifying problem or unwanted behaviour. However, before going any further, we need to be sure that we address the cause of the behaviour and the horse's underlying emotional state. To do otherwise would be unethical and potentially harmful; this is why great care should be taken when attempting behaviour modification.

First do no harm

Some experts in learning theory maintain that it is pointless trying to understand the underlying cause of behaviour in animals; it is enough to be able to modify it. I think this can be a dangerous approach. Take the example of the horse who bangs on his door. If this is only done at mealtimes we can ignore it (extinction) or put it on cue; the horse will still get his dinner once he stops banging. However, if the horse bangs on his door out of frustration at being cooped up in a stable, then eliminating or modifying the behaviour does nothing to ease the horse's frustration, which may be intensified and expressed in a different manner, possibly through stereotypical behaviour (such as weaving) or aggression. So *always* investigate the cause of unwanted behaviour. In some cases you can do this yourself, by observing and analysing the horse's actions; in others you may need to call in an animal behaviour specialist. Advice on how to find a reliable specialist is given in Appendix II.

Extinction

This is one of the most powerful 'tools' a trainer can have for dealing with unwanted behaviour. Unfortunately, while it is simple in principle, it has a number of drawbacks.

If a behaviour is not reinforced to the point where it becomes ingrained, or not reinforced at all, it will cease completely. For example, like many (perhaps most) colts, Nivalis could be very 'mouthy' when he was a youngster (I cover this in more detail under ***Nipping*** on pages 228–230). When he wanted attention he would nudge me and/or grab at my sleeve as I went past. It was tempting to respond with irritation but I ignored him and eventually the behaviour stopped because it was not being reinforced; in other words he was not getting anything out of the behaviour. This process is called *extinction*.

One problem with using extinction to deal with unwanted behaviour is that absolute consistency is necessary, or the problem may be made worse, not better. For example: suppose, in the case of Nivalis cited above, I ignored the behaviour but my husband did not. Nivalis would learn that sometimes the behaviour got the attention he wanted, but sometimes it did not. Because this effectively constitutes a *variable schedule of reinforcement* as described in Chapter 9, he would actually be more likely to escalate the behaviour in the hope that he might get what he wanted. This is exactly what happens when children throw tantrums in public places: their parents, wanting to avoid embarrassment, give in to their demands, whereas at home they might well not do so. The result is a child who knows they can get their own way by throwing tantrums in public places; the behaviour will therefore get worse until both parents consistently ignore it. (My own mother was iron-willed in this respect: no matter how severe my tantrum, she refused to give in. I soon learned that holding my breath and stamping my feet got me nowhere, and quickly stopped doing it.) One person, provided they have sufficient willpower and determination not to give in, can render an unwanted behaviour extinct; if even one other person lacks the willpower to do so, behaviour modification will not take place and the behaviour may even get worse. This makes it especially difficult to use extinction on a livery yard, because there is no guarantee that every person there will ignore the behaviour (some may stubbornly refuse to do so, believing that unwanted behaviour should always be punished). Many stallion owners, however, will not have this problem, as they are more likely than most horse owners to keep their horse(s) at home (or at least on their own land).

The other problem with using extinction is that the behaviour may (in fact, almost certainly will) get worse before it gets better; this is called an **extinction burst**. Again, this is caused by the effects of variable reinforcement: to begin with, the stallion will probably escalate the behaviour in the attempt to get the satisfaction he previously obtained from performing it. If he could think in words, it would probably be something like, 'This worked before; why isn't it working now? Maybe if I keep trying even harder it'll start working again…' (Before anyone starts feeling superior, let me say that humans do exactly the same, often with far less justification. As a species we have a remarkable capacity for continuing to repeat the same action, even when it doesn't bring us the result we want. That's one reason why there are so many 'difficult' horses.) The only way to deal with this is to persist in ignoring the behaviour; eventually it *will* stop. Unfortunately, at this point too many people give up, believing the tactic doesn't work. It does. You just have to hang in there. One essential – and challenging – aspect of using extinction as part of behaviour modification is identifying everything in the animal's environment that could be reinforcing the behaviour. It may not be immediately obvious what is reinforcing to the horse; often the only way to find out is by intensive observation (which should in any case form part of any behaviour modification programme). For example, the colt who nips because he wants attention might not respond to punishment, because that is giving him what he wants: attention. Unless the punishment is so severe that the severity outweighs the reinforcing aspect,[3] the colt will continue to nip as long as the nipping gets him the attention he craves.

Other methods of changing unwanted behaviour

Using conditioning to cure certain types of problem behaviour is a far more effective approach than punishment. One method involves training an animal to perform a behaviour that is physically incompatible with the unwanted behaviour. For example, Nivalis, like many stallions, could be quite nippy as a youngster. To counteract this we taught Nivalis, using +R, to stand still when requested. He could not stand like this and continue to nip; we thus got rid of the nipping without resorting to punishment. This is known as **counter-conditioning.**

Counter-conditioning

In Chapter 8, when I gave an example of what could be done to prevent a horse from barging, the example given contained an element of counter-conditioning. If a horse is taught to stand still and remain calm while the door to his stable is being opened, he cannot do so and barge at the same time. He has been conditioned to behave in a way that runs *counter* to his natural inclination, which is to rush out of the stable. It would be unfair and unrealistic to expect the horse to learn this while he is still desperately eager to get out, so the key to making this particular behaviour modification successful is to keep the situation low-key, and to start the counter-conditioning when the horse has been out and has been brought back in, sufficiently relaxed to absorb the lesson.

Counter-conditioning is often paired with systematic **desensitization.**

Desensitization

Systematic desensitization involves gradually exposing an animal to stimuli which elicit undesirable responses at a level low enough to prevent those responses from actually being triggered. In the example given on pages 185–187, how we trained Tariel to accept the halter after his frightening experience with one, the halter was presented to the foal in such a way that it did not trigger the fear response he had shown following his accident. Instead, he was encouraged to relax (being scratched, given treats) while the halter was gradually introduced. In this way, instead of responding to the sight of the halter with fear, he was conditioned to see it as something associated with good things (scratches, treats). This is an example of combining systematic desensitization with counter-conditioning.

As the desensitization progresses, the stimulus can be presented at gradually increasing levels; when the animal remains calm at a particular level, the stimulus level can be (again, very gradually) increased, until at the highest level it elicits no inappropriate or unwanted response.

This is effectively what we are doing when we introduce stallions to other horses: we wait until the stallion is calm at a distance before moving closer (and thus increasing the stimulus).

The key to successful desensitization and counter-conditioning is patience: being willing to proceed slowly and gradually and never to expect too much all at once (this of course applies to any

---

[3] Which, for the reasons stated in Chapter 9, is *not* recommended

aspect of training). Once the new behaviour is learned, the horse must be presented with a variety of stimuli in as many different situations as possible; in this way he can learn to generalize his new behaviour to different environments, and not just associate it with the situation and place where he learned it. In this way, stallions who become accustomed to behaving calmly around mares at home may be taught to remain calm even in more exciting situations, for example at shows.

Putting behaviour on cue

We can also try 'putting behaviour on cue', as mentioned in Chapter 10 under **Consistency is the key**. Suppose your horse persistently bangs his door at mealtimes, as described in Chapter 9. Using +R, you teach him to bang on cue, by reinforcing the behaviour when it occurs, then pairing the behaviour with a cue such as, 'Bang!' (or any other word you like). Once you can get the horse to bang on his door by saying 'Bang!' or whatever, and it has become an ingrained part of his behavioural repertoire to do this, you have effectively put the behaviour under the control of the cue. Then you simply never give the cue. This technique is often used to cure dogs whose barking has become a problem; like all training it requires time and patience but it is actually a very effective way of getting rid of unwanted behaviour.

What kind of problems are unsuitable for behaviour modification?

Actually, quite a few! Many so-called behavioural problems are caused by factors in the horse's environment. As we saw in Chapter 7, an inadequate social environment can cause an increase in reactivity, making a stallion more prone to 'act up' and become out of control; horses kept in a restricted environment are more likely to develop stereotypical behaviours, while in addition stallions and geldings may resort to self-mutilation (which in itself can be a form of stereotypical behaviour). Diet can also be a major factor in creating behavioural problems; the most obvious example is that of horses (not just stallions) fed a high-energy diet but given little opportunity to work off the resulting energy. I imagine most people with long experience of horses will at some time have had to deal with the resulting hyperactivity and explosiveness. However, it is not only high-energy feed that can cause problems; a startlingly high proportion of horses (and not just racehorses or high-level competition horses, but everyday leisure horses) suffer from gastric ulcers as a result of a diet with insufficient forage. This possibility will be looked at under specific behaviours which may be caused or exacerbated by ulcers.

To attempt behaviour modification of problems resulting from these physical factors without first of all changing those aspects of the environment could be considered unethical, as it would ignore associated welfare issues. The same applies to behavioural problems caused by pain or discomfort. For this reason, behaviour modification should only be attempted after thorough investigation has shown that it is the most suitable approach.

That being the case, before we look at various problem behaviours and some suggestions about how to deal with them, we will first of all consider some of the problems arising from physical and environmental (in which I include training and management regimes) causes.

Stress – what is it and how does it affect horses?

As we have seen, many management regimes, designed with the convenience of humans in mind rather than that of the horses themselves, deprive stallions of the ability to perform many of their natural behaviours. When everyday life produces stresses that individual horses are unable to cope with, physical and behavioural problems may arise.

What is stress?

In itself, stress is neither good nor bad. Hans Selye, pioneer in stress research, defined it as 'the non-specific response of the body to any demand'. This response is regulated by hormones released into the bloodstream by endocrine glands or specialized nerve cells. These hormones tell the body what to do in specific circumstances. For example, if danger threatens, the adrenal glands secrete adrenaline, which increases breathing rate and heart activity and intensifies muscle power. This prepares the body either to stand and fight or to flee – the famous 'fight or flight' syndrome. Stress can therefore be a source of energy as well as the body's system of raising awareness. In the short term this can be beneficial; however, when the demands on an individual exceed that individual's ability to cope with them, stress ceases to be beneficial and becomes *distress.*

Effects on physical health

Stress can affect physical health in many ways. For example, the stress response can increase acid secretions in the stomach, which may in turn increase the risk of gastric and duodenal ulcers. Some of the hormones and neurotransmitters produced during those stress responses have been proved to affect the immune system. The temporary suppression of the immune system which results from the release of these hormones may act, in the short term, to conserve the energy required for action appropriate to the crisis. But if the stress is constant, the effects on the immune system may be long-lasting, leaving the body prey to all manner of viral and bacterial infections.

Behavioural problems

Behavioural problems may also arise where stress levels exceed the ability to cope. An increase in aggression, general irritability, and the development of stereotypical behaviour (discussed later in this chapter) are common responses, and we can see some or all of these in horses who are under stress.

How do we know that these are responses to stress, and not caused by something else? We can observe the animals in question in a variety of environments and note how their behaviour differs in each case. If, for example, a high proportion of horses in a specific environment develop similar behavioural problems, we may suspect that the problems are linked to that environment. If the behavioural problems are alleviated or cured completely by a change of environment and/ or management regime, that suggests very strongly that our suspicions were correct. Behavioural scientists will try to gather as much information as they can before concluding that 'X' (where 'X' might be a specific situation or environment) is a significant cause of stress in horses.

Studying stress

Another way that scientists can study stress in horses is by taking blood samples at various times and analysing them for the chemicals and hormones which play a key role in the body's response to stress. So although we cannot ask horses directly whether they are suffering from stress, we can observe their behaviour and use the knowledge gained from the various scientific studies carried out on stress in horses and other animals to judge whether specific behaviours are the result of stress or whether they stem from some other cause.

The stresses of living in the wild

Horses living in the wild have to cope with different kinds of stresses from those experienced by horses living in a domestic setting. Although much has been written about the horse as a prey animal, there are actually very few places in the world where feral (i.e. domestic horses living in a wild state) or free-ranging horses face a significant amount of danger from predators. In some parts of the north-west USA mountain lions (pumas, or *Felis concolor*) may sometimes prey on foals and/ or sick and weakened horses. Bears may also sometimes attack horses, although they are not generally a significant risk to feral horses in the USA. Zebras, of course, may be attacked by large predators such as lions, cheetahs and, when crossing rivers, by crocodiles. In general, though, the kinds of large predator capable of bringing a horse down are not common in the lands inhabited by feral horses.

Shortage of food and water may produce what is called nutritional stress. Nevertheless, except in times of extreme drought even the horses inhabiting areas such as the Namib Desert manage to stay comparatively healthy in spite of the harshness of the environment in which they live.

In some situations feral horses may be stressed by the incursion of strange horses into their home range, especially if the 'invader' is a stallion attempting to take over a family group. If a stallion is deposed by the newcomer, the band mares may be harassed by the new stallion until they all get to know each other; this process, together with the loss of their own stallion, might conceivably produce high levels of stress in the band mares and their offspring. Stallions, too, must surely find the effort of protecting their family against intruders very stressful at times. However, these are short-term situations which do not arise every day. In general, feral horses left to their own devices would appear to live relatively stress-free lives. Certainly, the kind of stereotyped behaviours usually referred to as 'stable vices' (such as weaving, crib-biting, windsucking etc.), which result from long-term stress (and which we shall discuss later in this chapter), have not to date been observed in the wild.

Chronic ill-health

Among horses in a domestic setting, chronic ill health such as frequent viral infections, loss of appetite with no apparent cause, repeated bouts of colic and gastric ulcers, may be a result of long-term stress.

Gastric ulcers

Research carried out in Hong Kong, the USA, Australia and the UK suggests that a startlingly high number of horses used for racing and competition may be affected by gastric ulcers; the figures may be as high as 90 per cent of racehorses and up to 60 per cent of show and competition horses. Research carried out on horses not in race training, by a team of Danish and English scientists in Denmark, found that 53 per cent of the horses examined had severe ulcer lesions. Their conclusion was that 'This study confirms that gastric ulceration can be prevalent in a group of apparently clinically normal horses, not in intensive work.' (Luthersson *et al.*, 2009)

Ulcers are caused by an excess of acid in the upper part of the horse's stomach, which – unlike the lower portion of the equine stomach – is not well protected against the acids and enzymes which help to break down food. The main reason why racehorses, show and competition horses suffer such a high incidence of ulcers is that so many of them spend a high proportion of their time stabled up with limited amounts of forage to eat. A regular intake of feed such as grass, hay or alfalfa (lucerne) helps to neutralize stomach acids, as does water; Luthersson et al found that

> In the study population, 26% of the horses did not have water available in the paddock demonstrating that a simple intervention to make water available could have had a significant impact on the total number of horses with EGUS[4] in this group. (Luthersson, 2009)

Horses in hard work are usually fed a diet high in grain, the starch content of which actually stimulates the gastric secretions that cause ulcers. Even horses who are not in hard work may be fed in this way, because of a lingering perception that horses need grain. Most leisure horses do not do nearly enough work to warrant such a diet; even endurance horses can work efficiently on diets high in forage. Where extra energy is required, oils or fats can supply sufficient energy for their needs.

Although diet and prolonged periods without food are common causes of gastric ulcers in horses, stressful environments, and the stresses associated with intensive training, can also be factors. High levels of exercise decrease blood flow to the stomach, which lowers its protection against acid secretions. Travelling, changes of environment, lack of companionship, being turned out with incompatible companions – all of these can create sufficient stress to cause an increase in stomach acids, leading to the formation of ulcers.

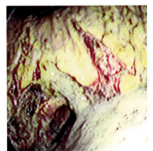

Gastric ulcer lesions in a horse's stomach.

Ulcers are caused by an excess of acid in the upper part of the horse's stomach, which – unlike the lower portion of the equine stomach – is not well protected against the acids and enzymes which help to break down food.

Stereotypies

The term 'stereotypy' is used scientifically to describe a series of fixed, repetitive, obsessive and apparently meaningless behaviour patterns. The disturbed child rocking back and forth, the dog spinning endlessly in circles, the zoo tiger pacing his cage for hours on end – these are all examples of stereotypical behaviour.

One might wonder what an animal gains by such behaviour, since to our eyes it may appear to be meaningless. Over the years many attempts have been made to provide explanations for stereotyped behaviour; what has emerged is that no single explanation is possible as there are many potential causes. Some of the behaviour may be learned: for example, if a horse becomes excited when he knows his dinner is about to arrive, he may start to nod his head in anticipation. If the food arrives while he is doing this, his behaviour is being rewarded (by the appearance of the food) and

---

4 Equine gastric ulceration syndrome

he is more likely to repeat it. If the food often arrives while he is nodding his head up and down, he may develop into a confirmed head-nodder: in other words his behaviour has been *reinforced* by the arrival of his food, and we would then say that he has been *conditioned* to repeat that behaviour when anticipating his dinner. However, he may not repeat the behaviour at any other time, so although this is stereotyped behaviour its performance is restricted to specific times, i.e. when the horse is anticipating food. Horses may display stereotyped behaviour when they are anxious, e.g. if they are waiting to be let out into the field, or for example a mare temporarily separated from her foal, but again the behaviour may be short-lived and may cease as soon as the cause of the anxiety is removed (horses let out into the field, the mare reunited with her foal). In these situations the horses concerned will usually still respond – even though they may be somewhat distracted – to nearby sights and sounds and to the humans who need to handle them. Other horses –and these are the ones giving rise to the greatest concern – may develop stereotypical behaviour that is more than a response to a temporary situation: such horses may spend hours engaged in these fixed, repetitive actions during which time they may be oblivious to anything else that is going on around them.

Whatever the immediate cause, one thing that has become clear is that stereotypies appear to be a response to a captive environment, since they have not been observed in the wild. The results of research carried out into stereotyped behaviour also suggest that each behaviour pattern has its roots in some form of behaviour that forms part of that animal's natural lifestyle: the animal appears to be 'acting out' some aspect of that behaviour in an attempt to alleviate frustration at being confined and unable to perform his natural behaviour. For example, the horse confined to the stable may want to leave his stable to run about in the field and get rid of his excess energy, or to socialize with other horses. He cannot get any further than his stable door and so cannot achieve his goal; however that goal is so important to him that he feels the need to make repeated attempts to achieve it, even though he cannot. He therefore 'acts out' the one part of the incomplete behaviour that he *can* perform: he walks towards the door then, unable to get any further, walks away again. This may develop into box-walking (see below). Crib-biting (also discussed below) appears to have its origins in an attempt to compensate for a diet high in concentrates but low in bulk fibre.

There is some evidence from the studies referred to above that horses may actually become addicted to their stereotype. Unlikely as it may seem, there is a link here to a certain aspect of human behaviour: people who like to run often do so not so much because they want to keep fit (there are other ways of keeping fit that do not involve as much stress on the joints) but because of the 'buzz' it gives them. Studies carried out on stereotypical behaviour suggest that animals who engage in stereotypies involving constant movement may be experiencing a similar 'buzz' to that felt by human runners; this may be what helps to alleviate their distress.

Boredom

One explanation that has often been put forward as a cause of stereotyped behaviour is boredom. This has frequently been dismissed by scientists, for two reasons. One is that horses who weave, for example, tend to perform more, not less, stereotyped behaviour when there is a lot of yard activity rather than when the yard is quiet. If the weaving (or whatever stereotypy may be performed) were caused by boredom, one would expect to see less, not more, of such behaviour when there is plenty going on for the horse to look at. So boredom cannot be the cause in such instances; the behaviour at such times seems to be triggered instead by a high level of emotional arousal, probably as a result of all the activity going on around the horse. Another reason for dismissing boredom as a cause is that many behavioural scientists have routinely discounted the idea that horses have any kind of mental life and surely one must have to have such an internal life in order to feel boredom.

However, we should not be too ready to rule out boredom. The more we learn about equine behaviour and physiology, the more it becomes clear that these are creatures with complex brains capable of far more than has generally been believed. We might wonder, though, how an animal which spends the greater part of its day eating could possibly feel bored. What could horses in the wild occupy themselves with when they are surrounded by nothing much but grass? It may be that where food is very scarce horses have to spend so much time finding and consuming food that they do not have much opportunity to amuse themselves in any other way. However, if we watch a group of horses who have unlimited freedom where grasses and shrubs are plentiful, we will see that in the intervals between grazing they find all kinds of things to investigate and play with (including their companions). As we saw in Chapter 7, horses not only need social contact, they also need the opportunity for play and relaxation in company.

Individual horses respond in so many different ways to similar situations that one cannot say that horses kept in a particular kind of environment will invariably tend to develop stereotypical behaviour. There is some evidence that certain horses are genetically predisposed to develop stereotypies but while such a tendency may appear to run in some families, it may simply be that such families belong to a breed frequently kept in a restricted kind of environment (e.g. Thoroughbred and Arabian racehorses, Arabian show horses, etc.)

In horses, stereotypies have often been thought of as vices (and in many countries must be declared as such if the animal is sold), as though they were mischievous actions resulting from a bad disposition. Sadly, some people still refer to them like this, even though we now know that they are not vices at all but the horse's attempt to cope with an inadequate lifestyle.

Stereotypical behaviour in horses may take the form of weaving, box-walking, head-nodding, crib-biting, and windsucking; in some cases a horse may perform more than one of these behaviours (e.g. weaving and crib-biting).

Weaving

The horse stands in his stable and weaves his head from side to side. He may also rock from one foot to the other. This is essentially a frustrated movement behaviour: the horse wants to move about freely but because he is confined to a stable he cannot fulfil his need for movement adequately. Weaving appears to have a hypnotic effect on the horse, who may stand for hours waving his head and/or rocking from side to side.

Many people attempt to 'cure' weavers by fitting an anti-weaving grille; with one of these in place, the horse can still look out, but can no longer weave his head from side to side. Another popular 'remedy' is to hang two bricks from the door frame so that if the horse attempts to weave he will hit his head on the bricks. Risk of injury aside, this and the weave grid are simply a way of masking the problem. Horses certainly tend to weave at the stable door, but just because a horse is prevented from weaving in the doorway this does not stop him from weaving further back in the stable! In fact most confirmed weavers will do this if they cannot weave at the doorway; this may actually make the problem worse, because the weaver's sense of frustration is increased by his being prevented from looking out over his stable door.

Chapter 11

Nivalis and his anti-weaving grille. as stated in the text, he has never weaved; the grille is there simply to prevent him from trying to jump over the stable door to get at horses out in the arena, should he ever take it into his head to do so. The grille slots into brackets fixed to the door (one bracket is just visible at the bottom of the photograph). Photo: Lesley Skipper

Box-walking

In many ways this is an even more distressing phenomenon than weaving. The horse walks round and round the stable, almost robotically, often keeping this up for hours at a time. Like weaving, this is an attempt to deal with the horse's frustrated need for movement. Box-walkers will often be poor doers because they are spending the time they should be eating in this travesty of equine movement.

Attempts to prevent box-walking usually involve either tying the horse up or placing obstacles in his way; a favourite 'remedy' is to place a series of rubber tyres in the stable where the horse normally box-walks. This may work in some cases but box-walkers are notoriously adept at finding ways to avoid the tyres while continuing with their robot-like walking. Furthermore, the tyres (or whatever other obstacles are placed in the stable) may prevent the horse from lying down and obtaining the rest he must surely need very badly.

Head nodding

The horse stands in one place and nods his head up and down repeatedly and for prolonged periods. He may stand still as he does this or he may perform a *piaffe*-like movement (i.e. alternately raising one diagonal pair of feet, as in the trot, but remaining in one place); sometimes the latter consists only of raising alternate forefeet. However, unlike a true *piaffe* this is not a collected movement but a hasty, agitated snatching up of the feet and then setting them down again; the feet may not be actually raised from the ground but simply half-lifted and then put down again.

Crib-biting

The horse takes hold of something (such as the top of his stable half-door, a fixed manger, a fence or the top of a gate) with his incisors (front teeth), arches his neck, pulls back and then lets go abruptly. He may grunt as he does so, although not all crib-biters do this. Crib biting is often associated with wood-chewing in general, but not all crib-biters actually chew wood and wood chewing does not always lead to crib-biting. Owners often attempt to cure crib-biters and wood-chewers by painting their stables with foul-tasting substances to put them off chewing the wood.

A crib-biter takes hold of something (such as the top of his stable half-door, a fixed manger, a fence or the top of a gate) with his incisors (front teeth), arches his neck, pulls back and then lets go abruptly. The horse in this photograph is not a true crib-biter; he only takes hold of the top of his stable door on rare occasions, and never progresses beyond simply taking hold of the top of the door. Photo: Lesley Skipper

Wind-sucking

Wind-sucking is often confused with crib-biting, possibly because so many crib-biters tend to grunt as they let go of whatever it is they are biting, giving the impression that they are gulping air. However, these are not the same thing. True windsucking is just that: the horse appears to lick or swallow the air, although recent research suggests that this is not in fact what is happening. It is not clear exactly what the horse is doing and perhaps this will only be explained when further research has been carried out. However this may be, it is certainly a bizarre and distressing behaviour and is often seen in horses who also crib-bite. Wind-suckers may have collars fitted to stop them from swallowing air, or even have operations to cut certain muscles in their necks to prevent them from windsucking. Both these 'remedies' may also be tried on crib-biters in the mistaken belief that they too are gulping air.

Attempts to cure stereotypies usually fail

Attempts to cure these stereotypies usually fail because they try to cure the symptoms without addressing the causes. Preventing a horse from performing his stereotypy is not only ineffective but also detrimental to the horse's welfare. By depriving him of his only means of coping with his situation it only drives the problem deeper inside and may actually cause total breakdown. ususally the only effective remedy is a change of management.

Self-mutilation

This is one of the most distressing and disturbing behaviours that horses can perform. Many other species self-mutilate; among domestic animals cats and dogs may lick themselves excessively, or chew their paws or tails. Birds, especially those of the parrot family, may resort to feather-plucking. Self-mutilation is common in some zoo animals. Humans self-mutilate: in its mildest form self-mutilation in humans may take the form of nail-biting; sometimes the nails are bitten down to the quick, and the surrounding area may start to bleed. Other self-mutilation behaviours, slightly more serious, may take the form of scratching, usually the arms, face and/or scalp. More serious forms of self-mutilation in humans include burns (usually cigarette burns) and cuts. Cutting behaviour is especially common. Typically such self-harm is a response to extreme emotional stress; the self-harmer is not trying to ask for help, as is often supposed (indeed, self-harm is often concealed from friends, family and health workers); in fact the self-harm is an attempt to obtain relief from a situation which feels unendurable.[5]

In horses, the self-mutilator is typically a stallion, although the behaviour has also been seen in geldings and, uncommonly, in mares. It is a type of stereotypical behaviour that is sometimes referred to as 'compulsive behaviour'

Causes of self-mutilation

Dr Sue McDonnell, who has made an extensive study of self-mutilation in horses, has divided self-mutilation behaviour into three types: Type I, where the root cause is physical discomfort and which can occur in stallions, mares and geldings; Type II, which is Dr McDonnell calls 'self-directed intermale aggression' and which is specific to stallions and geldings; and Type III, a less violent, more rhythmically repetitive behaviour.

Type I

This is an extreme behavioural response to pain, and, in addition to biting the flanks, may take the form of violent behaviour, such as bucking, kicking out, spinning in circles and nipping at the flank, shoulders or chest. (McDonnell, 2008) In extreme cases the horse may throw himself about violently. I have seen such behaviour in a horse suffering from severe colic; fortunately in that case the horse did not injure himself other than bruising his shoulders slightly, and he made a full recovery; however, it is extremely distressing and disturbing to watch. Some horses may injure themselves severely in this manner. The typical early signs of colic include turning round to look at the flank, so it is easy to see that if the pain is intense the horse might well proceed to actually biting at the flank in an attempt to obtain relief. Such behaviour typically stops when the painful condition is diagnosed and treatment given, which is why its origin can be traced to physical rather than

---

5 I have first-hand experience of this. In 2007 I was under extreme stress from a variety of causes, and took to cutting myself as a release from the stress (it is painful and embarrassing to admit to such behaviour, but if it helps people to understand what is going on the admission is worthwhile). Because the immediate sense of relief is so great, self-harm can become a habit. It can also lead to accidental (or even deliberate) harm of a much more serious nature, so it should never be dismissed as silly, neurotic or attention-seeking.

behavioural causes. In her review of self-mutilation behaviour Dr McDonnell included the following list of examples of physical discomfort causing self-mutilative behaviour in horses:

Abdominal/pelvic discomfort (includes colic, although Dr McDonnell does not specify this)
Adhesions
Aortic iliac thrombosis
Bladder disease
Epiploic foramen entrapment
Gastric ulcers
Impactions
Jejunal abscess
Limb pain
Myopathy
Nephroliths
Other causes of discomfort
Parasites
Pelvic fracture
Penile lesions (squamous cell carcinoma)
Penis bending over on itself within the sheath
Peripheral neuropathy
Scrotal hernia
Seminal vesiculitis
Skin allergies
Testicle in the inguinal ring
Testicular and scrotal lesions
Testicular torsion
Urethral lesions
Urogenital discomfort
Uroliths

Self-directed intermale aggression

Another form of self-mutilation is more specific to stallions and geldings. Sue McDonnell calls it Type II self-mutilation, or 'self-directed intermale aggression'. This is because it follows the sequence of behaviours typical of two stallions meeting in a wild or free-tanging situation, as described in Chapter 3. Dr McDonnell points out that the sniffing of each other's flank and genitals, and of each other's faeces, is an important trigger for the nipping and biting typical of such encounters. In the case of the self-mutilating stallion, however, the nipping and biting is directed against his own body, in the absence of another male. He may also spin in a tight circle, squealing and kicking out, sometimes even bucking – just as he would with another stallion. In this sense it seems to parallel some other stereotypical behaviours, in that it involves 'acting out' certain aspects of a natural behaviour that the stallion is unable to complete; in this instance, he cannot interact with another stallion, so he acts out the only part of the sequence that he can, directing the behaviour against himself and spinning, squealing, bucking, etc. Sue McDonnell says,

> It is common for episodes of flank-biting to commence with elimination marking and investigative sequences such as sniffing of feces of his own or of other stallions in shared turn-out facilities, or sniffing of his own groin. Oily body residues of self or other stallions on stall walls, fences, doorways or in trailers can similarly trigger episodes. Our clinic has been aware of cases of self-mutilation that appeared to have begun when a young stallion was first exposed without possibility to escape from the feces or oily residues of another stallion, for example during transport in a trailer or van. Episodes of Type II self-mutilation may be reliably provoked by the sight or sound of other stallions, or upon turn-out into a paddock used by other stallions. The author has observed several self-mutilating stallions whose episodes were set-off when they were exposed to their own reflection in glass or water. Similarly, tape-recorded sounds of their own vocalizations or those of other stallions reliably provoked the onset of episodes of flank-biting. (McDonnell, 2008)

In the article by Lucy Rees, cited in Chapter 2, about the Arabian stallion turned psychotic by mismanagement, Rees describes some of the stallion's more bizarre behaviour:

> Unlike hyenas, tigers and people, horses are not primary attackers: they are moony, peace-loving and paranoid, though young males in the football hooligan stage bite in play. This horse truly attacked with murderous, lunatic intent. Failing to find flesh, he thrust his head into his genitals, shrieked wildly and lashed out so violently that he nearly fell over. (Rees, 2000)

This horse had never been properly socialized; kept with his dam in a paddock until he was two-and-a-half, he was then stabled up. He had been fine until they tried to put him to a mare. When he showed no interest, his handlers had tried harder; the result was that the stallion mounted the man instead, and savaged him, almost killing him. Being alone with his mother, who had rejected his advances, had taught him that he was not allowed to mount an in-season mare.

> Faced with this most social of acts without any social training except her taboo, fired by the mare's pheromones into wild hormonal excitement, he had come to a unique solution: he had mounted the man. And the man, perceiving this as an attack, struck him. Adrenaline, as they taught us in politer days, is the hormone of fear, flight, fight and those activities associated with reproduction. Mustafa had only the third option. And when the fuss had died down, the ambulance gone, they had gone to 'teach him a lesson': that when you are quietly resting in your stable people come and attack you. He never let them in again. (Rees, 2000)

Observing the stallion's bizarre behaviour, especially what she calls the 'willy-shrieks', Lucy Rees remarks, 'With horror and pity, I recognised what they were: a mad version of what males do to each other when they meet, performed on himself.'

This behaviour did not erupt into full-blown self-mutilation; it simply contained some of the elements of the behaviour leading up to Type II mutilation. And the stallion's story did have a happy ending: by getting him to trust that she would not beat him, by teaching him to greet other horses sociably, and by introducing him to a world beyond the confines of his stable and a pen, Lucy Rees managed to reform this disturbed creature.

> Suddenly his inner self came shining through from beneath the welter of confusion and hatred people had imposed on him and he was what he should have been: a colt, bold and innocent, stepping forth with huge, delighted eyes to explore the world. (Rees, 2000)

Repetitive self-mutilative behaviour

Sue McDonnell calls this Type III self-mutilative behaviour. Because of its repetitive, often rhythmical nature, it seems more akin to the non-mutilative stereotypies described earlier in this chapter. McDonnell has observed stallions with

> fixed patterns of biting for example from flank to shoulder to chest to opposite shoulder to opposite flank and on. One stallion that was closely observed over a period of several weeks had daily episodes that occurred at the same place in the pasture at the same time of day for the same length of time, just as some horses walk the perimeter of their stall in very complex and fixed pattern day after day. (McDonnell, 2008)

In this photograph, Nivalis is scratching his flank. He only does this when he needs to scratch an itch; if you see a stallion doing this repetitively, or frequently find patches of damp hair in this region, suspect the onset of Type II self-mutilation and take action accordingly. Photo: Lesley Skipper

How can we find the cause of self-mutilation?

As Sue McDonnell points out, the only reliable way of finding the cause is through observation, which means watching the horse, and preferably recording his behaviour on video; it may take hours of observation to identify the problem. The areas selected by the horse for attention give clues as to where any pain might be located; veterinary examination can then proceed accordingly, although investigation should not be limited to the areas most affected. If the cause is physical, then treatment should make the self-mutilation stop very quickly.

If the cause is not physical, what can we do? Preventing the behaviour by means of some kind of physical restraint (e.g. protective wraps and blankets, bibs, muzzles and neck cradles) while the cause is investigated may be helpful in the short term (to stop the horse from injuring himself any further) but they should *never* be regarded as anything more than a temporary solution. They will not 'cure' the behaviour; indeed, if the horse cannot perform the behaviour that gives him relief he will seek relief in an alternative behaviour, which may be worse than the original behaviour.

Very often, as with the usual stereotypies, all that is required is a change in management – as Lucy Rees found in the case of Mustafa, the savage stallion described in Chapter 2 and on page 207. This is especially so where the self-mutilation is caused by frustration of the stallion's need to form social attachments. In particular, a self-mutilating stallion who is allowed to live in a natural family group may find himself so fulfilled by his family responsibilities that he will no longer feel the need to self –mutilate. Even turning the stallion out to grass may be sufficient, since he is also, in that situation, fulfilling a behavioural need – to graze, and to move about while grazing.

Careful observation of the self-mutilating stallion may reveal the triggers for the self-mutilative behaviour. If it is provoked by the sight or smell of another male horse, changes in housing may reduce or even eliminate the episodes of self-mutilation. Whatever the trigger, once it is identified, management changes can in most cases be made to ensure that the stallion is never exposed to the trigger.

Will gelding solve the problem?

Those who believe gelding is the solution to virtually all stallion behaviour problems will no doubt immediately think of gelding in the case of a self-mutilating stallion. Gelding is certainly an option, but it may not have any effect (after all, geldings can develop self-mutilative behaviour too, very often of Type II). Indeed, observations at the Equine Behavior Clinic, University of Pennsylvania School of Veterinary Medicine, suggest that gelding may make the self-mutilation worse.

Self-mutilation is, therefore, a difficult problem to deal with. Sue McDonnell says,

> In the author's clinical experience, no one treatment or management intervention alone is likely to satisfactorily reduce Types II and III self-mutilation. Clinical impression is that the cases for which the greatest relief has been achieved have involved simultaneously implementing as many of the treatment steps as possible. It is worth spending some time developing a custom plan based on everything that can be learned about the pattern of behavior in that particular horse, and to then implement planned interventions simultaneously. While it is then difficult to evaluate effectiveness of individual interventions, clinical experience has taught us that major change all at once is often more effective in interrupting self-mutilation than a systematic step-wise approach. (McDonnell, 2008)

If you have a self-mutilating stallion, I would suggest you contact Dr McDonnell (contact details can be found in Appendix II)

Changes in behaviour

Brain tumours

When faced with sudden behavioural changes, especially when the changes include savaging behaviour (whether towards humans or other horses) it is tempting to speculate that a brain tumour might be the cause. This may well be the case in some instances – and autopsies have revealed brain tumours in some horses who have undergone severe behavioural changes. However, anecdotally, brain tumours in horses are not that common. It is impossible to say how many dangerous horses are in fact being affected by a tumour, especially since such tumours are usually only detected when the horse is already dead, and then only if an autopsy is carried out. Part of the problem is that tumours are difficult to diagnose. Testing the white blood cell count or the protein levels in the cerebrospinal fluid may reveal a possible tumour, but tumours of the cranial vault only show up on radiography if they are very large and/or invade or distort the bone. Symptoms vary greatly, depending on where the tumour is; indeed the (scanty) scientific literature on brain tumours in horses is not very helpful in this respect. For example, a review of equine central nervous tissue tumours reported between 1970 to 1997 makes only one reference to behavioural changes, stating baldly among the clinical signs of invasive brain tumours of the cortex, 'behavioural changes' without stating what the changes were or how suddenly they appeared. Some of the cases cited showed no previous signs, while others showed a range of symptoms such as nerve dysfunction, seizures, loss of co-ordination and paralysis. (Paradis, 1998)

My personal thoughts are that, while brain tumours are always a possibility (if the symptoms really do fit), the majority of incidences of extreme aggression, especially in stallions, have their triggers either in some environmental factor or some aspect of learned behaviour. In some cases at least such explosive aggression is a release of extreme, pent-up emotion (from a variety of possible causes, constant thwarting of any attempt on the horse's part to express natural behaviour being only one of them). The problem of identifying the trigger, as I see it, is that such incidents tend to happen so fast that unless they are somehow captured on video (and sometimes not even then) it can be difficult to pin down exactly what was happening at the time.

Rabies

Rabies is not something that we in the UK would normally consider, because the last case recorded here (apart from those contracted abroad) was in 1902. However, in parts of the world where rabies is endemic, or at least not rare, horses can become infected with rabies, typically through being bitten by a wild animal while out at pasture, though it is very uncommon in horses.

In a recent case of a stallion attacking a man in Tennessee,[6] rabies was considered as a possible factor in the horse's behaviour, but post-mortem examination of the horse revealed that the horse was not infected.

It is difficult to say whether rabies could account for behaviour changes in horses, especially since the clinical signs of rabies are widely variable and include symptoms similar to those found in much commoner diseases, such as equine herpes virus, botulism, encephalomyelitis, lead poisoning, tetanus, trauma to the brain or spinal cord etc. Symptoms can show themselves and progress

6 See pages 219–220

to recumbency and death within as little as five to seven days, but sometimes the progress of the disease takes much longer (typically two to six weeks, but sometimes as much as 12 weeks). All of this makes it extremely difficult to diagnose rabies in horses. The clinical signs are:

Dullness, depression
Ataxia (lack of co-ordination)
Head pressing
Circling
Difficulty in swallowing
Muscle tremors or convulsions
Low-grade fever
Increased sensitivity at the site of the injury
Inability to rise (recumbency)
Coma

In addition, some horses may become fearful and aggressive, which is one reason why rabies is sometimes suspected where horses have shown a sudden onset of extreme aggression. However, dullness and depression are the commonest symptoms, so rabies would not be among the prime suspects as a cause of sudden, severe aggression, and veterinary surgeons would normally consider other possibilities before diagnosing rabies. Nevertheless, if you live in an area of the world where rabies is endemic, you should have your horse vaccinated against rabies as a precaution.

Aggression general

We hear a great deal about aggression in the horse world; aggression towards other horses – or to humans – is one of the commonest problems cited by horse owners, especially those who deal with stallions.

There is a popular belief among horse owners (and some trainers, as Chapter 8 showed) that horses – especially stallions, are naturally aggressive; indeed, some people appear to believe that aggression is a defining characteristic of all horses, not just stallions. Yet when asked to define aggression, surprisingly few people are actually able to do so convincingly. Often, people confuse it with *assertiveness*. Many years ago, when I was in the Civil Service, my colleagues and I spent hours on management courses being taught the difference between assertiveness and aggression. An assertive person will speak his or her mind, and will defend themself against the aggressive incursions of others, but will do so in a way that respects the rights and personal boundaries of others. An aggressive person does not respect the personal boundaries and rights of others, and will use force and intimidation to get his or her own way. Strictly speaking the term aggression should be reserved for behaviour between animals of the same species that is specifically intended to cause harm or pain. In spite of this, I will continue to use the term 'aggression' as it is normally used in popular discussions of this subject.

So can horses be aggressive to each other? Indeed, yes; although as we saw in earlier chapters, free-ranging and feral horses, and those in a domestic setting who are allowed to form close-knit, well-integrated groups, display very little aggression towards each other. Can horses be aggressive to humans, or animals of non-equine species? Received wisdom says yes, but it would be more accurate to call 'aggressive' behaviour towards non-equids 'agonistic' because that covers the range of behaviour normally associated with aggression: threat, attack, appeasement or flight. As we have seen, horses do not show the kind of appeasement behaviour used by, say, primates or canids; if they feel threatened, they are more likely to flee, or, if flight is not possible, to attack. They may use threats themselves, of course: to other horses, in the circumstances described in Chapters 4, 5 and 8; and to non-equids, to warn the non-equid to stop whatever it is doing that is upsetting or annoying the horse, or simply to go away. A horse who displays threat behaviour to a non-equid out of fear, or attacks the latter in self-defence, is not really being aggressive, but defensive. If more trainers would realize this, a great many of the problems associated with stallions could be avoided.

Stallion aggression

Testosterone is usually blamed for male aggression regardless of the species, hence the belief that castration will make a stallion easier to manage. However, as we have seen, that is not necessarily the case. Other hormones may affect aggression; for example, experiments involving male starlings found that aggression was more closely related to luteinizing hormone than testosterone (Simpson, 2001), while researchers at Pennsylvania State University have found that the cause of the spike in aggressive and insolent behaviour in human teenagers is probably oestrogen, not testosterone, and that aggressive behaviours are affected by both male and female sex hormones. (Finkelstein *et al.*, 1997)

Why are stallions aggressive?

A far better question would be, under what circumstances are stallions aggressive? One cannot say that stallions are basically aggressive, because no creature is *basically* any one quality. Certain qualities may predominate in different circumstances. Aggression is only one aspect of a stallion's emotional make-up, albeit a necessary one. Stallions are aggressive in much the same circumstances as any other mammal: when they feel threatened or fearful, when their families are threatened, or because of frustration (when this type of aggression is turned on a third party not connected with the source of the frustration or annoyance, it is known as 'redirected aggression', as described in Chapter 4).

So if a stallion shows aggression, whether toward another horse, a human or a non-equid animal, it is simply not ethical to assume that the stallion is just 'doing what stallions do' (or even worse, that he is being 'dominant'). Punishment is not (except in an emergency) a humane or ethical solution. In fact it is no solution at all, because – as with any other type of undesirable behaviour – suppressing the behaviour without addressing the cause is not solving or curing anything. It is merely 'papering over the cracks', and sooner or later (often very much sooner than later) the cracks will begin to show again, and the behaviour may escalate into something far worse.

Pain or discomfort-induced aggression

Pain and discomfort can induce aggression in any horse, not just in stallions. As always, before attempting behaviour modification of any kind, have the stallion thoroughly examined to eliminate physical causes. If the displays of aggression are confined to times when the stallion is in his stable, observe him to see whether or not they grow worse, or are triggered, by the approach of feeding time. Gastric juices flowing in anticipation of feeding can irritate an empty stomach; aggression around, or at, feeding time suggests that a gastric ulcer could be the cause. Gastric ulcers can also be the cause of a general deterioration in behaviour. (How many of us feel cranky when we are in pain or discomfort? And why should we expect horses to be any different?) It is worthwhile getting a veterinary surgeon to check for ulcers. It is a simple enough procedure: the horse is fasted for 17–23 hours prior to the procedure, then (in most cases) sedated, and a flexible endoscopy tube passed through one of the nostrils and down into the upper gastrointestinal tract. The veterinary surgeon can then see, by means of a tiny video camera sited at the end of the tube, whether or not any ulcerous lesions are present. Although the procedure is not pleasant (I have had several), horses do seem to accept it quite well (two of our horses, both highly-strung, have had the procedure and accepted it without fuss, even without sedation). Horses may be more tolerant of this procedure than humans because, although (contrary to what many people believe) they do have a gag reflex, it is very much weaker than in humans.

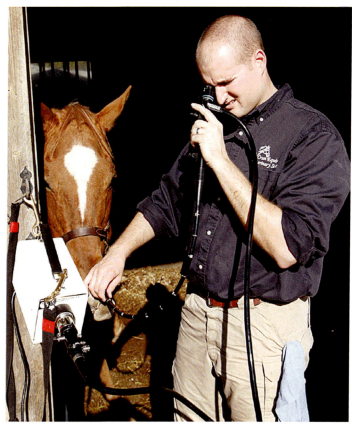

Equine endoscopy: Dr Adam Leininger, DVM, of Crum Equine Veterinary Service in Lancaster, Ohio, USA, performs an endoscopy on a patient. Photo: courtesy Dr Leininger and Crum Equine Veterinary Service.

Aggression caused by poor management

Much stallion aggression is caused directly by poor management. A stallion who is kept isolated from other horses and whose environment is impoverished (insufficient physical exercise and mental stimulation; limited or non-existent freedom to perform natural behaviours), may develop psychological problems which result in distorted perceptions of humans, other horses, non-equid animals or specific situations as being threatening. The stress created by his lifestyle may cause him to become aggressive to whoever comes his way, whether that be a human, another horse, or any other animal.

Research has shown that for humans in stressful jobs, the greater the degree of control they have over how they do their jobs, the better they are able to deal with the stress. This is why higher managers and executives can often hold down extremely stressful jobs and yet thrive on it; they have the power to dictate what they do and when and how they do it. By contrast, the middle or lower manager may have very little influence in that respect, and the poor worker right at the

The Natural Stallion

bottom may have none at all. The resulting stress can be overwhelming; some people become ill as a result, while others may experience a kind of psychological melt-down. The latter are typically those who become aggressive in response to stress;[7] they may not necessarily display aggression in the workplace (although see the footnote below regarding workplace violence), but rather where it may result in them being able to gain *some* control over their lives – or at least some feelings of control; it is usually families who suffer as a result of this.

In the same way the stallion who becomes aggressive through stress has achieved some degree of control over a part – however small – of his environment (because the human, horse or whatever has retreated, removing their threatening presence from his vicinity). Once the stallion learns that he can do this, he may show aggression more and more often. This small degree of control is all he has: it may not be much, but it helps him to deal with the stress he feels all day, every day.

When this behaviour has become established, attempts to deal with it by the use of confrontational methods or overt punishment may result in an escalation of the aggression, because the stallion expects – and will continue to expect – that his aggressive behaviour will get him the result he wants. A more subtle approach is necessary, which involves showing the stallion a) that he will not get what he wants simply by being aggressive, and b) that the people, horses, other animals or situations which he regards as threatening are not so. This may involve a complete change of lifestyle, and extensive counter-conditioning.

Aggression towards other horses

This is often, although not always, a result of poor socialization. This is partly a fear response: if the stallion feels threatened by other horses, he may respond to them with aggression rather than withdrawal, especially if he is physically prevented from removing himself from their presence (for example, in a crowded showring). Stallions may accept other horses in general, but develop a dislike of (or even hatred for) one or more particular horse(s). On pages 126–127 I described Nivalis's reaction to our Warmblood gelding; this is the only horse for whom he has shown implacable hatred.

Counter-conditioning and desensitization, as described on pages 196–197, should, if properly carried out, be sufficient to teach most stallions to accept the presence of other horses without fuss. To begin with, the stallion is introduced to the sight of other horses at a distance. Calmness is rewarded; displays of annoyance are ignored. In this way the stimulus (the sight of other horses) can be gradually increased in intensity until the stallion accepts their presence at close quarters. This may take a considerable length of time in the case of a stallion whose aggression towards other horses is extreme and deeply ingrained, but virtually all such cases can be dealt with in this way. Please note that this is not at all the same as 'flooding': the key is to keep exposure to the stimulus *gradual*.

Acceptance of other horses at close quarters does not, of course, guarantee that the stallion will accept them if turned loose with them. If you want to run your stallion with other horses (including mares) and he has shown aggression to other horses in the past, I would suggest that you first of all use counter-conditioning as described above, then try the introduction techniques suggested in

---

[7] The Michael Douglas film *Falling Down* depicts a brilliant example of this: Douglas's character, an unemployed defence worker, simply wants to get home in time for his daughter's birthday party. On the way he encounters so many of the frustrating situations that bedevil modern life that he becomes more and more aggressive and violent, eventually becoming totally unhinged as a result of all the petty annoyances, frustrations and injustices over which he has no control. The term *going postal* was coined as a result of a rash of violent outbursts, some culminating in shootings, on the part of US postal workers. However, this kind of workplace violence is becoming more common, at least in the US, and is by no means confined to postal workers. Workplace stress has been identified as one of the major causes of such violence.

Chapter 7. Sadly, some stallions may never accept such a degree of social contact; much depends on their age and life experiences. If this is the case, then turning them out in an adjoining paddock separated by a secure fence may be the best you can do to give them at least some social contact with their own kind, even if it is not at close quarters.

Aggression towards animals of another species (other than humans)

As for aggression towards other horses.

Aggression towards humans

Unfortunately, this is high on the list of the problems commonly experienced with stallions. As I said earlier in this chapter, it is tempting to attribute such aggression to a faulty temperament, yet the majority of cases it is actually the result

      a) of bad experiences with humans, whether in the present or in the past

      b) of poor or inadequate early training, or

      c) of an inadequate or inappropriate environment.

In Chapter 1 we saw how people's expectations can result in the inadvertent bringing about of the very situation they fear, and how stallions in particular suffer from the effects of the 'self-fulfilling prophecy'. Human aggression towards stallions, harsh and relentless training methods, and misplaced belief in the concept of 'dominance' can all, either separately or in combination, create aggression in stallions that is directed specifically towards humans (although it can spill over into aggression towards other animals as well).

In her splendid book, *The Classical Rider,* Sylvia Loch tells how, many years ago, she witnessed a magnificent stallion being ridden in a very aggressive manner. The horse was being prevented from moving freely by draw reins, a severe curb bit and some kind of martingale as well. The rider was 'clearly afraid of its boisterous power and rode it in the most aggressive but nervous way possible, spurring it forward in one instant only to punish it in the mouth the next.' (Loch, 1997) The horse, not surprisingly, seemed about to explode. Sylvia Loch learned from the rider's assistant that this rider treated all his horses like this; she was not surprised to learn, a few months later, that this particular stallion had killed him.

Some horses, while stopping short of actual slaughter, still manage to inflict considerable damage. In Chapter 8 I mentioned that I have personally witnessed stallions attack handlers savagely in retaliation against harsh treatment; and there have been countless similar incidents, some of them actually occurring in the show ring.

A Lipizzaner stallion called Maestoso Sitnica was more fortunate than the stallion cited by Sylvia Loch, though before he found his sanctuary with Lucy Rees he was violent and dangerous. Bred in Yugoslavia and trained in Germany for dressage, he passed through the hands of various trainers in Europe, gaining more and more of a bad reputation on the way for being almost impossible to handle.

> He would not be caught in the box, would not be bridled, could not be led nor mounted. He knocked people down, ran over them, crashed through barriers and created havoc. He had no fear of, nor respect for, anything. The scars and lumps on his head bear testimony to the efforts made to control him.

He could not be turned out as he could jump well and fences in any case meant nothing to him. He was extremely difficult to exercise as he was so explosive. Lucy Rees recognized that his problems stemmed not from fear but from the need to escape pressure. Her strategy for his rehabilitation required careful planning, making use of Maestoso's natural vigour, intelligence and curiosity, and constant thought on her part. 'Yet,' says Lucy Rees, 'we made steady progress, and finally he came to believe that whatever I wanted to do must involve something good for him in the end, and he became patient, willing and extremely interested in my ideas.' She goes on,

> Maestoso's problems stemmed from his immense strength, stamina and energy, coupled with unbending pride. Met by a domineering attitude and relentless overtraining, these made him violent and dangerous, as if he felt he was fighting for his life. After two or three years of exercise and freedom...his remarkable gentleness and nobility made it almost impossible to believe he was the same horse.(Rees, 1984)

Issues with personal space

Some stallions (and by extension this includes, of course, all horses) have what Sue McDonnell calls a 'large personal space requirement': that is, they react more quickly and more aggressively to the approach of anything (human or other animal) they perceive to be a threat. Such horses, if a human approaches their stable, will typically lunge at the intruder over the stable door; or, if they will allow a closer approach, they may turn their backs when the door is opened and threaten to kick. It is important to remember that this is a defensive act; it may be very tempting to react with punishment, but that simply confirms the horse's perception that humans are a threat, to be feared and shunned. Punishment administered quickly and severely enough may appear to solve the problem, but as I pointed out earlier, in fact all it does is suppress the behaviour. Instead, the horse must be taught that humans are not a threat and that allowing them to approach, and interact with them, can actually result in something good for the horse.

Again, counter-conditioning and desensitization are the procedures of choice when we deal with horses like this. One of the biggest challenges is actually getting close enough to the horse to interact with him in safety. Grabbing hold of his headcollar (assuming you can get one on him) is likely to do nothing more than confirm his belief that humans are not to be trusted, and may result in someone getting hurt, especially if the horse is the type who lunges at people threatening to bite (actually, in most cases it is not a threat as such – if they manage to make contact, they *will* bite). Instead – as always – make the lessons gradual. Start off by finding the maximum distance at which the horse's defensive reactions are triggered at low intensity. At this stage we do not want the horse to become too upset or he will be unable to learn. It is better if this can be carried out while the stallion is out in a paddock; if he feels as though he can get away from the 'intruder' if necessary, he will be less likely to become upset.

At this safe distance, a human – preferably the person who will be doing the training (although later we will want the stallion's calm acceptance of human presence to be generalized to all humans) should sit calmly on a chair, a bench, a bale of straw, or whatever, either in the stable yard or near the paddock fence, paying no attention to the stallion. As we have seen, they are curious creatures, and most will be unable to resist investigating – from a safe distance – this human who is sitting there quietly, paying them no attention, in fact doing nothing at all. When the stallion remains calm with the human at this safe distance, a conditioned reinforcer such as a clicker can be introduced; this enables us to tell the stallion, from a safe distance, that what he has done is good, and is what we want him to do. Obviously we can't pair the clicker with any of the normal positive reinforcers at this stage, so we make use of what we have: when the stallion remains calm, the human clicks and goes away. The human presence at this safe distance is a mild negative stimulus; removal of that stimulus acts as a negative reinforcer. The stallion soon learns that when he remains calm, the trainer clicks and goes away. The clicker thus comes to signal the correct action to produce the consequence the horse wants: for the trainer to go away, the horse must remain calm.

Once this has been achieved, the chair, bench or whatever can be moved a little closer; again, when this new safe distance is established and the stallion remains calm, the human clicks and goes away. In this way the stallion is gradually de-sensitized to the human's presence, until he will tolerate the human approaching closer and closer without reacting. The trainer should not outstay their welcome, but to begin with should click and move away the moment the stallion responds by staying calm and still. Gradually the stallion will come to tolerate the human's presence for longer and longer periods, but this process cannot be rushed; it certainly cannot be forced. Before long the stallion will start closing up the remaining gap himself, while remaining within what he considers his 'safe distance'. Once he has accepted the presence of a human at close quarters, the really challenging part of the training can begin.

I must stress here that safety must not be compromised. If the stallion is known to bite, the trainer must take precautions and wear thick padded clothing. A really savage horse bite can sometimes penetrate even this kind of protection, so we make it as thick as we can. To protect the head in the case of confirmed biters, we can wear a motorcycle helmet; although this may delay the stallion's acceptance of the human presence (because he must also adjust to the sight of the motorcycle helmet) it is preferable to getting bitten. If the stallion is accustomed beforehand to seeing humans wandering around wearing motorcycle helmets, he will be less likely to become upset at the sight of one. If necessary, use a soft rubber grazing muzzle (assuming the horse will allow this to be put on); this will prevent biting (and will not hurt so much if the horse punches you with his teeth) while initially working with the stallion at close quarters; it will still allow him to be given a food reward.

When we can approach the horse at close quarters without him lunging at us ready to bite, or whip round and kick out, we can start to use positive reinforcement to teach him that the presence of a human means something good for him. One of the best ways of doing this is to stand and hold a bucket of his favourite feed for him. Stroking, scratching those hard-to-reach spots and so on will also help to reassure him that having humans around isn't such a bad thing after all. Once he is accepting the presence of humans without any negative reaction, the trainer can progress to getting the stallion used to having different parts of his body touched, and to being handled in general. As always, each step in the right direction, no matter how tiny, is positively reinforced; and the trainer must take no action that will trigger the stallion's previous behavioural responses to the presence of humans. The stallion's new response (calm acceptance of a human's presence, and of being handled) should be well-established before he can start to generalize this response to humans other than the trainer, and everyone likely to be handling the stallion should be trained in the appropriate behaviour to maintain around him.

This is not a task to take on lightly, because it does entail risk to the trainer, and it also requires endless patience, willingness to take as much time as is required, and the ability to carry on even when progress seems slight or even non-existent. But the reward of seeing a previously unmanageable horse change his responses, and accept humans into his life without fear or aggression, is immeasurable. It must be a relief to the horse, too!

Universal principles

Because the principles underlying such techniques are universal, they can be applied to any animal, not just horses. Karen Pryor, for example, describes the 'approach-and-retreat' technique described above in the context of dealing with very shy animals such as llamas. ('Approach-and-retreat' is widely associated with Monty Roberts, and also with Native American methods of taming wild horse; however, it simply represents the judicious use of mild negative reinforcement, and as such the principle is, as I say, universal, not confined to any individual or culture).We have used these principles with outstanding success on feral cats and kittens; these may not be anywhere near as formidable as a stallion, or even a foal, but those razor-sharp claws and teeth can do a surprising amount of damage! The last time we used it on cats was with a litter of feral farm kittens that we had adopted. I spent what seemed like years (it was actually only a few days) sitting on the bathroom floor waiting for them to accept my presence without hiding behind the sink pedestal; it was a wonderful feeling when one of them suddenly, quite nonchalantly, ambled up to me and curled up on my knee. A few days more, and they were all climbing all over me. In fact, three years later, they still do.

A challenging case

Interestingly enough, one of the most challenging horses we have had to deal with in this respect was a mare, not a stallion. This mare is extremely protective of her personal space, to the extent that she used to attack, quite savagely, anyone who came near her stable door. She was not at all afraid of humans; in fact she was fine outside the stable, and could be handled without fuss. It would have been better to keep her out 24/7, but her mild chronic laminitis meant that turnout had to be restricted to a degree. The only way to get inside her stable was for someone to stand in the doorway and fend her off with a lunge-whip (of which she was not at all afraid; she simply did not like having it pointed at her). Gradually, my husband trained her to accept humans entering her personal space inside the stable without either lunging forward to bite them or whipping round to kick out. It is now possible to approach her stable door, to put a headcollar on her, and to go in her stable to change her water and give her hay, without risking injury, although care must be taken not to trigger any of her old responses by moving too suddenly or too close to her without warning. She does, however, remain defensive with strangers; and it is wise to muck her stable out while she is outside, or the activity becomes too much for her to deal with.

Sudden onset of extreme aggression

Some people insist that stallions, like some breeds of dog, can never be trusted as they can 'turn' in an instant for no reason. I do not believe that this is the case. *No* animal – human or non-human – does anything without a reason. Just because we cannot immediately see a reason for behaviour does not mean that no reason exists. A psychopathic human killer may murder another human simply because he can, and the feeling this engenders gives him pleasure. No matter how appalling this may seem to the rest of us, it is perfectly reasonable to the psychopath: his *reason* is the thrill he derives from violence. Although we may hear about the odd rogue among dogs or horses, it is extremely unlikely that dangerous behaviour ever arises from nothing. There is always either something in the external environment which triggers the behaviour, or it may stem from internal physical causes (for example, extreme pain, brain damage or in some cases, the effects of a brain tumour). To say that the dog or horse behaved violently 'for no reason' is to admit to a failure of understanding as well as demonstrating a regrettable tendency to blame the animal rather than look for the cause.

It is up to us to try to anticipate, and take steps to prevent, unwanted and/or dangerous behaviour on the part of any horse, whether entire or not.

True rogues: do they exist?

One often hears aggressive horses (not just stallions) being referred to as a rogue, but real rogues – the equine equivalent of the human psychopath – are *very rare*. This is not to say that they do not exist, but true psychopaths are rare in non-human animals anyway. In the wild, among such intensely social creatures as horses, they would seldom survive, let alone be allowed to reproduce, since they would disrupt the cohesion of whatever group they attached themselves to, and would almost certainly be driven out. But thanks to human interference in natural patterns of reproduction and survival, they *do* occasionally crop up in domestic horses. Even so, a stallion should not be branded as a rogue until *all* attempts have been made to reform him. All too often, humans who lack the knowledge to make such attempts – or are too lazy to do so – will cry 'rogue', and the unfortunate horse is not given a chance. As the case of Mustafa (described by Lucy Rees) shows, even the most dangerous horses can usually be rehabilitated by people with the knowledge, experience and empathy to do so. The late Vicki Hearne, an animal trainer for more than 25 years, remarked that 'I never encountered a horse in whose soul there was no harmony to call on.' (Hearne, 1986). However, this is not a task to be taken on lightly, even by someone with all the qualities mentioned above. If such a person cannot be found, then – and I hate to say this – euthanasia may be the kindest option. Even so, I feel very strongly that we owe it to such horses to take all steps available to us to prevent that situation from coming about.

In some cases, we will never know precisely what made a stallion turn against the humans who looked after him. In February 2010 a man from Tennessee was attacked by a stallion in the field, suffering severe injuries to his chest, abdomen and one leg. He also lost an arm in the attack; shockingly, it was found some distance away from the man, who was found by his son and a friend. The friend managed to drive the stallion away by hitting the horse with a rock; the son shot the stallion when he charged at them. The injured man was airlifted to hospital, but later died from his injuries.

What caused this terrible attack? Was this horse one of those rare, real rogues? As I said above, we will never know. The extreme severity of the attack makes us wonder about a brain tumour, but apparently the horse's head was sent to be tested for rabies, and as this involves parts of the brain being sectioned and stained to test for antibodies, one would imagine that the presence of a brain tumour would have been detected. If it was, no mention of this was made in the news reports, and one would think that such an explanation for the stallion's extreme behaviour would have been mentioned. Without knowing anything about the manner in which the horse was kept, how he was trained and how people behaved towards him, we have no idea what triggered this attack. We don't even know whether it was the result of pain or some undiagnosed internal problem. The only clue we have is the fact that the man who was killed reportedly carried a stick when he went to feed the stallion because the horse was 'mean'. Why was he 'mean'? What made him that way? Again, we don't know, and it is unlikely that we will ever find out. All we do know is that something, on that particular day, made this horse 'snap'[8] and the extreme severity of the attack has simply confirmed, in the minds of many, the stereotypical image of stallions set out in Chapter 1. If the attacker had been human, and had not been killed at the scene, the courts would no doubt have requested psychiatric

---

8 Apparently he attacked the man from behind when the latter turned to close the gate. No doubt this will confirm in the minds of some people (though not the author) the adage, 'Never turn your back on a stallion'.

reports on the attacker, and the latter's defence lawyer would no doubt be delving into reasons for the attacker's behaviour. In a case like this, while we are shocked and disturbed by the man's injuries, and naturally feel great sympathy for him and his family, we cannot help wondering: in such a situation, who will speak for the horse?

Barging

Barging was dealt with in Chapter 8.

Biting

True biting should be distinguished from nipping (see under **Nipping**). Whereas nipping, which is usually relatively mild, is often used in play, in courtship (see Chapter 6) as part of a friendly greeting, or as a bid for attention, real biting is reserved for more serious intent. The biter will typically lunge without any real warning, with the ears flattened and the mouth open. A horse is capable of inflicting a serious injury with a bite, making this a real problem if you have to deal with a confirmed biter.

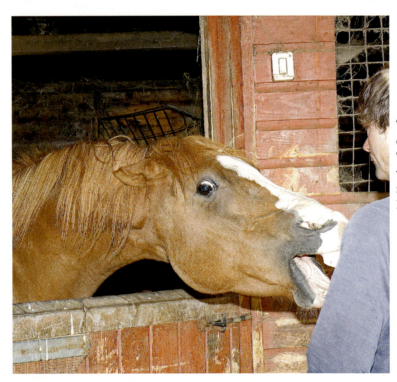

True biting should be distinguished from nipping. The real biter typically lunges wthout real warning, with ears flattened and the mouth open. Photo: Lesley Skipper

Why do horses bite? Some people believe that it is a means of establishing dominance, but that is part of the belief system which sees dominance issues in virtually everything the horse does. This often goes hand-in-hand with the idea that horses bite and kick each other all the time. But this is simply not true. Feral and free-ranging horses do *not* bite and kick each other all the time; in fact, within a natural family group agonistic interactions are few and far between. I have spent many years studying the behavior of my own horses and those belonging to the riding school next door, and have found aggressive acts in either group to be rare and mostly confined to the odd occasions when one horse inadvertently invades another's space, or where concentrate feed has been given in the field. Even then, there has been very little kicking and almost no biting. If I saw a group in which there was a lot of biting activity I would be very concerned that something was seriously upsetting that group's equilibrium, and investigate accordingly.

Unfortunately, the 'dominance issues-as-explanation-for-virtually-everything' school of thought is so pervasive that all too many people use it to explain biting (and other potentially serious behaviour) without properly investigating potential causes. For example, here is one trainer's explanation: 'Horses bite for many reasons. They may bite looking for a treat, or they may bite as a means of establishing dominance... while a horse may bite because of the occasional mistake of looking for a carrot, more often than not a horse is biting because they are asserting dominance.' But that explanation encompasses only two potential reasons, not 'many reasons' and, as we have seen, it is based on faulty assumptions about the nature of horses.

So why do horses – especially stallions, for they are the most likely biters – bite?

Pain and discomfort

As we have already seen, aggression may be caused by pain or discomfort. If stomach ulcers are the cause, then the biting is especially likely to be associated with feeding-time. Fortunately this is comparatively easily investigated (see pages 199–200 and 213). In any case, as with any severe behavioural problem, a confirmed biter should always be thoroughly examined to exclude physical causes.

Fear and insecurity

Biting is very often a stallion's reaction to fear, since it is not only a means of self-defence, but also a way of controlling his environment (that is, by keeping humans – or any other living source of fear – away). Sadly, it can often be caused by attempts to correct nipping in colts, ponies or even mature stallions. This is ironic, because books, magazine articles and various trainers often state that nipping must be corrected instantly or it will lead to savage biting. So why should such attempts at correction lead to the opposite result?

As we saw in Chapter 9, punishment must be applied appropriately, correctly and at exactly the right time, or it will be either ineffective or actually harmful. Unfortunately, attempts to correct nipping usually involve punishment, often incorrectly applied (for more about such attempts to correct nipping, see pages 228–229 under **Nipping**). The more severe the punishment, then – especially if it is not carried out correctly – the greater the degree of fear the horse will experience. If, in addition, he is confused about the reason for the punishment (for example, because the person inflicting the punishment has poor timing), then the punishment will seem arbitrary, and it is very likely that he will feel that the only course of action is to defend himself. Since stallions typically do this by biting, it is not difficult to see how the biting behaviour begins. If further punishment results, this is likely to confirm the stallion's belief that he needs to defend himself against humans. He may well become head-shy, and may resort to swift attacks with his teeth in order to pre-empt the punishment he now fears. Typically, stallions making such attacks will then move out of the way very quickly, in order to avoid further punishment.

The stallion may come to fear humans for a variety of reasons, not just poor attempts to correct nipping. Punishment during training, severe and/or abusive handling, poor timing during training, resulting in confusion, stress and fear (especially as a result of ill-conceived attempts to 'dominate' the horse) – all of these can create distrust, fear and even loathing of humans.

The Natural Stallion

The fearless biter

While their biting may still be the result of inappropriate punishment, some stallions who bite show no fear of humans at all. For example, Lucy Rees cites the case of an Arabian stallion who neither disliked nor feared people. However, he was a vicious biter when handled. He was cured by being worked in a round pen; he had to be worked hard and fast to get his attention. When he was allowed to approach the trainer he soon started to bite when he was rubbed and stroked. When this happened he was driven angrily away. He soon learned that he was allowed to nuzzle and lick the handler, but that biting was not acceptable. Lucy Rees says, 'His delight in finding an acceptable way of making contact with people was almost laughable: he even licked the vet tenderly.' She goes on to say,

> Fire's need to make contact with his mouth is typical of stallions. As often happens, it had built up to such a point that, combined with the certainty of punishment, it was expressed violently. In a herd, older mares teach colts how to approach and nuzzle politely in exactly the same way, by driving them away angrily when they are too rough. But when a horse is restrained by a lead rope, he cannot go away, and so cannot learn. (Rees, 1984)

Lack of socialization

As we have seen, colts who are brought up with their fathers, in a proper family group, or at least with older male horses in a bachelor group, quickly learn that while nipping may be tolerated to a degree, real biting will not. Unfortunately, all too many stallions are deprived of this kind of social learning just at an age when they are starting to explore the world with their mouths; they never get the opportunity to learn from other horses, so have no idea that rough contact with the mouth is not acceptable. Human attempts to teach them this are often poorly-timed, and even if they are not, the colt or stallion is not shown an acceptable alternative – as proved to be the case in Lucy Rees's example given above. I give some examples of how to let colts and stallions use their mouths in an acceptable manner later in this chapter, under **Nipping.**

Dealing with a biter

Although I would never advocate punishment as a first resort, there are occasions – such as when dealing with a confirmed biter who suddenly attacks without warning (as real biters usually do) – when the only way of staying safe may be to retaliate, sharply and swiftly, so that the horse is left under no illusion that what he is done is unacceptable.[9] This will at least buy some time while the cause of the biting is investigated and an acceptable solution is found. Sometimes, that 'short sharp shock' may – especially if it involves a colt who has not yet turned into a real biter – be sufficient to stop the behaviour dead in its tracks – hence the insistence of so many people that instant punishment is the only effective treatment for a horse who nips or bites. However, it is very unlikely to cure a real biter, because, as usual, the punishment has done nothing to address the underlying cause of the behaviour. The type of solution adopted in the case of the Arabian stallion cited by Lucy Rees

---

9 Sometimes all that is required to make such a horse back off is a really loud vocal sound. I have found that shouting 'GAAAAGH!' at the top of my voice is very effective in such cases. I would not normally recommend shouting at horses in other circumstances than these – and of course it does not address the actual behaviour.

may be very effective and is certainly worth trying for all but the most severe cases; it lets the horse know clearly when his behaviour is unacceptable and reinforces the good behaviour. Where biting has escalated to the level where it is dangerous to go near the horse, it may be better to adopt the kind of approach I described in the case of horses who aggressively guard their personal space. In either case I would be wary of attempting to cure a real biter without the support and guidance of a real expert in dealing with such problems (see Appendix II).

Charging

To be charged at by a stallion – especially if he belongs to one of the bigger breeds – can be a terrifying experience. In the wild, a stallion would normally only charge at a potential rival during serious fighting (see page 60); charging does not usually form part of the preliminaries to a fight. It is a serious attempt to drive off an opponent, and it signals that if the said opponent does not turn and flee, the charge will be followed through with a serious attack. If you are ever charged by a stallion in this manner, don't try to face him down; get out of the way as fast as you can, because he means business. A stallion who charges at a human like this wants the human out of the way, and is prepared to do whatever he has to in order to achieve that goal.

What makes a stallion charge?

Although charging is an *offensive* move, it has its roots – like so much aggressive behaviour – in *defence*. The band stallion charging at a potential rival is protecting his mares and offspring; he wants the rival out of the way as soon as possible, and unless his opponent is supremely confident of his fighting skills, he will usually back down and flee – remember that the band stallion has more to lose than his rival, and so will fight harder to protect what he has. But why would a stallion in a domestic situation charge at a human?

This sometimes happens when stallions are turned out with mares and think a human is going to take the mares away. The stallion would have no reason to think a human was going to do so unless he has had prior bad experience in this respect, and if his life experiences with humans have not given him confidence in human behaviour. This is why I stress that if mares are to be removed from fields where they are running out with the stallion, he must have confidence, from experience, that he will not be parted from his mares indefinitely (see Chapter 10 under **Teaching stallions to accept separation from mares**).

However, this is only one reason why a stallion might charge a human. If he has had previous bad experiences with humans and has learned to distrust them, he may be protective of his personal space[10] and simply want to keep the invading human away. This is what appears to have happened in the case of Mustafa, the stallion whose extreme aggression was described by Lucy Rees on pages 207–208. Such cases can be dealt with in a similar manner to that described on pages 216–217; as with all such situations, I would strongly recommend enlisting the aid of someone who really understands stallions and has experience of dealing with such cases.

There is a world of difference between the stallion who charges and a boisterous colt who has just not learned to respect the personal space of others, whether of humans or of other horses. I deal with these on pages 235–236

---

10 As we have seen, horses are not territorial as such; what the stallion is protecting here is not territory, but an extension of his personal space and that of his family (if they are present).

Dropping' and sexual excitement at shows etc.

See under **Masturbation**

Head-rubbing

We have already dealt with head-rubbing in Chapter 10, but I will just reiterate here: attempts to rub his head on you are *not* a sign that the horse is trying to dominate you. A great deal of nonsense is talked – and written – often by people who are otherwise very knowledgeable – about herd dynamics and how a horse who invades another horse's – or a human's – personal space, is showing dominance, because a horse who does this is ranked higher in the herd. In fact, if we look back to the chapter on dominance we can see that it is the opposite that happens: the dominant horse in a dominance relationship *may* invade the personal space of another, but only to displace him or her – in other words, to say, 'Go away!' This is not related to head-rubbing, or grooming, or any of the other situations in which 'dominance' is put forward as an explanation for a behaviour. Horses rub their heads on each other, or on humans, because they feel itchy and because they can. If you see it as a problem (and not everyone does) simply do as I suggested in Chapter 10 and put the behaviour on cue – then never give the cue. The current obsession with dominance and ranks does nothing more than cloud issues and prevent people from getting to the real root of problems.

Kicking

Like biting, kicking is a form of self-defence (a stronger way of saying 'Go away!'). Stallions typically resort to biting or striking out with the fore feet rather than kicking out with the hind feet (as the old saying has it, beware of the front feet of a stallion and the hind feet of a mare), so kicking out with the hind feet may be regarded as a kind of 'escalation of defence', if you like. As always, the key to dealing with this behaviour is to find out, through careful observation, what triggers this behaviour, which will in turn suggest how it can effectively be dealt with.

Case study

In February 2009 Nivalis developed sudden, very severe, acute laminitis. Surgical intervention was required to alleviate the pressure inside the hoof capsule, so a dorsal wall resection was performed on both front feet. This was successful, and Nivalis appeared to be making a good recovery, when in June 2009 he suffered a relapse. The pedal bone in his right fore foot rotated to the extent that it had actually penetrated the sole, and initially it seemed as if euthanasia was the kindest option. However, thanks to some superb work on the part of our inestimable farrier, Neil Jackson, in re-shaping the hoof so as to realign the pedal bone, disaster was averted. We had to wash the feet every day, dry them and spray the soles with a strong solution of iodine, to keep infection at bay and help to harden the hoof. Before long the split in Nivalis's sole had healed and he was walking well, without any sign of pain or discomfort and without the need for painkillers.

All throughout the acute phase of his illness, no matter what we humans (the vet, the farrier, my husband and I) did to him, he remained calm and co-operative, enduring all the discomfort with what I can only describe as equine heroism. However, once he started to recover, his behaviour changed. He was fine outside the stable; I could (still can, for that matter) hold him for Brian to wash his feet and spray them with iodine with nothing more than a lead-rope around his neck. But it was getting hold of him in order to do so that proved problematic. We could go in the stable with him without any problems, as we have done all his life, and do whatever was necessary; but the moment he sensed even a hint of the iodine being produced, he would turn his back and threaten to kick, sometimes actually doing so, kicking out with both hind feet. This is a horse who adores having his backside scratched by humans, indeed who loves being groomed all over, and who under normal circumstances would never threaten to kick. Eventually this was generalized to having his headcollar put on, or even a lead rope slipped round his neck, because he associated both of those events with having his feet sprayed.

I can't blame Nivalis for reacting in this way. As anyone knows who has ever splashed it on their skin, iodine, even at lower concentrations, stings like mad – and we were using a strong concentrate. It was inevitable that when Nivalis's feet were being sprayed, some iodine splashed on the surrounding skin, and sometimes even higher up (on occasions his elbows have been dyed bright yellow with the stuff). He had come to regard the appearance of the iodine spray with fear and loathing, and was only trying to protect himself from it. The most effective way for him to do this was not to threaten to bite (which would in any case have been ineffective) but for him simply not to allow us to get hold of him.

We solved this in the short term by putting his morning feed of chaff and alfalfa[11] in a bucket outside his stable, so that if he wanted his breakfast he had to step outside his stable. Once his nose was in the bucket I could (provided I was quick enough) slip the lead-rope around his neck and then, having got hold of him, put the headcollar on, giving me much better control. I would then allow him to eat his breakfast in peace. Once he was relaxed, Brian would clean and spray his feet, and he was then allowed the freedom of the yard while we attended to all the usual stable chores. In the long term, having got him to allow us a) to catch him and b) to put the lead rope or headcollar on, we made a point of doing so at random *without* treating his feet. In this way the automatic association of lead ropes and headcollars with iodine was broken, and we can now approach him with either of those items in our hands without triggering the automatic defence reaction. Things got even better when Nivalis's feet had grown and hardened sufficiently for him to be allowed, for a limited amount of time each day, the freedom of the stallion paddock, or to be taken for gentle walks in hand. He now associates the headcollar with going out, and especially with the freedom to have a really good roll in the dust of the stallion paddock (or the mud, depending on the weather), and even though we still have to treat his feet with iodine as a precaution, we no longer have any difficulty catching him in his stable.

Leading problems

If a stallion is properly trained he should lead without any problems. However, bad habits can develop, so it is as well to know how to deal with them when they do arise.

Opinions vary enormously regarding the correct place to position oneself when leading any horses, not just stallions. Some trainers insist that one should take up a position ahead of the horse, because horses follow the leader (who is almost always, in this way of thinking, equated with a dominant horse). Others say no, this is not a good idea, because dominant horses 'lead' by driving from behind! As we have seen, neither of these is correct, being based on faulty perceptions of both dominance and leadership in horses. Social facilitation (and the chance that you might have some goodies for him, or be ready to give him a rub, or a scratch, or whatever – or because he just likes being with you) may make a horse follow you, but that has nothing to do with equine social organization. The correct position to take up when leading a horse is the one which combines the maximum effectiveness with the maximum safety, and these factors will depend on individual horses and individual circumstances. I have found that the safest and most effective place to walk

11 We feed Happy Hoof, a chaff and alfalfa mix approved by the Laminitis Trust.

The Natural Stallion

is roughly parallel with the horse's shoulder; with some horses you might need to move forward a little slightly ahead of the shoulder.

Crowding

This is useful when dealing with horses who tend to crowd one; an elbow in the neck (not jabbing, just held there) can effectively discourage a horse from crowding.

However, it is preferable not to have to stick your elbow in a horse's neck like this; I am sure the horse would agree! Fortunately, teaching a horse not to crowd, either when being led or when simply coming close to the handler, is relatively easy, and is covered on pages 235–236 under **Teaching a colt or stallion to respect the handler's personal space**.

Circling

What about the horse who circles in front of the handler? This may be caused by impatience to get somewhere, or the opposite, a desire *not* to go somewhere; it is surely related to the actions of a foal trying to get his dam to stop so that he can take milk. If you watch foals doing this, you will see them dart in front of the mare, who will usually stop; the foal then nips to the udder and starts to suckle. He has learned – probably in one lesson – that this is the way to get something he wants. And while it is exceedingly unlikely that a stallion, or even an immature colt, would mistake a human handler for his dam, he may remember it as an effective strategy for getting something he wanted. In some cases – especially with stallions, who like to look around them and assess a situation – it might be that he just wants to stop and look around. It is a good idea to let him do this, as long as he understands that he must move forward again when you ask him to. Otherwise if he becomes rooted to the spot, attempts to make him go forward may result in him running backwards or even rearing.

Stallions need to look around and assess a situation; this is part of their vigilant role in the family group. It is a good idea to let them do this, as long as they understand that they must move forward again when asked. Photos: Lesley Skipper

To stop a horse from circling, carry a schooling whip in your free hand (the horse should be taught to lead from both sides). Hold this just in front of his chest, so that he runs into it as soon as he tries to circle (or to get ahead of you). I must emphasize that the whip is there purely as an extension of your arm, as a barrier, not as something to hit the horse with. The moment he stops trying to get ahead of you or circle in front of you, move the whip away (mild negative reinforcement).

Eventually he will get the idea that every time he runs forward, the whip is there as a barrier, while if he walks quietly by your side the whip is removed. When he understands this, as soon as he starts to walk quietly, switch to positive reinforcement; it helps if you have already established the use of a clicker or other conditioned reinforcer.

Going forward

Every horse, whether stallion, mare or gelding, should be taught to go forward, whether in-hand or under saddle. This is one of the earliest lessons we teach foals, even before they learn to accept the halter, using positive reinforcement as described in Chapter 9 under **Getting the timing right**. However, positive reinforcement can be used to ingrain the forward movement at any age. Teaching a control cue for walking on, like the 'stop' cue mentioned in Chapter 8, is a very powerful way of getting a horse that is 'stuck' to the ground to move forward. See also under **Rearing**; a rearing horse is a prime example of one who has become 'stuck' and can't or won't move forward.

Masturbation

I include masturbation in this chapter with some reluctance because, as we saw in Chapter 6, masturbation is part of normal equine behaviour and is not harmful in any way. It is therefore not really problem behaviour at all. However, many people insist on trying to eliminate it, either because they feel it is inappropriate and/or embarrassing, or because they feel it *is* somehow harmful. To this end, all kinds of devices designed to prevent masturbation in stallions have been designed and are readily available in some parts of the world, especially the USA. These typically take the form of devices fitted over the penis and may include rings, cages, spike pads and brushes (please note that in the UK the term 'stallion ring' usually refers to a ring-bit known as a Chifney, rather than an anti-masturbatory device). It is truly depressing to see how far humans will go in order to eliminate perfectly natural behaviour which does no harm. One manufacturer has even produced an electric shock collar as an anti-masturbatory device!

Sue McDonnell has this to say about the use of anti-masturbatory devices:

> Our observations and systematic studies (McDonnell and Hinze, unpublished observations, 1996–1997) indicate that anti-masturbatory devices rarely reduce spontaneous erection and penile movements, but in most cases increase the frequency and duration of episodes. Nonetheless, horse managers continue to try to stop the behavior. In our clinic we see many cases each year involving penile injury associated with anti-masturbatory devices, presented for libido, erection, and/or ejaculation dysfunction. (McDonnell, 2000)

It is also very sad to see how many people are prepared to use such devices simply in order to prevent embarrassing behaviour at shows. Show judges vary in their attitude towards stallions who drop the penis during a class; some ignore it, while others penalize such behaviour, in some instances even going so far as to ask the handler to remove the horse from the class. This seems to be more prevalent in the USA than in the UK; I have seen stallions 'drop' numerous times at shows here in the UK and have never seen anyone being penalized or asked to leave as a result. On one memorable occasion[12] at a regional breed show for Arabian horses, a stallion 'dropped' very noticeably during

---
12 Memorable, for me, for more than one reason: the colt I was showing had trodden heavily on my foot during our trot-up in his championship class, breaking my big toe. The whole foot swelled up like a football and I was in considerable pain, so the incident referred to above caused enough amusement to distract me from the discomfort.

The Natural Stallion

the Supreme In-hand Championship class (being close to an obviously oestrus mare no doubt did it for him). He did not misbehave in any way, apart from fidgeting a little, but his 'fifth leg' did cause considerable amusement among spectators. This did not affect his chances, though; as far as I recall, he won the championship.

I would ask anyone who is considering using an anti-masturbatory device to think very carefully before doing so, and to consider objectively their reasons for wanting to prevent the behaviour. We have seen that masturbation does not affect fertility, and that the use of preventative devices may not only be ineffective but may cause actual harm. Even if no injury results, is it fair to the stallion to cause him discomfort simply in order to prevent a harmless, very natural behaviour? And if the intention is to prevent such behaviour in the showring, is it worth compromising the stallion's welfare in order to gain a rosette? Some people may feel that it is; I leave it to their conscience to decide.

Young stallion 'dropping' at a show. This does not seem to be so frequently penalised in the UK and elsewhere as it is in the USA. Photo: Lesley Skipper

Mouthiness

Mouthing at things (other horses, people, inanimate objects) is normal for colts and stallions. See under **Nipping** below for more about this.

Nipping

As I said above, mouthing at things is normal for colts and stallions; one of the ways in which they explore the world is with their mouths. If they get excited, it is therefore quite possible that they will grab hold of something with their teeth (such as sleeves and puffy jackets, which they seem to find irresistible – see below).

Nippy behaviour frequently has its roots in an attempt to attract attention (perhaps as an extension of play behaviour). Responding to it – even with punishment – may, as we have already seen, actually intensify the behaviour, because the colt has got what he wants – attention.

We can certainly discourage such behaviour using punishment; what is usually advocated is a smack on the nose. However, if this is forceful enough to act as a deterrent, it may simply make the colt headshy and afraid of humans. It may also create resentment (in his world, the colt is doing nothing wrong) and may actually create, rather than prevent, aggression. A colt thus punished may learn to take a quick nip and then dodge rapidly out of range of a smack (few humans have reflexes to match those of a horse!).

It is of course true that stallions use their teeth in fighting more than mares or geldings do, but it is necessary to read the horse's body language, and to judge whether real aggression is involved: is a colt or stallion who nips or bites angry or annoyed? If so, why? Is he biting from frustration caused by an unnatural lifestyle, or is it simply playful nipping caused by a lack of mental stimulation and/or a need to mouth at something? Or is it just bad manners on the part of a horse who has never been taught the limits of acceptable behaviour? Many colts start off with playful nips that are misinterpreted as actual aggressive biting; the usual 'cure' for this (normally a whack across the nose) does not in fact cure anything, because while it may discourage the horse from nipping (though in my experience it seldom does), it does nothing to remove his reasons for doing so. It may actually make the situation much worse, and turn a 'nipper' into a really vicious biter; there is a strong probability that it will also make him headshy

My Arabian gelding Zareeba and his half-brother Kruger were both very 'nippy' as young colts. This was caused by nothing more than youthful exuberance and a need to explore things with their mouths. One must remember that to a horse, the mouth, with its extremely mobile lips, is his only means of manipulation. Sometimes the nippiest, 'mouthiest' colts are the cleverest when it comes to undoing stable doors and untying the knots in the ropes with which they are tied up. We found that both Zareeba and Kruger were nippy not because they were being in any way aggressive, but because they needed to play with things with their mouths. Zareeba in particular could never resist the kind of puffy padded jackets often worn around stables in winter. He would also pick one's pocket, and several times I have had to rescue a pair of gloves that were being well and truly chewed. His favourite trick (which he will still do, given half the chance) was to whip my woolly winter hat off my head, wave it up and down a few times, then lower it to the ground and proceed to wipe the floor with it (is this evidence of an equine sense of humour? One does wonder). But puffy jackets were always his greatest temptation. If I (or any other unsuspecting person) walked past too close to his stable door while he was looking out, we might find our progress suddenly arrested as a playful colt grabbed a sleeve in his mouth. On one occasion he took this a little too far; his breeder's small daughter was standing near him one day when he casually picked her up by the hood of her anorak, and lifted her clear off the ground! There was absolutely no malice or aggression in any of this; it was simply born of a need to mouth at things and play with them, and it would have been stupid as well as wrong to punish it. I ignored well-meant advice to 'give him a good clout whenever he nips'. Instead I worked at diverting his mind by teaching him things; simple 'tricks' like shaking hands, as well as giving him things to play with; the often recommended turnip was a great success, with only one problem – it lasted all of five minutes. (Nowadays we use something like the Likit Boredom Breaker, pictured on page 230). I taught him that if he wanted to mouth at my hand or my arm – licking, nuzzling, mouthing with his lips, or even a gentle nibble – that was fine; but if he nipped, he would be pushed away and all attention withdrawn. Eventually he stopped nipping altogether, though even now, at the age of 22, he still likes to lick and mouth at people's hands and arms. Smacking would not have cured him (it had already been tried, and failed, before I acquired him); in time it might well have turned him into a real, frustrated biter. Gelding did not cure him, either; as we have seen, it does not necessarily eliminate coltish or stallion behaviour. What he needed was some outlet for his need to mouth and nuzzle at people and other animals, as well as something to occupy his mind. Lungeing, long-reining, being taken for walks through the woods (where he learned to ignore the 125 Express that came screaming past only a few metres away from the path on its journey out of Darlington station), as well as teaching him a few basic tricks, helped to develop his mind to the point where being boisterous and nippy were no longer such attractive options as they had once been. We have tried the same tactics with other 'nippy' colts, with great success.

Likit Boredom Breaker. This holds several variously flavoured blocks similar to salt licks, although those used in the Boredom Breaker consist mainly of flavoured glucose. Because the hanging lick and the ball beneath it move when the horse licks at them, he has to make some effort to get his treat. We have found these invaluable for horses who, for whatever reason, have to be stabled for some time. They are also very useful for giving colts and stallions something to mouth at. Photo: Lesley Skipper

Extinction, which forms part of the technique described above, is extremely effective at stopping colts from nipping. The photograph on page 231 shows me ignoring a colt who was determined to get my attention by nipping at my sleeve. I wore the puffy jacket partly for protection and partly because it would encourage him to nip – the irresistible puffiness referred to above – which I could then ignore; in this way I 'set up' the lesson that nipping would be ignored no matter how intense it became. This does work as long as the nipping is ignored with absolute consistency, as described under **Extinction** on pages 195–196.

Many people fear that feeding treats will cause nipping, or 'mugging', where the horse will waylay the handler looking for treats. As I said in Chapter 9, this will only be the case when treats are fed indiscriminately, but if a horse has already been spoilt in this way, some other kind of positive reinforcement will have to be found until he can be retrained. This can be done by feeding treats *only* as a reinforcer, using a conditioned reinforcer such as a clicker, and teaching the horse that treats come only from a special container (e.g. a pouch, a special bag or even from something like a small Tupperware container) rather than from people's hands or pockets. This problem tends to be more common in children's ponies than in horses, because children are more likely to feed treats indiscriminately.

It is a shame that fear of inducing nipping prevents some people from using treats as a positive reinforcer, because a small amount of the horse's favourite food is one of the most powerful reinforcers there is. If the simple guidelines outlined above are followed, there should be no problem with treats causing nipping. We have been using treats with colts and stallions for more than 20 years without any problems; and as I pointed out in Chapter 9, the riders of the Spanish Riding School have been giving the stallions sugar lumps without adverse consequences for hundreds of years.

Pawing

Stallions, mares and geldings may all paw occasionally, but pawing seems more common in stallions. Sometimes it may be related to striking out, seen in stallions who are greeting and investigating each

Chapter 11

Extinction: I am allowing Tariel to nip at my jacket; by ignoring him steadfastly I aim to extinguish the behaviour. Because I, together with everyone else handling him,- was consistent in ignoring this behaviour, it did indeed extinguish, and has never resurfaced. Photo: Brian Skipper

other (pages 56–57). It is not normally a problem unless the pawing is so frequent that it causes excessive wear to a hoof or shoe, or if the horse paws in a place where he could hurt himself (e.g. pawing near a fence and getting a foot stuck as a result). If the latter is the case, consider running a strand of electric tape or rope along the bottom rail of the fence, as described in Chapter 7.

As with any such behaviour, observe carefully to see when and where the horse paws. If it occurs at mealtimes, it may simply be anticipatory behaviour, although in that case it would usually stop once the horse has been fed (some horses paw while eating, which could possibly indicate anxiety about other horses taking the food). It might be a displacement activity; while grazing, horses are on the move all the time, seldom staying for more than a few seconds in exactly the same place. Pawing during feeding might be the horse's way of maintaining some degree of movement while eating. Some horses paw when prevented from moving; Nivalis will normally stand very quietly for most routine care procedures, but if such procedures are too prolonged for his liking (for example when he is being bathed, or sometimes when having his feet trimmed) he may start to paw the ground. We have found that the best cure for this is to halt the procedure for a while and lead him around for a few minutes, perhaps allowing him to nibble some grass; when we come back to the procedure he is normally very patient again.

If a horse paws excessively at times other than during (or prior to) feeding or while being asked to stand still for any period of time, suspect a physical cause. Gastric ulcers appear to be the culprit in many horses who paw excessively, so – as with generalized bad temper – it would be worthwhile asking your vet to investigate this possibility. Diet in general is a suspect in such cases; a diet high in forage and low in concentrates (if at all possible, eliminate concentrates altogether) is recommended.

Some people advocate shock collars or hobbles to eliminate pawing; these are not humane solutions and cannot be recommended; the same applies to any form of punishment.

Rearing

This is one of the most frightening, as well as dangerous, of behaviours. As we saw in Chapter 4, stallions rear when fighting, even if it is only a play-fight. Because of this, it is easy to conclude (as many people do) that when a stallion rears in the presence of a human he is doing so in an attempt to dominate. However, as with all such explanations, this is much too simplistic. The only way a

The Natural Stallion

stallion rearing is trying to dominate is in the very specific sense of trying to control the situation, not in the 'social dominance' sense. Bearing this in mind, why do stallions rear in a domestic setting?

Rearing in-hand

I have seen – all too often, although it is now less common than it used to be – irresponsible handlers inciting, or at the least encouraging, stallions to rear during in-hand showing classes (most notably at Arabian breed shows), in the mistaken belief that this adds excitement to the class and enhances the stallion's 'macho' image. In reality it is simply stupid and dangerous. The presence of strange stallions in close proximity, within the confines of the show ring (even a large ring can seem too small at such times), can cause even a normally calm, well-behaved stallion to feel a rush of adrenalin. Most, if they are well-trained and properly handled, will be able to deal with the situation without getting out of hand; however, there will always be some who simply find it all too much to cope with. They may find the presence of other stallions – whom they can neither drive away nor escape from – overwhelming, and rearing in such a situation is an attempt to perform at least part

Some stallions rear in protest at the too-close presence of other stallions in the showring. A moment after this photograph was taken, order was restored and the stallion was calm again. Photo: Lesley Skipper

Above left: A moment of unruliness at a show. Above right: this is dealt with quickly and efficiently by the handler, who gets the horse moving forward again. Photos: Lesley Skipper

of a stallion's normal behaviour in a situation which he feels calls for fight-or-flight. A good stallion handler will know how to calm a stallion and bring his behaviour under control again.

At a very large, prestigious show in the north of England, I recently saw an exemplary response on the part of a handler to over-excited behaviour on the part of a big Cleveland Bay colt. The charged atmosphere of the show ring was simply too much for the colt, who reared and broke away from the handler in the show ring. Another handler, who evidently knew the colt well, stepped in from outside the ring, and managed to get hold of the colt (who to his credit had not gone charging round creating mayhem, but had simply darted about a bit before trotting over to the side of the ring). The new handler caught hold of the colt; remaining utterly calm himself, he led the colt around for a few minutes until he quietened down, to show him that there was really nothing to get upset about, and led him, still calm and quiet, out of the ring. The stewards and the rest of the competitors likewise remained calm and patient; there was no fuss, and no unseemly hustling of the colt out of the showring.

Rearing may also be a form of protest at being asked to go somewhere the colt or stallion does not want to go, for example, away from mares or into a situation he finds strange or alarming. Stallions will sometimes rear in an attempt to escape restraint.

Solution

The stallion must be taught that the handler is someone he can trust, who will not put him in a position where he feels the need to defend himself. Potential sources of conflict must be identified and dealt with; for example, if the stallion rears in protest at being led away from mares, he should be taught that this is nothing terrible, and that the mares will still be there when he comes back (see page 187). If the situation is one which inspires fear, again this should be dealt with through a course of systematic desensitization and counter-conditioning. In a tense situation such as the show ring, the handler must take care not to let the stallion get too close to other stallions; the horse should be exposed to smaller shows with less exciting show ring conditions before being asked to cope with the tense atmosphere that prevails at many larger shows. In all cases, the stallion should, as a matter of course (and certainly before any tendency to rear manifests itself) be taught to go forward in response to a request from the handler. A horse cannot move forward and rear at the same time (unless he is an exceptionally athletic horse who has been taught the *courbette*[13] which in any case is a highly collected movement, not a proper rear). Teaching a 'forward' control cue can be of inestimable use here; the use of such a cue can work wonders even in a very tense situation.

Under saddle

Rearing under saddle often has its roots in pain, usually in the neck and back but also on occasions in the limbs as well. In some cases simple loss of balance is a factor; I have seen horses rear to try to regain lost balance (most typically on a slope of some kind) just as I have seen them buck for the same reason. Sometimes freshness can be a cause: the horse wants to have a fling but is restrained by the rider, so he rears in protest; or he may simply be unwilling to go forward.

This is one of the most common and frustrating of the many problems experienced by riders. The rider whose horse does not go forward has to work so hard just to keep him going that instead

---

13 The *courbette* is one of the 'airs above the ground' which certain talented horses perform at the Spanish Riding School and some other academies of equestrian art. The horse raises his forehand off the ground with his forelegs tucked in evenly and his hind legs flexed; he then leaps forward several times on his hind legs. The hind legs must be flexed in order for him to do this, which is why the *courbette* is not a proper rear. In a rear the hind legs are straight, and it is impossible for a horse to jump forward without bending his hind legs.

of being an enjoyable experience riding becomes an exhausting battle. Some riders simply become discouraged and ride less and less as a result, while others may become so annoyed and frustrated that they take their frustration and annoyance out on the horse.

Lack of forward movement can also be physically injurious to the horse, since a horse who is not using himself properly will not develop the proper muscles to carry a rider without physical damage.

Riders and trainers often regard a horse's refusal to move forward freely as a sign of laziness, stubbornness and a general unwillingness to co-operate. However, there are many possible causes of this lack of co-operation and as always we must investigate them thoroughly and eliminate the cause before we attempt a cure.

Possible causes

Pain Reluctance to move forward may be caused by pain occurring almost anywhere in the body, and as with most problems this possibility must always be thoroughly investigated.

Lack of energy Some horses may simply be lacking sufficient energy to carry a rider.

Fear of loss of balance Horses who have just been started under saddle, or those who are recovering from an injury, may be reluctant to move forward because they fear a loss of balance under the rider's weight. This is one of the commonest reasons why horses may 'act up' when first ridden.

Lack of strength If the horse has not been adequately prepared for ridden work, or has not been in regular work, he may simply not have sufficient strength to carry a rider efficiently.

Lack of motivation Many people believe that horses cannot become bored as they do not have sufficiently complex mental processes. However, there is ample evidence from recent research that this is not the case and that horses are in fact capable of a certain degree of reasoning and abstract thought.

Solution

Have the horse's back, neck and legs checked by a veterinary surgeon, have his feet looked at by a good farrier, and get a properly qualified equine dentist to examine his teeth, since the horse may be hanging back because he is trying to avoid contact with the bit. An equine dentist will also be able to look at the size and shape of the horse's mouth and check to see whether the bit fits properly. The horse's tack should also be checked to ensure that it fits correctly, since ill-fitting tack is a common cause of reluctance to move forward.

If the cause is a lack of energy, this may be a simple matter of adjusting the amount/type of the horse's feed, but since a lack of energy may be a sign of some underlying health problem, this should be discussed with the vet at the same time as the horse is examined for possible causes of pain.

Where loss of balance appears to be the cause, the rider must ensure their position in the saddle is correct and that they sit as still as possible, because an unbalanced rider who bumps around in the saddle will make the horse feel even more 'wobbly' and reluctant to move.

After all the necessary checks have been carried out to eliminate pain as a cause, the horse should first of all be taken back to basics on the lunge in order to build up his muscle strength and tone and improve his balance. Once he is moving forward freely on the lunge, his muscles have become more toned and he can stay on a circle without either hanging back or rushing to regain his balance, ridden exercises may be started which will help to establish and maintain forward movement and impulsion.[14]

Horses, especially stallions, need mental stimulation, and some horses may simply 'switch off' when being worked in an arena or other enclosed space. The same horses, when ridden out in the country or on the road, may become much more animated and forward-going, because they find the change of scenery exciting and even entertaining. Other horses may be quite happy to work in an arena as long as the work is varied and interesting and they are challenged by their work without being over-taxed. By varying the type and location of their work, and ensuring they are rewarded when they have done well, the rider can encourage such horses to enjoy their work and even look forward to it.

Some – perhaps most – stallions never rear either in hand or under saddle. Others may only rear once or twice, and never repeat the behaviour. However, a confirmed rearer can be very difficult to retrain, and if you have such a stallion, seek help from someone with the kind of credentials outlined in Appendix II. Horses who only rear occasionally can still be very alarming and it is a problem that needs to be dealt with quickly if it is not to become a habit.

Striking out

As stated under **Pawing**, this is normal behaviour for stallions who are greeting and investigating each other. In the absence of another stallion, it may be a sign of frustration (the horse wants to move, but is prevented from doing so because he is restrained). The best way of dealing with it is to ignore it (extinction) and reinforce good behaviour (i.e. when the stallion is standing quietly with all four feet on the ground) with something the horse likes. In any event, don't stand directly in front of a stallion who is likely to strike out! I don't see any point in making a big fuss about this behaviour, which (unless it becomes a habit) is unlikely to harm himself or anyone else (unless they are foolish enough to stand in front of him).

Teaching a colt or stallion to respect the handler's personal space

As I said in Chapter 8, the terms 'respect' and 'disrespect' are now used so indiscriminately by horse trainers that they are now virtually meaningless, and for that reason I dislike using them almost on principle. However, where personal space is concerned I think we can legitimately use the word 'respect' in the dictionary sense of 'polite or kind regard'. Just as it is polite for humans to respect each other's personal space, so it is polite for horses to respect each other's personal space, which is something they learn from other horses. However, they are not born understanding the need to respect ours; this is something they need to be taught if they are not to be continually barging into us, pushing us around or otherwise getting in our way. This is a two-way thing, of course; in turn we must be respectful of their personal space, and not simply assume we can barge into a horse's stable and do whatever we like with him. This type of attitude is often at the root of the kind of extreme distrust of humans manifested by some horses. Instead we need to teach him that our presence can mean something nice for him. Suppose we need to enter a horse's stable, say, in order to change his water, or to give him hay. All we need to do is to teach him to go back when asked, so that he can stand quietly while we do whatever is necessary. In this way his personal space and ours are both respected. We can also teach the horse to come to us, inviting him into our personal space. This is not at all difficult if we use the principles of reinforcement outlined in Chapter 9, to teach the

---

14 *Exercise School for Horse and Rider*, Chapters 6 to 8

horse to stand still, go back or come forward. If he knows this will result in something good for him (positive reinforcement) he will readily learn to respond to our requests.

Out of the stable, we can use exactly the same principles to teach the horse not to crowd us, or to barge, as described earlier in this chapter and in Chapter 8. In general, there is no need to make a big song-and-dance about it, as some trainers do, or, in most cases, to use twirling ropes and the like.

However, there *are* occasions when the twirling (or waggling) rope can come in very useful. Suppose you have a colt (or a mature stallion) who has never been taught to respect a human's personal space. Twirling a lead-rope (it doesn't have to be very long) between yourself and the horse can be very effective in making him keep his distance until you work out how to deal with the situation. If a colt comes running at you playfully (as opposed to a full-blown charge) in the field, making yourself 'big' (by standing tall and square and holding your arms out or up – see the photographs on page 147) and holding up a hand can be extremely effective at stopping him dead in his tracks. The usual explanation for this is that increasing your size in this way makes him think of a stallion 'puffing himself up' in display, and that holding a hand up imitates the action of a hoof raised in threat. Enchanting as these ideas are, I don't really think they are an accurate depiction of what the horse is thinking. There is no way in which a puny human can begin to imitate a stallion displaying to a rival, or a raised hand be the equivalent of a raised hoof. In any case, if the colt did think of the human as a displaying stallion, he might conceivably regard the 'puffing up' as a challenge, which could have undesirable results! But I do not think this is at all what happens. It is really much more likely that the colt is sufficiently startled by this change in the human's appearance – and that the raised hand is something he wants to avoid, as horses will tend to back away from hands, or anything else, raised in their faces – that such actions have a powerful 'stopping' effect.

In any case, such actions are not in themselves a solution, because although they will stop the horse from approaching you, they will not tell him what to do instead. What you need to do is to teach the horse to stand still while you hold him, then gradually move away from him until you are standing at what you consider a comfortable, acceptable distance from him. Then, having already taught him to understand a conditioned reinforcer such as the clicker, you can teach him to stay at that distance, using a control cue, until you invite him to approach you. In exactly the same way, you can teach him to keep his distance when being led.

Non-confrontation is *not* a 'soft' option

There will be people who, on reading through this chapter, will feel that I am much too 'soft' in my approach, and that what is really needed to solve the kind of behavioural problems outlined here is a much 'tougher' approach, if necessary involving punishment.

Yes, punishment does work – if it is applied properly. But as we have seen, it does nothing to address the underlying cause of the behaviour; it merely suppresses it, leaving it free to emerge again if the stresses which created the behaviour in the first place should ever return. If you ever hear someone say something like, 'Whenever my horse does *X* I simply give him a whack, and he stops doing it' think about what they have just said. *Whenever he does* X: that means that whatever behaviour '*X*' might represent, the horse is still doing it – until he is whacked, when he stops – until the next time. So the punishment hasn't really worked – it has merely suppressed the behaviour *at that time*. Furthermore – and I know I have repeated this several times, but I feel it can't be emphasized enough – punishment can't ever teach the horse an alternative, more acceptable behaviour. And if the emotional state which caused the behaviour is not dealt with, the horse may simply find other (and possibly even less acceptable) ways of dealing with it.

We also need to consider how much equine aggression (especially on the part of stallions) is actually the result of attempts to punish (or 'discipline') the horse for some behaviour deemed unacceptable. If punishment and/or the use of harsh, coercive training methods is really so effective, why do so many of the people who advocate such measures continue to think of stallions as inherently untrustworthy? On the other hand, those of us who use (and advocate) non-confrontational methods, with an emphasis on positive reinforcement, find the opposite: that stallions are inherently *trustworthy*, provided they are treated properly.

In 2007 a paper was published giving the results of a survey of records of children bitten by dogs. The researchers found that 59 per cent of the dogs examined had responded to disciplinary measures with aggression. (Reisner *et al.*, 2007) And researchers have also found that the use of punitive training methods predisposes dogs to aggression (De Keuster and Jung, 2009). Now certainly, horses are not dogs; but the circumstances which trigger aggression are very similar in many species. Is it worth taking the risk of creating aggressive responses in any animal, simply to avoid being thought of as 'soft'?[15] As Lucy Rees says, '... unpleasantness breeds fear, fear tension, tension inability to respond and thus resistance – and training becomes a desperate, dangerous and unpleasant struggle.' (Rees, 1984)

By contrast, when the non-confrontational approach is used, the worst that can happen is that nothing changes – for better or for worse. The trainer will then have to re-think their approach, but at least they will not have created further problems, or made a bad situation worse.

A colt's redemption

Finally, I will end this chapter with a story which illustrates nicely how problem behaviour can be solved without resorting to force, through the simple application of patience, common sense and a real understanding of colts and stallions.

> I am sorry to tell you that I am seriously contemplating the gelding of Rose of Sharon's 1906 colt by Harb, that I named Rodan. He is a magnificent appearing colt, but has a nasty temper, something entirely new in our experience with Arab horses. From a very young colt he has been ready to kick or strike any one who came near him, and I am afraid he may hurt some of my men as he gains in strength. No one can touch him to groom his quarters, neither kindness nor discipline affects him... (Blunt, 1986)

Thus wrote Colonel Spencer Borden in May 1907 to Lady Anne Blunt of the famous Crabbet Arabian Stud, from whom he had bought several horses. Lady Anne replied, 'Surely it is too soon to despair about the Rose of Sharon colt. I have never met with a bad-tempered Arabian horse in all my thirty years' experience...' She had consulted with her stud manager in Egypt, she said, 'an Arab of the Muteyr, the most famous horsebreeding tribe in the S. Eastern Nejd, about your colt. He declared that no Arabian horse could be innately or permanently ill tempered, although young colts may sometimes be violent to begin with, from being above themselves and to let off high spirits, "before their intelligence is developed", as he expressed it.' She went on to tell Colonel Borden about a colt that the Stud Manager, Mutlak el Battal, had dealt with when working for the late Ali Pasha Sherif in Cairo, that had started life very much like the Rose of Sharon colt, by behaving

---

15 In any case it is not at all clear why being thought of as 'soft' is such a terrible thing. This seems to be a cultural response by people who are conditioned to believe that 'being tough' (even when such 'toughness' is either irrelevant or counter-productive) is somehow a virtue.

Young colts may sometimes be unruly from being above themselves and to let off high spirits. Photo: Lesley Skipper

savagely, but that he had cured by exercise and work (it is important to realise here that Mutlak did *not* use coercion – just a vast amount of patience and persistence). Lady Anne's remedy for Rodan was similar. 'Of course,' she wrote, 'Rodan is too young to be mounted but all the preliminary processes could be gone on with and the sooner the better. No "discipline" other than the firmness necessary to keep him in check and never to let him have his own way.' (Blunt, 1986)

Colonel Borden took Lady Anne's advice; part of his course of action involved changing Rodan's groom for another. 'This latter, a Portuguese, is very gentle with him, but patient and firm, never letting him get the upper hand, persisting always until the colt does what he wants him to do. He never raises his voice, Rodan likes him, and is a changed animal.'

On being told the story of Rodan, Mutlak, the *bedawin* stud manager, said 'Ah, *I* like to see them nice and bold.' (Blunt, 1986)

This passage is interesting on several counts. Firstly, there is the wisdom shown by both Lady Anne and her stud manager in not attributing Rodan's 'nastiness' to any inherent bad temper, but rather to the bumptiousness of a young colt who had simply, as Mutlak would put it, got 'above himself'. Then, one is struck by the way in which both Mutlak and Lady Anne took it for granted that horses *have* an intelligence to be developed. Finally, there is the absence of any suggestion of 'breaking' the colt's spirit in order to tame him; this was to be done by awakening and expanding his mind by means of work suitable to his age and level of physical maturity. Some of the modern-day trainers who insist on 'dominating' the horse, and who decry so-called 'traditional' methods, would do well to take heed of all this.

Chapter 12

The stallion's role in the horse world in general

Look, what a horse should have he did not lack,
Save a proud rider on so proud a back.

– William Shakespeare, Venus and Adonis

I HOPE the preceding chapters have shown that a stallion's role need not be confined to breeding, and that entire male horses can – if trained and managed properly – have a major role to play in the horse world in general.

The stallion's capacity for co-operation with his human caretakers has long been recognized by those who make use of stallions in their daily work. For example, here is Andy Beck of the White Horse Ethology Project talking about his experience using stallions in a trekking operation (Beck, 2005):

> When the Project was established in 1972 I had already worked three Andalusian stallions together in a trekking operation, and had found them excellent work partners that could very easily have taken advantage of many of the 'greenhorn' tourists that two of them regularly carried – but very politely forbore to do so. This was somewhat surprising to say the least given the general expectation for entires. The third of the trio – my mount – guided and controlled rides including strings of up to 17 horses so well that I rarely had to do anything other than enquire as to the tourist's wishes regarding pace and rest stops. I had assumed that this degree of co-operation was due to the fact that our interests coincided reasonably well – for my part, I fed them the best balanced feed I could put together, made certain they had regular breaks, never had to work through the mid-day heat, got a couple of days off whenever they seemed stressed and were never abused by any rider. In return they gave me their co-operation and loyalty. At no point was there any real need for a clash of interests, unless it was on those very rare occasions when a ride passed a mare in season in some field bordering the trail, and even then there was always the dual urge to keep up with the rest of the group rather than to stop.

There are some spheres of equestrian activity in which stallions have always been paramount, for example the equestrian academies of Spain and Portugal, and of course the Spanish Riding School

The Natural Stallion

of Vienna. There is one sphere of equestrian activity in which stallions reign supreme: this is the *corrida* of Spain and Portugal. I refer not to the bullfight on foot, where the only horses involved are the unfortunate, broken-down horses of the *picadors*, but to the mounted bullfight (in Spain this is referred to as the *rejoneo* to distinguish it from the bullfight on foot; in Portugal it is the only form of bullfight, and is there known simply as the *corrida*).

The mounted bullfight

This is not the place to discuss the ethics of bullfighting; that discussion belongs elsewhere. It is sufficient to say here that while in Spain the bull is still killed in the *rejoneo*, in Portugal he is spared. In the Portuguese *corrida* the fight is not so much a pitting of wits against the bull, as a test of the skill and courage of the *cavaleiro*[1] and his horse combined – the idea of the partnership being paramount. The *cavaleiro* must be able to rely utterly on his horse's unswerving courage and loyalty, for he is literally riding for his life, and the slightest hesitation may prove fatal. It is a testimony to the skill of these horsemen – a skill which dates back to ancient times – and to the valour of their horses, that injuries to horses are very rare, and it is considered a terrible disgrace for the *cavaleiro* to allow this to happen. Sylvia Loch, describing the exploits of these daring horsemen, says 'Great bullfighters, who at the height of their summer season, daily court death with their beautiful horses, are unreservedly emotional about the relationship they share with their fighting horse.' (Loch, 1986)

Stallions are used almost exclusively in the mounted bullfight, although every now and then a mare such as Espléndida, with whom Alvaro Domecq, one of the most renowned *rejoneadors* of the twentieth century, fought many bulls, will overturn this tradition. However, this is very rare; for the most part, the mounted bullfight belongs to stallions.

The Portuguese *corrida*: Antonio Ribeiro Telles on El Viti. Photo: courtesy of Arsénio Raposo Cordeiro

Competing with stallions

Competing with stallions can bring with it certain challenges, such as the obvious one of bringing stallions into close contact with other horses, and show personnel who may have little if any experience of dealing with stallions. The less obvious challenge is that of combining a career at stud with competition; traditionally, entire racehorses who have proved themselves on the track then retire to stud and are seen no more by the general public. At a higher level, it may be difficult to organize a competing stallion's stud activities so as to allow him to continue competing; a stallion who is fully booked for stud duties may simply not have the time to intersperse these with competition

---

1 Horseman; in Portuguese, literally 'knight'.

Chapter 12

(although some have managed it), so for many, the only practical way is to offer chilled or frozen semen (a recent example of this being the dressage stallion Moorlands Totilas – see page 251). However, unless a stallion has to cover a great many mares in a season, combining stud activities with competition need not be an insurmountable problem, as demonstrated by people like Ann Hyland with her Arabian stallion Nizzolan (see page 253) and Patti Demers Bailey with her legendary Arabian stallion Remington Steele (see page 259).

Even at comparatively low levels of competition, more and more people are bringing stallions out to compete – and proving that their behaviour in a competition setting can be as good as – if not better than – that of the more usual mares and geldings. In May 2006, for example, dressage classes held at Eden Hall in Kelso on the Scottish borders as part of the Borders Festival of the Horse, saw two stallions competing among the usual bevy of mares and geldings. These two stallions, a Lusitano named Quem Foi and an Appaloosa called Elljay Indiana (known as Max), behaved in an exemplary manner, as well as delighting the audience with their performances.

Katharine Duckitt with her Lusitano stallion Quem Foi at the Borders Festival of the Horse, 2006. Photo: Lesley Skipper

Daune Bronte-Stuart wih her Appaloosa stallion Elljay Indiana (Max to his friends) at the Borders Festival of the Horse, 2006. Photo: Lesley Skipper

More and more people are bringing stallions out to compete: coloured stallion Login Lucky Lad not only won his class (Native Cob/Traditonal Type Ridden Pony) at the Great Yorkshire Show in 2010; he went on to win the Coloured Horse and Pony Ridden Championship.   Photo: Lesley Skipper

Stallions in demonstrations and displays

The Spanish Riding School

Perhaps the most famous displays given by stallions worldwide are those of the 400-year-old Spanish Riding School in Vienna. The Lipizzaner stallions, born at the School's stud at Piber in Styria, Austria, leave the stud at the age of four to be trained at the famous Winter Riding School in Vienna. After a long and distinguished career (for Lipizzaners are long-lived horses, and their classical training keeps them fit and sound), the best of them return to the stud at Piber to pass on their bloodlines; having completed their stud duties, they go back to Vienna and resume their life at the Riding School.

Sylvia Loch and Prazer

Sylvia Loch regularly holds demonstrations with her Lusitano stallion Prazer, who is also sometimes used as a schoolmaster horse for Sylvia's pupils. The photographs on page 243 show Sylvia and Prazer in demonstration; on page 244 we see Prazer giving a lesson to one of Sylvia's pupils.

Chapter 12

The Spanish Riding School: Siglavy Mantua I, ridden by Ober-Bereiter (Chief Rider) Klaus Krzisch. Photo: J.J.A. Hohmann

Above left: Sylvia Loch and her Lusitano stallion Prazer give a demonstration of classical riding. Above right: Sylvia and Prazer. Photos: Lesley Skipper

The Natural Stallion

Prazer and Sylvia give one of Sylvia's pupils a lesson. Photos: Nathalie Todd

The Classical Riding Club's 15th Anniversary event, 2010

At the Classical Riding Club's[2] 15th Anniversary event, 'Perfect Your Position; Perfect Your Horse' held at Myerscough College, Lancashire on 11th July 2010, six horses took part in sessions with three trainers (Sylvia Loch, Heather Moffett and Mary Wanless); Pedro Neves also gave a demonstration of Portuguese classical in-hand work. Of the seven horses who took part, three were stallions (all

Above left: Sylvia Loch riding Lusitano stallion Safões. Above right: Helen Kettleborough and Lusitano stallion Quite. Both photographs were taken at the Classical Riding Club's 15th Anniversary event. Photos: Lesley Skipper

---

2 For more about the Classical Riding Club, see Appendix II

Lusitanos); their behaviour was impeccable, even when another stallion was in the arena (albeit a short distance away).

Stallions of the Spanish Riding School

The Spanish Riding School has produced many great stallions, some of whom have been immortalized by Alois Podhajsky in his delightful and moving book, *My Horses, My Teachers*. The first of the school stallions trained by Podhajsky after he joined the Spanish Riding School as director, was Neapolitano Africa. Podhajsky says of him:

> Neapolitano Africa was very good-natured and willing to learn but as touchy as a prima donna. Any small trifle was enough to excite him and make him nervous. If he happened to make a mistake he was beside himself so that I had to calm him by patting and caressing and to comfort him by giving him to understand that everybody makes mistakes now and then and that there is nothing tragic about them. I called him 'my sensitive little soul' and treated him with even more care and tenderness than my other horses. (Podhajsky, 1997)

Although Neapolitano Africa was so excitable when faced with anything new, Podhajsky always felt he could rely on him. He was the solo star of many performances during the Spanish Riding School's tours abroad from 1948 to 1949, and he went with Podhajsky to the Olympic Games in London in 1948, together with Podhajsky's Hungarian gelding Teja. Although the result of the Grand Prix with Teja was disappointing to Podhajsky, he was asked to give a demonstration with Neapolitano Africa, which he did to great acclaim. The following year Podhajsky, once again in London with Teja and Neapolitano Africa, was asked to give a demonstration riding in the spotlights. Podhajsky recalls, 'Although I had never tried anything like it and there was no possibility of rehearsing before the show, I agreed, trusting in my good Neapolitano Africa.' Podhajsky was rather apprehensive, because the great showjumper Harry Llewellyn had described how his horse, Foxhunter, had been blinded by the dazzling light during their lap of honour in the spotlights, and had been afraid to go into the complete darkness in front of him; Foxhunter had also tried to jump over his own shadow when it appeared in the spotlight. Podhajsky goes on to say:

> I admit that it was with some forebodings that I cantered into the pitch-dark stadium of White City surrounded and followed by a circle of four blinding spotlights which embraced horse and rider. I could see barely two yards to the front. When one of the flower pots that marked the arena appeared in the circle of light, I knew that this was the end of the line and I had to turn. Neapolitano Africa had to remain absolutely straight and not miss a single one of these marks, otherwise we would have lost our direction in the vast arena. I am sure this was the most severe test of going straight and in perfect balance. The slightest swaying in the lateral work or in the change of leg at the canter, or a pirouette not executed correctly would have meant not meeting the flower pot and getting lost. Moreover, this display was the greatest proof of Neapolitano Africa's obedience and confidence. He allowed me to take him at the extended trot or the canter into the black darkness in front of him without hesitating for a fraction of a second. (Podhajsky, 1997)

Another very great Spanish Riding School stallion was Pluto Theodorosta. Initially a very difficult horse, he became one of the stars of the School. In 1949 he went to London with Podhajsky, together with Teja and Neapolitano Africa, and participated in displays at the International Horse Show at

Alois Podhajsky with Neapolitano Africa, his 'sensitive little soul', in *piaffe*.

White City. The following year Pluto Theodorosta appeared at the spring show of the Royal Dublin Society. Podhajsky says of him:

> Pluto Theodorosta had a sparkling temperament, which enhanced his lively and impulsive paces and gave a special brilliance to his whole appearance. His obedience was exemplary and he had unlimited confidence in his rider, which prevented him from shying or giving trouble by sheer gaiety.

He goes on to recount an amusing anecdote about the return from Dublin:

> He [Pluto Theodorosta] revealed his lively temperament in a very spectacular way on his trip home from Dublin. Quite obviously he took the rather dilapidated state of the French Railway Company car as an insult and not in keeping with his rank. Maybe it was also the continuous rattling and jolting that disgusted him. For a while his groom, my faithful Flasar, succeeded in calming him, but then he had enough of it. With a tremendous leap he tore his halter and gave vent to his rage. The poor man who had been the horse's best friend had no choice but to take flight. He squeezed himself through a narrow opening in the sliding door, pushed it closed again, and hanging outside on the step of the carriage in the brisk air of spring, frantically tried to catch the attention of the personnel of the train. When at last they noticed him, the train was halted on the spot. Flasar bravely ventured into the carriage again and tried to put order into the mess which the horses had produced and to calm them down, because rebelling Pluto Theodorosta had excited Teja, too, and instigated a veritable riot. His rebellion had a positive result, however, for at the next station their defective carriage was exchanged for a better one. (Podhajsky, 1997)

In 1953 the Spanish Riding School was invited to give a display at White City in London. At a reception after the display, Podhajsky was presented to Her Majesty Queen Elizabeth II, who impressed him with her knowledge of horses and of the Spanish Riding School. Podhajsky asked the Queen if she would like to ride Pluto Theodorosta. The Queen accepted, and on July 25th, 1953, she rode

Chapter 12

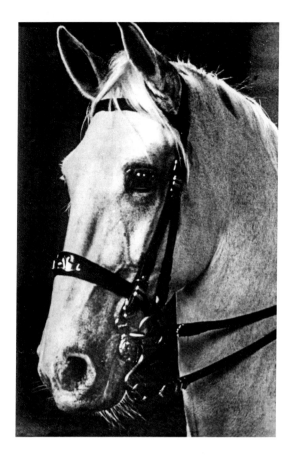

Pluto Theodorosta. Photo courtesy of the late Mme Eva Podhajsky and Sylvia Loch.

Pluto Theodorosta, the only person to have done so, apart from Podhajsky, in ten years. The Queen was thrilled with Pluto Theodorosta; Podhajsky commented,

> I felt royally rewarded in the true meaning of the word when the Queen praised the softness of Pluto Theodorosta's movements which, of all things, had been so unimaginably hard in the beginning. (Podhajsky, 1997)

After this, Pluto Theodorosta became so famous that many months later Podhajsky received a letter addressed simply to 'Mr Pluto Theodorosta, Austria'!

When Pluto Theodorosta reached the age of 29, Podhajsky wanted to retire him, thinking he deserved a well-earned rest. But Pluto Theodorosta thought otherwise.

> One day he took advantage of the fact that the door of his box was always open and trotted through the time-honoured courtyard and across the street to the indoor riding school. The groom who raced after him stood horror-struck when a bus rolled through the busy narrow street that the stallion was about to cross. But Pluto Theodorosta paused, waited until the traffic had passed, and crossed the street when he had convinced himself that there was no danger. Appreciating his zeal, I continued to ride him for another year in the beautiful riding hall, taking care not to demand too much and gradually making him accustomed to his retired life. The last year of his life I had him exercised at the walk without a rider and without a saddle. When he was thirty-one years old his gallant heart gradually grew tired until at last, on a hot summer day, it ceased to beat. (Podhajsky, 1997)

The Natural Stallion

Robyn Walker with Dervatiw Gwyddion at the Arab Horse Society's National Show, Malvern, in 2008. Photo by Lesley Skipper

Chapter 12

Some great stallions

There have been many, many great stallions in all fields of competition and equestrian endeavour. It would take more than one book, let alone one chapter, to do justice to them all, so I will simply mention here a very few who have earned a place on that list of ambassadors for their sex.

Dervatiw Gwyddion (1995–)

I first saw Dervatiw Gwyddion (AJ Ibn Negatiw x Dervona) at the Horse of the Year Show in 2007, and was impressed not only by his commanding presence but by his correctness of conformation and type. He is the kind of Arabian stallion you want to take home with you! 'Mr Gwiddy', as he is known to his friends, was bred in the USA, where Jean Peck of Paslow Arabians acquired him as a young horse who was still quite green under saddle, yet already athletic, powerful and balanced. However it was not only his athleticism that impressed Jean, but also his lovely, unspoilt, gentle nature.

Gwyddion began his dressage training in 2001, and at Scottsdale in February 2002 he won five Training Level tests with an average score of 66 per cent. He also came second in his debut First Level test with a score of 64 per cent. On top of that, he was the Scottsdale Champion Sport Horse Stallion – a resoundingly successful start to his ridden career. Of that day at Scottsdale, Jean says, 'He amazed people by having his stall door open all day with just a mesh guard in front, attesting to his wonderful temperament and dislike of bars.' (Liz Salmon, 'The Dervatiw Gwyddion Story').

More successes and championships followed; 'Mr Gwiddy' became the 2004 US National Champion Sport Horse Stallion, USEF Horse of the Year, Region 3 Champion in Arabian Speciality, and the winner of the Ann T Bowling Memorial Trophy at the 2004 California State Dressage Championships. In 2005 Dave and Jean Peck returned to the UK, bringing Gwyddion with them. He continued his ridden career in the UK partnered by Fiona Grant Chivers, who had wisely suggested to Dave and Jean that mixing both showing and advanced dressage might be difficult for their talented stallion. After competing at HOYS in October 2006 with Fiona, and earning a creditable third place, Gwyddion continued to be ridden by Fiona, with whom he won many ridden championships all over the country. The pair were virtually unbeaten, and became known, as Jean Peck puts it, for their 'trademark big gallop'.

In autumn 2006 Gwyddion was introduced to a talented young dressage rider, Robyn Walker. At the time Robyn was only 13, very slight, small and shy; however, she confidently got on Gwid and put him through his paces. As Jean Peck says, 'The pair had a few trial outings and were greatly admired, but it was questioned as to whether a 16hh, high powered Arab stallion, with a devilish sense of humour, was a bit too "high octane" after Robyn's previous partner, a 13hh pony!' (Jean Peck, personal communication)

Neverthess, after Gwyddion's successful show season with Fiona in 2007, Dave and Jean asked Robyn if she would like to compete with Gwid in the dressage at the Arab Horse Society's National Show at Malvern, with Fiona riding him in the Open Stallion class. Robyn readily agreed and, after a few practice runs at local shows, she and Gwid delighted everyone with a win in the Elementary Class and a second place in the Medium test at Malvern. The stallion's versatility was demonstrated by his second place with Fiona in the Open Stallion Class.

In the meantime Robyn had qualified Gwid for the region's Pet Plan Area Festival, which was to be held at Towerlands on the 11th and 12th October 2008. Again, they delighted everyone by winning the Open Elementary class and coming second in the Open Novice class; this was a remarkable achievement, since she was competing against all adults on mainly Warmblood horses.

The Natural Stallion

Above left: Fiona Grant-Chivers with Dervatiw Gwyddion, Malvern 2008. Above right: Robyn Walker and Gwiddy about to start a dressage test. Photos: Lesley Skipper

These results qualified the pair for the British Dressage National Championships in April 2009 at Hartpury, an amazing feat in itself: Robyn and Gwiddy had beaten many horses and riders who had been trying to qualify at dressage events all over the UK. They turned in a very creditable performance at Hartpury, gaining eighth place out of more than 30 horses in the Open Elementary test. The Open Novice Class was even more hotly contested with over 60 entered in two divisions. Robyn and Gwid made it through to the final 30, being placed third by one judge; sadly, the other judge did not place them but they still gained a very creditable 13th place out of the original sixty.

Robyn and Gwid have gone from strength to strength, adding to their triumphs not only dressage but showing classes too. At the Arab Horse Society's National Show at Malvern in 2010 they won a hotly contested Elementary dressage with 68.80 per cent, and then went on to gain second place in the Medium Test. To top that, they were pulled in first in the Horse of the Year Qualifier Senior Stallion class, during which they gave a display of what Jean Peck calls their 'trademark "proper" gallop. They were ultimately placed second after Darren Crowe, but as Jean says, 'it would take a VERY brave judge to put up a 16-year-old above all the pro riders!' (Personal communication).

I saw Robyn and Gwid at Malvern in 2008 and loved the way they had developed such a harmonious partnership. Robyn was only 14 at the time, yet this powerful Arabian stallion, who is not only a multi-champion in the USA and in the UK as well as being approved by the American Warmblood Society, as a 'Preferred Sire', responded to her in a way that was beautiful to watch.

Downlands Cancara (1975–2006)

One of the most moving sights I have ever witnessed was at the Great Yorkshire Show some years ago, during a display given by the Riding for the Disabled Association. The famous Lloyds Black Horse of the 1980s TV adverts, Downlands Cancara, was ridden by a young woman who – although the precise nature and extent of her disability was not clear – could scarcely hold the reins in her hands. It was also quite apparent that her aids were virtually non-existent. Yet this horse –

a powerful, high-spirited Trakehner stallion – carried her with grace and dignity around a large showring, to tremendous applause.

Moorlands Totilas (2001–)

In July 2009 the spectacular Dutch Warmblood stallion Moorlands Totilas, owned by Tosca and Kees Visser and ridden by Edward Gal, scored a world record 89.4 per cent in the freestyle dressage to music in the World Dressage Masters at Hickstead. In August the same year Totilas and Gal broke their own record at the Alltech FEI European Jumping & Dressage Championships at Windsor, scoring 90.70 per cent to win the Freestyle gold medal; then in December 2009 they caused a further sensation by breaking their own record again at the Olympia Horse Show World Cup Dressage Qualifier, with a remarkable score of 92.3 per cent. They went on to win the dressage World Cup final at 's-Hertogenbosch on 27 March 2010. There has been ongoing controversy in the dressage world about Totilas's way of going; but whatever one's opinion about this it cannot be denied that he is a very talented horse with immense presence. Gal says of Totilas ('Toto' to his friends): 'Totilas is a very special horse. He has an incredible amount of talent; it's simply a pleasure to ride him. Totilas is everything a rider could want!'

Edward Gal with Moorlands Totilas.
Photo: Bob Langrish

Nizzolan (1967–2001)

One of the most successful endurance horses of the 1970s, Nizzolan (1967–2001) was a grey 15 hh Arabian stallion of 75 per cent Crabbet breeding. Born in North Carolina, USA, he was by Lewisfield Nizzamo out of Solange, a mare from Harwood Arabian Stud. Nizzolan was brought back from the USA by Ann Hyland when she returned to England in 1968, having lived in the USA for a number of years. From the start, 'Nizzie' was an easy horse. Ann Hyland says of him, 'He was never "broken in", just accepting things as if it was the natural thing to do.' For the first six months of his ridden life Nizzie was ridden in a halter as Ann was unable to find a bit small enough to fit his tiny muzzle.

A very versatile horse, Nizzolan's forte was long distance. His career in this discipline began in 1972; in his first big event, the British Horse Society Golden Horseshoe Ride, he gained a silver award, followed by three successive gold awards, in every case without incurring a veterinary penalty. In 1974 the Endurance Horse and Pony Society began a points system for their series of rides around the country, and in 1974 and 1975 Nizzolan came top of the league, winning the Manar Trophy for the leading endurance horse of the year; 1976 he stood reserve champion because, as Ann points out, she lost her way and earned time penalties in the course of a ride. In 1975 he won the first ever 100-mile endurance race to be held in Britain, travelling at an average speed of 8.33mph with a riding time of 12 hours 1 minute – a speed not bettered for nine years. In the same year Nizzolan represented the discipline of long distance riding at the Horse of the Year Show, taking part in the Parade of Champions; the same year, as the Arabian breed's top endurance horse, he appeared at the Arab Horse Society's National Championships, as well as in an Arabian extravaganza at Olympia in London. In 1976 Nizzolan and another horse, Margaret Montgomerie's Tarquin, took part in the Hamburg to Hannover 100-mile ride. Ann Hyland remarks, 'Despite not getting an accurate translation of the rules we both survived the distance and some of the rather strange obstacles, including swimming the River Aller 2 km from the finish'. Riding as a team she and Margaret Montgomerie finished together; at the vetting the following day, Tarquin was placed first, with Nizzolan second.

At the time Nizzolan was shown in-hand, it was still the fashion to show Arabian horses with too much condition. Nizzolan, lean and fit for endurance work, did not always show to advantage against some of the overweight show horses. However, Lady Anne Lytton, daughter of the celebrated Lady Wentworth, having on one memorable occasion the opportunity to examine Nizzolan, praised his type and conformation, comparing him favourably to some of the top show winners of his day. This was praise indeed coming from such a knowledgeable source.

Nizzolan. Photo: Robin Nicholson

Chapter 12

In an article which appeared in Arabian Horse News in 1984, Dr P.M. Ellis, M.V.Sc. wrote of Nizzolan:

> During my daily work as a vet with horses of all breeds shapes and sizes, I am often asked why I am particularly interested in and admire the Arabian horse. Owners Arabians never have to ask that question, they share the same disease HIPPOPHILIA ARABI! My love for the breed evolved over a period of time from a love of horses in general. The Arabian horse chose me rather than vice versa, as a result of one ride through the New Forest. That single ride triggered an interest that changed the course of my life... Shortly after the hundred mile ride, Ann Hyland, owner of the winner, purebred Arabian stallion Nizzolan (Lewisfield Nizzamo x Solange) allowed me to ride the stallion on a twenty mile jaunt through the New Forest. It is to Nizzolan I owe my dedication to the Arabian horse – the progression of *Hippophilia generalis* to *Hippophilia arabi*!
>
> What a ride! He moved in a ground-eating, effortless comfortably trot, so obedient but with overdrive if required. My sprit soared and I never have and never will forget that horse. In his trlim state of that time he might not have carried off first prize in a show ring but he was a superb athlete with an exceptional temperament and the best horse it has ever been my privilege to ride. I was hooked!
> (Ellis, 1984)

Nizzolan (on the left, with Ann Hyland) being ridden out with his long-time companion Katchina. Photo: courtesy of Ann Hyland

Nizzie combined stud duties with a versatile career in a number of different disciplines. At that time it was comparatively unusual for stallions to be ridden in open competition, and as Ann says, 'It was ... found very strange that a stallion standing at stud with a full book of mares would also engage in a very full round of ridden activities.' (Hyland, The Endurance Horse, 1988). Nizzie was shown successfully in both English and Western classes with many wins and numerous placings. He was also a superb hunter; Ann hunted him for several seasons with the New Forest Foxhounds and he did his regular stint leading the Master's horse when Sir Newton Rycroft was Master of the New Forest Hounds. Nizzie was also extremely good at working cattle, being adept both at cutting a calf from a bunch and at driving cattle across country, something he did regularly when he and Ann lived in the New Forest. However, as Ann says, his *piece de resistance* was being ridden bridle-less with only a cord around his neck.

> He gave many demonstrations doing this and could be worked at speed, in figures of eight, with flying changes and rapid rollbacks. In fact, he went better without a bridle than with one and was completely trustworthy, even when working as a pair with another stallion (bridled) at a demonstration. (Hyland, 2001)

Nizzolan being ridden bridle-less by Ann Hyland. Photo: Peter Connolly

In his later years, one of his occasional roles was in what is called 'experimental archaeology'.

> Original and facsimile equestrian artefacts from the past are put to a practical test to prove or disprove their functions. As I write on the history of the horse from ancient times onwards this was a great help. He and his friend Katchina got used to carrying Roman equipment and working out military manoeuvres from Arrian's *Ars Tactica*, a second century AD military treatise I analysed for my publishers. Nizzolan also worked with a variety of ancient bits, ranging from the 12th to 18th century, some of which are held in the Museum of London. (Hyland, 2001)

Nizzie ran out with two geldings and a mare, Ann Hyland's Standardbred Magnet Regent. Over the course of many years Magnet had nine foals by him. Several of them won national and international awards in endurance riding and showjumping.

Ann says of Nizzolan,

Chapter 12

I can honestly say he was the easiest horse I have ever worked with. He combined stud and performance duties – often on the same day if necessary. He did his stint at babysitting weaned foals, even tolerating cheek from one bumptious six-month-old that challenged him. His last years were spent running out with his friend Katchina, alas also gone at the age of 31, and his last son Granicus. I do not think his place can ever be filled. (Hyland, 2001)

Palomo Linares (1973–2001)

Anyone who joined the Classical Riding Club during the 1990s, or who followed Sylvia Loch's monthly column in the magazine Horse and Rider during much of the same period, could not fail to be aware of the influence one special horse had had on his owner. This was Sylvia's Lusitano x Arabian stallion, Palomo Linares. It was Palomo whose correctness and balance, and his ability to help everyone who sat on his back – provided they were properly humble and respectful – that made Sylvia decide to return to teaching, which she had abandoned after the sudden death of her husband, Lord Henry Loch, in 1982.

Palomo was 14 when Sylvia acquired him in Portugal. He had been a bullfighting horse, but had also taken part in Iberian sports such as javelin-racing, which dates back to Roman times. He had then gone to stud, and finally been sold on. However, his new owner found his explosive nature under saddle too much to handle, so Sylvia was given the chance to buy him.

Sylvia Loch with Palomo Linares Photo: courtesy of Sylvia Loch

The Natural Stallion

From the moment she sat on his back, Sylvia knew that Palomo was something special. 'He was king,' she said in an interview for the magazine Horse and Hound in 1996, 'and I felt I was sitting on a throne. The horse knew everything about classical dressage and just lifted up his front, sat down on his hocks and performed.' (Lithman, 1996)

Sylvia brought Palomo back to England, to her small yard in Suffolk. To begin with, Sylvia simply concentrated on forging a partnership with Palomo.

> If the riding was sometimes unpredictable, Palomo was an absolute gentleman in every other way. Shoeing, boxing, and grooming ... like most Iberians, he was the perfect horse. And all who visited at my tiny two-horse yard were rapidly captivated by his winning ways over the stable door.
>
> Whenever I was stumped or mystified about a certain technique or principle, I would simply ride my horse. It may sound trite, but with him I always found the answer to the most technical of questions. It was as though he bared his soul and allowed me the privilege of looking into it – not for his sake, but to help all horses. I can only say it was as though he was speaking through me. (Loch, 2001)

Eventually Sylvia started using Palomo to teach her pupils. He was not so much a schoolmaster as a professor – in the same sense that the *Bereiters* of the Spanish Riding School refer to the stallions who are best at teaching young riders as 'professors'. As well as giving lessons, Palomo won classes at shows, excelled in dressage to music, appeared on television and 'starred' in several books and countless magazine articles. He also, memorably, gave a full high school display in front of 400 people with nothing more than a silken cord in his mouth, repeating the performance later at the Royal Mews in London, first in a double bridle and then with just the cord in his mouth.

Palomo ridden by Annabel Weller-Poley. Photo: Event Print

But it is as an equine professor that he will chiefly be remembered, especially by those of Sylvia's pupils who were privileged to ride him. Of his ability as a teacher, Sylvia says,

256

Chapter 12

No one respected the ethos of classical riding more than Palomo, and by his own self-discipline, he kept us all up to scratch. Even in his last lesson on the 1st November, you could sense the pride and desire for perfection. And that was why he helped everyone who sat on his back.

Nothing was done improperly or shoddily. He was a true master and showed the way. It was awe inspiring. No matter how novice or how advanced the pupil, he tried to make each step correct. Regardless of mistakes, he always indicated what was needed. The best thing for me was to watch each pupil's face – after watching his.

People who knew him, said he always looked to me for guidance, but it was a two way thing. He simply trusted me to put into words what they needed to know, but it was him who showed me through his eye and body language. (Loch, 2001)

**Palomo giving one of Sylvia's pupils a lesson.
Photo: courtesy of Sylvia Loch**

Fellow equestrian author Anne Wilson has this to say about Palomo:

> I first sat on Palomo Linares around 1995 and the experience was to change my life! I had been reading the books of the masters such as Alois Podhajsky and of course Sylvia Loch, and was captivated by the theory, ethos and beauty of classical riding. However, I had never really experienced true lightness and classicism in the way that Palomo demonstrated to me. Being well-read in the masters' books, I appreciated how much of a novice – classically speaking – I was. Therefore I was quite nervous when first mounting Palomo – not least because he was the first stallion I had ever ridden.

257

> I needn't have worried; from the moment I settled gently into the saddle I experienced a strong aura from this wonderful creature, as if he was saying 'Don't worry, I'll show you, and I'll take care of you'. This he certainly did. He showed me what not to do, which was extremely valuable. When I did it wrong, then so did he. When my weight was not even he went sideways – what better way could he tell me I wasn't sitting straight! When I eventually got it right, it was wonderful beyond belief.
>
> Never once did this very intelligent, kind and brilliant horse ever show any annoyance at, or resistance to, my ineptitude. He was patience personified. Sylvia had told me that he had actually dislodged many a rough and arrogant rider, so I feel extremely privileged that he treated me with such kindness and was so generous in his paces.
>
> To me, Palomo Linares showed all the attributes that any classical rider should aspire to – patience, humility, generosity and love, and yet had strength of character to not allow himself to be bullied.(Anne Wilson, personal communication)

I only met Palomo twice: once at Sylvia's home in Suffolk, and again after she and her family had moved to Scotland. But even on such brief acquaintance, I could tell that Palomo was a very special horse indeed.

Anne Wilson with Palomo. Photo: courtesy of Anne Wilson

Remington Steele (1982–2007)

Pure-bred Arabian Remington Steele (Gaffizon x Jordjina) was a remarkable stallion in every respect. Owned by Patti Demers Bailey of New Hampshire, USA (www.remingtonsteele.org), he combined beauty, grace and a superb temperament with astonishing versatility. As well as being a US and Canadian Top Ten Halter Champion, winning many championships in Open Halter and Sport Horse in-hand classes, he took part in – and won – many different performance classes and championships. One of his most remarkable achievements was taking part in the gruelling Tevis

Cup 100 mile 24-hour ride in California's Sierra Nevada, a mere 9 months after being a US National Top Ten Halter Stallion – an achievement previously unheard of for a multiple halter champion.

Remington's rider in the Tevis, veterinary surgeon Elaine Dornton, remarks:

> Each person has his own little phobias about riding the Tevis. For some, it's the night riding; others, the American River crossing; others, the physical fatigue. For me, it's always the start of the race. There you are, sitting on a dynamite stallion, with more than two hundred horses snorting and prancing in the dark on a steep and narrow ski road waiting for the signal to go, being bumped and pushed along with everyone else in the struggle to keep your place in line. Remington, however, did fine in that tense situation, even when another stallion came between us and his favorite mare, Patti's horse, Cola Bay. (Bailey, 1990)

Remington Steele tackles Cougar Rock, one of the toughest sections of the gruelling Tevis Cup 100 mile endurance ride. Photo: courtesy of Patti Demers Bailey

Because of his extreme versatility, 'Rem' was chosen to represent the Arabian breed at Kentucky Horse Park's *Horses Of The World* exhibit. He was also named a Living Legend (awarded to only 10 Arabs out of a population of 650,000 in the USA, and only once every 25 years). Every year, the World Arabian Horse Organization (WAHO) donates a trophy to each of its member countries, for an Arabian horse which has itself in some way been an excellent 'ambassador' for the breed or, in the case of older horses, has achieved the same through its immediate progeny. Rem became the first WAHO Trophy Winner for the USA. On top of all this, 'Rem' sired many outstanding offspring internationally who went on to compete – and win (including many championships) in a variety of disciplines including endurance, competitive trail, hunter/jumper, Western pleasure, English pleasure, driving and dressage. 'Rem' even managed to complete a breeding season while being conditioned for the Tevis Cup!

Remington's owner, Patti Bailey, calls him the 'gift of a lifetime'.

> To me, the best thing about Rem's story is that he was owned by a middle class person of "normal" means...he had to 'earn' his way to shows by being leased to junior riders and pros alike, sometimes showing in many different styles of classes at the same show.' (Patti Bailey, personal communication).

The Natural Stallion

Remington's versatility extended far beyond taking part in different disciplines. At the 1995 Diablo Stallion Extravaganza

> Remington Steele had been named Liberty Challenge Champion, after flying around the show arena and doing his fiery stallion thing, to the great delight of the crowd, when I heard several children crying to their mothers that the pony rides had closed. Rem could save the day. We put a barn halter on Rem and I carried a two-year-old to him. 'Baby, Rem!' I told him. 'Baby!' Time to be gentle, he knew. He immediately changed gears and we spent the rest of the afternoon giving pony rides to children. That's what this horse is all about. (Bailey, The Tough Get Going)

Remington Steele. Photo: Lynne Glazer Imagery

Beyond all his achievements in the showring and on the trail, and as a sire, Remington embodied the best of stallion qualities, not least of which was courage. During Remington's lifetime, Patti Bailey recalled that

> ... watching him cross the finish line at Tevis 100-miles-in-one-day ride, 9 months after being a US National Top Ten Halter Stallion, was a spiritual and emotional high in admiration for what incredible heart this great stallion carries. I thought this could not be topped until the following happened. Our farm, Phase II, is remote and very near where a lady trail runner was killed by a mountain lion, in 1994; the forest service rangers have coached us on encountering lions ... 'Never ride alone and if you see a lion scream and yell, make a lot of noise, try to intimidate it but DO NOT turn your back or try to run'. I teach this to my clients when we venture into the wilderness on horseback. One day at a ride I found myself alone on Remington face to face with a huge male lion on

260

a plateau above us up the steep ascent we were making! He was only about 12 feet away from our faces, flipping his tail, pinning his ears and snarling down at us. Remington stopped still. I tried to yell but I was so terrified I could not make a sound come from my voice, nor paralyzed with fear, could I take my eyes off the lion long enough to find my mace can spray I carry for such occasions. Remington took charge – from the depths of his ancestral being came a primal stallion scream I have not heard before or since AND he charged the lion striking repeatedly with both front feet until the lion turned and sauntered down the trail. Then Remington instinctively did the correct thing, he boldly followed the lion down the trail until the cat disappeared in the underbrush and we could trot safely away! (Bailey, Remington Steele)

An English breeder recalls her first sight of Remington Steele:

I first saw 'Rem' in his senior years as he waited patiently in his stall to be called to parade before the huge crowd at the 'Living Legends' presentation in Denver in 2005. Children were anxious to touch this beautiful silky white stallion and climbed up his legs, hung on to his tail and pushed fingers into his soft nostrils.

He just looked on benignly and never moved a hoof. But once Patti was saddled up and on board, he galloped into the arena every inch the champion to roars of applause. What a star!

(Anne Brown of Gadebrook Stud, owner and breeder of Magic Domino, the only British horse also to be made a 'Living Legend'; personal communication)

Remington Steele out for a ride in the snow. Photo: Lynne Glazer Imagery

This is only a tiny, and very personal, sample of the very many stallions who, all over the world, are quietly proving not only that stallions are not the aggressive monsters of legend, but the contrary: they can be among the kindest, most responsive riding horses of all.

Conclusion

Sometime he trots, as if he told the steps,
With gentle majesty and modest pride

Anon he rears upright, curvets and leaps,
As who should say 'Lo, thus my strength is tried,
And this I do to captivate the eye
Of the fair breeder that is standing by.'

– William Shakespeare, Venus and Adonis

IN his celebrated poem *Venus and Adonis*, Shakespeare captures the true spirit of the stallion far better than those modern commentators who see in the stallion's behaviour only aggression and the desire to dominate. We have seen how false that perception is, yet in spite of all the evidence against it, it still prevails among many of those in a position of influence in the horse world. In the summer of 2010 there was an uproar about the treatment meted out to a young stallion, during a public demonstration, by a very high-profile trainer. Complaints were made and a furious debate ensued on many online forums. Predictably, excuses were made by and on behalf of the trainer concerned, one of them being 'it's a stallion'[1] as though that explained the necessity for subduing a horse who, on the evidence, was doing nothing that justified such treatment.

Why should this be? Why are so many people ready to defend a course of action that so many knowledgeable people considered indefensible? And why, given that there is so much evidence that treating stallions harshly is counter-productive and may even provoke (or reinforce) the dangerous behaviour the proponents of such harsh behaviour fear and wish to avoid or eliminate, do so many people still advocate such treatment?

We have already seen the power of the self-fulfilling prophecy: harsh treatment may provoke the very behaviour it is supposed to prevent/cure, thus reinforcing the belief that stallions are dangerous. If the stallion is the saintly type who does not retaliate or behave in a dangerous manner, the advocates of harsh treatment believe it must have worked, again reinforcing the belief that it was necessary in the first place.

Cognitive dissonance

But there is something else at work here: a mental process that we all – without exception – use to maintain psychological equilibrium: self-justification. This is the mind's way of dealing with acts and beliefs that are not consonant with our self-image. This lack of consonance leads to *dissonance*; hence the term used by psychologists to describe this phenomenon: *cognitive dissonance*. Faced

---

[1] Although as far as I am aware, the trainer himself did not put forward this excuse; only his followers did so.

with such dissonance, people either admit they were wrong and change their beliefs/behaviour (something that can be extraordinarily difficult to do) or they (usually subconsciously) rearrange facts in their minds so that the dissonance disappears. Suppose I behave badly towards a friend. I believe I am a good person, who would not do anything to harm or upset a friend. So if I behaved in this way, the person to whom I have behaved badly must have done something to deserve it. In this way our minds justify our actions, allowing us to continue to believe that we are good people. The alternative – accepting that we have hurt someone who really doesn't deserve it – is simply too painful for the mind to accept – 'I'm not like that; I just wouldn't behave like that to someone who had done nothing to deserve it.' In this way, whole groups of people have managed to justify their ill-treatment of other groups of people: by persuading themselves that the people in the other group somehow deserved such treatment because of who or what they were. None of us is immune from this process; it is the mind's way of protecting itself, of preventing us from constantly going over past mistakes and tormenting ourselves with the memory of our errors of judgement. In many cases, it does no harm. But when it distorts reality to the extent that it prevents us from seeing important issues clearly, and from taking responsibility for our actions, its effects can be devastating.[2]

Cognitive dissonance explains why people like the trainer mentioned above, and the many people who admire him and his methods, can continue to justify his treatment of the stallion in the demo, no matter how much or what kind of evidence is produced to demonstrate that there were other, much better ways of dealing with the situation. No one likes to think they are wrong; but this goes beyond that feeling to the very heart of a person's self-image. This trainer believes – and I am convinced of his sincerity – that his actions are carried out for the benefit of the horse, even when they have the opposite effect from that intended. He cannot admit he was wrong, because that would destroy his self-image; his supporters cannot admit he was wrong either, because that would destroy *their* self-image; after all, they care about horses, and they would never support someone whose actions were harmful to a horse, would they? Yet what if this trainer were to announce, publicly, something on the lines of: 'I made a mistake. I thought this was the way to deal with this horse's problems, but I was wrong. As soon as he started to resist, I should have backed off and re-assessed the situation, and if necessary called off the demo. It would have disappointed the audience, but we could have worked with another horse, and I could have taken more time to assess just what help this particular stallion needed to overcome his problem. I didn't do that, and for that I apologize.'

Would this trainer have lost credibility in the eyes of the horse world? I'd be willing to bet that he wouldn't. Instead, he would probably have gained far more respect for being willing to stand up in public and admit he made a mistake. We all make mistakes, especially where horses are concerned. It *is* painful to admit one's mistakes, and the greater one's self-esteem, the more difficult it is to do so. But once we become aware of cognitive dissonance and its effect on our thinking, it becomes easier to identify – and admit – where our preconceived ideas and prejudices have led us astray.

Learning to admit mistakes

In my life with horses, I have learned quite a few painful lessons in cognitive dissonance. Many years ago, I was persuaded, against my better judgement, to buy a dressage saddle for my Arabian gelding that was simply too narrow. The person who persuaded me was a very experienced saddle-fitter; who was I to argue with her judgement? I knew from the start that the saddle wasn't quite right, yet I couldn't bring myself to admit that I had made an error in judgement by allowing myself to be

---

[2] *Mistakes were made (but not by <u>me</u>)* is a superb book by Carol Tavris and Elliot Aronson which explains what cognitive dissonance is and how it works. They give some chilling examples of how it has led to terrible political mistakes and some ghastly miscarriages of justice. See the Bibliography for details of this book, which I recommend to everyone.

persuaded. I began to find all kinds of reasons why it was an excellent saddle (it was – it just didn't fit my horse) and why I had made the right decision to buy it. Then one day I was riding my little gelding – the sweetest-natured, most willing horse one could ever wish for – and he started to back off – so much so that at one point I feared he might actually go up – something he had never done before. A sudden flash of insight made me realize it had to be the saddle. I jumped off and untacked him right there, in the *manège*, vowing never to use that saddle again. I exchanged it for a different saddle that really did fit him, and he never backed off again. I lost money over that – not a lot, but more than I could afford at the time – but how much more would I have lost if my beloved horse had been injured as a result of my inability to recognize that I had made a mistake!

When I first started to write about horses I used to maintain that we never used negative reinforcement with our horses. I now cringe to think that I could ever have written that, because of course we *do*. As I pointed out in Chapter 9, it is not the fact that negative reinforcement is used that matters so much as *how* and *when* it is used. Yet because I thought of myself as someone who would never use an aversive method with a horse, I could not accept that much of what I really did do consisted of negative reinforcement, albeit of a very mild nature. As I admitted on page 177, I was initially dismissive of clicker-training, and said so in some of my writings; yet once I found out more about the principle I realized what a powerful tool it can be when used correctly. So I held my hands up and said: I was wrong. It wasn't a pleasant experience, but it didn't kill me to do so, and I don't believe I lost credibility as a result.

Konrad Lorenz: everything I've written about dogs is wrong

Konrad Lorenz, whose book on dogs was, as we saw in Chapter 5, very influential in its day, also held his hands up and admitted he was wrong. When Ray and Lorna Coppinger met Lorenz in 1977, he greeted them by saying, 'So you are the dog biologists. Before we start our talks I just want to say, everything I've written about dogs is wrong.' (Coppinger, 2002) Lorenz may have been an unrepentant old Nazi, but he was also a scientist, and a world-renowned one at that. He was not afraid to make such an admission, because he knew that science is not static, that as our knowledge grows it will confirm some theories and hypotheses while compelling us – if we are honest – to reject others.

Nuno Oliveira on making mistakes

One of the greatest equestrians of the twentieth century, Nuno Oliveira, wrote 'I have made countless errors in the training of literally thousands of horses … I know that I still have much to learn, and will go on learning until my dying day.' (Oliveira, 1976) Oliveira was not only a great equestrian, but – where it mattered – a humble one. He knew he had made mistakes, but he learned from them – and how to correct them – and it made him a better equestrian as a result.

Changing perceptions

So in order to change perceptions about stallions, it is not enough to present evidence that so many entrenched management and training practices are detrimental to the stallion, and to human relationships with them. Cognitive dissonance also has to be dealt with, by showing people how their beliefs act to protect them, and that discarding some of these beliefs doesn't mean their world has to fall apart. Of course if they have invested a great deal of time, effort and money (not to mention emotion) in those beliefs, it is going to be much more difficult for them to change. But it *can* be done; Carol Tavris and Elliot Aronson give examples of people who have changed their beliefs, sometimes at considerable initial cost to themselves, but ultimately to their benefit.

Welfare issues

It is not only the harsh treatment to which so many stallions are subjected that needs to change, but also the management methods that effectively deny stallions the opportunity to perform their natural behaviours.

The Five Freedoms

The Farm Animal Welfare Council has identified a number of conditions which it deems essential for the welfare of farm animals (Farm Welfare Council, 1996). These are known as the Five Freedoms and have been adopted by a number of other organizations, notably the RSPCA, and extended to non-agricultural animals such as horses. They are:

◊ Freedom from hunger and thirst by ready access to fresh water and a diet to maintain full health and vigour

◊ Freedom from discomfort by providing an appropriate environment, including shelter and a comfortable resting area

◊ Freedom from pain, injury and disease by prevention or rapid diagnosis and treatment

◊ Freedom to express normal behaviour by providing sufficient space, proper facilities and company of the animal's own kind

◊ Freedom from fear and distress by ensuring conditions and treatment which avoid mental suffering

Many – perhaps most – responsible stallion owners manage to fulfil the first three welfare requirements listed above. However, the last two are more problematical. How many stallions, one may ask, are allowed the freedom to express normal behaviour, and to enjoy the company of their own kind? And how many stallions are trained and managed in ways that avoid mental suffering?

There are many stallion owners who do fulfil these conditions and who allow their stallions a rich, full life, managing and training them in humane, ethical ways which ensure the horse's wellbeing and contentment. But for every stallion kept in such a manner there are many more whose lives are rendered miserable by a restricted lifestyle and training and management methods which are virtually guaranteed to produce fear and distress – even though the people looking after them may genuinely believe they are doing their best for the stallion(s) in their care.

Yet such attitudes are slowly changing. Lurking (as I often do) on numerous online forums devoted to the training and management of horses, I have sometimes been appalled by the levels of ignorance displayed by some horse owners. At the same time, though, I have been impressed by the number of stallion owners who post on such forums and make it clear that they have a humane and

The Natural Stallion

enlightened attitude to training and managing their stallions. These are the people whose voices need to be heard. There is already an online stallion care group, which can be found at http://pets.groups.yahoo.com/group/stallioncare/ on which enlightened stallion owners from all over the world share their experiences and help others with queries and problems. Wouldn't it be wonderful if, one day, such people became the majority, and the bad old beliefs were consigned to oblivion?

As Andy Beck says,

> Stallions, far from being sociopaths or maniacs, can be one of the most delightful, and predictable, of domestic animals to work with. Perhaps it is time that the welfare ethics of traditional horse industry breeding barn methods are questioned. Although vested interest is such that it is not at all surprising that the old status-quo is perpetuated. It is my firm belief we owe these equine family men better treatment – and that those of us who are lucky enough to work with stallions owe ourselves the unforgettable experience of achieving a brotherhood across the gulf that divides species. (Beck, 2005)

Owning a stallion entails a great deal of responsibility, but once you have accepted that responsibility and have established mutual understanding with your stallion, the result can be one of the most rewarding relationships a human could possibly have with another living creature.

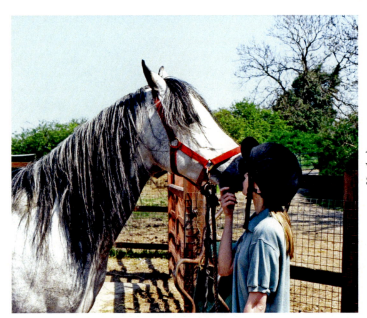

A rewarding relationship: Nivalis with his friend Joanne. Photo: Lesley Skipper

Appendix I: Safety

MOST of what is set down here regarding safety issues applies regardless of whether one keeps stallions, mares or geldings; however, safety awareness is even more important when one is dealing with stallions. We look at some of the practicalities as well as the legal obligations facing horse owners.

Some basic handling safety

Hard hats and gloves

I mentioned the use of hard hats and gloves in Chapter 6; I am ashamed to say that my husband and I don't always take our own advice, although we invariably wear a hard hat when riding. No matter how placid or well-behaved a horse is, he might trip or fall (no horse is immune from such mishaps); even a fall from a horse who is standing still can be fatally damaging to the human skull. If you are lunging, or leading a skittish horse, gloves are a good idea – I gave an example in Chapter 6 of how easily rope burns can occur if gloves are not worn.

Jewellery

It is also a good idea to remove jewellery when handling horses, especially sharp, lively horses who may react suddenly to some unanticipated stimulus. Earrings can easily become caught in manes or in various items of tack; having an earring ripped out of a pierced ear is an extremely painful experience. Chains around the neck, while they may not result in quite such a painful injury if they become caught up, may nevertheless cause soreness and bruising before they break.

It is really not a good idea to wear rings, as I found to my cost a few years ago. Although I never wore any other kind of ring while handling horses, for many years I continued to wear my wedding ring at the stables. Then one day my friend and I were leading our senior stallion out into one of the fields together with Tiff, the mare he lives with on-and-off. They were used to being led out together, and there were no problems until they actually got out into the field. Then something happened to upset Nivalis, who was being led out on the long lunge line. He half-reared and pulled away; startled, my friend dropped the lunge line. Not wanting to see Nivalis tear off up the field trailing a long line, I made a grab for the line with my left hand. Just as I got hold of it, Nivalis, still upset, pulled away again, hard enough to sprain my left hand. I got him under control again, and we were able to let both horses go without further incident. However, the ring finger of my left hand was now swollen to almost twice its normal size, and as a result my wedding ring was so tight that it threatened to cut off the circulation. It was obvious that the ring would have to be cut off, and a visit to the hospital also revealed a rather impressive fracture of the ring finger. Having a ring cut off is not a pleasant experience, especially if the finger it is being removed from is broken. Although I might still have ended up with a nasty sprain, had I not been wearing my ring I would have been saved a great deal of discomfort, and it is quite possible that the finger might not have been fractured. This was a minor injury, but if the ring itself had been torn off – which has happened to people in similar circumstances – the result could have been the loss of the finger, or at least a part of it. Some people may find it difficult or impossible to remove a ring which has been worn on the same finger for a number of years. If you feel you must continue to wear a ring when handling horses, gloves might prevent a serious injury, but may not provide sufficient protection from sprains of the kind described above.

Footwear

Adequate footwear is also something to consider, especially when handling lively colts and stallions. It is sometimes difficult to position oneself in the right place to avoid being trodden on, because a horse who is upset or excited may move unpredictably and it is all too easy for human feet to get in the way. There are various makes of boots with steel toe-caps available, but I have found these rather too heavy and cumbersome for freedom of movement. There is the added disadvantage that most of them do not protect the instep, which in my experience is just as vulnerable as the toes. Strong shoes or boots may offer almost as much protection; flimsy shoes are definitely not recommended.

Extra vigilance is required

Keeping a stallion requires extra vigilance on the part of the keeper. When leading a stallion out when there are other horses in the yard, it makes sense not to take him too close to the other horses. Even where stallions are accustomed to being turned out with other horses, there may still be rivalries and antagonisms that are exacerbated by the fact that when horses are together in a confined space such as a stable yard, they cannot get away from each other and accidents become more likely.

For example, Nivalis is normally very easy to handle when being led in and out of the yard. However, he does have his moments. In Chapter 7 I described what happened when he got away from Brian in the yard (the first and only time this has happened with Brian). However, there was a similar incident one day very soon after that, when my friend, who was leading him back into his stable, let go of him too soon, before he was properly through the door. Immediately he made a dive towards his arch-rival Toska, then in his box across the yard. Toska prudently retreated to the rear of his stable, but Nivalis was determined to get at him, kicking at the stable door, roaring in fury and half-rearing as if he was going to try to climb over the door. A handler attempting to intervene in a situation like this runs the risk of being injured, because an infuriated stallion, no matter how much he may like and respect his handler, may simply forget about the handler's presence and could injure them, not out of malice, but simply because they get in the way. The only way we could get Nivalis away from Toska was to bring his mare, Tiff, to the yard gate. He immediately ran over to her and was sufficiently distracted that I was able to catch hold of his halter without being kicked or bowled over. Once I had hold of him he became extremely docile, allowing himself to be led back to his stable without fuss.[1] Fortunately no horses or humans were injured in this incident, but it was a salutary reminder of how easy it is to become complacent. My normal practice is to lead Nivalis right into his stable and turn his head towards me before taking off his halter. In this way, if he becomes excited by the sight of his mare Tiff (with whom he might have been grazing until only a few moments before) and kicks out in his excitement, I can get out of the way quickly. He rarely does kick out, and never with the deliberate intention of kicking a human,[2] but as I said above, he

---

1 We have observed that colts and stallions frequently react like this to being caught after a bit of a fracas; it's almost as if they are relieved at not having to go on being responsible for dealing with the situation.

2 Apart from the situation described in Chapter 11; this, however, is an exception to his normal behaviour and only occurs in that specific context.

could easily injure me or another human by accident, simply because we were in the way. No matter how well-behaved a stallion is, it makes sense not to take unnecessary risks.

Leading a stallion in a bridle

Many sources advise leading a stallion in a bridle at all times. At first glance, this might seem like good advice, since one may indeed have a greater degree of control with a bridle. However, this may not automatically be a good idea. There is the danger that a horse rearing or pulling away could damage his mouth on a bit. Some horses may subsequently fear the bit which would compromise their ability to accept a bit when being ridden. Many people believe that horses do not need bits, and I would certainly not insist that they are at all times necessary for ridden horses. Bitless bridles can be just as effective for all but the most advanced High School work (where the rider can give the horse extremely subtle signals down the reins via the bit); even then, some very advanced horses can be ridden with just a silken cord in their mouths (like Palomo Linares) or even without a bridle at all, like Nizzolan. However, a bitless bridle is not a substitute for good horsemanship, and if a rider cannot guide a horse with finesse using a bit, they are not likely to be able to do so using a bitless bridle.

In any case, why risk damaging the horse's mouth at all? And if the horse does hurt his mouth on the bit, this may make him try to avoid it immediately. He may then become even more difficult to handle. If you are going to lead your stallion in a bridle (and many breed shows stipulate that stallions and colts aged three and over being shown in-hand must be bitted) first of all ensure that he is controllable in a headcollar or a lunge cavesson. Teach him the kind of control cues suggested in Chapters 8, 10 and 11, and you will find leading him in a bridle much easier.[3]

The legal aspect: what happens if your horse gets loose and injures someone?

Until the mid-1990s, horse owners living in the UK were unlikely to find themselves being sued if their horse escaped from a field and injured someone or caused damage to property, provided they had not been negligent in any way. This was because of the way the 1971 Animals Act had generally been interpreted. Section 2 (2) of this Act deals with animals belonging to species classed as 'non-dangerous'. Farm animals and horses are not classed as dangerous because they are domestic animals, unlike, for instance, lions or tigers, which are not commonly domesticated in the UK and would therefore be classed as dangerous animals. Section 2(2) of the Animals Act states that the keeper of an animal belonging to a non-dangerous species is liable for any damage (to land, property or a person) where:

a) The damage is of a kind which the animal, unless restrained, was likely to cause or which, if caused by the animal, was likely to be severe; and

b) The likelihood of the damage or of its being severe was due to characteristics of the animal which are not normally found in animals of the same species or are not normally to be found except at particular times or in particular circumstances; and

c) Those characteristics were known to that keeper or were at any time known to a person who at that time had charge of the animal as that keeper's servant, or, where that keeper is the head of the household, were known to another keeper of the animal who is a member of that household and under the age of 16.

---

[3] The same cautions apply to the use of stud chains over the nose, commonly used in the USA and Australia.

The Natural Stallion

In 1995 a man was walking his dogs (which were on leads) along a public pathway which ran through a farmer's land. He was attacked by a suckler herd (i.e. having calves with them) of cows, and was severely injured. He sued the farmer and was awarded damages of £46,000. The court held that although the cows in question were 'normal' cows and therefore not normally dangerous, they had displayed characteristics (in this instance, aggression) in particular circumstances (i.e. they had calves with them and there was a dog nearby). The farmer was held to be liable because he was aware that these cows could display such behaviour in such circumstances; only three weeks prior to the incident described above they had chased and frightened someone else – an incident which had been reported to the farmer, so he could scarcely say that he was unaware that his cows might react like this to someone else walking across the land. In any case, it is hardly likely that a farmer keeping a suckler herd would be unaware that such behaviour was possible in such circumstances, so even if the earlier incident had not occurred, the court would probably still have held the farmer liable.

Because this case involved cattle rather than horses, most horse owners remained oblivious to it, until 2003, when the possibility that they, too, could be held liable for damage caused by their horses was brought home to them by a controversial decision made by the Court of Appeal.

This was the now notorious case of *Mirvahedy v. Henley*. What happened was that three horses owned by the Henleys were frightened by something – the actual cause of their fright remaining unknown – and in their panic escaped from their field, in the process breaking through an electric fence, barbed wire and some undergrowth. They ended up on a dual carriageway, where one of them collided with Mr Mirvahedy's car; Mr Mirvahedy was seriously injured as a result (the horse, sadly, died). The Henleys were not held to have been negligent in any way, as they had taken what would normally have been adequate precautions to prevent their horses getting out of the field. However, the Court of Appeal held that they were nevertheless liable for Mr Mirvahedy's injuries, because although these horses usually displayed 'normal' behaviour, their behaviour in this instance (fleeing from real or perceived danger in a panic) was what might be expected of terrified horses.

Following this decision, for a time it looked as though there would be few situations in which owners could escape liability. However, the Mirvahedy decision remains controversial; in a court of appeal case heard in 2006 (*Clark v Bowlt*) Lord Justice Seely remarked that Section 2(2) of the Animals Act is not intended to render the keepers of domesticated animals routinely liable for damage which results from characteristics common to the species. And it is still necessary to identify a specific characteristic and a specific circumstance which led to the accident; it is not enough just to claim that the animal caused an accident.

A claim would also probably fail if the injured party's actions contributed to the circumstances which led to the accident. If, for example, someone is injured by horses while trespassing on the land where the horses are kept, they could then be said to have brought the injury on themselves by their own negligent or reckless behaviour.

Even though the Mirvahedy case has not proved as disastrous as it might have done, it must surely make every horse owner think hard about what would happen if their horse(s) injured someone and/or or caused damage to property. In these litigious times people can no longer rely on the concept of a pure 'accident' that is no-one's fault. Suppose, for example, you have a stallion who is turned out in a field through which a public footpath runs. Walkers are subsequently attacked and injured by the stallion (it may not even be necessary for physical injury to occur; it could be that a claim for psychological distress caused by being attacked and/or chased might succeed, although it would clearly be more difficult to prove). It might be no defence to claim that your stallion was not normally aggressive; a competent lawyer could argue (no doubt with the assistance of expert witnesses) that stallions are likely to be more protective of their personal space than mares or geldings and that a stallion whose field is invaded by strange people could be expected to react aggressively. You could argue that your particular stallion would *not* normally react in such a way, but you would still have to prove that such a reaction was not a normal reaction in such a situation, and it is by no means certain that you would win the case.

It would really be better not to take any risks, and to refrain from turning a stallion out in a field with a public footpath running through it. Or, if this was unavoidable, a sensible precaution would be to fence off part of the field so that walkers would have no occasion to go near your stallion (unless they chose to do so, in which case you could claim that any resulting injuries were the result of their own recklessness).

Exactly the same applies with regard to keeping stallions in fields crossed by other ights of way such as bridleways. The British Horse Society offers a number of free advice leaflets, including the following regarding the keeping of stallions in fields crossed by rights of way:

ArowS06/1: Stallions on Bridleways

This advisory statement is mainly directed at the keeping of stallions in enclosed fields crossed by rights of way or other such routes used by riders but owners of stallions which run on unenclosed land are also asked to take note of the problems which can arise.

It is well known that entires of any description (bulls, stallions, rams, ganders etc.) can behave aggressively at some times and amorously at others. Such behaviour can cause distress and/or injury to humans and animals present at the time, as well as a risk to the stallion.

Where stallions are kept in enclosed fields crossed by bridleways, this kind of behaviour can be increased by the riding of horses along the bridleway. If unfenced there is nothing to prevent the stallions from approaching the rider(s) and attacking or attempting to recruit the horses(s).

This can be extremely dangerous for the rider, whose horse may try to defend itself, shy, or bolt. Even experienced riders may have difficulty in dealing with such situations, while the young, the elderly or the disabled are at a grave disadvantage. Several instances have occurred where injury has resulted to either horse or rider or both.

Legislation exists to prevent the running of certain breeds of bull in fields crossed by rights of way (Section 59, Wildlife & Countryside Act 1981). While no legislation covers the running of stallions or other entires in these fields, the situation is exactly the same for ridden horses and the Society feels that owners of stallions should give serious consideration to keeping their entire away from fields crossed by bridleways, along which there is a public right to ride.

If an animal (not being of a dangerous species) acts in such a way as to cause injury or damage to humans or their property it is then known to have this propensity. If the act is repeated, the keeper of that animal may be liable under the Animal Act 1971 for the damage or injury caused. Some cases have resulted in the award of high sums to persons injured.

It is hoped that owners of stallions will appreciate that their entires can cause distress, damage and sometimes lifelong disablement by their behaviour. Moreover, the owner of a stallion must be aware that such behaviour is likely to occur if horses are ridden through a field in which a stallion is kept.

It is recommended, therefore, that owners of stallions do not keep their stallions in fields crossed by bridleways.

It has been noted that action on "statutory nuisance" has been taken against the owner of a stallion under the Environmental Protection Act 1990. A bridleway had been denied to riders for many years because of the presence of a stallion in a field crossed by the bridleway. The County Council, who felt it had no powers in the matter, passed the case to the relevant District Council who was empowered to take action under the Act. The problem was solved in a week, following a letter threatening action under the Act.

The information in this leaflet applies to England and Wales only. For information on Scottish Law, please consult the BHS Access Officer for Scotland:

Mrs Pat Somerville,
The Loaning
Auchengate
Irvine
KA11 5BH.

Tel: 01294 270891
Mobile: 07712 139795
Email: p.somerville@bhs.org.uk

The British Horse Society
Stoneleigh Deer Park
Kenilworth
Warwickshire
CV8 2XZ

Tel: 01926 707700
Fax: 01926 707800

The legal situation may well be very different in countries other than the UK, but I think it is always wise to take out insurance against the possibility of your horse injuring people and/or property. The cost of such insurance need not be prohibitive and some breed societies and other equestrian organizations include third-party insurance as part of their membership fees. For instance, as a Gold member of the British Horse Society I am automatically insured, and the same applies to my husband and me as members of the Arab Horse Society in the UK. Gold members of the British Horse Society also have access to free legal advice. Wherever you live, I would strongly advise that you check out the kind of liability you are likely to face, as a horse owner or keeper, in the event of injury or damage caused by your horses(s), and to take out the necessary insurance.

Fencing

In Chapter 2, I mentioned some of the factors which may make keeping stallions difficult if not impossible for people who do not own (or rent) their own land and stabling. In addition to these factors, livery yards may not have a suitable enclosure where stallions can be turned out safely. However, it may sometimes be possible to negotiate a secure turnout area by volunteering to pay for modifications to existing fencing. There may be other possible solutions, depending on individual circumstances. In Chapter 6 I mentioned keeping our own horses at livery temporarily while our present stable block was under construction. Zareeba was still entire when we moved to the livery yard; fortunately the owner had her own stallion, and she was kind enough to let me turn Zareeba out overnight in her stallion paddock; he would be brought in during the day so that the owner's stallion could go out. This arrangement worked very nicely. The stallion paddock was separated from the other paddocks by a double row of high post-and-rail fencing, the two rows being separated by a six-foot gap.

What type of fencing?

The case of *Mirvahedy v. Henley* highlights the need for secure fencing. The Henleys' horses broke through an electric fence *and* through barbed wire, which in most normal circumstances would have been enough to keep horses in. Ordinary post-and-rail fencing is not, on its own, enough to keep a stallion in should he decide to break out and go in search of mares. Some years ago, the people who at that time owned the land adjoining ours had a rather nice three-year-old Thoroughbred colt, whom they had kept entire and who lived out in the summer with a group of geldings. The colt was very good-natured, albeit a little boisterous, and got on very well with his gelding companions. One day, however, he broke through our fence and chased one of our mares, Roxzella. I described what ensued in Chapter 7; had Nivalis and Zareeba (who thinks he is still a stallion to some extent) caught up with the colt, a serious fight and severe injuries could have been the result.

In this particular case the fencing was quite inadequate to keep two entire males apart, or to separate a stallion from mares. The photograph on page 274 shows our own stallion, Nivalis, confronting the colt described above (on an earlier, different occasion). The fence is quite flimsy, and we would never have put Nivalis in that field had we known that the owners of the other colt were going to turn the latter out in the adjoining field. Fortunately no harm was done on that occasion, because Nivalis at the age of three was only just beginning to realize what being a stallion is all about, and as the photograph shows, his reaction to the other colt's aggressive stance suggests that he was rather taken aback by the challenge.

High quality modern electric fencing, in conjunction with good old post-and-rail,[4] will deter most stallions from going walkabout. Siting the turnout paddock away from mares will also lessen the temptation to roam. In addition, stallions who are kept mentally occupied, with suitable companionship and lots of human contact, will usually be content enough to want to stay put, although this must never be taken for granted.

Now that Nivalis is a mature stallion and the land adjoining ours has changed hands, our turnout strategy has been revised several times to take account of changing circumstances. Until laminitis struck, Nivalis lived with his mare, Tiff; they were normally turned out either in the grassed-over

---

4 A good example of this type of fencing is shown in the photograph of the two stallions on page 135.

The Natural Stallion

manège or in the stallion paddock, which at the time had triple strands of electric tape (see the photograph on page 46). The time came, however, when we had to let our younger stallion, Rigel, out in the same paddock. As I mentioned in Chapter 7, Rigel is an escape artist, and the existing fencing, although more than adequate to keep Nivalis contained, had to be replaced. Post-and-rail fencing, with two rails and two strands of electrified rope, has proved successful in preventing any more of Rigel's 'adventures'.

Nivalis, aged three, confronting another entire. the fence is far to flimsy to separate stallions from other horses safely. Photo: Brian Skipper

What height should the fencing be? Much depends on the size of the stallion. For some of the larger breeds, the fence should ideally be a minimum of six feet high, and preferably more; eight feet would not be excessive. For smaller breeds, a lower height should be sufficient, although much depends on the individual stallion. Our fence is four feet six inches high, which is adequate for us, because although both the stallions can jump well, neither has shown any inclination to jump out of the paddock, or even attempt to do so, even though on occasions (such as strange horses getting into the field adjoining theirs) there has been plenty of temptation for them to do so. If in doubt, make the fence higher rather than lower.

If you are electrifying the fence (which I strongly recommend), do you choose tape, rope or wire? Personally I dislike wire, because if it breaks and gets wrapped round a horse's leg, it can do some really horrific damage. Tape or rope can also cause damage, of course, but of the three wire is the most dangerous. Tape is excellent, and easy for horses to see;[5] it is also easy to handle. Its main drawback is that even when the tensioners are closely spaced, tape flaps about in the wind, and it can quickly become frayed and break. For this reason we prefer rope, which also has the advantage of being easy to mend (kits can be obtained to mend broken tape and rope). To set up an electrified fence, you will need a suitable energizer, tape or rope, tensioners, an earth spike and, if electrifying the gate, gate handles and anchors. You can also get posts but I would not recommend these for stallions, as they are more suitable for temporary fencing (for example when sectioning off part of a field). However, they might be useful to have in case you need to separate the stallion temporarily

---

[5] I once read an exceedingly silly statement in a horse magazine to the effect that tape should be coloured because horses cannot see white. I can assure people that horse can see white; my own have proved this on numerous occasions. In any case, there is no physiological or behavioural reason why they should be unable to see white. This statement does not make sense on any level.

in another part of the field or paddock. You should also put up a warning sign if the fence is to be left on when you are not about; it would be a good idea to put a sign up anyway.

If you are not sure which type of energizer you need, or what gauge tape or rope to use, talk to some of the companies which supply electric fencing kits for horses. Information can be obtained from:

Fieldguard
Norley Farm
Horsham Road
Cranleigh
Surrey, GU6 8EH

Tel: 01483 275182
Fax: 01483 275341

Email: info@fieldguard.com
Website: http://www.fieldguard.com

Agrisellex UK,
116 North Park,
Fakenham.
Norfolk.
NR21 9RH

Tel: 01328 853266

Email: sales@agrisellex.co.uk

Website: http://www.agrisellex.co.uk/

For readers outside the UK, a trawl through the internet (http://www.google.com is the most comprehensive search engine) should produce information about electric fencing suppliers in your area. Look out for companies who have specialist knowledge of what is suitable for horses.

Bolting the stable door *before* the horse gets out

For anyone keeping horses, elementary safety precautions should always be taken, and for stallion owners they are absolutely essential. For example, at our own small private yard, our checklist before turning our senior stallion out with his equine family (or his son with the latter's girlfriend) would be:

◊ Is the fence secure in the turnout paddock?

◊ Is the battery which powers the electric fence charged up, and is the fence turned on and working?

The Natural Stallion

- ◊ Is the gate leading to the road secured?

- ◊ Is the gate leading to the *manège* properly closed?

- ◊ Is the gate leading to the big field secured? This is important as this field adjoins that belonging to the riding stables next door.

- ◊ Are there any horses still out in the field adjoining the stallion paddock? If so, these will have to be sent through into the far field which does not directly abut on the stallion paddock.

- ◊ Is the fence separating the far field from the big field adjoining the stallion paddock secure?

- ◊ Are the dogs safely out of the way? Some stallions are tolerant of dogs but Nivalis is not and would chase and try to kill any dog that got into his paddock.

On leaving the yard at night (or for periods during the day), we check the following:

- ◊ If the stallion (or his son) is still out, is the fence still secure and do the safety considerations above still apply?

- ◊ If they are in their stables, are the doors securely bolted and the kick-bolts at the bottom of the doors secure?

- ◊ Is Nivalis's back door secure and is the weave grille up? This is put in place not because he weaves (he has never done so) but as an extra precaution should he take it into his head to try to jump out. He has never shown signs of doing this but when horses are turned out in the neighbouring field, especially mares, we take no chances. He can still communicate with his mare Tiff through the centre 'V' of the grille (see photograph on page 203)

- ◊ If any of the other horses are in their stables, are their doors also secured?

- ◊ If the other horses are out, is the field gate secure? On one memorable occasion one of our geldings discovered how to open the field gate; he and another of the geldings 'raided' the yard, in the process demolishing the dog kennel (fortunately uninhabited at the time) and breaking into the tack room in search of food (they found none as it was all securely stored in tamper-proof feed bins, but they did quite a bit of damage to the tack room furnishings). No horses were injured but Nivalis was in his stable and must have been extremely stressed by the close presence of his enemy Toska. Had the latter got within range Nivalis would undoubtedly have attacked him.

All this may seem like a lot of trouble to go to but in reality such safety checks take up very little time and in due course become second nature. Then of course one has to guard against doing things automatically and effectively going onto 'autopilot'. When this happens it is easy to think one has carried out a safety check when one has in fact forgotten to do so, so it's best not to let the process become too automatic.

Appendix II

Seeking professional help

No matter how experienced you are with stallions, there may come a time when you need to seek help or advice from someone else. This is particularly so if you are trying to deal with problem behaviours, especially if those behaviours are, or may become, dangerous; Chapter 11 gave some instances of such behaviours. But who do you turn to? Given some of the inaccurate perceptions of stallions, how do you know who to trust?

Equine Behaviour general

The Equine Behaviour Forum

The Equine Behaviour Forum was founded in 1978 and based in the UK. Its present Chairman and Scientific Editor is Dr Francis Burton of the University of Glasgow in Scotland. The EBF is an entirely voluntary, non-profit-making, international group of people interested in equine (not only horse) behaviour. Its membership comprises vets, scientists, professional and amateur horsepeople, breeders, casual riders and horse owners, 'weekend riders' and also people who have no access to equines or who simply prefer to observe them from a safe distance! All you need to enjoy the Forum is a genuine interest in equine behaviour.

The EBF produces a journal entitled, appropriately enough, *Equine Behaviour*, which contains both scientific and 'amateur' sections. Edited by Alison Averis and Francis Burton, Equine Behaviour is written and illustrated mainly by its members and comprises letters, articles, views and experiences, book reviews, requests for and offers of help and advice, and much more.

The Forum organizes optional projects for members to carry out informal talks and discussion groups and visits to places of interest in the horse world.

It is very much a member-participation group. Without the active participation of its members, particularly in relation to the production of its newsletter, it cannot exist. Because of this, members are asked to contribute at least one item per year for publication in Equine Behaviour, although this not a condition of membership. Contributions certainly do not have to be professionally written. Anything is interesting, from a full article or scientific paper to a short comment or query. Photographs and artwork are also most welcome.

The membership subscription for 2010 is £15 payable in sterling for UK members, £16 in *sterling only* for the rest of the world.

For details of how to join, articles, photographs, useful links etc., please visit the Forum's website at http://www.gla.ac.uk/external/EBF/

Advice regarding ridden work

The Classical Riding Club

If you have problems with your stallion's ridden work – or just want general advice regarding riding stallions – the Classical Riding Club may be a good place to start, as many of its members not only ride stallions, but teach classical riding using schoolmaster stallions.

The Classical Riding Club was started by Sylvia Loch in January 1995 as a means of bringing together like-minded people who were interested in a more philosophical approach to riding. This approach puts the happiness and pride of the horse above all else: even above winning and being seen to be successful. This does not mean that the CRC is anti-competition; on the contrary, it recognizes that competition, when participated in for the right reasons, can be a very healthy way of giving oneself and one's horse a goal to aim for, and of proving the correctness of training and riding. However the CRC also recognizes that the pressures of modern equestrian sport have all too often meant that the great classical values and traditions seem in danger of being forgotten or swept away, and it is these values and traditions that the CRC seeks to communicate and to help preserve.

The Classical Riding Club membership is composed of people from every walk of life, and with widely differing equestrian backgrounds and levels of ability. Members range from those who do not own or even ride horses, but simply have an interest in the classical philosophy, to those working at High School level, with every possible combination of ability and level of knowledge in between. Although the bulk of the members are resident in the UK, there are members as far afield as the USA and Australia, as well as mainland Europe. The CRC welcomes everyone with a genuine interest in the classical ethos, but above all its aim is to bring this ethos to the everyday rider to enhance our understanding of the horse.

The Classical Riding Club can be contacted at:

Eden Hall
Kelso
Roxburghshire
TD5 7QD,
UK.

Fax: +44 1890 830667

Email: crc@classicalriding.co.uk
Website: www.classicalriding.co.uk

Telephone advice

Most reputable animal behaviour consultants will be very wary – and rightly so – of giving advice over the telephone. I am often asked for advice in this way (even though I do not regard myself as an animal behaviour consultant, and do not advertise myself as such), as well as by email, and while it is very tempting to rush into a diagnosis, I resist the temptation. I am happy to give general advice which may or may not help to provide a solution to the problem, but as far as the individual horse is concerned, I have to restrict myself to those generalities. This is because – as I hope the rest of the book has made clear – every horse is unique, as are his individual circumstances. Without knowing the horse, or at least spending some time with him, I might inadvertently give advice which could prove disastrous for both horse and owner.

Quackery

There are too many individuals who dispense advice according to a 'one-size-fits-all' concept of equine behaviour and then pretend that this will solve all problems. It won't. This is the equestrian equivalent of 'snake-oil': in the late 1800s a man named Clark Stanley sold a liniment allegedly made from oil extracted from rattlesnakes, which was supposed to be a wonderful cure-all for pain and lameness, such as rheumatism, neuralgia, sciatica, lumbago, toothache, sprains, swellings, etc. as well as curing frostbite, chilblains, bruises, sore throats, and the bites of animals, insects and reptiles. It cost 50¢ a bottle, which was a lot of money in those days. Needless to say, there was no snake-oil in the product, which was mostly plain mineral oil, and in 1915 the US government shut Stanley down for making false claims. Sadly, there is as yet no regulatory body to oversee the activities of those claiming to be able to solve equine behaviour problems.

Accountability

One good thing about the internet and the way it can disseminate information instantly is that, thanks to online forums and sites such as YouTube, evidence of a trainer's activities can be quickly uploaded and shared with the equestrian world at large. If – as has happened in recent years – a trainer is caught out on video using unacceptable methods, the equestrian world is quick to learn about it. Not all of this evidence should be taken at face value: video clips can be taken out of context, and the trainer may be explaining something to the audience which puts his or her actions in a different light. However, some of the videos we have seen in recent years cannot be explained away so readily. Trainers are becoming more and more accountable for their actions, which can only be a good thing for horses.

Experience and qualifications

Unfortunately, anyone can set themselves up as a trainer or as an animal behaviour consultant. You do not have to have a string of letters (or any letters at all) after your name in order to do so. (I don't, but then I don't call myself an animal behaviour consultant, or a trainer. I simply study, and write about, horses.) And even if someone does have a string of letters after their name, that does not necessarily mean anything (although it usually does). Find out what their qualifications are. Just because someone has a PhD, giving them the right to call themselves 'doctor', this does not mean that they are an expert in animal behaviour. Find out in what field of study their PhD was gained. Of course, the fact that someone has gained a doctorate in some field does tell us something about them: it says that they have the ability to do research, to analyse that research and derive conclusions from it. It does not automatically mean that they have any practical, everyday experience of their subject, although very many people who have PhDs in animal behaviour sciences do have such 'hands-on' experience. Look into their background. What have they done with horses?

Never be afraid to question the person you are thinking of consulting. You have read this book; you have a good idea (if you did not already) of the principles underlying behaviour modification. Find out what your potential consultant knows about these principles. Ask about

◊ What education/training they have received in animal behaviour. Just because someone does not have qualifications in this field does not mean that they are not competent to deal with your horse's problems; equally so, just because someone does have such qualifications is not automatically a guarantee that they can give effective help. In either case you need to know more about what experience they have, what kind of problems they have tackled, how they dealt with them, etc.

◊ The consultant/trainer's philosophy of training. Do they advocate the use of aversive methods, or do they emphasize positive reinforcement? Do they understand about behaviour modification techniques and when to use them? Ask if they use (for example) counter-conditioning/desensitization techniques, and when they would use these.

◊ Look for honesty in their assessment of your horse's problems. If they appear to promise quick and/or specific results, look elsewhere. No-one can guarantee either of those things.

◊ Beware of anyone who seems condescending and/or talks to you as if they think you are ignorant, and especially if they adopt an intimidating manner. If they talk to you like that, it is unlikely that they will respect your horse.

◊ Don't let anyone intimidate you into taking a course of action that feels wrong to you. If a consultant/trainer suggests such a course of action, ask them to explain exactly why they are recommending it.

◊ If at all possible, watch them at work before you let them see your horse. It is not uncommon for someone to talk as though they use only humane, positive methods, then demonstrate that in fact they use the opposite approach in practice.

Who are you going to call?

UK and Europe

The Association of Pet Behaviour Counsellors

Based in the UK, the APBC is an international network of experienced and qualified pet behaviour counsellors who work on referral from veterinary surgeons to treat behaviour problems in dogs, cats, birds, rabbits, horses and other pets. APBC members are able to offer the time and expertise necessary to investigate the causes of unwanted behaviour in pets, and outline practical treatment plans that are suitable for their clients' circumstances.

The APBC also runs seminars and workshops for its members, veterinarians, and members of the public interested in the field of pet behaviour therapy and dog training. Books, videos and other products related to the pet behaviour are sold through the APBC website.

Although the emphasis is on smaller domestic animals such as dogs, cats, rabbits etc, the APBC does provide information about horses, and has members specializing in horses.

Address:

PO Box 46
Worcester
WR8 9YS
UK

Telephone   +44 (0) 1386 751151

Fax   +44 (0) 1386 750743

Email   info@apbc.org.uk
Website: http://www.apbc.org.uk/apbc

USA

Certified Applied Animal Behaviourists

In the USA, you can seek help from a certified animal behaviourist.[1] Details can be obtained from their website:

http://www.certifiedanimalbehaviorist.com/

Certified Applied Animal Behaviourists are non-veterinary (although some may have veterinary qualifications) who have graduate training in animal behaviour, together with supervised, hands-on experience with a wide variety of species. The information they provide is based not only on personal experience but also on the scientific principles of animal behaviour. Unlike many self-proclaimed behaviour experts, CAABs will also have ready access to, and will make use of, the most up-to-date information on the latest scientific findings and literature about animal behaviour.

After your veterinary surgeon has examined the horse fully and determined that there is no underlying physical problem that is causing the unwanted behaviour, a certified Applied Animal Behaviourist will work with your vet to determine, and provide advice on, the best course of action. CAABs work closely with vets through veterinary referrals, so they know how important it is to keep the vet informed of their findings. Their training also enables them to provide useful case summaries to vets.

(Dr Sue McDonnell may be contacted via this organization.)

---

[1] Strictly speaking, the term 'behaviourist' should be reserved for someone who follows the behaviourist school of psychology, which confines itself to the study of observable and quantifiable aspects of behavior and excludes subjective phenomena, such as emotions or motives. However, its use to describe people who study, and work with, animal behaviour in general, is now so widespread that it seems unlikely to change in the foreseeable future.

Australia

In Australia, a good source of information about equine behaviour problems is the

Australian Equine Behaviour Centre

730 Clonbinane Road
Broadford
Victoria 3658
Australia

Tel.: +613 5787 1374

Email: via website

Website: http://www.aebc.com.au

Just remember the following points:

◊ There is *no* such thing as a 'quick' fix or magical method that will solve problems in one session

◊ Modifying problem behaviour takes time, patience and a lot of effort

◊ You have to be prepared to persevere. If, in spite of sticking to a programme, you feel you are not getting anywhere, seek further advice from the person you consulted. If they are unable to help further, seek help from someone else – just don't give up!

Bibliography

Books (the books marked* are especially recommended)

Asa, Cheryl S (2002) Equid Reproductive Biology In Moehlman, P.D. (ed.), *Equids: Zebras, Asses and horses – Status Survey and Conservation Action Plan* (pp. 113–117) World Conservation Union

Bayley, Lesley, and Maxwell, Richard (1996) *Understanding Your Horse* David & Charles

Berger, Joel (1986) *Wild Horses of the Great Basin* University of Chicago*

Blake, Henry (1975) *Talking with Horses* London: Souvenir Press

Blunt, Lady Anne (1986) *Journals and Correspondence 1878–1917* (ed. Rosemary Archer and James Fleming) Alexander Heriot

Budiansky, Stephen (1997) *The Nature of Horses: Exploring Equine Evolution, Intelligence, and Behavior* The Free Press

Burch, Mary R. and Bailey, Jon S. (1999) *How Dogs Learn* John Wiley & Sons*

Coppinger, Raymond and Coppinger, Lorna (2002) *Dogs: A New Understanding of Canine Origin, Behavior, and Evolution* University of Chicago Press

Dawson, Paul L. (2011) *Au Galop! Horses and Riders of Napoleon's Army* Stockton-on-Tees: Black Tent Publications

De Keuster, T. and Jung, H. (2009) Aggression towards familiar people and animals In Horwitz, D.F. and Mills, D.S., *BSAVA Manual of Canine and Feline Behavioural Medicine* 2nd ed. British Small Animal Veterinary Association

Dougall, Neil (1999) *Stallions: Their Management and Handling* J.A. Allen & Co Ltd (New edition)

Eaton, Barry (2002) *Dominance: Fact or Fiction?*

Evans, Nicholas (1995) *The Horse Whisperer* Bantam Press

Fisher, John (1998) *Diary of a 'Dotty Dog' Doctor* Alpha Publishing

Fraser, A.F. (2010) *The Behaviour and Welfare of the Horse* 2nd Revised edition CABI Publishing

Hall, R. (1972) *Wild Horse: Biology and Alternatives for Management, Pryor Mountain Wild Horse Range* Billings, Montana, USA: Bureau of Land Management

Hart, Ben (2008) *The Art and Science of Clicker Training for Horses: A Positive Approach to Training Equines and Understanding Them* Souvenir Press

Hearne, Vicki (1986) *Adam's Task: Calling Animals By Name* London: Heinemann

Herbermann, Erik F. (1989) *Dressage Formula*, 2nd ed. London: J.A. Allen

Hilberger, Oliver (2009) *Schooling Exercises in Hand: Working Towards Suppleness and Confidence* Cadmos Equestrian*

Hinrichs, Richard (2001) *Schooling Horses In-hand: For Suppling and Collection* J.A.Allen

Hogg, Abigail (2003) *The Horse Behaviour Handbook* David & Charles

Hyland, Ann (1988) *The Endurance Horse* London: J.A. Allen

Karl, Philippe (2003) *Long Reining* tr. Anthony Dent New edition J.A.Allen

Kathrens, Ginger (2001) *Cloud: Wild Stallion of the Rockies* Irvine, California, USA: Bowtie Press

Kiley-Worthington, Dr Marthe (1987) *The Behaviour of Horses in relation to management and training* London: J.A. Allen *

Kiley-Worthington, Dr Marthe (1997) *Equine Welfare* J A Allen *

Kiley-Worthington, Dr Marthe (2005) *Horse Watch: What it is to be Equine* J.A. Allen *

Kurland, Alexandra (2001) *Clicker Training for Your Horse* Ringpress*

Lethbridge, Emma (2009) *Knowing Your Horse: A Guide to Equine Learning, Training and Behaviour* Wiley-Blackwell*

Lijsen, Henrik J. (1993) *Classical Circus Equitation* (originally published in Dutch as *De Hooge School*, 1949; tr. by Anthony Hippisley-Coxe; ed. by Sylvia Stanier) London: J.A. Allen

Loch, Sylvia (1986) *The Royal Horse of Europe* London: J.A. Allen

Loch, Sylvia (1997) *The Classical Rider: Being at one with your horse* London: J.A. Allen

Loch, Sylvia (2000) *Dressage in Lightness* London: J.A Allen*

MacSwiney, Owen, Marquis of Mashanaglass (1987) *Training from the Ground* London: J.A. Allen

Masson, Jeffrey and McCarthy, Susan (1996) *When Elephants Weep: The Emotional Lives of Animals* Vintage

McBane, Susan (1994) *Behaviour Problems in Horses* David & Charles

McCall, James P. (2001) *The Stallion: A Breeding Guide for Owners and Handlers* Jimani Publications

McDonnell, Dr Sue M. (1999) Stallion sexual behaviour In J. C. Samper, *Equine Breeding Management and Artificial Insemination* (Chapter 4) Saunders

McDonnell, Dr Sue M. (2002) *The Equid Ethogram* Eclipse Press*

McDonnell, Dr Sue M. (2005) *Understanding Your Horse's Behavior* Eclipse Press.*

McGreevy, Paul (1996) *Why Does My Horse?* Souvenir Press

McGreevy, Paul (2004) *Equine Behavior: A Guide for Veterinarians and Equine Scientists* Saunders

McLean, Andrew (2003) *The Truth About Horses: A Guide to Understanding and Training Your Horse* David & Charles

Bibliography

Midgley, Mary (1995) *Beast and Man* (rev. ed.) Routledge

Mills, Daniel, and Nankervis, Kathryn (1999) *Equine Behaviour: Principles and Practice* Blackwell Science Ltd *

Mills, Daniel and McDonnell, Dr Sue M. (eds.) (2005) *The Domestic Horse: The Evolution, Development and Management of its Behaviour* Cambridge: Cambridge University Press

Newcastle, William Cavendish, Duke of (2000) *A General System of Horsemanship* (Facsimile reproduction of the edition of 1743) London: J.A. Allen

Oliveira, Nuno (1976) *Reflections on Equestrian Art* London: J.A. Allen

Podhajsky, Colonel Alois (1967) *The Complete Training of Horse and Rider,* (tr. Colonel V. D. S. Williams and Eva Podhajsky) Harrap

Podhajsky, Colonel Alois (1997) *My Horses, My Teachers* (orig. published 1967 as *Meine Lehrmeister die Pferde*) tr. Eva Podhajsky J.A. Allen

Pryor, Karen (2002) *Don't Shoot the Dog!: The New Art of Teaching and Training* 3rd Revised edition Ringpress Books*

Pryor, Karen (2009) *Reaching the Animal Mind: Clicker Training and What It Teaches Us about All Animals* Scribner Book Company*

Rees, Lucy (1984) *The Horse's Mind* Stanley Paul*

Sagan, Carl (1974) *Broca's Brain: Reflections on the Romance of Science* Random House

Sax, Boria (2000) *Animals in the Third Reich: Pets, Scapegoats, and the Holocaust* Continuum International Publishing Group

Schäfer, Michael *The Language of the Horse: Habits and Forms of Expression* tr. Daphne Machin Goodall Kaye & Ward 1975

Schultz, D. (1965) *Sensory Restriction* New York: Academic Press

Semyonova, Alexandra (2009) *100 Silliest things people say about dogs* Hastings Press

Sidman, Murray (2000) *Coercion and its Fallout* rev. ed. Authors' Cooperative Inc.

Skipper, Lesley (2005) *Let Horses Be Horses* J.A. Allen

Skipper, Lesley (2008) *Exercise School for Horse and Rider* London: New Holland Publishing*

Smythe, R. H. (1974) *The Mind of the Horse* J.A. Allen

Syme, G.T. and Syme, L.A. (1979) *Social Structure in Farm Animals* Amsterdam: Elsevier

Tavris, Carol and Aronson, Elliot (2007) *Mistakes were made (but not by me)* Pinter & Martin

Waran, Natalie K. (2001) The Social Behaviour of Horses In Keeling, L.J. and Gonyou, H.W (eds), *Social Behaviour in Farm Animals* (pp. 247–274) CAB International

Waring, George (1983) *Horse Behavior* Noyes

Wentworth, Judith Anne Dorothea Lytton, Lady (1962) *The Authentic Arabian Horse* (2nd ed.) George Allen & Unwin

Wilson, Anne (2009) *Riding Revelations: Classical Training from the Beginning* Stockton-on-Tees: Black Tent Publications*

E-books:

Beck, Andy (2005) The Secret Life of the Horse (e-book) Equine-Behavior.com.*

Articles in magazines

Arab Horse Society News (2006, Spring), Letters page

Archer, Rosemary (1996) *Arab Horse Society News,* Summer

Bailey, Patti (1990). 'When the Going gets Tough' *Arabian Horse World,* July

Beck, Andy (2006) 'The Secret Life of Stallions' *Planète Cheval Au Naturel* April–May–June

Dunbar, Dr Ian (2010) 'The appliance of science' *Dogs Today,* March, pp. 20–24

Hicks, Diane (2008) 'Herd Observation: A Week in Spain with Lucy Rees' *Equine Behaviour,* Autumn, pp. 17–19

Hudson, M. (2004) 'Wake up call' *Horse & Rider,* March

Hyland, Ann (2001) 'Nizzolan' *Arab Horse Society News,* Summer

Isaac, Nikki (1997) 'Submissive signalling' *Equine Behaviour* 35, Spring

Lithman, Adella (1996) 'Horses of a lifetime:the bullfighter who became a classical professor' *Horse and Hound,* February 8, p. 110

Loch, Sylvia (2001) Goodbye, Dear Friend *Horse & Rider*

Mech, L. David (2008) 'Whatever Happened to the Term Alpha Wolf?' *International Wolf* Winter, 5

Rees, Lucy (2000) 'Mustafa's Story' *Equine Behaviour* 48, Summer

Russell, Bob (1998) 'Understanding Herd Mentality: Pecking Order' *Classical Riding Club Newsletter* No. 14, Summer

Articles downloaded from websites

Bailey, Patti (n.d.). Remington Steele*++ Retrieved from http://www.remingtonsteele.org/Stallions/Remington/sporthorse.htm.

Bailey, Patti (n.d.) The Tough Get Going Retrieved from http://www.remingtonsteele.org/Stallions/Remington/ttgg.htm

Houpt, K. (2000) Equine Maternal Behavior and its Aberrations In K. Houpt, Recent Advances in Companion Animal Behavior Problems International Veterinary Information Service (www.ivis.org).

Keiper, Ronald and Boyd, Lee (n.d.) Behavioral Ecology of Feral Horses Retrieved from http://research.vet.upenn.edu/HavemeyerEquineBehaviorLabHomePage

McDonnell, S. M. (n.d.) Sexual behavior dysfunction in stallions 668–671 Retrieved from http://research.vet.upenn.edu/Portals/49/92sexualU.pdf

McDonnell, Dr Sue M. (2001) Mare Savages Foal Retrieved from TheHorse.com, June 1 Article # 235

McDonnell, Dr Sue M. (2003) Abusive Training for Stud Colts Retrieved from TheHorse.com (Article # 4749): www.thehorse.com , December 1

Parelli, Pat (n.d.) Article 15, 'Stallions Demand Savvy' Retrieved from www.parelli.com

Parelli, Pat (n.d.) Become a Natural Horseman Without Strings Attached (Article 12) Retrieved from www.parelli.com

Petura, Barbara (n.d.) A Talk with Ray & Lorna Coppinger Retrieved from WorkingDogWeb: http://www.workingdogweb.com/Coppinger.htm#Interview

Salmon, Liz (n.d.) 'The Dervatiw Gwyddion Story', http://www.paslowhallarabians.com/DervatiwGwyddionStory.html)

Semyonova, Alexandra (2003) The social organization of the domestic dog; a longitudinal study of domestic canine behavior and the ontogeny of domestic canine social systems The Carriage House Foundation, The Hague, www.nonlineardogs.com , version 2006

Scientific monographs, papers and theses

Altmann, M. (1951) The study of behavior in a horse-mule group *Sociometry* 14, 538–545

Altmann, Stuart A. (1981) Dominance relationships: The Cheshire cat's grin? (in: Bernstein: Dominance: The baby and the bathwater) *The Behavioral and Brain Sciences* 4, 431

Anderson, T.M., Pickett, B.W., Heird, J.C. and Squires, E.L. (1996) Effect of blocking vision and olfaction on sexual responses of haltered or loose stallions *Journal of Equine Veterinary Science* Vol. 16 no. 6, 254–261

Antonius, Otto (1937) Über Herdenbildung and Paarungs eigentumlichkeiten der Einhufer *Zeitschrift für Tierpsychologie* 1, 259–289

Appleby, Michael C. (1983) The probability of linearity in hierarchies *Animal Behaviour* 31, 600–608

Baenninger, Ronald (1981) Dominance: On distinguishing the baby from the bathwater (in: Bernstein: Dominance: The baby and the bathwater) *The Behavioral and Brain Sciences* 4, 431

Baer, K.L., Potter, G. D., Friend, T. H. and Beaver, B. V. (1983) Observation effects on learning in horses *Applied Animal Ethology* 11 (2) November, 123–129

Baker, A.E.M. and Crawford, B.H. (1986) Observational learning in horses *Applied Animal Behaviour Science* 15 (1) , 7–13

Bartlett, Thad Q., Sussman, Robert W. and Cheverud, James M. (1993) Infant killing in primates: a review of observed cases with specific reference to the sexual selection hypothesis *American Anthropologist* 95, 958–990

Berger, Joel (1977) Organizational systems and dominance in feral horses in the Grand Canyon *Behavioral Ecology and Sociobiology*, 2, 131–146

Berger, Joel and Rudman, Rebecca (1985) Predation and interactions between coyotes and feral horse foals *Journal of Mammalogy* 66 (2), 401–402

Berger, Joel, and Cunningham, Carol (1987) Influence of familiarity on frequency of inbreeding in wild horses *Evolution* 41 (1), 229–331

Bernstein, Irwin S. (1981) Dominance: The baby and the bathwater (includes peer reviews) *The Behavioral and Brain Sciences* 4, 419–457

Blakeslee, J.K. (1974) *Mother-Young Relationships And Related Behavior Among Free-Ranging Appaloosa Horses* MSc Thesis, Idaho State University

Boy, Vincent and Duncan, Patrick Time-budgets of Camargue horses I. Developmental changes in the time-budgets of foals *Behaviour* 71, 3–4, 187–202

Boyd Lee E. (1980) *The natality, foal survivorship, and mare-foal behaviour of feral horses in Wyoming's Red Desert* MSc Thesis, Univ. of Wyoming, Laramie

Boyd, Lee E. (1986) Behavior problems of equids in zoos *The Veterinary Clinics of North America: Equine Practice* 2 (3), 653–664

Boyd, Lee E. (1991) The behavior of Przewalski's horses and its importance to their management *Applied Animal Behaviour Science* 29, 301–318

Bradshaw, John W. S., Blackwell, Emily J. and Casey, Rachel A. (2009) Dominance in domestic dogs – useful construct or bad habit? *Journal of Veterinary Behavior* 4, 135–144

Bristol, F. (1982) Breeding behaviour of a stallion at pasture with 20 mares in synchronized oestrus *Journal of Reproduction and Fertility* (Supplement 32), 71–7

Cameron, Elissa Z., Linklater, Wayne, Stafford, Kevin J. and Minot, Edward O. (2003) Social grouping and maternal behaviour in feral horses (Equus caballus): the influence of males on maternal protectiveness *Behavioural Ecology and Sociobiology* 53, 92–101

Chaya, Layne, Cowan, Elizabeth and McGuire, Betty (2006) A note on the relationship between time spent in turnout and behaviour during turnout in horses (Equus caballus) *Applied Animal Behaviour Science* 98, 155–160

Chen, Yuncai, Dube, Celine M., Rice, Courtney J. and Baram, Tallie Z. (2008) Rapid loss of dendritic spines after stress involves derangement of spine dynamics by corticotrophin-releasing hormone *Journal of Neuroscience* March 12 2008, 28 (11), 2903–2911

Clutton-Brock, T.H., Greenwood, P.J. and Powell, R.P. (1976) Ranks and relationships in Highland ponies and Highland cows *Zeitschrift für Tierpsychologie* 41, 202–216

Crowell-Davis, S.L., Houpt, K.A. and Burnham, J.S. (1985) The ontogeny of flehmen in horses *Animal Behavior* 33, 739–745

Crowell-Davis, Sharon and Houpt, Katherine A. (1985) Snapping by foals of Equus caballus 69 *Zeitschrift für Tierpsychologie*, 42–54

Dagg, Anne Innes (1998) Infanticide by Male Lions Hypothesis: A Fallacy Influencing Research into Human Behavior *American Anthropologist* New Series, Vol. 100, No. 4, 940–950

Dierendonck, Machteld van, Vries, Hans de and Schilder, Matthijs B.H. (1995) An analysis of dominance, its behavioural parameters and possible determinants in a herd of Icelandic horses in captivity *Netherlands Journal of Zoology* 45 (3–4), 362–385

Dobroruka, L. (1961) Eine Verhaltensstudie des Przewalski-Urwildpferdes (Equus przewalskii Poliakov 1881) in dem Zoologischen Garten Prag. *Equus* 1 (1), 89–104

Doren, Janine van (2000–2001) *Factors Affecting Dominance and Aggressive Interactions Among Castrated Male Domestic Horses (Equus caballus)* BSc Thesis Hartwick College, Oneonta, NY

Duncan, P. (1980 Time-budgets of Camargue horses II: Time-budgets of adult horses and weaned sub-adults *Behaviour* 72, 1–2, 27–49

Duncan, P. (1982) Foal killing by stallions *Applied Animal Ethology* 8, 567–570

Duncan, P. (1992) Horses and Grasses: The Nutritional Ecology of Equids and Their Impact on the Camargue *Ecological Studies* 87 Springer-Verlag

Duncan, P., Feh, C., Gleize, J.C., Malkas, P. and Scott, A.M. (1984) Reduction of inbreeding in a natural herd of horses *Animal Behavior* 32, 520–527

Ebhardt, H. (1954) Verhaltensweisen von Islandpferden in einem norddeutschen Freigelände *Säugetierkundliche Mitteilung* 5, 113–117

Farm Welfare Council (1996) Report on the welfare of dairy cattle

Feh, Claudia (1988) Social behaviour and relationships of Przewalski horses in Dutch semi-reserves *Applied Animal Behaviour Science* 21, 71–87

Feh, Claudia and Mazières, Jeanne de (1993) Grooming at a preferred site reduces heart rate in horses *Animal Behaviour* 46, 1191–1194

Feh, Claudia (1999) Alliances and reproductive success in Camargue stallions *Animal Behaviour* 57, 705–713

Feh, Claudia (2001) Alliances between stallions are more than just multimale groups: reply to Linklater & Cameron (2000) *Animal Behaviour* 61, F27–F30

Feh, Claudia and Munkhtuya, Byamba (2008) Male infanticide and paternity analyses in a socially natural herd of Przewalski's horses: sexual selection? *Behavioural Processes* 78, 335–339

Feist, James and McCullough, Dale (1976) Behavior Patterns and Communication in Feral Horses *Zeitschrift für Tierpsychologie* 41, 337–371

Finkelstein, J. Susman, E., Chinchilli, V. Kunselman, S., D'Arcangelo, M. R., Schwab, J. Demers, L. Liben, L. Lookingbill, G. and Kulin, H.E. (1997) Estrogen or testosterone increases self-reported aggressive behaviors in hypogonadal adolescents *Journal of Clinical Endocrinology and Metabolism* Vol. 82, No. 8, 2433–2438

Freire, R, Buckley, P and Cooper, J.J. (2009) Effects of different forms of exercise on post inhibitory rebound and unwanted behaviour in stabled horses *Equine Veterinary Journal* May; 41(5), 487–92

Grassian, Stuart M.D. (1983) Psychopathological effects of solitary confinement *American Journal of Psychiatry* 140:11, November, 1450–1454

Gray, Meeghan E. (2009) An infanticide attempt by a free-roaming feral stallion (*Equus caballus*) *Biology Letters* 5, 23–25

Greyling, Telané (1994) *The Behavioural Ecology of the Feral Horses in the Namib Naukluft Park* MSc Thesis University of Pretoria

Greyling, Telané (2005) *Factors affecting possible management strategies for the Namib feral horses* PhD (Zoology) Thesis North-West University (Potchefstroom)

Grzimek, Bernhard (1944) Rangordnungsversuche mit Pferden Zeitchrift fur Tierpsychologie, 6, 455–464

Haag, Ellen L., Rudman, Rebecca and Houpt, Katherine Albro (1980) Avoidance, maze learning and social dominance in ponies Journal of Animal Science 50, 329–335

Hanggi, Evelyn B. (1999) Interocular transfer of learning in horses Journal of Equine Veterinary Science 19 (2), 518–523

Hausberger, Martine, Gautier, Emmanual, Biquand, Veronique, Lunel, Christophe and Jego, Patrick (2009) Could Work Be a Source of Behavioural Disorders? A Study in Horses PLOS One (4) (10)

Hoffman, R. (1983) Social organization patterns of several feral horse and feral ass populations in Central Australia Zeitschrift für Saügetierkunde 48, 124–126, 124–126

Houpt, Katherine A., Law, Karen and Martinisi, Venera (1978) Dominance hierarchies in domestic horses Applied Animal Ethology 4, 273–283

Houpt, Katherine A. and Wolski, Thomas R. (1980) Stability of equine hierarchies and the prevention of dominance related aggression Equine Veterinary Journal 12 (1), 15–18

Houpt, K.A. and Keiper, R. (1982) The Position of the Stallion in the Equine Dominance Hierarchy of Feral and Domestic Ponies Journal of Animal Science 54, 945–950

Houpt, K. A. (1984) Flehmen Equine Practice March, 32–35

Houpt, K. A. (1993) Aggression and intolerance of separation from a mare by an aged gelding Equine Veterinary Education 5 (3), 140–141

Innes, L. and McBride, S. (2007) Negative versus positive reinforcement: an evaluation of training strategies for rehabilitated horses Applied Animal Behaviour Science 87, 357–368

Keiper, R. (1979) Population dynamics of feral ponies Conference on Ecology and Behavior of Feral Equids September 6–7, Laramie, WY

Keiper, R.R. and Sambraus, H.H. (1986) The stability of dominance hierarchies and the effects of kinship, proximity and foaling status on hierarchy rank Applied Animal Behaviour Science 16, 121–130

Kiley-Worthington, M. (1998) Communication in Horses: Cooperation and Competition Publication 19, Eco-Research and Education Centre, University of Exeter

Kirkpatrick, J.F. and Turner, J.V. (1991) Changes in herd stallions among feral horse bands and the absence of forced copulation and induced abortion Behavioral Ecology and Sociobiology 29, 217–219

Klingel, H. (1969) Reproduction in the Plains zebra, Equus burchelli boehmi, Behaviour and ecological factors Journal of Reproduction and Fertility Supplement 6, 339–345

Lindsay, Flora E.F. and Burton, Francis L. (1983) Observational study of "urine testing" in the horse and donkey stallion Equine Veterinary Journal 15 (4), 330–336

Line, Scott W., DVM; Hart, Benjamin L., DVM, PhD and Sanders, Linda, BA, MA. (1985) Effect of prepubertal versus postpubertal castration on sexual and aggressive behavior in male horses *Journal of the American Veterinary Medical Association* 186 (3), 249–51

Linklater, W.L., Cameron, E.Z., Minot, E.O. and Stafford, K.J. (1999) Stallion harassment and the mating system of horses *Animal Behaviour* 58, 295–306

Lloyd, Adele Sian, Martin, Joanne Elizabet, Bornett-Gauci, Hannah Louise Imogen and Wilkinson, Robert George. (2007) Evaluation of a novel method of horse personality assessment: Rater-agreement and links to behaviour *Applied Animal Behaviour Science* 105, 205–222

Luthersson, N., Nielsen, K. H., Harris, P. and Parkin, T. D. (2009) The prevalence and anatomical distribution of equine gastric ulceration syndrome (EGUS) in 201 horses in Denmark *Equine Veterinary Journal* 41 (7), 619–624 and 625–630

Mackler, S.F. and Dolan, J.M. (1980) Social structure and herd behavior of Equus przewalskii Poliakov, 1881 at the San Diego Wild Animal Park *Equus* 2 (1), 55–69

Mader, D.R. and Price, E. O. (1980) Discrimination Learning in Horses: Effects of Breed, Age and Social Dominance *Journal of Animal Science* 962–965

Marinier, S.L., Alexander, A.J. and Waring, G.H. (1988) Flehmen behavior in the domestic horse: discrimination of conspecific odours *Applied Animal Behaviour Science* 19, 227–237

McDonnell, S. M., Kenney, R.M., Meckley, P.E. and Garcia, M.C. (1985) Conditioned suppression of sexual behavior in stallions and reversal with diazepam *Physiology & Behavior* Vol. 34, 951–956

McDonnell, S. M. (1986) Reproductive behavior of the stallion *Equine Practice* Vol. 2 no. 3, December, 535–555

McDonnell, S.M., Henry, M. and Bristol, F. (1991) Spontaneous erection and masturbation in equids *Journal of Reproduction and Fertility* Supplement 44, 664–665

McDonnell, S. M. (1992) Normal and abnormal sexual behavior *Veterinary Clinics of North America: Equine Practice* Vol.8, no. 1, April, 71–89

McDonnell, S.M. and Haviland, J.C.S. (1995) Agonistic ethogram of the equid bachelor band *Applied Animal Behaviour Science* 43 147–188

McDonnell, S.M. and Murray, S. (1995) Bachelor and Harem Stallion Behavior and Endocrinology *Equine Reproduction* v.I Biol Reprod Mono 1, 577–590

McDonnell, S. M. (2000) Reproductive behavior of stallions and mares: comparison of free-running and domestic in-hand breeding *Animal Reproduction Science* 60–61, 211–219

McDonnell, S.M. and Poulin, A. (2002) Equid play ethogram *Applied Animal Behaviour Science* 78, 263–290

McDonnell, S. M. (2008) Practical review of self-mutilation in horses *Animal Reproduction Science* 107, 219–228

Mech, L.David (1999) Alpha Status, Dominance, and Division of Labor *Canadian Journal of Zoology* 77, 1196–1203

Mech, L. David (2000) Leadership in Wolf, Canis lupus, packs *Canadian Field-Naturalist* 114 (2), 259–263

Miller, R. (1981) Male aggression, breeding behavior and dominance in Red Desert feral horses

Zeitschrift für Tierpsychologie 57, 340–351

Mills, D.S. (1998) Applying learning theory to the management of the horse: the difference between getting it right and getting it wrong *Equine Veterinary Journal* Supplement 27

Mills, D.S. and Davenport, K. (2002) The effect of a neighbouring conspecific versus the use of a mirror for the control of stereotypic weaving behaviour in the stabled horse *Animal Science* 74

Montgomery, G. G. (1957) Some Aspects of the Sociality of the Domestic Horse *Transactions of the Kansas Academy of Science* (1903–), Vol. 60, No. 4 Winter, 1957, 419–424

Mosley, J. C. (1999) Influence of Social Dominance on Habitat Selection by Free-Ranging Ungulates Grazing Behavior of Livestock and Wildlife *Idaho Forest, Wildlife & Range Exp. Sta. Bull. #70.* Univ. of Idaho, Moscow, ID

Paradis, M. R. (1998) Tumors of the central nervous system *Veterinary Clinics of North America: Equine Practice* Vol.14, No.3, December 1998, 543–561

Paredes, R.G., Lopez, M.E. and Baum, M.J. Testosterone Augments Neuronal Fos Responses to Estrous Odors throughout the Vomeronasal Projection Pathway of Gonadectomized Male and Female Rats *Hormones and Behavior* 33, Issue 1, February 1998, pp. 48–57

Penzhorn, B. (1979) Social organization of the Cape Mountain zebra, Equus zebra zebra, in the Mountain Zebra National Park *Koedoe* 22, 115–156

Pluháček Jan and Bartoš, Ludek (2000) Male infanticide in captive plains zebra (*Equus burchelli*) *Animal Behaviour* 59, 689–694

Pluháček, Jan and Bartoš, Ludek (2005) Further evidence for male infanticide and feticide in captive plains zebra, Equus burchelli *Folia Zool.* – 54(3), 258–262

Pozor, M.H., McDonnell, S.M., Kenney, R.M. and Tischner, M. (1991) GnRH facilitates copulatory behavior in geldings treated with testosterone *Journal of Reproduction and Fertility* 44, 666–667

Reisner, Ilana R., Shofer, Frances S., and Nance, Michael L. (2007) Behavioral assessment of child-directed canine aggression *Injury Prevention* 13, 348–351

Rho, Jeong Rae, Srygley, Robert Boxter and Choe, Jae Chun (2004) Behavioral ecology of the Jeju pony (Equus caballus): Effects of maternal age, maternal dominance hierarchy, and foal age on mare aggression *Ecological Research* 19, 55–63

Rowell, T. (1988) Beyond the one-male group Behaviour, Vol. 104, No. 3/4 (Mar.), 189–201

Rubenstein, D. (1981) Behavioural ecology of island feral horses *Equine Veterinary Journal* 13 (1), 27–33

Sax, B. (1997) What is a "Jewish dog"? Konrad Lorenz and the cult of wildness *Society and Animals* Vol. 5, no.1, 3–21

Schilder, M. (1988) Dominance relationships between adult plains zebra stallions in semi-captivity *Behaviour* 104, 300–319

Schilder, M. (1990) Interventions in a herd of semi-captive plains zebras *Behaviour* 112, 53–83

Simpson, K. (2001) The Role of Testosterone in Aggression *McGill Journal of Medicine* 6, 32-40

Stahlbaum, Cathi C. and Houpt, Katherine A. (1989) The role of the flehmen respoonse in the behavioral repertoire of the stallion *Physiology & Behavior* Vol.45, 1207–1214

Tyler, S. J. (1972) The behaviour and social organization of the New Forest ponies *Animal behaviour monographs* vol.5, pt.2. London: Baillière Tindall

Verrill, Sarah, BS, and McDonnell, Sue,MS, PhD (2008) Equal Outcomes with and without Human-to-Horse Eye Contact When Catching Horses and Ponies in an Open Pasture *Journal of Equine Veterinary Science* Vol 28, No 5 , 309–312

Waran, N. K. (1997) Can studies of feral horse behaviour be used for assessing domestic horse welfare? *Equine Veterinary Journal* 29 (4), 249–251

Wells, Susan M. and Goldschmidt-Rothschild, Bettina von. (1979) Social behavior and relationships in a herd of Camargue horses *Zeitschrift für Tierpsychologie* 49, 363–380

Welsh, D.A. (1975) *Population, behavioral and grazing ecology of the horses of Sable Island* MSc Thesis Dalhousie USA

Woods, G.L. and Houpt, K.A. (1986) An abnormal facial gesture in an estrous mare *Applied Animal Behaviour Science* 16, 199–202.

Zeeb, K. (1959) Die "Unterlegenheitsgebärde" des noch nicht ausgewachsenen Pferdes (Equus caballus) *Zeitschrift für Tierpsychologie* 16, 489–496

Index

Entries in **bold** indicate the name of a horse; italics indicate photographs; n. indicates a reference in a footnote.

A

abuse, 147, 148, 167
adrenal glands, 32, 38, 198
adrenaline, 198, 207
aggression, 15, 41, 49, 53, 66, 71, 80, 84, 86, 91–92, 95, 97, 99, 101, 105, 125, 126, 127, 128, 169, 170, 192, 194, 211–220, 228, 229, 237, 270
    avoidance of, 99, 99, 149, 155
    caused by poor management, 198, 210, 213–214
    caused by stress, 198
    fear-induced, 18, 212
    hierarchy of, 86, 95, 100
    inter-male, 41, 47, 56, 63, 79, 95, 135, 205–208
    pain or discomfort-induced, 212–213, 221
    redirected, 53, 70, 76, 212
    in stallions, 11, 26, 32, 62, 63, 72, 73, 75, 212–213, 262
    sudden onset of, 218
    towards animals of different species, 215
    towards humans, 34, 35, 215–220
    towards other horses, 34, 35, 43, 214–215
alpha
    animal, 51
    horse, 88, 145–146, 153
    intelligence, 160
    status, 87, 88, 145
    wolf, 87
'alpha roll', 148
Andalusian (PRE), 141, 239
Assateague Island, 68, 94
Association of Pet Behavior Counsellors, 280
Assyrians, 20
Audaz, *140*
Australian Equine Behavior Centre, 282
aversive training techniques, risks of, 148, 158, 264, 280
Azrek, 120

B

bachelor bands, 43–44, 46, 48, 54, 94, 97, 119, 125, 126, 131, 222
bachelors, 41, 43, 48, 54, 62, 63, 119
    adopting foals, 75–77
    attempting to steal mares, 41, 48, 60
    challenging band stallion, 47–48
    encounters with band stallions, 48, 55, 63
    establishing family group, 48
    influence on young colts, 43
    interacting with band stallion, 47, 48, 95
    interaction of young colts with, 44–45
    interactions among, 45, 46–47
    male-male mounting. *see* homosexual mounting
    taking over established bands, 48, 95
Bailey, Patti Demers, 241, 258–261
Balthasar, *132*
band, family, 42–43, *43*, 48, 51, 53, 54, 63, 68, 69, 77, 78. *see also* family group
    multi-male, 58, 78–81
    size of, 42–43
barging, 153, 196, 220
Beck, Andy, 13, 33–34, 44, 45, 46, 48, 55, 56, 64, 71, 72, 73, 74, 76–77, 125–126, 131, 192, 239, 266
Bedouin, 20, 154
behaviour
    abnormal, 125
    castration and, 192
    changes in, 137, 210ff
    brain tumour, 210
    rabies, 210
    modification, 192, 194–197, 212, 216
        problems which are unsuitable for, 197
    problems, 12, 29, 32–33, 34, 38, 113, 122, 123, 134, 138, 151, 164, 169, 173, 183, 184, 191ff, 221, 277–282. *see also* problem behaviours

diagnosing, 193–194
    taking responsibility for, 193
    temperament and, 182, 191–192
    putting on cue. *see* cue
    suppression of, 150, 151, 212
    undesirable, 34, 35, 125
Berger, Joel, 41, 42, 43, 44, 48, 51, 56, 60, 63, 68, 75, 77–78, 95–96, 97, 99
Bernstein, Irwin S., 86, 90
biter, 217, 220–221
    dealing with, 222–223. *see also* biting
    fearless, 222
bite-threat, 146
biting, 47, 60, 62, 64, 68, 69, 110, 148, 153, 154, 205, 206, 208, 217, 220, 220–223
    causes of, 220
        fear and insecurity, 221
        lack of socialization, 222
        pain and discomfort, 221
    as self-defence, 221
Blake, Henry, 28, 59, 63, 120
Blunt, Lady Anne, 120, 237–238
body-language, 17, 175, 257
    aggressive, 150, 172
    equine, 102, 145, 229
boss, 17, 49, 50, 51, 83, 146, 148
brain tumour. *see* behaviour, changes in
bribe, 174
bribery, 174
brutality, 148, 151
bucking, 168, 205, 206, 207
bullfight
    mounted, 137, 240
        corrida, 137, 240, *240*
        rejoneo, 137, 240
Byerly Turk, 20

C

Camargue, 64, 67
    horses, 64, 67, 79, 96
casting a horse, 148
castration, 22, 32–36, 38. *see also* gelding
    effectiveness of, 33–35, 38, 192, 212
    forbidden by Islamic law, 22
    as a matter of routine, 24
    process, 36
    before puberty, 34
    after puberty, 34
celibacy, 119
Certified Applied Animal Behaviorists, 281
charging, 60, 69, 153, 223, 236
Classical Riding Club, 141, 244, 255, 278
clicker, 175, *178*
    as marker, 175
clicker-training, 139, 175, 176, 177–178
cloning, 24
coercion, 12, 30, 151, 166, 167, 170, 171, 178, 187, 238
cognitive dissonance, 158, 262–263, 264
companionship, 26, 200, 273
    of another species, 136
competitiveness, lack of in horses, 96
conditioning, 161, 163–164, 196
    classical, 164
    operant, 164
conflict
    avoiding, 41
    creating, 97, 99, 149–150, 153, 172, 233
consistency, 183, 195, 230
control cues. *see* cues, control
cooperation, 41, 80, 81
Copenhagen, 21
Cornell University, 94
counter-conditioning, 196, 214, 216, 233, 280
courtship behaviour, 102, 105–110
covering in hand, dangers of, 116
Coward, Mrs Pat, 22
cryptorchid, 37
cryptorchidism, 37–38
    abdominal, 37
    bilateral, 37
    inguinal, 37
cue, 143, 161, 164, 165, 176, 178, 181
    control, 133, 143, 156, 183, 187, 227
        and formal/informal contexts, 156–157
    poisoned, 168, 179
    putting behaviour on, 184, 194, 197, 224, 236, 269

D

Darley Arabian, 20
defensive
    actions, 137, 153, 216
    alliances, 78
    posture, 60
Dervatiw Gwyddion, *248, 250,* 249–251
desensitization, 163, 196–197, 214, 216, 233, 280
dimorphism, sexual, 31, 56, 94
Dino, *35*
disobedience, 168
disrespect, 144, 147 and n., 151, 153, 157, 183, 184, 235
DNA, 24, 40 n., 41
dog
    pack, 87
    trainers, 87, 88
    training, 87, 148
dogs, 57, 85, 86, 87, 88, 136–137, 145, 148, 156, 157, 164, 176, 192 n., 197, 237, 264, 270, 276
    sled, 52
dominance, 40, 49, 50, 57, 145, 149, 151, 157, 160, 215, 220, 221, 224, 225, 232
    definition of, 83, 88–89
    hierarchy, 17, 57, 82–83, 84ff, 89, 93
    alpha animal in. *see* alpha animal
    alpha status. *see* alpha status
    identifying (bucket test), 100
    measuring, 90–92, 93
    ranks in, 82, 83
    and leadership, 50–51
    learning ability and, 160
    mythology of, 147 n., 148
    not an abstract quality, 41
    relationship, 41, 81, 84, 86, 89ff, 101, 146, 155
        linear, 48 n., 89
        triangular, 89
    role of, 95
        access to food and water, 96–97
        access to potential mates, 95–96
        reduction of aggression, 97–99
dominance-based training, 144, 151 n., 152, 153, 158

dominant, 50, 89, 160
Downlands Cancara, 250–251
'dropping' and sexual excitement at shows. *see* masturbation
Dunbar, Dr Ian, 156
dungpile
    investigation, 103–104
    ritual, 54, 55, 57–58, 62

E

Egyptians, 20
Elljay Indiana, *241*
Equine Behaviour, 27, 277
Equine Behaviour Forum, 8, 27 n., 277
Equus przewalskii. *see* Przewalski
erection, spontaneous. *see* masturbation
Eric, 76–77
estrus. *see* oestrus
ethologists, 42, 45, 50, 52, 70, 71, 83, 84–85, 86, 90, 161
ethology, 84, 85
Evans, Nicholas, 148
expectation, power of, 30
extinction, 179, 194, 195–196, 230, *231*
    burst, 195

F

family group, 11, 13, 17, 27, 41, 42 and n., 43, 48, 50, 54, 55, 56, 60, 63–64, 71, 72, 75, 77, 87, 95, 114, 125, 126, 128–129, *129*, 151, 199, 209, 220, 222
    interaction between groups, 54
Feh, Claudia, 65, 66, 67, 79, 80–81, 89
fencing, 127, 134, 273
    height of, 274
    types of, 273
        electric, 273
        post and rail, 273
feral, 8, 41
    definition of, 41
    populations, 41, 42
fertility, higher in pasture-breeding stallions, 119
fight, fights. *see* fighting

fighting, 40, 41, 47, 48, 54, 56ff, 60–62 and 62 n., 62, 63, 79, 149, 151, 229, 231
    to the death, 40, 41
    mock, 47, 48
    play, 59, 63, 231
    serious, 47, 60–62, 63, 79, 223
Five Freedoms, 265
flehmen, 14–105, *106*, 109
flight responses, suppression of, 15
flooding, 148 n., 163, 185 n., 214
foal-face, 92, 97 and n., 109. *see also* submission
foals
    attacks on
        by mares, 71
        by stallions, 64–71
    stallions killing, 64–71
    stallions savaging, 64–71
folk beliefs, 15, 40
folk knowledge, 15
food, effects of on social structure, 83, 94, 95, 96–97
formal/informal contexts, 156–157, 183

G

gastric ulcers, 197, 198, 199–200, *200*, 206, 212, 231
    endoscopy to diagnose, 213, *213*
gelding, 22, 232
    age at which carried out, 36
    effects of, on growth, 36
    process, 36
    routine, 22
geldings, 11, 20, 21, 24, 25, 26, 31, 32, 33
    aggression
        towards humans, 34
        towards other horses, 34
    with stallion characteristics, 34
genes, 40 and n., 65
genetic inheritance, 182, 191, 202
genome, 24
goats, as companions, 136, 137
Godolphin Arabian, 20
Grand Canyon, 51, 94
Granite Range, 41, 42, 43, 60, 63, 77, 78, 96
Greyling, Telané, 42, 48 n., 50, 54, 55, 56, 62, 63, 68, 75, 94, 97

grooming, mutual, 46, 72, 102, 154–155, 156, 175, 224
    partner, 79, 153, 154
group cohesion, 95, 101, 219

H

habituation, 162–163, 184, 187, 189
harem, 46 n., 48, 49, 50, 53ff, 72, 76, 81, 89, 94, 99, 126
    stallion, 46, 47, 65, 95, 119
Hart, Ben, 177
head-rubbing, 183–184, 224
herd, definition of, 42
herding behaviour
    in geldings, 34
    'snaking', 53
    in stallions, 49, 50, 51, 53–55, 56
Highland ponies, 89, 96
hippocampus, 152
Hlayyil Ramadan, *123*
homosexual mounting, 44
Houdini, 72, 73
Houpt, Katherine, 94, 104
Husband, Joanne, *155, 183, 266*
Hyland, Ann, 241, 251–255

I

Iberian
    horses, 141, 171, 256
    Peninsula, 22, 141
Icelandic ponies, 50
imprinting, 161 and n.
Imzadi, 113, 114, *114*, 117, *117*, 118, *131*
incest, 77–78
India, 21
infanticide, 65
    evolutionary explanation for, 65ff
    in lions, 65–66
    possible causes of, in horses, 66ff
    in primates, 66
in-hand work, 139–141, *140*

J

Jacobson's organ. *see* vomeronasal organ

K

kicking, 47, 54, 62, 68, 69, 105, 132, 148, 153, 221
    case-study, 224–225
    in self-defence, 224
Kiley-Worthington, Dr Marthe, 15, 18, 24, 78, 83, 99 n., 100–101, 121, 130, 161, 162, 192
Kiri, 127
Kruger, 100, 229
Kurland, Alexandra, 139 and n., 177, 178

L

leader, 47, 48
leadership, 48ff
    definition of, 49
leading problems, 225–227
    circling, 226
    crowding, 226
    not going forward, 227
learning, 35, 152, 160
    imprinting. *see* imprinting
    insight, 161–162
    latent, 161
    one-trial, 162
    principles of, 30
    process, 148, 151, 152, 158, 160
    silent, 161
    social, 162
legal cases
    Clark v. Bowlt, 270
    Kinley v. Bierly, 18
    Mirvahedy v. Henley, 270
libido, 31, 131, 227
    natural suppression of, 119
Likit Boredom Breaker, *230*
Lipizzaners, 120 and n., 121, 175, 215, 242
Loch, Sylvia, 137, 142, 215, 240, 242–258
Login Lucky Lad, *242*
Lorenz, Konrad, 85 and n., 87 and n., 88, 161, 264
Lusitano, 137, 141, 241, 242, 245, 255
Lyons, John, 148

M

MacSwiney, Owen, Marquis of Mashanaglass, 24
Maestoso Sitnica, 215–216
Magic Domino, 261
mare
    'boss', 83
    dominant, 49, 50, 83, 88, 89
    leading, 49, 50, 51, 52
Marengo, 20
mares
    adverse effects of restraining during copulation on, 115–116
    interfering with mating process, 111
    maiden, 114–115
    oestrus behaviour of, 102–103, 105, 106, 107, 109–110
    savaging foals, 71
    and stallions, 77, 102, 112–113, 115–116, 129–130
        introducing to each other, 117–118
        separating. *see* stallions and mares, separating
    take the initiative in mating, 102–103, 106–107, 111
masturbation, 119, 227–228
    not harmful, 119, 227
    at shows, 227–228, *228*
McCall, James, 144
McDonnell, Dr Sue M., 44, 46, 47, 103, 106, 107, 111, 115, 116, 117, 119, 149, 187ff, 194, 205ff, 216, 227, 281
Mech, David, 87
Merlin, *132*
Midgley, Mary, 40
'mind games', 14, 145
mistakes, learning to admit, 263–265
Mongols, 20
monorchid, 37
Moorlands Totilas, 241, 251, *251*
Most, Konrad, 87 n.
mountain lion, 199, 260–261
mouthiness, 228

Mustafa, 207, 209, 219, 223

N

Namib desert, 43, 199
Namib horses, 48, 50, 52, 54, 56, 62, 63, 68, 94, 97, *98*, 199
Namib Naukluft Park, 42, 50, 62, 68, 94, 97
Napoleon Bonaparte, 20 and n., *21*.
Nazi
    ideals, 85 n., 87
    Party, 88
Neapolitano Africa, 245, *246*
neck-wrestling, 59
negative
    attitude, 30
    expectations, 30
    perceptions, 18
negative reinforcement. *see* reinforcement
neurons, 152
Neves, Pedro, *140*, 244
New Forest, 50, 253, 254
    ponies, 50, 67, 76, 96, 111
Newcastle, William Cavendish, Duke of, 117–118
    on covering mares, 118
nipping, 196, 220, 221, 222, 228
    causes of, 228–229
    dealing with, 196, 228–230
    feeding treats and, 173, 174–175, 230
Nivalis, 15, *16*, 22, 23, 25, *26*, 28–29, 44, 46, *58*, *60*, 72, 73, 74, 75, *93*, *98*, 100, *106*, *108*, 109, *110*, *111*, 113, *113*, 115, 120, 121, 126–128, *127*, *129*, *130*, 133, 134, 135 n., 136–137, *137*, 138–138, *141*, 142, *142*, 145, 154, *154*, 155, *155*, 156–157, *159*, *177*, 179, *180*, *183*, 190, 195, 196, *203*, *208*, 214, 224–225, *226*, 231, *266*, *267*, *268*, 273–274, *274*, 276
Nizzolan, 241, 251–255, *252*, *253*, *255*
non-confrontation not a soft option, 236–237
Nonius, 120–121

O

oestrus, 28, 34 and n., 43, 65, 73, 80, 102, 103, 104–105, 109, 121, 134, 189–190, 228

olfactory stimulation, 103–104
Oliveira, Nuno, 264

P

Palomo Linares, 137, 255, 255–258, *256*, *257*, *258*
Parelli, Pat, 40, 145
pasture breeding, 113–114
pawing, 56, 134, 138, 230–231, 235
Peck, Jean, 249–250
penis, 32 and n., 44, 119, 187–189, 206, 227
personal space, 45–46, 54, 95, 97, 146, 147, 172, 216–217, 218, 223 and n., 224
    contact species and, 45
    distance species and, 45
    interacting with a stallion within, 155–156
    teaching a colt or stallion to respect, 235–236
personality, 18, 22, 182, 191
    trait, dominance not a, 89
Pharis, *132*
pheromones, 104, 207
Pluto Theodorosta, 245–247, *247*
Podhajsky, Colonel Alois, 120 and n., 121, 169, 187, 245–247, *246*, 257
poisoned cue. *see* cue, poisoned
Portugal, 22, 30, 124, 137 and n., 139, 239, 240, 255
posturing and display, 41, 47, 54, 55, 56, 58–59, 62, 97
Prazer, 242, *243*, 244
predators, 81 n., 96, 136, 147, 199
pressure-and-release, 171
problem behaviours, 32–33, 151
    defining, 191
Pryor, Karen, 177, 218
Pryor Mountain horses, 53, 54, 56, 59
Pryor Mountain Wild Horse Range, 42, 50, 58, 94
Przewalski horses (Equus przewalskii), 41, 42, 64, 65, 66, 73, 75, 76, 81, 89, 107
puma (Felis concolor). *see* mountain lion
punishment, 148 n., 151, 165ff, 172, 188, 196, 212, 216, 221, 222, 228, 231, 236, 237
    appropriate, 169, 170

arbitrary, 221
combining reward and, 179, 181
confused with negative reinforcement, 170
difficult to administer effectively, 166, 169
effective, 169
inappropriate use of, 166, 167, 222
limitations of, 166, 168, 181, 236
may lead to aggression, 169, 214, 228
negative, 165
physical, 150
positive, 165
reasons to avoid, 169, 179
unjust, 166, 169
pushing and shoving, 54, 59

Q

Quem Foi, *241*
Quinito, *135, 143*
Quite, *244*

R

rabies. *see* behaviour, changes in
rank, ranking, 82, 83, 84, 86, 89, 90, 91, 92, 95, 96, 97, 99, 147 n., 224
reactivity, 125, 150, 171, 197
rearing, 59, 60, 133, 226, 227, 231–235, *232*
  in hand, 232–233
    causes of, 232–233
    solution, 233
  under saddle, 233–235
    causes of, 234
    solution, 234–235
received wisdom, 15, 30, 40, 49, 211
Red Desert, Wyoming, 53, 56, 80
  horses of, 57, 58 n., 79
Rees, Lucy, 27, 28 n., 57, 72, 73, 161, 207, 208, 209, 215–216, 219, 222, 223, 237
reification, 201 and n.
reinforcement, 161, 235
  conditioned, 176–177
  negative, 164, 165, 170–173, 174, 264
    benign use of, 172, 172–173, 218, 226
    on the ground, 171–172
    problems with using, 171–173
    under saddle, 173, 176
  positive, 25, 88, 151 n., 153, 164, 173–176, 217, 227, 230, 236, 237, 280
    selective schedule of, 138 n., 179
    timing of, 176
    variable schedule of, 179, 195
reinforcers, 164
Remington Steele, 241, 258–261, *259, 260, 261*
  Living Legend, 259, 261
  and mountain lion, 260–261
  and Tevis Cup, 259
respect, 49, 144, 147, 148, 157, 223, 235, 236
  lack of, 147, 151
retaliation, 215
rewards, 25, 52, 165, 170, 176, 178, 179, 181
  do horses understand?, 173, 175
  food, nipping and, 173, 174–175
  nature of, 173–174
ridden work, 141
rig, 36
  false, 38
  true, 37
Rigel, 44, *61, 93, 106, 110,* 113, 114, *114,* 117, *118,* 130 n., *131,* 135 and n., *147,* 155 n., *183,* 274
Risqué, 76–77
Roberts, Lord, 21, *21*
Roberts, Monty, 26–27, 27n., 148, 218
rogues, 218, 219
Romadour II, 24–25
Romans, 20
Rosie, *110*
Rossigkeitsgesicht, 92, 109–110
round pens, 172, 197, 222
Roxan, 22, *23*
Roxzella, 100, 114, 120, 128, 273

S

Sable Island horses, 50, 51, 55, 58, 88–89
safety, 26, 116–117, 126–127, 134, 135, 142, 185, 194, 216, 217, 225
  basic handling, 267
    footwear, 268
    hard hats and gloves, 267

jewellery, 267–268
checks, 275–276
leading a stallion in a bridle, 269
legal aspects, 269–273
horses classed as non-dangerous species, 269
insurance, 272–273
liability for damage, 270–271. *see also* legal cases
vigilance, need for, 268–269
Safões, *244*
sā'is, 154
Saudi Arabia, 141
Schenkel, Rudolf, 87
Schjelderup-Ebbe, Thorleif, 84, 85, 89
self-fulfilling prophecy, 17, 30, 123, 145, 192, 215, 262
self-mutilation, 122, 197, 205–209
causes of, 205–209
change in management and, 209
finding the cause, 209
flank-biting, 208
gelding and, 209
repetitive, 208
self-directed inter-male aggression, 206–208
Type I, 205
Type II, 206–208, 209
Type III, 205, 208, 209
Seligman, Martin, 150
Selye, Hans, 198
Semyonova, Alexandra, 85–86, 87 n., 88, 90–91, 148 n.
shaping, 178, 179, 184
free, 138 n., 179 n.
sheath, washing, 32, 187–189
sheep, as companions, 136, 137
shows, going to, 142–143
Sidman, Murray, 170
Siglavy Mantua I, *243*
Siglavy Neapolitano, 120–121
smegma, 32, 187, 188
Smythe, R.H., 48–49
'snapping', 92, *93*, 109. *see also* foal-face
social
cohesion, 55. *see also* group cohesion

contact, 25, 123, 125, 214–215
facilitation, 51–53, 225
hierarchy. *see* dominance hierarchy
integration, 46, 48, 125–126
status, 45, 84, 87, 95, 97, 99, 144, 152, 153
Spain, 72, 124, 139, 239, 240
Spanish Riding School, 119, 120, 124 n., 139, 169, 175, 230, 233 n., 239, 242, *243*, 245–247
stallion
is still a horse, 12
stallions
adopting foals, 75–77
aggressive, 15
alliances, 78–81
allowing s. to nibble, 154
amateurs and, 27
assisting with movement of mares, 55
attacking foals, 64–71. *see also* foals, s. attacks on
attacks on humans, 15, 19 n., 130, 149, 207, 210, 215, 219–220, 220 n., 221, 222, 270–272
avoiding physical conflict, 41
in battle, 20–21
bonds with humans, 25, 139, 153–154
in cavalry, 20
children and, 22–23, *23*
competing with, 240–241
confidence and, 25–26, 28–29, 126, 184
considered dangerous, 15, 18
cultural perceptions of, 18, 20–21
driving behaviour. *see* herding behaviour
dungpile ritual. *see* dungpile ritual
encounters between, 48, 54–55, 56–63
fights between. *see* fights
folk beliefs about, 15. *see also* folk beliefs
harsh treatment of, 28, 122, 215, 237, 262, 265
herding behaviour. *see* herding behaviour
investigating humans, 73
investigating other horses, 56, 59, 68
killing foals, 64–71. *see also* foals, s. killing
and leadership, 48–53
likes and dislikes, 120–121
livery yards and, 25, 192, 195, 273
and mares, separating, 130–131, 187

301

myths about, 14, 15
novices and, 22, 27
playing, 63
playing with foals, 73
professionals and, 26–27
protecting foals, 75, 77
protective behaviour, 34, 41, 46 n., 48, 49, 54–55, 63, 64, 78, 79, 95, 100, 126, 130, 199, 223
role in family group, 27, 41, 42, 46 and n., 48ff, 53
running with mares, 129–130
savaging foals, 64–71. *see also* foals, s. savaging
sharing food with foals, 75
sharpness, characteristic of, 25
as social example (role model), 72, 73–74, 133
as status symbol, 25
subordinate position of, 93–94
trusting, 18, 144, 237
turning out with mares and foals, 128–129
turning out with other s., 131–135
women and, 28–29, 29
stereotypical behaviour, 124, 133, 194, 197, 198, 199. *see also* stereotypies
stereotypies, 125, 200–204
    definition of, 200
    possible causes of, 200–202
        anxiety, 201
        boredom, 201–202
        environment, 202
    types of
        box-walking, 203
        crib-biting, 204, *204*
        head nodding, 203
        weaving, 202
        wind-sucking, 204
stress, 65, 66, 70, 71, 125, 126, 150, 151, 153 and n., 158, 171, 173, 176, 197–200, 205 and n., 213–214, 214 n., 221, 236, 239
    behaviour problems as a result of, 198
    chronic ill-health and, 199
    definition of, 198
    effects on ability to learn, 143, 151–152, 184
    effects on physical health, 198–199

    gastric ulcers and. *see* gastric ulcers
    studying, 198–199
    striking out, 57, 59, 60, 134, 135, 153, 224, 230, 235
submission, 92–93, 97, 110, 147 n., 157
    forcing, 148

T

target training, 177–178
Tariel, *16, 60, 61, 73, 74, 93, 111, 115, 129,* 133, 185–187, *186,* 196
telephone advice, dangers of, 278–279
temperament, 53, 134, 172, 182, 191–192, 215
territorial, horses not, 54, 57, 81, 223 n.
territory, 54, 57, 95
testes, 31–32, 36, 37–38
testosterone, 25, 31–32, 38, 47, 119
    and behaviour, 32–33, 34, 37, 38–39, 212
    and growth, 36
Tevis Cup, 258–529, 260
Thoroughbred, 20, 21, 120, 128, 171, 202, 273
Tiff, *16, 98, 108, 111, 113,* 114, *115, 129, 130,* 133, 267, 268, 273, 276
'Tit-for-tat', 100
Tigre, *135,* 143
timing, 176, 177
    importance of, 153, 155
    poor, 151, 171, 221
Toska, *61,* 126–128, 133, 135, 268, 276
Tour du Valat herd, 96
Turkey, 20
turnout, importance of, 124–125

U

universal principles, 218
Unterlegenheitsgebärde. *see* foal-face

V

vasectomized stallion, 121
vomeronasal organ, 104
Vonolel, *21*
    awarded Kabul medal and Kandahar Star, 21

W

walk, going out for a, 142–143
Walker, Robyn, *248,* 249–251, *250*
Warmbloods, 36, 126, 133, 134, 135, 171, 214, 249, 250, 251
Waterloo, 21
weaning, effects of isolation at, 123
Wellington, Arthur Wellesley, Duke of, 21
Welsh, D.A., 51, 55, 57, 58–59, 75, 88–89
White Horse Equine Ethology Project, 13, 33, 44, 46, 55, 72, 73, 76, 192, 239
Wilson, Anne, 142, 257–258, *258*
wolf, 87, 88
    society, 87

Z

Zareeba, 77, 78, 112–113, *127,* 128, 134, 229, 273
zebra, 50, 92, 97, 107, 109, 110, 199
    Grevy's, 42
    Hartmann's, 50
    mountain, 42, 50
    plains, 42, 50, 64, 65, 81, 90
Zeeb, K., 92